DEFENDING THE MOTHERLAND

By the same author

A Writer at War: Vasily Grossman with the Red Army 1941–1945 (2005)
(with Antony Beevor)

LYUBA VINOGRADOVA

DEFENDING THE MOTHERLAND

THE SOVIET WOMEN WHO FOUGHT HITLER'S ACES

With an Introduction by Antony Beevor

Translated from the Russian by
Arch Tait

MACLEHOSE PRESS
QUERCUS · LONDON

First published in Great Britain in 2015 by

MacLehose Press
an imprint of Quercus
55 Baker Street
7th Floor, South Block
London W1U 8EW

The publication was effected under the auspices of the Mikhail Prokhorov Foundation
TRANSCRIPT Programme to Support Translations of Russian Literature

ISBN (HB) 978 0 85705 192 9
ISBN (TPB) 978 0 85705 193 6
ISBN (Ebook) 978 0 85705 194 3

10 9 8 7 6 5 4 3 2 1

Designed and typeset in Quadraat by Libanus Press, Marlborough
Plates designed by Carr Design
Printed and bound in Great Britain by Clays Ltd, St Ives plc

In memory of
Nikolai Menkov and
Valentina Krasnoshchyokova,
two extraordinary people it was my good fortune to know

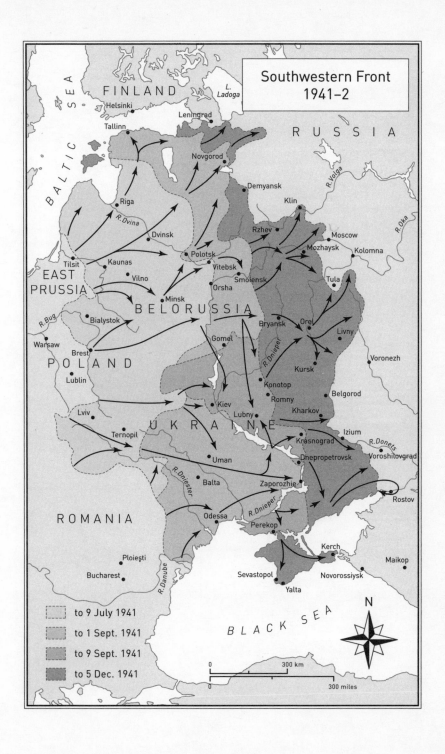

Southwestern Front
1941–2

FINLAND

L. Ladoga

BALTIC SEA

Helsinki

Tallinn

Leningrad

RUSSIA

Novgorod

Demyansk

R. Volga

Riga

R. Dvina

Dvinsk

Polotsk

Vitebsk

Smolensk

Orsha

Klin

Rzhev

Mozhaysk

Moscow

Kolomna

R. Oka

Tilsit

Kaunas

EAST
PRUSSIA

Vilno

Minsk

BELORUSSIA

Tula

R. Bug

Bialystok

Brest

Bryansk

Orel

Livny

Gomel

R. Dnieper

Warsaw

POLAND

Lublin

Konotop

Romny

Kursk

Voronezh

Belgorod

Lviv

Kiev

Lubny

Kharkov

Ternopil

UKRAINE

Izium

Krasnograd

R. Donets

Uman

Dnepropetrovsk

Voroshilovgrad

Balta

Zaporozhie

R. Dniester

Odessa

R. Dnieper

Perekop

Rostov

ROMANIA

Kerch

Maikop

Ploiești

Bucharest

Sevastopol

Yalta

Novorossiysk

R. Danube

BLACK SEA

to 9 July 1941
to 1 Sept. 1941
to 9 Sept. 1941
to 5 Dec. 1941

N

0   300 km

0   300 miles

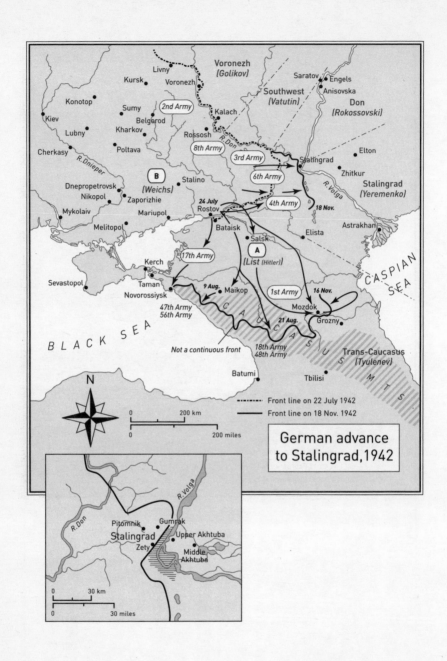

German advance to Stalingrad, 1942

Southwest Russia,
1942
Soviet Winter Offensive
13 Dec. 1942–18 Feb. 1943

Russian offensive
Front line on 13 December 1942
Front line on 18 January 1943
Front line on 12 February 1943
Front line on 18 February 1943

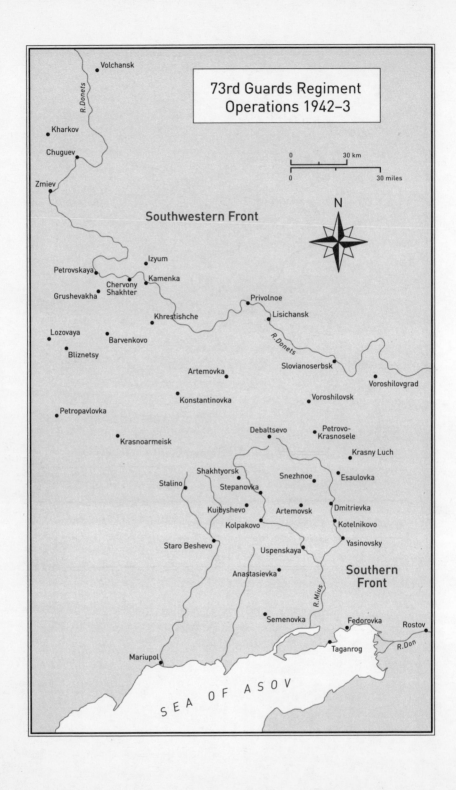

73rd Guards Regiment Operations 1942–3

Volchansk

R. Donets

Kharkov

Chuguev

Zmiev

Southwestern Front

0   30 km

0   30 miles

N

Izyum

Petrovskaya

Kamenka

Chervony
Shakhter

Grushevakha

Privolnoe

Khrestishche

Lisichansk

R. Donets

Lozovaya

Barvenkovo

Bliznetsy

Slovianoserbsk

Artemovka

Voroshilovgrad

Konstantinovka

Voroshilovsk

Petropavlovka

Debaltsevo

Petrovo-
Krasnosele

Krasnoarmeisk

Krasny Luch

Shakhtyorsk

Snezhnoe

Esaulovka

Stalino

Stepanovka

Kuibyshevo

Artemovsk

Dmitrievka

Kolpakovo

Kotelnikovo

Staro Beshevo

Yasinovsky

Uspenskaya

Southern
Front

Anastasievka

R. Mius

Semenovka

Fedorovka

Rostov

Taganrog

R. Don

Mariupol

SEA OF ASOV

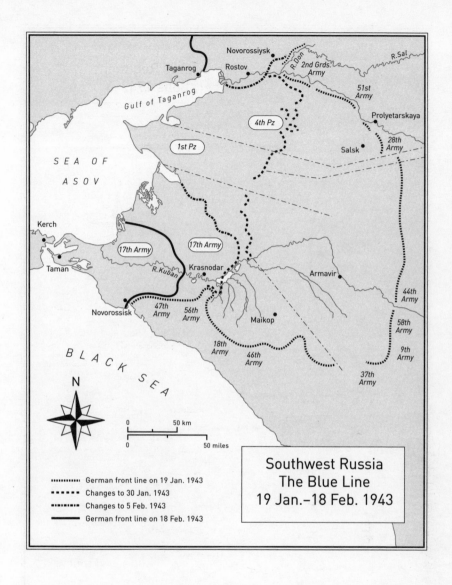

Southwest Russia
The Blue Line
19 Jan.–18 Feb. 1943

Novorossiysk
Taganrog
Rostov
R. Don
2nd Grds. Army
R. Sal
4th Pz
51st Army
Prolyetarskaya
1st Pz
Salsk
28th Army
SEA OF ASOV
Kerch
17th Army
17th Army
Taman
R. Kuban
Krasnodar
Armavir
44th Army
Novorossisk
47th Army
56th Army
Maikop
58th Army
18th Army
46th Army
9th Army
BLACK SEA
37th Army
Gulf of Taganrog

N

0   50 km
0   50 miles

············· German front line on 19 Jan. 1943
- - - - - Changes to 30 Jan. 1943
-·-·-·-·- Changes to 5 Feb. 1943
———— German front line on 18 Feb. 1943

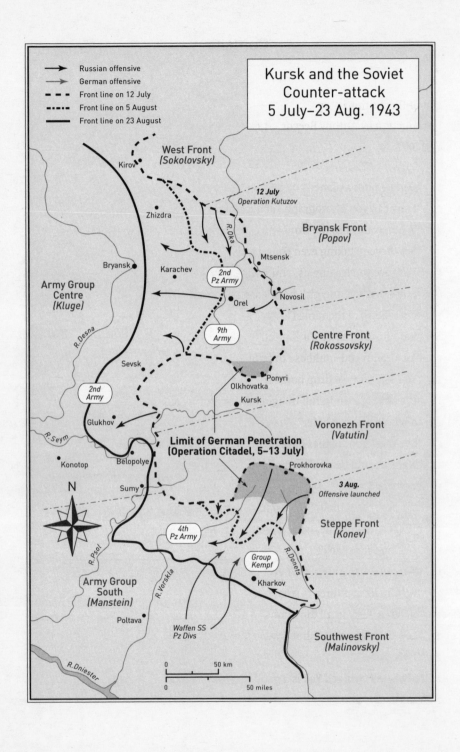

Kursk and the Soviet
Counter-attack
5 July–23 Aug. 1943

Russian offensive
German offensive
Front line on 12 July
Front line on 5 August
Front line on 23 August

West Front
(Sokolovsky)

Kirov

12 July
Operation Kutuzov

Zhizdra

R. Oka

Bryansk Front
(Popov)

Mtsensk

Bryansk

Karachev

2nd
Pz Army

Orel

Novosil

Army Group
Centre
(Kluge)

R. Desna

9th
Army

Centre Front
(Rokossovsky)

Sevsk

2nd
Army

Ponyri

Olkhovatka

Kursk

Glukhov

R. Seym

Limit of German Penetration
(Operation Citadel, 5–13 July)

Voronezh Front
(Vatutin)

Konotop

Belopolye

Prokhorovka

3 Aug.
Offensive launched

N

Sumy

4th
Pz Army

Steppe Front
(Konev)

R. Psol

Group
Kempf

R. Donets

Army Group
South
(Manstein)

R. Vorskla

Kharkov

Poltava

Waffen SS
Pz Divs

0   50 km

0   50 miles

R. Dniester

Southwest Front
(Malinovsky)

Contents

List of Illustrations

Introduction

Antony Beevor

Defending the Motherland is the fascinating story of the female pilots who fought for the Soviet Union in the Second World War, a unique phenomenon in the history of modern conflict. Inspired by the intrepid aviators of the inter-war years, young women had flocked to join flying clubs in the 1930s. For many, their dream was to emulate the great Marina Raskova, a beautiful aviatrix and famous Soviet heroine, whom we soon discover was also secretly an officer in Lavrenty Beria's dreaded N.K.V.D. secret police.

Following the Nazi invasion of June 1941, Raskova used her prestige and contacts in Moscow to form a group of three all-women aviation regiments in the autumn and winter of 1941. There was to be a fighter regiment, a night bomber regiment, and a long-range bomber regiment. Raskova was clearly a natural leader, and when she issued her call for volunteers, hundreds of young women from different walks of life travelled from all over the Soviet Union in the hope of being accepted. They were not downhearted when they found themselves issued with uniforms and greatcoats that were far too large and made them look ridiculous, nor even when handed Red Army underwear for men. They fashioned their own, ideally from German parachute silk.

Russian machismo did not pay much attention to Soviet theories of sexual equality. The 'girls', as they were always known, were mercilessly mocked and teased, yet they had far fewer crashes in training than any of the male units. Raskova's young women, most of whom were in their early twenties, had to prove themselves by being more skilled and more courageous than the men, yet male commanders remained deeply reluctant to allow them to engage in combat.

Raskova's little air army assembled in southern Russia at the large airbase outside Engels. Almost all her volunteers with flying experience wanted to become fighter pilots. Only the most experienced and intrepid were selected. Raskova commanded the long-range bomber regiment herself. Exploiting her contacts in the Soviet hierarchy once again, she managed to obtain the new Pe-2 dive bomber for her regiment although it was not an easy aircraft to fly. But perhaps the greatest courage was needed by the pilots and navigators of the 'night bomber regiment', which flew flimsy U-2 biplanes. Navigation in the dark, with only the most basic instruments, required a very cool head and their crews were not allowed parachutes until late in the war. Their main combat mission was to fly over enemy lines at night, switching off their engines to glide in like ghosts and drop small bombs. The Germans, on hearing that the pilots were women, dubbed them the 'Night Witches'.

The stories of these courageous young women also tell us so much about Soviet society under Stalin. It is Lyuba Vinogradova's great achievement after so much research to have been able to assemble such a detailed picture of their lives, their hopes, their idealism and also their disappointments. I am not surprised since, having worked with her on and off for just on twenty years, I have seen how brilliant she is in archives, cleverly handling the dragons who guard them, and then, with her instinct for the telling description, spotting the nuggets which make all the difference to bringing the period to life. I greatly look forward to her next book, which will be on the young women snipers in the Red Army.

Preface

I first started my research into Soviet female wartime pilots in the spring of 2009. Incredibly, in spite of having collaborated for many years as a researcher with various historians and focusing closely on WWII (which involved reading thousands of pages of documents and hundreds of books), I was not even aware of their existence – or that of American and British female ferry pilots. I learned about them from the French historian Claude Quétel, director of the Mémorial de Caen in Normandy and a specialist in the history of WWII. Claude was convinced that someone had to write a biography of Lilya Litvyak, the "White Rose of Stalingrad", as she was very often referred to in publications – a girl who achieved great renown as a fighter pilot before she was killed in her early twenties. He suggested this project to Antony Beevor, my own friend and mentor, and Antony in turn suggested it to me.

Of course I was interested. I am not a historian, but I have always been fascinated by stories about peoples' experiences, and at no other time did people have such dramatic experiences as during the war. Lilya's seemed such a remarkably powerful story. This slender, blonde girl with shining eyes and a courageous heart, a gifted pilot – another pilot tried to convey a sense of Lilya's rare talent by explaining that she could "see" the air – and a rebel who was never afraid of her commanders. And she had had a love affair with a young, brave pilot who also died too soon.

But straightaway I realised that one could not really write a book about her alone. Lilya died at the age of twenty-one, when her life was just beginning, and before she had the chance to experience all those things that might make up a volume of biography. Together with this realisation there came an idea: I should tell the story of Lilya and her comrades, those who died and those who survived the war. I did not want it to be simply a collective biography; I was keen to use the experiences of these young women pilots and their mechanics to help give an account of the first two years of the war. I also ended up writing some chapters about male pilots, those whose regiments Litvyak and her squadron joined at Stalingrad in 1942.

I started reading up and, as I did so, looked for veterans of Marina Raskova's three female regiments who might still be alive. It turned out that the pilots themselves were almost all dead. Because they needed to clock up a lot of flying hours to be allowed to join Raskova's regiments, they were generally older than their crews.

But I was very lucky to meet Valentina Neminushchaya (née Petrochenkova) from the female fighter regiment. She was the first person to explain to me the kind of qualities a girl needed to be able to fly a fighter. Unfortunately there was no second visit, but it was through her that I met Elena Kulkova (née Malyutina), a heroic bomber pilot and a very special, generous and strong, intellectual person, who is now and will always be my dear friend. Elena introduced me to "Hero of the Soviet Union" Yevdokia Pasko, from the night bomber regiment, who told me how she and her friends flew at night in tiny plywood and canvas training aircraft.

Elena also gave me addresses in Saratov where I met navigator Olga Golubeva-Teres, who became a writer in her later years, and Elena Lukina from the heavy bomber regiment. Across the Volga from Saratov, I was able to see the town of Engels, the place where Raskova's regiments were first stationed.

I called Stepan Mikoyan who was a young pilot during the war (and after the war became a famous Soviet test pilot). It was to Stepan's regiment, the 434th, at Stalingrad, that four of the girl pilots were sent in September 1942. We have met several times, and I am extremely grateful to this amazing man, a fearless pilot and a great storyteller, for letting me catch a glimpse of the atmosphere in which he lived in September 1942 and for sharing some fleeting memories of the four girls who fought alongside him during several incredibly hard weeks.

And now it is time to write about two people who brought my main characters to life, and made my book what it is now: a story based on the recollections of some of those who were there, who saw the dramatic events with their own eyes. I still cannot believe my luck, not only because these two people fought alongside Litvyak and Katya Budanova (who also flew fighter planes with great distinction), but also because they were such special, rare people, people who make the world a better place with every step they take.

I found Nikolai Menkov's name in the semi-fictional account of Lilya Litvyak's life written by Valeriy Agranovsky, who quoted Menkov's letter giving details about the missing girl (whose aircraft he serviced) and the plane. The letter (written in the seventies) mentioned that he lived in Cherepovets. What happened next was nothing short of a miracle. I found Nikolai within twenty minutes of learning of his existence: his telephone number was in the Cherepovets online database. When I called, he answered immediately and invited me to come and see him. I visited him and his daughter Tatyana several times, and each time was unforgettable: a kind, warm reception and fascinating conversations that ranged well beyond the war and aviation. On one of these visits I brought along the regiment's documents, and Nikolai read and commented on them. All of a sudden the documents came to life.

"I am so sorry, but I don't let strangers into my apartment," Valentina Krasnoshchyokova explained politely when I called her first. However, I did not visit alone: Lidiya Zaitseva, the record-setting Soviet sports pilot, a lovely, kind person, brought me along to Valentina's tiny flat in Kaluga. There were portraits of Litvyak and Budanova on her shelf and I made a beeline for them. Some are included in the book. Kaluga is only 150 kilometres away from Moscow, to the south-west, and it was my great luck that I was able to visit Valentina often. We would talk about the female fighter regiment, and about the 437th, and 9th regiments, as well as the 73rd, which she left in 1944 when she was badly wounded. The two girl pilots who died in the summer of 1943 were sometimes present in our conversations, but not always. Valentina had memories to share that were a lot more important to her than Litvyak and Budanova. I came to love her dearly and so was willing to listen. I recorded and will keep many of her stories about events that happened long after Lilya and Katya had died:

for example, how, when Valentina was working at the Oblast Party Committee, she rescued the Soviet bard Bulat Okudzhava from a teaching position at a village school where he had been exiled by the authorities; or how she sat all night comforting a new arrival at the boarding school for children with hearing problems, where she was for many years director (Valentina was almost completely deaf as a result of concussion in 1944). Once I accompanied her to a supermarket and two girls greeted her in sign language. They were too young to have been her students at the boarding school so she asked them how they knew her. The girls explained using signs: *people say that a long time ago there was a kind director at our school*. I felt very touched, this exemplified my friend: a kind and active person who always helped those who needed her.

Valentina Krasnoshchyokova and Nikolai Menkov, who both died in 2012, will always be in my thoughts. I believe they would have been glad to know of the existence of a book that would tell the world a little about them, about their comrades and about the regiments in which they served so hard and risked their lives, in order to bring victory closer.

LYUBA VINOGRADOVA
November 2014
Maputo, Mozambique

I

"Girls – pilot a plane!"

Moscow was expecting the Wehrmacht. The huge shop windows on Gorky Street were piled high with sandbags. Above the Kremlin, barrage balloons floated like huge, motionless fish. Mother Russia looked down from propaganda posters, doleful but stern. The city seemed to have died. The only places bustling with life were food shops and warehouses being plundered by looters who had run amok in an unexpected interval of freedom; and railway stations and roads leading east. Terrified Muscovites and refugees from regions already occupied by Hitler's troops sought desperately to flee the city.

The panic that gripped Moscow on 15 October 1941 was comparable with the chaos of September 1812 when Napoleon's troops entered the city. Having taken Moscow without a battle, the French emperor was forced immediately to withdraw his troops as the city was engulfed by a huge fire, supposedly started by the Muscovites themselves to prevent their ancient capital falling into the hands of the enemy. Napoleon grimly observed the conflagration, which almost completely destroyed the timber-built Russian capital, from his headquarters at Petrovsky Palace on the north-western outskirts of the city.

This squat neo-Gothic castle was still standing in 1941, but now its windows looked out, not onto the St Petersburg High Road, but at the expanse of the Leningrad Highway. The highway was deserted. There were rumours that the previous day a detachment of German motorcyclists had advanced along it as far as the Northern River Station before encountering any resistance.[1] It was also said they were followed by two armoured personnel carriers. Those reconnoitring units had immediately been destroyed but others would doubtless follow, because the Germans had taken just three and a half months to reach the Soviet capital. They had effortlessly captured almost all the country's major cities and were now at the very gates of Moscow. To many Muscovites it seemed that only a miracle could save them. There were people who insisted they had heard with their own ears Yury Levitan, the official Soviet news announcer, admitting on the radio that: "The Germans are entering Moscow."

All the more surprising then were the noise and bustle prevailing in the old Petrovsky Palace. Vaulted ceilings that had once echoed to the music of balls held by Catherine the Great, now reverberated to women's voices from a more motley assembly than they had ever witnessed. The proceedings were being directed by a few women in military uniform: the "very beautiful and slender" Captain Militsa Kazarinova; plump, stubby Captain Yevdokia Rachkevich; the celebrity aviatrix Vera Lomako, and one or two others. They were all young, the oldest only a little over thirty, but those they were organising were younger still. Besides these military officers, several dozen women wore the beret with a red star and the blue tunic of the flying clubs. These were instructors, their uniform familiar to the whole country from the posters of Osoaviakhim, the "Association for the Support of the Defence, Aviation and Chemical Industries", which was responsible for the sporting and military education of Soviet youth and the training of reservists for the armed forces. The rest were in civilian clothes, wearing dresses or skirts, in shoes with or without high heels. Almost all had long hair, braided into plaits or pinned up in buns. They could hardly have looked less military, yet within a few hours these girls would be donning uniforms, foot wrappings and army boots.

Having ploughed her way through a vast amount of business that morning, another beautiful young woman was being chauffeured in an official black limousine to meet this mixed gathering.

She had grey eyes, dark thin eyebrows, and an elegantly smooth hairstyle. She wore a well-fitting uniform, the red-starred beret and, on her chest, the gold star of a Hero of the Soviet Union. Despite her youth and beauty, she was not being driven in a GAZ-M1 limousine because she was the wife of some factory director or military bigwig. The car had been allocated for her personal use by the Soviet Government, and although she was only twenty-nine years old, newspaper photographs had made her face familiar the length and breadth of the U.S.S.R. Everybody knew the name of Marina Raskova. For millions of Soviet citizens there was magic in it and they associated it with heroism, and the romance of long-distance flights. Every schoolchild knew that this was a woman for whom no exploit was too daunting and who could rise to any challenge. "I want to be like Marina Raskova," hundreds of thousands of young Soviet women wrote on their application forms to join flying clubs and branches of Osoaviakhim. Raskova had flown first the breadth and then the length of the largest country in the world. She tested the latest aircraft. She had spent ten days alone in the forests of Siberia with almost no food, and none of those assembled in Petrovsky Palace had any doubt that she would cope with the new and challenging task she had set herself. She was to bring together women of her own kind, fearless and in love with their homeland and the heavens, to turn them into wartime pilots, and release them into the skies to deal death to the enemy.

In the Moscow courtyard where Raskova grew up, the children would stop playing and gaze up at the sky on the rare occasions a plane crossed it. They would sing a silly song:

> Aeroplane, aeroplane,
> Fly me faster than a train
> If I fall out of the bed
> I will really bang my head.

The children all wanted to be aviators, but Marina, the daughter of a deceased music teacher, wanted to be an opera singer and intended to study at the Conservatory.

Although she had many talents and was good at all her school subjects, besides music she especially loved chemistry. In those years when the Soviet Union was industrialising, this was a discipline as important as computer science is today. A time came in the life of the young Marina when she had to choose between music and chemistry and, as she needed to earn a living, she opted for chemistry.

She worked for a time as a laboratory technician at a chemical plant before marrying a chemist from the same factory. Marina Malinina became Marina Raskova and gave birth to a daughter. She later divorced. When her daughter was a little older, Raskova returned to work, this time as a draughtswoman at the Air Force Academy, and there she discovered a whole new world. The Academy was swarming with young men who wore leather raglan coats, talked about the latest aircraft, flights at high altitude and great speed, new weaponry, and the enormous distances that could now be travelled. These were people whose faces featured in the newspapers, and they included heroes the whole country knew. More importantly, as far as Marina was concerned, there were also women pilots.

The government, pushing through the industrialisation of a huge, backward country, proclaimed total equality of the sexes. There were no jobs from which women were barred: they could work in any branch of the economy on equal terms. "Girls – the building sites need you!" "Girls – drive a tractor!" "Girls – pilot a plane!" they were urged by "visual propaganda media", the Soviet government's posters. Girl pilots began to appear, but there were as yet no girl navigators. Nor any male navigators either, come to that. There had been no time to train people to assist with flying the first large airships or, if the need should arise, to bring an aircraft to a target and bomb it effectively. The young draughtswoman saw an opportunity and Marina Raskova became the first female navigator in the U.S.S.R.

She sat the examination as a non-resident student, and also graduated from the flying school at Moscow's Tushino Aerodrome, but had little opportunity to actually fly. That did not prevent her from rubbing shoulders with a new Soviet elite, the aviators. With her beauty, intelligence, and an attractively strong personality, she was soon fully accepted in this exclusive circle. Indeed, it was not long before her fame eclipsed that of almost all her new friends.

In 1938 Raskova took part in two record-breaking long-distance flights with legendary Soviet women pilots. She first flew from Sebastopol in the Crimea to Arkhangelsk in the Soviet Arctic with Polina Osipenko and Vera Lomako. After this success something even more spectacular was envisaged: a flight from Moscow to the Russian Far East.

Valentina Grizodubova, in command, and her co-pilot Polina Osipenko took Raskova on as their navigator. The graceful Valentina was a long-standing aviatrix who, at twenty-eight, already had a great deal of flying experience. Polina, who at first sight could easily be mistaken for a man, had until quite recently been a penniless poultry maid but, with steely determination, got herself enrolled in the Kacha Flying School and made her own way to the heavens. She was now an experienced pilot, and in 1937 alone, flying in a range of aircraft, had set five different world records for altitude, speed and distance of flight.

The sheer ambition of the new project took away the breath of even experienced pilots. The Soviet Union extended over one-sixth of the globe, and they decided they would fly across nearly the whole of its European and Asian territory, from Moscow to Komsomolsk-on-Amur, which was almost on the Pacific Ocean. It was to be a non-stop flight of 6,000 kilometres.

The expectation was that the flight, in a huge silver Tupolev ANT-37 long-range bomber that was given the name of *Motherland*, would take about twenty-four hours, but it was late September and the weather was unpredictable. On the day of the flight, conditions were worse than anticipated, and sixty kilometres after take-off all sight of the ground was lost under cloud cover. They flew by their instruments to the Urals, but then faced an additional hazard as the plane began to ice up. Encountering strong turbulence in the night they had to fly above the clouds and rose to a height of 7,500 metres, where it was desperately cold. At this point, nine hours into the flight, the plane's receiver and transmitter froze and they lost radio contact. The whole country was on tenterhooks. By dawn, as they approached the Manchurian border, an indicator light warned that their fuel would run out in at most another half hour. Grizodubova ordered Marina to bail out as her navigator's module, separate from the cockpit and at the front of the aircraft, would almost certainly be crushed in an emergency landing. Raskova was reluctant but, having no choice, opened the trapdoor in the cabin floor. In her pockets she had a pistol, a compass, a pocket knife, matches which would light even when wet, and one and a half bars of chocolate.[2]

Landing in thick forest, Marina spent ten days searching for the plane. She battled her way through dense undergrowth in her heavy, fur-lined flying suit, heading slowly for where she thought she should find *Motherland*. On the first day, in the belief that she would soon locate the aircraft, she ate half a bar of chocolate, but in the days that followed rationed herself to a single segment. Sometimes she came upon berries, and once found mushrooms, but when she tried to cook them started such a fire in the forest she was lucky to escape with her life.

During one of her last nights in the forest Marina dreamed of Comrade Stalin, who reproached her for being a poor navigator. She was terribly shamed by the words of this "dearest person of all", as she called him, and promised to improve her work.[3] On the morning of the tenth day, Marina saw planes overhead and heard shots. By now she was barely able to move without the support of a stick, but shortly afterwards glimpsed the silver tail of a plane, "our beautiful *Motherland*". When they spotted Marina, the pilots, mechanics and doctors by the plane rushed to meet her. She was wearing warm long johns and a jersey, with a woollen sweater over it and the Order of Lenin pinned to her chest. One foot was in a high fur boot but the other was bare. They wanted to carry her, but Marina proudly refused and walked to the plane on her own.

Her fellow crew members told her that Valentina had managed very skilfully to land the aircraft on its fuselage in a swamp without lowering the undercarriage. When they looked at their watches and instruments, the airwomen calculated that *Motherland* had been airborne for twenty-six hours and twenty-nine minutes, a world record.

Valentina and Polina had settled to wait for Marina, who they thought must have parachuted down nearby. Alas, she did not appear and neither did anyone else. The whole country was looking for *Motherland*, but it took time to find them. The pilots' only visitors were creatures of the *taiga*,* first a lynx, which they nicknamed *Kisya* ("Pussy"), and then a bear. When they heard the bear rubbing itself against the plane the young women believed they had finally been found. With the words, "Please come in!" they threw open the cabin door. Terrified to find their visitor was a bear, they fired a signal flare and it ran off back into the woods.[4]

It took a week of searching before the silver fuselage of *Motherland* was spotted by a young pilot called Mikhail Sakharov. Nobody dared land next to them on the swamp, and equipment and food were parachuted down instead. The news that *Motherland* and two members of the crew had been found spread across the land like wildfire, and for the next few days everybody was anxiously waiting for news of Raskova. By the time Marina staggered into view, Valentina and Polina had almost given up hope of ever seeing her again. After the doctor had fed her a few spoonfuls of chicken broth, she fell asleep next to her friends and all the newspapers prepared front pages with the news that Marina Raskova was alive!

The first women to be awarded the title of Hero of the Soviet Union arrived at Belorussky Station in a special carriage. Marina emerged with a cage in which a squirrel was jumping around, a gift for her daughter Tanya from the Young Pioneers of Komsomolsk-on-Amur. They were driven to the Kremlin in an open limousine down Gorky Street, which was strewn with flowers and leaflets.

In reporting their return to Moscow, the press made no mention of the collision of two aircraft above *Motherland*'s emergency landing site. A Douglas DC-3 sent to the aid of *Motherland* by an Air Force research institute collided head on with a Tupolev TB-3 bomber with parachute troops on board. Sixteen men died, with just four of those on board the TB-3 managing to jump clear as their plane tumbled to the ground. It seems they did not want to spoil the holiday atmosphere.[5] The victims's remains were honoured instead by a ceremony at the workers' club at the No. 199 Shipbuilding Plant in Komsomolsk-on-Amur.[6]

* A boundless coniferous forest.

In her *Notes of a Navigator*, which became the favourite reading of millions of Soviet women, Raskova gave a detailed account of her adventures in the forest and of how she met Grizodubova.[7] Raskova writes of how she and "Valya" took to each other at first sight and soon became close friends. Together they planned their record-breaking flight in Valya's cramped room after she had put her little son to bed. Valentina Grizodubova, however, tells a different story.

Grizodubova outlived Raskova and Osipenko by many years, surviving to the ripe age of eighty-three. By the time she died in 1993, it had become possible to say things one could never have dreamed of mentioning before. And the famous aviatrix did talk, to people she considered worthy of her revelations, about many things, including Marina Raskova.

Grizodubova was a wonderfully honest and magnanimous woman, a fearless champion of people who had been wronged, someone who saved many people in the field of aviation from the Stalinist purges, including the spacecraft designer Sergey Korolyov. She spoke of Raskova, the companion with whom she had undergone such tribulations and side-by-side with whom she had lived the best moments of her life, with manifest dislike. Grizodubova's revelations go a long way towards explaining Marina Raskova's meteoric career.

According to Grizodubova, Raskova, who had little experience as a navigator, was "imposed" on her and Osipenko because in the Soviet Union any team engaged on an important mission had always to include an N.K.V.D. (secret police) officer. Few people were aware that at the beginning of the war Air Force Major Marina Raskova was also a senior lieutenant of state security – a rank that corresponded to a major in the Red Army. For four years her workplace had been an office in the Lubyanka. From 1937 she was on the N.K.V.D.'s payroll as a staff consultant and by February 1939 she had become a fully fledged officer of the N.K.V.D.'s Special Department. Raskova had probably been working for the N.K.V.D. even before 1937, because most staff consultants had previously been engaged as freelance consultants or, more simply, informers. The documents that would shed light on Senior Lieutenant Raskova's duties, if they still exist, are not publicly available, but it is likely they would have included informing on those with whom she socialised, the aviators. It is perhaps no coincidence that it was in 1940, when repressive measures against them were at their height, that Raskova's N.K.V.D. career took off spectacularly. By the beginning of the war, hundreds of aircraft designers, managers of aircraft factories and top Soviet Air Force officers had been arrested. Many were shot.

"I have no idea how Marina gained her navigator's licence," Grizodubova remarked. "Neither do I know what other work she was doing in parallel, but I have no doubt that many people suffered because of her. You could say she and I worked in tandem: she put people in prison and I ran around all the offices and tried to get them back out."[8] She continued, "If Polina Osipenko was a top-rate pilot, Marina Raskova had no specialist training as a navigator and had clocked up a total of only thirty or so flying hours. She knew absolutely nothing about flying in extreme weather conditions, let alone at night. She was a member of our crew only because she had been 'recommended' to us."[9]

In 1941, however, the Soviet public knew Raskova as a heroic airwoman, a legend, the idol of a generation. She showed the whole world that aircraft built by the new Soviet industries could set world records, and that they could be flown by women. She was the darling of the U.S.S.R. and received enormous numbers of letters from Soviet women. After the outbreak of war, the stream became a flood. Among these were many letters from female pilots who had unsuccessfully done the rounds of bureaucracy trying to get to fight at the front. They were not wanted: in 1941 there were plenty of male pilots, just not enough aircraft for them to fly.

Marina Raskova hit on the idea of forming and heading a regiment of female military pilots. Unlike Valentina Grizodubova, who by this time commanded a force of men, Raskova would recruit the best Soviet women pilots, who would be more than a match for anyone. Fortunately, the beautiful Marina Raskova, the heroic aviatrix who was also a secret police officer, was on such good terms with Stalin that she took her proposal straight to him in the Kremlin.

Stalin approved the idea and Raskova immediately set about implementing it. She had so many volunteers it was decided to set up three units: a fighter regiment, a heavy bomber regiment, and a night bomber regiment.

By mid-October 1941 the preparations were complete and the future pilots, together with college-educated girls who were to be trained as navigators and mechanics, were assembled in Moscow.

2

"How can you photograph such misery?"

On 19 July 1941 Masha Dolina became a military pilot in an unusual way.[10] Earlier that month German troops, implementing the Barbarossa campaign plan, broke through the last line of defence in Soviet Byelorussia on the River Berezina and, heading into the Ukraine, dashed towards the line formed by the Western Dvina and Dnieper rivers. Here they encountered unexpected resistance from regrouped forces of the Soviet Western Front, but these were unable to hold them back for long. Further up the Dnieper, German armies, which in early July had taken the cities of Zhitomir and Berdichev in Western Ukraine, soon came close to the Dnieper itself, encircling and capturing two Soviet armies along with their commanders at Uman. Beyond the Dnieper lay Kiev, the capital of the Ukraine, which Stalin had only recently assured the Allies would never be surrendered.

That same July, Konstantin Simonov, a young but already well-known and fashionable poet, prose-writer and playwright, and now war correspondent, witnessed the terrible chaos of the retreat over the Dnieper. He saw refugees whom he was powerless to help and, like most of the soldiers, felt terribly ashamed. Many years later, Yakov Khalip, a photographer for the Army newspaper Red Star, who had been with Simonov, asked him, "Do you remember that old man at the crossing on the Dnieper?" Simonov suddenly did remember an old man who had harnessed himself in place of a horse and was pulling a cart with children in it. Khalip had started photographing the scene when Simonov snatched the camera and pushed him back into their car, yelling, "How can you photograph such misery?"

Thinking back now, Simonov saw they had both been right: he in saying it was unforgivable for a man in uniform to climb out of a vehicle and start photographing "this appalling refugee exodus" and the old man hauling children in a cart. It had seemed immoral. He could not imagine how to explain to the disconsolate people going past why they should be photographed. With the war in the past, however, he accepted that, if it was legitimate for him to write about these things, the only way a photojournalist could capture the misery was by photographing it.[11]

At the flying club* in Nikopol where Masha was working there was total confusion. As the fighting had already reached the suburbs of Kiev, Nikopol, which was 400 kilometres away, was hastily evacuated, but the flying club was completely overlooked. Masha, who found herself in charge as all the more senior instructors had been sent to the front, did not know what to do. With German tanks only eighty kilometres away, she rushed in desperation to the commander of the retreating fighter division. "Comrade Colonel! Take us together with our aircraft as volunteer pilots." The colonel had no time for her and just waved her away angrily, saying he was far from certain he would be able to save even his own aircraft.

The next day, by which time the Germans were even closer, Masha appealed to him again. In the division everyone was "running around in disarray". At first the colonel did not even notice her, giving her his attention only when she shouted in tears at his back that to abandon the flying club members and leave their three U-2 aircraft to fall into enemy hands would be treason. The colonel stared at her very intently, before ordering

* Flying clubs had first appeared in the U.S.S.R. in the early 1930s and were immediately extremely popular. Although they trained amateur pilots, they also offered a route to the flying schools, both military and civilian, where one received professional pilot's training.

her to destroy the flying club's hangars and fuel tanks, and fly her planes across the Dnieper at night. If her pilots managed that he would enlist them in his division. Masha and her friends destroyed their beloved flying club with their own hands, not looking at each other in order not to break down. That night, with no experience whatsoever of night flying, she and two colleagues flew their first and most terrifying combat mission.

She was to remember the Dnieper in 1941 for the rest of her life: the flash and thunder of explosions, the impenetrable smoke and blood-red glow. Down below, blown-up ferries flew into the air, tanks burned like huge black bonfires, planes fell from the sky like wood shavings. The water of the Dnieper, which they glimpsed through breaks in the smoke, seemed also to be engulfed in flames. Miraculously, they managed to get all three of their planes through this vision of hell and land them safely at the airfield, which was completely blacked out because of the bombing. The divisional commander was as good as his word and duly enrolled them in 296 Fighter Regiment.

Many of the regiment's pilots had fought in the Russo-Finnish war and were already highly decorated. And a good number, like the commander, Nikolai Baranov, had been fighting since the day the war began in June. At first, finding herself alongside these battle-hardened fighter pilots, Masha's throat was dry with excitement. She began to develop a crazy determination, which grew stronger by the day, to become a fighter pilot herself. From her earliest days she had told herself that, "to live without a goal is completely pointless."[12]

Masha Dolina was the eldest in the family of a whole horde of children. Her mother could neither read nor write and earned a living for them by taking in washing; her father was paralysed from the waist down and confined to an invalid's cart. It was a hard, hungry life. There was no food for Masha to take from home to eat at school, but sometimes kind classmates shared theirs with her. Her clothes had been endlessly patched, and her first real felt boots were bought for her by a whip-round among her teachers after her feet were frostbitten. For years her family huddled in a corner of the village pottery, until they made a dugout for themselves that had walls of bricks which her mother and all the children, from the oldest to the youngest, made together from clay mixed with horse dung. They were thrilled with their new house, which rose seventy centimetres above ground level and had a tiny window – but in darker moments Masha feared she would never escape such dire poverty. When she completed seventh grade at school she had to go in search of work to feed the family. Masha sensed that only the currently fashionable profession of aviation, with its seemingly limitless prospects, offered a way out. Now, at twenty years of age already a seasoned pilot and flying instructor determined to devote her life to aviation, Masha wanted to scale the heights of her profession and become a fighter pilot.

This, however, was not a good moment to fulfil that dream. The regiment was in constant retreat, abandoning one airfield after another. They abandoned the Ukraine, Masha's homeland, to the Germans. "God forbid you should ever witness a retreat and have to see that dismay, that child-like helplessness and forlorn hope in the eyes of your fellow countrymen."[13] When they were very close to Masha's village of Mikhailovka, where her family were still living, she plucked up the courage to ask Baranov to give her leave to say goodbye to them before the Germans came. She promised she would just fly there, give them food, hug them, and come straight back. Baranov, a broad-shouldered man of thirty or so, with curly, slightly ginger hair and a big round head, fixed his grey eyes on Masha "as if checking my trustworthiness". He would be risking not only a pilot but also a plane, and yet he could hardly refuse.

"Just mind that when you land in your village you unload your gifts, hug your parents, but under no circumstances turn off the engine," he said. He knew from that morning's intelligence report that the Germans had already reached the station at Prishib, just seven kilometres from Mikhailovka. Masha was given the coordinates that would enable her to catch up with the regiment.

Baranov was an intrepid pilot and an extremely able commander who was loved as well as respected. After his talk with Masha, he gathered the other pilots and had a word with them. Straight away, one after the other, they came over to Masha's plane bearing an extraordinary array of gifts. They brought out the emergency rations of chocolate, biscuits and tinned food stored in their aircraft against the eventuality of a forced landing. They brought all the food they had, as well as greatcoats and tunics, soap and first aid kits and piled these offerings into the plane. It was after midday before Masha took off for Mikhailovka in her overloaded U-2.

As she flew over her home she could see no people in the village streets, but spotted the airfield where she had flown a glider, then the school, then her family's humble dugout. Masha circled and saw people beginning to come out of their homes. She landed the plane in the street by the village soviet and people came running from all directions. Her father was brought in his little cart, with Masha's mother running beside him, heavily pregnant again. Masha tearfully hugged all her relatives, unloaded the presents, and ran back to the plane saying, "I have to go!" but people swarmed round and it was evening before she was able to take off.

By the next day Mikhailovka was in German hands, and from then on Masha lived in constant fear for her family. Now, however, she had another family of loyal front-line friends among whom she already felt thoroughly at home. This meant she was stunned when Baranov summoned her one day to relay an order: "Comrade Junior Lieutenant, you are required to report for duty to Hero of the Soviet Union Raskova!"

Masha burst into tears. The name of her icon was no consolation; she could not forgive even Raskova for taking her away from the front to waste time on a lot of square-bashing when she was within striking distance of becoming a fighter pilot. Baranov knew her for a fine, courageous U-2 pilot and needed her for liaison – a complex and challenging role that involved everything from communicating with division headquarters to transporting the wounded and ferrying supplies. He had no wish to lose her, but told her he could not disobey orders.

3

"When you get to the front you can wrap your feet in newspaper"

There had always been more girls than boys in teacher training colleges. "You're never going to find yourself a husband there!" Valya Krasnoshchyokova was warned, half-jokingly, half in earnest, by a girlfriend when she decided to be a history teacher. And by the summer of 1941 the only boys left on the course were those unfit for military service. Some had been conscripted, others had volunteered for the front. The girls themselves were sent in September to build defence works, and brought back to college in Moscow in early October. Before classes even started, however, the Komsomol (Young Communist League) administrator asked, not altogether unexpectedly, "Well, girls, who wants to go to the front line?"

Valya was not entirely sure she did. Certainly she wanted to do her bit for the country. She wanted to fight the Germans who had occupied her home town, but was reluctant to abandon her college course, and what was to become of her two younger sisters and little brother? Their mother had died and their father had been drafted into the Army. To refuse was, however, impossible, Valya decided. When she and several other girls put themselves forward, the administrator told them to come the next day to the Komsomol Central Committee building on Maroseyka Street in central Moscow. He warned them to be sure to say they were there as volunteers.

Facing such an abrupt change in the direction of their lives, the girls were barely able to sleep that night. In the morning they walked to the Komsomol building, where they were asked what they wanted to be at the front. Valya replied for herself and her friend, "machine gunners". She received a nod of acknowledgement, which she took to signify agreement.

There were a lot of girls in the conference hall. "What are they going to be doing?" Valya wondered. "Are they all going to be machine-gunners?" At this point Nikolai Mikhailov, the First Secretary of the Central Committee of the Komsomol, and Raskova came out onto the stage.

Mikhailov announced simply that Marina Raskova would now address them. There was no need to introduce her: everybody knew her from photographs and *Notes of a Navigator*, which most of them had read in *Newspaper Novels*.* Raskova said she had spoken to Comrade Stalin, and he had given her permission to form women's air regiments. "But Comrade Stalin warned that they must consist only of volunteers," she added, which made clear to Valya why their Komsomol administrator had been so emphatic about that point.

Raskova told the girls to obtain their parents' consent, but Valya had no one to ask. Her college headmaster, however, gave her and her friends a great send-off, as if they were members of his own family. He assembled the college students and, in front of them all, bade a solemn farewell to those leaving for the front. Friends who were staying behind boiled porridge for them, albeit without salt or sugar because there were already major difficulties with food supplies, and they ate a final meal together. The volunteers collected their "rucksacks", ordinary bags to which shoulder straps and a drawstring had been added. Valya's only "smart" item of clothing was a white batiste blouse. She left it with a friend who was not going to the front, telling her she would be back for it when the war was over.

The weather was already cold when, the next day, the students were led through the centre of Moscow, from Maroseyka Street to Petrovsky Palace. On the way there were several air-raid alerts, during which they went down into the recently built Metro stations. These were very crowded. Trains were still running, but at Mayakovskaya Station what caught their eye was not the ornate mosaics on the ceiling glorifying the achievements of Soviet aviation, but the fold-up beds on the marble floors. The stations were being hastily converted into air-raid shelters.[14] Within a few days the trains had stopped running and people were sleeping on the tracks.[15]

The Red Army soldier escorting the girls made fun of them. "What are you thinking of, girlies? When you're in a greatcoat and boots no boy will

---

* The immensely popular project, founded in 1927, which serialised classic and contemporary books (usually fiction) with a view to introducing them to a wider audience.

dream of taking you to the pictures!" At Petrovsky Palace they were met by uniformed women who seemed to be sterner and more authoritative than anyone they had met before. The girls were in gladiatorial mood, expecting to be issued with uniforms and guns on the spot so they could go out and fight the enemy straight away. When they saw their uniforms, however, their spirits fell.

The uniforms were new, and the girls were also issued with a creaking leather belt and boots, but everything was designed for men. The trousers reached to their breasts, the huge tunic collars flopped down almost to their navels, and there were no boots smaller than Size 7. The boys who were being assembled at the palace to form a men's unit sniggered, "Never mind, girls, when you get to the front you can wrap your feet in newspaper." They were dismayed. Their overcoats were too long and came down almost to the heels of the more petite girls. Each was issued with an empty pistol holster, a flask and various useless items that the bureaucracy evidently considered essential equipment. They looked at each other in disbelief. "It would have been difficult to design a uniform to make young women look less feminine."[16]

Before being taken to the canteen for dinner, they were ordered to put on all their equipment. There was nothing for it: in their stiff new uniforms and steel-studded boots (which clattered terribly on the palace's stone floors), with their empty holsters, they passed the line-up of boys, who viewed them with a mixture of curiosity and amusement. It was an uncomfortable intimation of the disparagement they were yet to face.[17]

The next day the organisers started making soldiers of them. They were put through their paces on the drill square and began learning the army's endless regulations. Already, however, Moscow was so threatened that neither the instructors nor the students could concentrate. On 15 October, just a couple of days after arriving at the unit, they also learned that Air Group 122, as Raskova's regiments were being called, was being evacuated to the city of Engels. Engels, across the Volga from Saratov, is 800 kilometres south-east of Moscow and 300 kilometres upriver of Stalingrad.

The following morning they marched through the city singing. It was very cold and the trams, no longer running, were half covered in snow. The few passers-by stopped to watch, and old ladies "came to the edge of the pavement and stood there silently, making the sign of the cross over us", and looking sadly after them.[18] If most young Muscovites believed Moscow would not fall and that the enemy would be defeated, an older generation, which had already suffered much during the Great War and the brutal Russian Civil War that followed, was pessimistic. The German advance had been too swift and unchallenged for them to remain confident that Moscow was impregnable.

The general German offensive against Moscow had begun on 30 September 1941 and developed rapidly. Soviet troops surrendered the cities of Kaluga and Vyazma, leaving the Germans with another 600,000 soldiers and officers as prisoners of war. On 13 October German troops crossed the Volga in the vicinity of Kalinin where it was relatively narrow, and on 15 October Kalinin itself was taken. They were only 150 kilometres from Moscow. The Germans immediately brought up reinforcements and, breaking through weak Soviet defences, headed straight down the Leningrad Highway towards the capital. They gave the Russians no time to establish the Kalinin Front to protect their capital.

The same day, Stalin signed a decree of the State Defence Committee, "Evacuation of Moscow, Capital City of the U.S.S.R." The decree indicated that Stalin would leave Moscow the next day or later, depending on the situation. The Government was to be evacuated on the day the decree was published. Muscovites themselves were certain the entire Government had already decamped. The rumour in the food queues was that the Germans were dropping leaflets declaring, "You will go to bed Soviet and wake up German." This was exactly what had recently happened in Oryol, and many feared it would be repeated in Moscow. One young Muscovite wrote in her diary, "Everyone is totally confused. Even those in authority have no idea what to do, to say nothing of those under them."[19] Citizens who were not planning to flee "watched everyone else leaving from morning to night" and "saw people losing all their human dignity".[20]

From the beginning of October, Lazar Brontman, a *Pravda* war correspondent, and other members of the paper's staff had been watching the Germans close in. Even so, they "had not appreciated the extent of the threat".[21] On 15 October the Germans made a sudden breakthrough and reached Naro-Fominsk, seventy kilometres south-west of Moscow. Brontman was advised that the newspaper was being evacuated, but that he and a few others were to remain in Moscow to "continue publishing until the last possible moment". Bringing out each issue proved inordinately difficult, and it had to be followed immediately, without any time for sleep, by the next. On the evening of 16 October Brontman drove from door to door, collecting people who were to be evacuated by train that evening. Everybody was "terribly jittery, getting their belongings and all sorts of junk together, weeping". On the streets there was "terrible confusion. Everybody was in a rush to get somewhere, carting rucksacks around," and many were leaving Moscow on foot. Brontman noted tersely in his diary, "At the station everything was a diabolical shambles, with stray people swarming everywhere!"

He added that the *Pravda* journalist Semyon Gershberg took down the photos of his wife and son from the wall, saying, "The Germans will only deface them." Brontman did not share his pessimism, and Gershberg's confidence returned too in the days that followed, as the authorities overcame their paralysis.

The Moscow through which Air Group 122 marched was anticipating surrender and planning urban guerrilla resistance. During the night of 16 October the Bolshoy Theatre was hurriedly packed with explosives. Numerous factories, warehouses, institutions, bridges and major shops had been previously readied for blowing up. To ensure that the city's food reserves did not fall into enemy hands, Alexander Shcherbakov, secretary of the Moscow Party Committee, gave orders for flour, cereals, canned food, warm clothing and footwear to be distributed free to Muscovites (although he was subsequently reprimanded for this "defeatism").[22] The entrance to the Kremlin was barricaded with logs, and the complex itself was camouflaged to ensure it was unrecognisable both from the air and on the ground.[23] Its walls were covered over to make the buildings look like ordinary city apartment blocks. Next to it a fake bridge was built over the Moscow River. Roofs and façades of the Kremlin buildings and walls that had not been covered were made to look more ordinary. Red stars no longer shone atop the towers but were hidden behind wooden shuttering, and the crosses were taken down from church domes. Although it had long been empty, the Lenin Mausoleum was enclosed in a fake villa made of fabric, wood and cardboard.

As early as 3 July, that holiest of Soviet relics, the body of Lenin, had been evacuated to Tyumen in Siberia in a special train.[24] The body was accompanied by Lenin's heart; the bullet that had been extracted from his body in 1922, four years after the Socialist Revolutionary, Fanny Kaplan, had attempted to assassinate him; his preserved brain; the body's principal guardian, Professor Boris Zbarsky, and a whole team of support staff. Ensconced with his relic far from prying eyes in a mansion guarded by the militia and N.K.V.D., Zbarsky reported to the Government that his "project" was "in a very good state".[25]

Greatly alarmed by the Germans' rapid advance, the Soviet leaders hastened after the corpse of their former leader. The upper echelons of the Party and government loaded their large black cars to the gunwales with possessions and headed east along Enthusiasts' Highway. Alongside them, hundreds of thousands of people festooned with bundles and knapsacks were on the move in cars, on carts and bicycles, or on foot.

It became more and more difficult to make progress and the mood became desperate. Nobody was directing this traffic and mob violence broke out. Enraged crowds brought official cars to a standstill, robbed the occupants and dumped them in the ditch. In Moscow too during the night of 15 October people smashed windows, broke down doors, and carted everything out of the shops and food stores. Gangs of looters materialised, occupying evacuees' apartments and helping themselves to anything of value in warehouses and enterprises. The mob was galvanised by the wholly unexpected freedom and a sense of complete impunity.

On 16 October Radio Moscow was back on air again after a long silence.

The announcer advised that Moscow was in grave danger and recommended that all residents should leave the city. Order was restored a couple of days later and the blind panic subsided. Contrary to rumour, Stalin was still in the city, which earned him considerable respect, but Moscow remained in imminent danger for a further month.

The mess tins tied to their backpacks clinked in time to the girls' less than military marching. At their sides dangled the empty holsters, flasks, and bags for gas masks. They tried to keep in step but were not very good at it yet. It was bitterly cold and a light snow stung their faces as they marched past the immobile trams, past the air-raid shelter Metro stations, past parks hosting anti-aircraft guns, past closed shops. They made their way through crowds of people to their platform at the Kazansky Station and spent hours loading mattresses, bags, and food supplies into their heated goods wagon. It was evening before the train pulled out, and they found a song to fit the occasion:

> Farewell, beloved Moscow,
> To fight the foe I leave you now . . .

4

"So, they are taking even young girls"

"Beyond the mountains and the forests, far across the mighty main, but not in heaven, here on earth . . . " Zhenya Rudneva recited in a thin, singsong voice. Yershov's "Little Humpbacked Horse" was one of those tales everyone loved but which was just too long to learn by heart. Except that Zhenya had. They whiled away their long train journey singing songs and telling stories. Many joined in. Valya Krasnoshchyokova recited Pushkin's "Tale of Tsar Saltan":

> A playful wind gusts on the sea
> chasing their little ship along . . .

But it was Zhenya who knew the most, treating them to an inexhaustible repertoire of tales, myths and poems. Whether the train's wheels drummed on the tracks, or were silent as they stood in sidings, day after day Zhenya told them stories of knights and damsels fair; legends about the constellations; recited poetry; and recounted what she had read in many books. They could not believe one head could contain so many things. Her new friends gathered round, listening intently, gazing at her in admiration. Zhenya was not like other people, as everyone could see.

"Not quite of this world," was Valya's first impression.[26] Zhenya had large, pale blue eyes and a long, tightly braided plait encircling her head. She was not tall, had a slender neck, and a slow, awkward way of moving. Grey-blue eyes shone with intelligence and kindness.

Zhenya had been eager to get to the front from the first days of the war. Her simple, sensitive heart was full of the ideals inculcated in her generation by Soviet ideologists. While still at school, after watching the film "Lenin in October", she noted in her diary:

> I know very well that, if the hour should come, I shall lay down my life in the cause of my people, as those unknown heroes did in this wonderful film!
>
> I want to dedicate my life to science, and I shall. Soviet Power has provided all the conditions necessary to enable everyone to realise their dreams, no matter how ambitious, but I am a member of the Komsomol and the common cause is dearer to me than my own career. That is how I look on my profession, and if the Party and the working class require it, I shall set astronomy aside for as long as necessary and become a soldier, or an orderly, or nurse the casualties of gas warfare.[27]

That hour did come and Zhenya, one of the brightest students in her year at Moscow University, gave up her intended career in astronomy to become a soldier. She was the only daughter of well-educated parents. Her father had been ill and, as she left for Engels, she felt unable to tell them the truth. She said she was going to train militia volunteers to fire machine guns. Her parents were astonished, and wondered if there was really no one else who could have done the job.

By Soviet standards Zhenya's parents were not poor, so this was the first time she had travelled in a goods truck. For many of the other girls, those from impoverished working-class families or the countryside, this mode of transport was nothing new.

Nowadays few people have any idea what such a truck was like, but in the first half of the twentieth century no explanation was needed. Ordinary goods wagons like these were constructed from wooden planks but with a double layer of insulation, an iron stove and bunks. Millions of Russians travelled the length and breadth of their vast country in them, and even lived in them. Before the revolution peasants were transported in goods wagons to cultivate new lands. After the revolution they were used to take young people to Komsomol construction projects; exiles to their place of deportation; and, of course, millions of prisoners destined to build new cities and fell lumber in the forests of Siberia were transported in them, often deprived for days of food or even water. Strong young soldiers were taken to the front in these wagons, and the wagons brought back the sick and wounded. The common people invented a word for them, the kindly-sounding "*teplushka*". Derived from the word for "warm", it also suggests gratitude for that warmth, for the insulated walls and the stove blazing in the middle, without which life would have been that much harder for the travellers.

Warm as they may have been, they did nevertheless lack a toilet. To relieve yourself, you had to ask your friends to hold your hands while you shoved the appropriate part of your body out through the open door. Valya Krasnoshchyokova never forgot the time Tanya Sumarokova's foot slipped and they almost lost their grip on her. When they got over their fright, Tanya hooted with laughter with the rest of them. Their journey went on and on but none of them would have dreamed of complaining.

45

They were soldiers now, and soldiers do not expect to travel first class.

Most, like Valya Petrochenkova, a future fighter pilot, had grown up in penury. Valya was a pretty girl with dark, bright eyes, curly black hair and dimples on her cheeks. In the summer of 1941 she applied to fight in the war but was turned down on the grounds that she would be better employed using what she had learned at her flying club to train pilots for the front. As she left for her new job, she had had a few hours to look in at the room in Moscow into which her parents were crowded with their younger children. The only gift Valya's mother could give her eighteen-year-old daughter, as she embarked on adult life and a dangerous career, was kind words. She could give no blouse, no pillow or towel, only a few dry crusts. Valya had a uniform from her flying club, so left her only dress to her younger sister. She was the eldest of the children and hoped soon to be in a position to help support her family.

When she arrived at her new workplace, she found everything in a state of chaos. Valya was instructing thirty young men whom she was to train as paratroopers. Some were her age, others older. Nearly all the male instructors had left for the front and the flying club's future was uncertain as it had been allocated no funding by the government. For a month and a half, while things were being sorted out, she had to fend for herself, with little to eat, sleeping at night on a straw mattress in a lean-to attached to a barn. She had no blankets, pillows, sheets, or towels, and no clothes other than those she was wearing. Valya scrubbed them with a wet cloth, and tried to dry her underwear overnight by sleeping on top of it. She put it on still damp in the morning. Valya couldn't even wash herself properly: she was first issued soap two weeks after arriving.[28] She stayed at this flying club for two years training male cadets, and little by little life became better, although it remained hard and hungry. In 1943 she was called up and joined the women's fighter regiment as one of the many reinforcements they needed after suffering so many losses.

For the girls of Raskova's unit, the main thing was to get their training over quickly and start fighting. Like Raskova herself, they had only the vaguest idea of what the front would actually be like, and although the Germans were at the gates of Moscow, they were worried that the war might be over before they could get started. Whenever their train stopped at a station, Raskova would immediately set off to find the military commandant and demand that they should be allowed to proceed as soon as possible. Her face was highly recognisable (and prettier than it looked in the photographs), and her confident demeanour had an instant effect. Invariably the commandant would promise to send them forward just as quickly as he could.

It was not always a simple matter to reach the station building in the first place if their train was on some faraway track. What were you to do if, as was common at Soviet railway junctions at the time, there were no recognised crossings over a dozen tracks, all of which were occupied by seemingly endless trains? Militsa Kazarinova, Raskova's chief of staff, recalled the night the two of them climbed down and asked the track inspector how to reach the station. "Count a dozen or so tracks under the wagons and that'll be the station," he replied.

Raskova immediately set off under the wagons. Kazarinova, scurrying after her, counted: one train, two, three . . . before losing count. Some of the trains were being moved and they had to wait. When the commandant saw Raskova he asked in surprise how they had managed to reach him. "We crawled under the trains," Raskova said, laughing. The commandant shook his head. Raskova knew very well that the trains might at any moment have started moving and crushed her, but she had long grown used to risking her own and other people's lives. "We are in a hurry to reach the front." No further explanation was needed.[29]

For all that, they often had to wait, their train standing interminably in sidings, allowing other, even more urgent, trains to take priority. The whole country was on the move, in different directions but in the same teplushka wagons. Ceaselessly the troop trains moved westwards, while trains carrying the wounded and evacuees went east. Entire factories were being evacuated with all their machinery.

The food issued on the train journey was exactly what they would receive throughout the war up until the opening of the Second Front by the

Western Allies: grey bread, herring, and millet porridge. Instead of tea there was boiling water, but they took that in their stride. Many were familiar enough, if not with starvation, then with living hand to mouth.

There was, of course, no opportunity to wash on the journey or to launder what few items of clothing they had brought with them. Although it was not forbidden to bring civilian clothing, few had brought anything other than a change of underwear (which quickly became dirty). What would be the point? It would hardly be needed at the front, so it made better sense to leave it for a younger sister, or for their mother to sell if times got really hard. In any case, Communist ideology condemned excessive attachment to material goods, seeing it as a symptom of bourgeois mentality. Good Communists had no business treasuring pretty clothes.

Valya Abankina was accepted into Marina Raskova's group for training as an aircraft mechanic, and she too left behind a large family and a minimal wardrobe of clothes. When she was asked to write a résumé of her life she replied that she had not yet had a life: what was there to list? She had been born, attended school, and then gone to work in a motorcycle factory. Now, however, in her as yet short biography, as in those of all Raskova's young warriors, there was about to be inscribed the most testing, but also the most vivid and memorable, chapter of their entire lives.

That first day, before they had got to know each other, the future mechanics and armourers kept to themselves: the girls from the motorcycle factory, from the aircraft factory, from teacher training college, from Moscow University. Besides Zhenya Rudneva, sixteen other girls from Moscow University had presented themselves at Raskova's rallying point. They were undergraduate and postgraduate students from the faculties of mathematics, physics, chemistry, geography and history.

Of them all, Sasha Makunina was the eldest – she was five or six years older than the seventeen- and eighteen-year-olds who formed the majority of the unit. The outbreak of war had found her on a geological expedition in the Urals, in a place so remote that it was three days before she heard of the German invasion. Sasha was a short girl with big eyes.[30] She could fly a glider and jump with a parachute, and she had chosen to study geography at university because that profession held out the promise of travel, discovery, and adventure. The war, however, looked to be more of an adventure than any expedition and, as Sasha was returning from the Urals, her only thought was to get back to Moscow as quickly as possible. Like most young people brought up on Soviet propaganda, she was sure any war would last no more than two weeks. It would be fought wholly on German territory, and the enemy would not hold out for long. For her too, the main thing was to get to fight in the war before it was over.

By October it was becoming clear that victory was still some way off, but that did not change Sasha's sense of urgency: she wanted to be part of the war effort as soon as possible and in any capacity. On 10 October her friend Irina Rakobolskaya called her away from teaching her students to say, "They are enlisting volunteers. Be as quick as you can. Enrolment is at six."[31] Sasha's mother had already been evacuated. Her father was, of course, distraught but could hardly oppose his daughter's decision and only said quietly, "So, they are taking even young girls?" The neighbours in their shared apartment gave Sasha a send-off as if she were their own daughter. They wept, and put together an artless kitbag, the usual parting gift for those heading for the front. They dried bread for her to take and ironed her underwear.

On their long journey the girls talked endlessly about the families they had left behind, the factories where they worked, the universities where they studied. They talked also about what they would do when the war was over, but with most animation they talked about the fact that they would surely fly with Raskova. They had heard there were real, professional female pilots on the train with them who only needed now to be taught how to fly military aircraft. These were evidently in a different wagon, and everyone was intrigued as to what they must be like. The young girls who only yesterday had still been students imagined them to be very special beings, much older, immeasurably more experienced and braver, cleverer and more educated than they were. If Raskova was a goddess, these women must be demi-goddesses at least.

In reality, the pilots were much more down-to-earth than the students.

Very few had finished even secondary school. Most, like Katya Budanova, had joined flying clubs from working in factories and workshops. Katya was a simple village girl, very energetic and intelligent, but she had had a grim childhood. Her father died when she was young and her mother, unable to feed a large family, sent her out to work from the age of nine, minding other people's children. Her only respite from work was when she was at school. After seven years of village education, Katya was packed off to an older sister in Moscow. She got a job as a mechanic in an aircraft factory, and was eventually able to start realising her dreams when she joined a flying club. This was followed by flying school, where she went on to become an instructor. She performed at air shows and notched up a respectable number of parachute jumps. Flying changed her life beyond all recognition.

Katya became the proud owner of a long leather raglan coat whose flaps could be buttoned round the legs so it could be worn while parachuting. A raglan was what every pilot aspired to, but a separate room in Moscow's convenient Sivtsev Vrazhek street, which Katya was also awarded, was the height of luxury and beyond most people's wildest dreams. According to her friends, she now developed a certain attitude and arrogance which had not been there before. The village girl, the factory worker, had become a pilot.

"High in the clouds, intrepidly . . ." Katya would sing in her low, melodious voice, and the others on the train bound for Engels would take up the song. When her friends reminisced about her, they recalled that fine, strong voice and the songs she loved to sing, her dense, wavy hair and dazzling smile.

While they were still on the train, many had been struck by the appearance of a small, slender girl who, despite her male soldier's uniform, could never have been mistaken for a boy. She had light-brown curls, green eyes, an elegant figure, and a pleasing, self-possessed way of moving. Her name was Lidia but she introduced herself as Lilya. She too was a pilot, although nobody knew that. Who was she to compete with Yevgenia Prokhorova's famous aerobatic quintet who, it was said, were also on their way to join

Raskova's unit? Those girls were nationally renowned as a result of the air shows held each year on 18 August, Aviation Day, at the Tushino Aerodrome.

"We present the women pilots, Popova, Belyaeva, Khomyakova, and Glukhovtseva. Their leader is Yevgenia Prokhorova, world record holder in gliding," the announcer declared. "These five daring women will now demonstrate their skill." Five small planes in tight triangular formation began to execute advanced aerobatic stunts, looping loops without for a second losing the perfection of their formation. "As if a single person were flying five aircraft," the announcer exclaimed rapturously.[32]

The public too was enraptured. From the stand of the Central Flying Club of Moscow, the Government, who had duly arrived in their black GAZ-M1s, looked on. They were all wearing white: white civilian suits, or white military tunics with white caps; even their shoes were white. Only Stalin wore his inevitable khaki tunic, standing right in the middle and noticeably shorter than everybody else. Everyone was talking about the flying, gesticulating, imitating the way the aircraft flew. Valentina Grizodubova was there in a light-coloured dress and with a fashionable hairstyle. A head shorter than her was Raskova in her signature military uniform and beret. They talked animatedly and laughed when they noticed they were being filmed. Like everybody else that day, they were agreeably excited.

On the ground and the hills around the aerodrome huge numbers of spectators were sitting in places allotted them by tickets they had gone to great lengths to secure. The grass was divided into squares by white ropes. The public had reached the remote airfield on trams packed with people inside and festooned with people outside, or in the back of trucks, and even on foot.

Planes wrote in the sky, "Glory to Stalin!" Huge flags were raised aloft showing Stalin's face to best advantage, in three-quarters profile. The announcer talked bombastically of Stalin's Falcons and declared that, "In the name of Stalin, at the first call of the Party and Government, Soviet pilots will swoop into battle like flights of eagles to defend the Soviet borders, and the enemy will be annihilated on its own territory."

Yevgenia, more often called just Zhenya, Prokhorova, a regular participant in such air shows, went to defend her country just as described, "at the first call of the Party and Government". Her quintet split up: only Raisa Belyaeva and Lera Khomyakova joined Zhenya on the journey to Engels. All three were to perish.

Despite Raskova's best efforts, the 800-kilometre journey to Engels took a full ten days. She soon recognised that she would need a lot of time to turn her charges into real combatants. Even before they embarked on the train Kazarinova had gone to inspect the sentries guarding Air Group 122's property as it was waiting to be loaded. It was Katya Budanova's duty to see to the change of guards, but she was lying on a table in a cold shed, fast asleep. As Kazarinova marched her to where the crates, bags and mattresses that comprised the group's property were piled up, she saw no sentries at their posts. There was an air raid, and when it was over and the anti-aircraft guns had fallen silent, Budanova's shouts finally got through to her sentries, whose sleepy heads appeared from a pile of mattresses in which, as they explained, they had been hiding from the cold. Kazarinova reported the delinquent sentries to Raskova but she just laughed and said, "My dear Captain, you want them to become soldiers in an instant but it will not be that simple."[33]

In the course of the journey Raskova had time to arrive at a number of momentous decisions in respect of her soldiers. One was that they were not to braid their hair.

She had noticed two girls in uniform jump out at one of the stops and run along the side of the train. When they saw Raskova and Kazarinova they stopped to ask permission to post letters. This Raskova granted and, holding hands, they ran on their way. Long curls, matted from the journey, crowned their young heads. Kazarinova remarked that she would not want them to be seen bare-headed like that by the station commandant and, in any case, she considered long hair impermissible in a military unit. With a sigh, Raskova instructed her to draft an order that upon arrival in Engels all personnel were to have their hair cropped.[34]

The other girls also sent letters home when the train stopped, to the civilian life they had left behind only a few days before. As they hurried back to their wagon, they asked people on the platform for news. What was happening at the front? Was Moscow holding out?[35]

5

"Why are you leaving us, children?"

In the days immediately after Raskova's departure, the Germans were driven back from the city, but soon re-launched their advance. On 19 October 1941 a state of siege was declared. The decree of the State Defence Committee stated, "Anyone guilty of disorder is to be charged without delay and their case referred to the Military Tribunal. Spies and other enemy agents inciting disorder are to be summarily shot."[36]

On 20 October units of the Bryansk Front, some 380 kilometres south-west of Moscow, surrendered after being cut off by the advance of German tanks. The pitiful appearance of the Soviet prisoners of war shocked even Field Marshal von Bock who was in command of the advance. He wrote, "The sight of tens of thousands of Russian prisoners of war dragging themselves, almost without guards, towards Smolensk makes a dreadful impression. Endless columns of these unfortunates wandered exhausted and starving along the road past my motor car. Some collapsed and died right there on the highway from wounds they had suffered in battle."[37]

Towards the end of October the German advance was slowed by heavy rains that made many roads impassable. Soon afterwards, severe winter cold arrived to sap the morale of troops unaccustomed to such conditions. Nevertheless, even on 7 November (the date on which, after reform of the old calendar, the Revolution of 25 October was now celebrated) fresh Soviet units went straight from the Red Square parade marking the anniversary of the Revolution into battle to defend Moscow. Along with them went a Muscovite volunteer militia of people not conscripted into the regular army, either because they were too old, in poor health, or in reserved professions important to the functioning of the country. Some were in military uniform, often far from new, others in quilted jackets or civilian coats, some with fur hats, some in peaked caps, some just wearing an ordinary hat. Most were going to their deaths. It is difficult to be entirely confident about the figures, but it is believed that of 120,000 members of the Moscow volunteer militia 100,000 were killed.

The possibility that Moscow might fall was seen as a catastrophe almost tantamount to losing the war. Anna Yegorova could not imagine the consequences, though she had already been watching the collapse of Russia's defences in disbelief. After the German Army Groups South and Centre had succeeded in September 1941 in encircling, southeast of Kiev, the main forces of the Soviet Southwestern Front, which lost more than 600,000 men dead, missing or, even more disastrously, taken prisoner, the Germans launched an offensive in the autumn on the Donetsk coal-basin.[38] Taking the Donbas was a key priority in Hitler's pre-war planning. It produced 60 per cent of the Soviet Union's coal, 40 per cent of its iron, and 23 per cent of its steel. Hitler believed the outcome of the conflict would be decided by the conquest of this territory between the Sea of Azov, the lower reaches of the Don, and the lower and middle reaches of the River Seversky Donets. He was certain that if the Soviet side could be deprived of Donbas coal it would be unable to carry on fighting.[39]

Anna Yegorova had found herself in Stalino (formerly and subsequently Donetsk) shortly before its surrender. She could not believe that a city with that name could fall to the enemy, but on 16 October it did. Advancing on their major objective, Rostov-on-Don, on 8 October the Germans had suddenly captured the major Russian port of Mariupol on the Sea of Azov and, after a skirmish with Soviet troops, on 17 October, took Taganrog, another important port. The advance faltered after this because the rains of autumn reduced the roads to quagmires and the Germans were also short of fuel, but Hitler insisted on pressing forward with the offensive.

Even while she was at the front, in Stalino, Anna's thoughts kept turning to Moscow, where she had helped to build the first stations of the Metro, and which she regarded as her second home.

Anna had come to stay with her older brother in Moscow as a long-legged teenager wearing a faded Young Pioneer scarf and elastic-sided boots her uncle had made for her. She found life in the capital amazing: intense and challenging, and very different from her experiences in the village among the pine forests of Tver. Her mother allowed her to leave the village on condition that she studied in college, but the Komsomol summoned her to work on a construction project, and for every Muscovite the main project in the pre-war years was the Metro.

Stalin had decided the Moscow Metro was to be completely unlike the utilitarian systems in other European capitals, where colourless stations with their economical decor were indistinguishable from each other. The Moscow Metro was to be the most technically advanced and beautiful in the world. What did it matter that people in villages were living in primitive log huts, and even in Moscow were crammed into overcrowded barracks without water or toilets, or into communal apartments with ten people living in a single room? The Metro would belong to the people, its stations in no way inferior in beauty and sumptuousness to the palaces of the former nobility, and anyone entering it would be happy and proud of their state and take a pride in themselves.

The building and designing of the Metro attracted the best architects, sculptors and artists of the time. There was no stinting on marble – which was transported thousands of miles – on crystal, or gilding. Soviet ideologues calculated that these underground palaces would be a substitute for the churches destroyed by the Soviet order, simultaneously exalting and crushing the human spirit and instilling a sense of awe. The new deity, however, was a pockmarked little man with a withered arm.

Of all Stalin's megalomaniac projects, the Metro was the only one that did not exploit the labour of prisoners of the Gulag. Instead it was built by people like the boys and girls of the Komsomol.

At that time all occupations were open to women, and Anna Yegorova became a steel reinforcement fitter at the construction site of the Krasnye

Vorota Metro station. Like other girls she lugged the steel reinforcement bars on her shoulders, bent double under the weight of her burden. No one complained, as they proudly demonstrated that girls could cope with any work a man could do. As the project advanced Anna, like almost everyone else, mastered new trades. Later, when tilers and plasterers were needed they turned their hands to these skills too, eager to build their own Metro station from start to finish. When the two red carriages of the Metro's first train ran down the line in October 1934, Anna and her friends ran after them, dancing and hugging each other. On 6 February 1935 the builders of the Metro sped through thirteen of the stations they had built, the first stops of a Soviet underground railway.[40]

At the age of sixteen Anna had joined a flying club, and as she toiled in the shafts of the deepest Metro stations she dreamed endlessly of flying. After training on gliders and U-2 trainer planes and making her first parachute jumps, she decided to enrol at a flying school. She passed the entrance exams with distinction, survived the close scrutiny of a medical panel and became a cadet, only for her studies to come to an abrupt end when the authorities learned that her elder brother had been arrested by the secret police. She was expelled from the school that same day.

Despite this setback, she did graduate from flying school with the help of good people, but had to travel to Kherson in the Ukraine to do so. From then until the war Anna Yegorova worked as an instructor at a flying club in Kalinin, near her mother and the village where she was born. On Sunday, 22 June 1941 she was sitting with friends on the bank of the Volga when she heard from the radio of a passing ship that the Soviet Union was at war. She decided instantly to do everything she could to be a pilot at the front. This was how she could best help a Motherland that had given her so much. In combat she would be able to show the skill she had acquired during her years as a student and instructor.

At the military recuitment office Anna heard the same story as other women pilots: there will be time enough for you to fly combat missions later. For the present what was needed was to train male pilots for the front. She was directed to work as a flying instructor in Stalino but even before she got there she heard that the flying club, together with factories, institutions, and people, had been evacuated. Stalino, the capital of Russia's coal industry, was on the verge of falling into enemy hands.

Arriving in Stalino, Anna walked through the deserted flying club and, with nothing else to do, went to the opera house's last performance. A day before being evacuated the theatre was performing "Carmen", but Anna felt she was watching it "through glass", and was unmoved by its tale of love and death. The next day she fortuitously encountered a lieutenant from a flying squadron who was scouting for pilots at the flying club and in the hospital. She offered herself as a candidate, much to his surprise, but eventually she and others were accepted into the Signals Squadron of the Southern Front. The decision was taken reluctantly, but in the chaos of retreat in the early days of the war there was no time to look for male pilots. By the time the Germans were threatening Moscow, Anna had already been flying for a month close to the front line, carrying orders to the retreating troops, transporting liaison officers, and establishing the location of army units. She was flying a U-2, the same plane in which she had learned to fly and in which she had taught her students.

The U-2 was an insubstantial little biplane that was designed in the late 1920s, and all the heroes and heroines in this book learned to fly in it. The plane had two cockpits, one for the student and one for the instructor, both of whom could control the aircraft. When the instructor felt the student was ready to fly solo, he was replaced in the rear cabin by a sandbag, universally known as Ivan Ivanovich, which was used as ballast. The U-2 was a small, lightweight, low-speed aircraft made from plywood and percale, a finely woven cotton fabric, so it was very cheap to manufacture. Nobody had any complaints about it before the war and when, with the outbreak of hostilities, the flying clubs' U-2s were requisitioned for the front, the "crop duster", "the duck" or, as the Germans came to call it, "the Plywood Russ", was recognised as an irreplaceable little workhorse. It transported the wounded, was used for communications, dropped supplies to encircled units and partisans, and was even adapted to carry bombs under its wings and function as a night bomber. It could take off from a small forest clearing and land on a roadway.

Nikolai Polikarpov, the designer of this immensely useful small plane, was rewarded in a peculiarly Soviet manner. He was the first of the Soviet aircraft designers arrested in 1929, probably not helped by the fact that his father was a priest.[41] He designed his next several aircraft in prison, a location which the N.K.V.D. leaders believed would make him and his fellow designers far more productive, since they would have nothing but their work to focus on. "Only in a militarised environment can such specialists work effectively, as opposed to the corrosive environment of civilian institutions," Genrikh Yagoda, one of the initiators of the repressions of the Stalin period, wrote in a letter to Molotov.[42] Polikarpov was fortunate because the I-5 fighter, designed under his leadership, was demonstrated to Stalin by test pilot Valeriy Chkalov, a favourite of the public and authorities, and he was pardoned. Two other aircraft designers, Andrey Tupolev and Vladimir Petlyakov, spent much longer in prison, while Sergey Korolyov, the creator of the spacecraft which took Yury Gagarin into space, would have died in the Gulag had he not been transferred to work in an N.K.V.D. prison facility.

To Anna Yegorova, flying close to the front line, the small, nimble U-2 seemed completely defenceless. At any moment you might meet a German fighter, and the U-2 could be shot down even with a rifle. It was not fast enough to escape a German fighter plane and the only chance of escape in daylight was to dive and fly as close to the ground as possible.

On 19 September 1941 the Germans occupied Kiev. The Soviet troops retreating through the Ukraine hardly resembled an army. The units Anna Yegorova was sent out to find were not marching in columns but in bedraggled groups. Ragged, exhausted and starving, they could barely walk as they dragged their weapons and the wounded with them. Given new hope by the sight of the little plane with its red star, the soldiers waved their hands, caps and helmets. Several times she had to land in villages in imminent danger of capture, but the U-2 never failed, sometimes taking off with bullet holes in its wings.

When she found she was bringing orders to retreat, Anna always wondered why they were necessary since the army had already been retreating for a long time. On one occasion she flew to the headquarters of the Southwestern Front at the Kharkov aerodrome to find everything in chaos, and discovered that in wartime a plane can be rustled as easily as a horse.

A pilot from her squadron had previously flown to Kharkov with secret correspondence, but when it was time to go back his plane was nowhere to be seen on the apron. A lot of "horseless" pilots were wandering around. Some had lost their planes in battle and others because the Germans had bombed huge numbers of aircraft on the ground. Anna and her colleague were sent to look for the missing plane but found nothing. Returning via the airfield at Chuguev, where she failed to get anything to eat at the canteen, Anna went back to her U-2 and, to her surprise, found a major sitting in the cockpit shouting, "Contact!" A second airman, also a major, was turning the propeller by hand to help start the engine. Surprise turned to rage and, forgetting her subordinate rank, she jumped onto the wing of her plane and set about the major with her fists, shouting "Stop thief! You bandit! Have you no conscience?"

The major took this calmly. He turned to face her and said, "Why are you yelling like that? This is not the bazaar! Just tell us politely this is your plane and we will go and look for one which is stray." As the two majors walked off, one striding manfully and the other trotting behind him, Anna even felt sorry for them.

When a U-2 pilot who survived the war was describing his adventures at the front, his wife, who spent the whole conflict with ground units, would tell him he had not seen the worst of it, as he flew from one airfield to another with his pilot's ration of special Cola chocolate.[43] On 24 October 1941 Kharkov fell. The filth and horror of a war with nothing remotely romantic about it was something the soldiers of the retreating units, which Anna Yegorova viewed from above, saw only too clearly.

Among these crushed, exhausted people retreating from Kharkov was Anya Skorobogatova, tramping with them in boots too large for her. She was just eighteen years old, a slip of a girl with a straight nose, thick black hair and lively eyes as blue as forget-me-nots. Since she was a child Anya had dreamed of being a pilot, and went on to complete a course at a flying club.[44] At the outbreak of war she reported to the recruitment centre but was told they were not at present taking on girls as pilots, but she could enrol on a course for radio operators with airborne units. She settled for that, hoping to see combat and imagining the time might come when her flying experience would be needed.

Anya Skorobogatova had begun her course in Kharkov but these were disconcerting times. The streets of this beautiful city were already full of military hardware, the local hospitals full to overflowing with wounded people, while day and night a distant thunder, "the voice of war", was audible. Soviet troops were retreating to Stalingrad, and it was this time of retreat, not the fighting, that many eyewitnesses remember as the most desperate days of the war. The retreating soldiers were hungry and exhausted and many were totally dejected. Vladimir Pivovarov, command-ing a reconnaissance squad, recalls the day he and his comrades found a beehive by the roadway, instantly tore the honeycomb apart and ate their fill of the honey. This made them even thirstier. At just the wrong moment they heard the shout, "Communists and Komsomol members, forward with your weapons!" The Germans were nearby, but as the Russians advanced they spotted a small pond ahead, ignored their commanding officers and the threat from the enemy, and rushed to drink, hopelessly muddying the water.[45]

Anya's course for radio operators also retreated. She was dismayed when she heard they were being ordered to evacuate to Rossosh, a town in the steppe between Kharkov and Stalingrad. It meant moving further away from her parents, whom she had to leave behind in a village near Taganrog. Very young and now with no one to turn to for support, she was precipitated into adulthood.

Anya struck up a close friendship on the course with three girls: Frida Katz from Gomel, Anya Stobova from Poltava, and Lena Bachul from Mol-davia. They were immediately nicknamed "The Four Sisters" and swore never to be parted for the rest of their lives. Only Anya survived the war.

The would-be radio operators were each given a rusty rifle but no ammunition. That did not matter much, because nobody had yet taught them how to shoot. They were issued with oversized boots and greatcoats "to grow into", and told to put what they would need in kitbags. Before leaving Kharkov, Anya sent her mother a letter, not knowing whether it would ever reach her. Its message was in verse, banal, emotional, and heartfelt and ended, "And so, farewell, I shall return – victorious!" Their group of about a hundred boys and girls covered the 250 kilometres to Rossosh on foot. To start with they marched by day, which was terrifying. Enemy aircraft with crosses on their wings flew low overhead. In the villages they passed through, the local women gave them boiled sweetcorn to eat, but wailed, "Children, who are you leaving us to?" They shared the roads with refugees burdened with their pitiful possessions, pulling children along and driving their cows ahead of them. It started raining and for a day they were soaked through. Then the officers decided it was too dangerous to proceed like that and they spent the daytime sheltering in sheds and moved on only after dark. They found it difficult, and would fall asleep on their feet. All the time they were accompanied by the lamentation of the village women crying, "Why are you leaving us, children?"

When finally they reached Rossosh, which had been far to the rear, they found it was now no distance at all from the front line. The Germans too had been on the move. It was a day's march to Stalingrad, with only the River Don barring the way.

They again settled down to learn to transmit and receive radio messages and to use Morse code.[46] Anya calculated how much longer the training would take her and determined to make sure she was attached to an aviation unit. She had not given up hope of flying.

6

"She's just a young girl, hasn't seen people die"

It was night when Raskova's Air Group 122 finally arrived in Engels and there was not a soul on the platform. It was raining and foggy and, in the absence of any lights, Raskova was far from certain that they were actually in the right place.[47] Blundering around in the dark, she eventually came upon the military garrison's duty officer and was assured that they were expected. The officer showed them to their quarters, the sports hall of the officers' club where, as in their railway wagon, the girls would be sleeping on two-tiered bunks. A comfortable room had been prepared for Raskova with a large bed and a carpet. She caustically dubbed it a boudoir, ordered that the carpet should be removed, and had the bed replaced by two narrow bunks for herself and her chief of staff.

After the endless packed meals on the train the girls were glad to be served hot "blondie" – millet porridge – in the garrison canteen. They began settling in. The men in other flying units stationed there were "greatly entertained" by their arrival.[48] An all-female unit, and an airborne one at that, seemed simply unbelievable. The men immediately nicknamed Raskova's girls "Dollies". When the Dollies' Komsomol administrator, earnest, chubby-faced Nina Ivakina, told their instructor, a senior lieutenant, that she was their political officer his eyes "grew wide with astonishment and he exclaimed, 'What? You even have political officers, like in a real regiment?'" When Vera Lomako, a famous Soviet pilot who, like Raskova, set records in long-distance flights, heard that the male trainees at the Engels military flying school, who looked down pityingly on the girls, were calling them the Death Battalion, she encouraged the girls to treat the men with a withering condescension of their own. Raskova smiled, confident that when the time came her wards would show they were the equals of men.[49]

At the time they arrived, Engels was still far behind the front lines. The Germans were already close to the Volga further upriver, but that was a good thousand kilometres away. In this backwater, as the women pilots immediately disparagingly described it, there were the usual privations of life in wartime: men were being seen off to the front, and just to survive involved an unremitting struggle. Food was in short supply, and the mothers of young children were only too glad to cook and do the laundry of the service personnel billeted on them, in return for even a very small amount of the semolina in their rations.[50] The little town that bore the name of one of the founders of communism was, the airwomen generally agreed, "a hole". "The squalid little houses were made of clay and had their heads bowed to one side from age," Nina Ivakina wrote in her diary. The walls of most of them were made of the clay mentioned by Nina, mixed with straw and brushwood. There were four stone buildings in the town centre: the N.K.V.D. headquarters, the headquarters of the town's Party Committee, the Young Pioneers Palace, and the Motherland Cinema. Engels' shops were single-storey stone hovels full of the usual village bric-a-brac, each one identical to the rest and unlikely to satisfy the fashion sense of even the most undemanding and provincial of the girls.[51] The town was also full of exceptionally cowardly stray dogs.

But in most other respects, Engels was an ideal location for training pilots. The dry steppe surrounding it was as flat as a pancake: it was effectively one enormous airfield on which you could land wherever you pleased. In the winter there was also the immensity of the iced-over Volga, another possible landing strip. There were many more days of flying weather than in Central Russia and, for the time being, the front was far away.

The girls' new home was a barracks where each had their place on wooden planking, a grey flannel blanket, and a straw mattress. They were all accommodated in a single large hall. For a small number of the new recruits, of course, these conditions were almost intolerable, but few of the rest of the girls were accustomed to anything much better. Girls from peasant families had grown up in houses without any furniture beyond a wooden table and benches. Needless to say, no one had a room of their own, although the parents might live behind a curtain or in the separate "guest" part of the hut. Everyone else slept on the stove, on the benches or on the floor. Nobody had sheets or pillowcases. Everybody ate communally with wooden spoons from a large bowl, drinking their soup in turn. Meat, when there was any, was shared out by the head of the family.

When peasants left the countryside to work in factories in the cities, they would be accommodated in workers' barracks, where many people lived in a shared room without amenities. Even those who succeeded in finding a place to live in an apartment usually had the whole family living in a single room. In the communal kitchen each family had its own table and cupboard and cooked on a large stove. There was one toilet shared by everyone, and a single sink with water. They went to the bathhouse to wash because the apartments had no bathroom. Before the war many Soviet citizens had known real hunger.

The first thing Raskova did when they all arrived in Engels was to send the girls off for a bath and a haircut. The order drawn up by her chief of staff specifying that their hair was to be no longer than halfway down their ears was read out almost before they left the station platform. An elderly barber duly snipped away, and gradually the floor was carpeted with long tresses, light-coloured and dark, straight and curly.

When the barber finished snipping and stepped back from the mirror, Natasha Meklin, a future navigator, saw a boy looking straight out at her. "That just could not be me. Someone completely different was clutching the arms of the chair and staring at me in surprise and alarm."[52] The boy had a funny tuft of hair sticking up on the back of his head that Natasha could not get to lie down. "Nothing to worry about," the barber assured her. "It's because it's a new style. That will soon settle. Next!"

Next in the chair was Zhenya Rudneva. She took her time unwinding a long, tight, blonde plait before shaking her head. Golden hair cascaded down over her shoulders. Everybody froze. Was this too destined to end up on the floor? The barber looked at Zhenya and hesitantly opened and closed drawers for a time in silence, before asking, "All off?" Zhenya looked up in surprise and nodded.[53]

Most of the girls parted with their plaits just as serenely as Zhenya, but some were in tears, either at the fate of their own hair or someone else's. They could keep a plait only with Raskova's personal permission, and very few had the temerity to bother her over such a trivial matter. Most, even if they regretted the loss of their tresses, were well aware after ten days in the goods wagon that plaits were not a good idea in wartime.

That autumn hundreds of thousands of Soviet women bade farewell to their plaits, exchanging the saying that "a woman's hair is her crowning glory" for the stern reminder that "If the head is cut off you don't weep for the hair." As they departed for the front, nurses, signallers and radio operators, telephonists, clerks and anti-aircraft gunners parted with their tresses. Shura Vinogradova in all her eighteen years had never cut her hair, but the day came when she begged for a pair of scissors to get rid of it. She had just started teaching at a village school when her call-up notice arrived. She had no wish to go to the war, leaving her school without a teacher and her family to look after themselves, but you could not argue with the enlistment commission. In defiance of the truth, her documents stated she had volunteered for the front. It took an interminable time to reach her posting on the Leningrad Front. Within ten days she had lice, and two weeks later her plait was teeming with them. In desperation she walked down a column of trucks in search of a pair of scissors. Eventually a driver cut it off for her and hastily threw it under a bush. "I'll grow it back when the war is over," she consoled herself but, of course, never did – like the rest of the girls, her waist-length hair had taken almost twenty years to grow. Neither, though, did she forget that long blonde plait, discarded under a bush in Malaya Vishera.[54]

Having settled her troops in the hall of the officers' club, Raskova immediately got down to business: aircraft, engines, armaments, aeronautical studies, and drill. At her first meeting with Badaev, the commander of the air garrison, she was told he had received an order giving the titles of three regiments she was to command. These were 586 Fighter Regiment, 587 Bomber Regiment, and 588 Night Bomber Regiment. At present they existed only on paper and she needed to allocate personnel to them. She also needed to decide who, among those with flying experience, would be a pilot and who a navigator, and to determine whether those without flying experience should be trained up as navigators or mechanics. These decisions were taken jointly by Raskova and Vera Lomako and created much disgruntlement, but Raskova had not only great personal authority but was also a skilled communicator, capable of persuading anyone to do almost anything.

All her new servicewomen wanted to fly, if not as pilots then at least as navigators. All the navigators wanted to be pilots. All the pilots wanted to be fighter pilots. Raskova listened to everyone who was aggrieved and brave enough to approach her with a request for a transfer. She talked to each in a serious and respectful manner. Galya Dokutovich wanted to be a pilot, but Raskova explained how greatly the bomber regiment needed navigators with flying experience. To forceful, chubby Faina Pleshivtseva she explained that, even though she had graduated from her flying club, the country presently had a pressing need of her detailed understanding of the mechanical aspects of aircraft. Pleshivtseva had joined Raskova from her fourth year at aviation institute but was talked round, although she still hoped eventually to fly. Raskova did not dash that hope, and even encouraged it. The hopes of armourers and mechanics that one day they would take to the sky were often realised. There was a war on and, in the night bomber regiment at least, the groundcrew were often retrained as navigators, and navigators retrained as pilots to replace senior colleagues lost through illness, injury, or death.

Almost all the professional pilots with many flying hours who had come to Raskova from civil aviation or had been flying club instructors were drafted into the heavy bomber regiment. Those with less experience became pilots in the night bomber regiment or navigators. Only the very best, competitive pilots with extensive experience had any prospect of being accepted into the fighter regiment. Everything was decided on the basis of test flights. Although Raskova had little flying experience herself, she had great intuition and was an excellent judge of character. She believed a real fighter pilot could be recognised immediately from the boldness of her "signature" in the air, the skill with which she manoeuvred the aircraft and controlled its speed. She was assisted in these decisions by Vera Lomako, a professional aviatrix who had been one of the pilots on the first non-stop flight from the Black Sea to the White Sea, on which Raskova had been the navigator.

Although she did not remain in the regiment for long because a recent crash had undermined her health, everybody well remembered the colourful figure she cut. Lomako was tall but thickset, wore a leather raglan coat and boots, and a flying helmet with earflaps and lined with grey astrakhan. Her most memorable feature, however, was her face: the girls thought she looked like a real warrior, with the unflinching gaze of her hazel-brown eyes and the gauze bandages on her nose and eyebrow. People found Lomako so intimidating that on one occasion Valya Krasnoshchyokova, nervously reporting that she had safely delivered a package to Lomako's husband, Major Bashmakov (a pilot also stationed at that time in Engels, whose surname means "shoes" in Russian), accidentally called him "Major Boots", incurring Lomako's wrath.[55] Few dared to question Vera Lomako's judgements. Those who made it into the fighter regiment were women in whom she and Raskova detected lightning-fast reactions, an ability to improvise (which could save the pilot's life in an unanticipated situation), and tremendous courage. By temperament a fighter pilot must always be a leader. She is alone in the cockpit with no one other than herself to rely on and no one to follow. In a dogfight decisions have to be taken and implemented in a fraction of a second, and there is a high price to pay if they are wrong.

The decisions of Raskova and Lomako could be unexpected: Lyuba Gubina, an experienced instructor, was not acepted for the fighter regiment. She was told that, with her flying hours, she would be capable of piloting "our most sophisticated aircraft, the heavy bomber". She was disappointed to be drafted into 587 Regiment, feeling there could be no comparison between flying even the most advanced bomber and the kind of aerobatic skill required of a fighter pilot. Valya Kravchenko, with thousands of flying hours, was also despatched to the bomber regiment, while Larisa Rozanova, an experienced flying instructor, even ended up in the night bomber regiment. To those who were disappointed Raskova explained that the other regiments too needed experienced pilots. With the Motherland under threat, personal preferences had to be put aside in order to do what had to be done.

By 27 November the fighter regiment had almost been formed and the pilots assigned to their squadrons, but many of the pilots allocated to the bomber regiment were still unhappy. If we can rely on the testimony of Nina Ivakina, the Komsomol administrator whose jobs included reporting to her seniors on political attitudes amongst the recruits, pilots Makarova, Tarmosina and Gvozdikova were indignant that their aerobatic skills had not been considered sufficient to include them as fighter pilots.[56] Valya Gvozdikova, an instructor at the Moscow Flying Club, "a bright, statuesque, cheerful girl", was one of the first pilots to be assigned to Raskova. Together with Anya Demchenko and Larisa Rozanova she had needed to get to Moscow from the village in Ryazan Province to which the club had been evacuated. When they received the summons they dashed to the club treasurer for their fare, but found there was a total of only 60 rubles 80 kopecks in the kitty. This was not enough to hire a horse and cart to get them to the station. Nothing daunted, they walked the twenty-five kilometres to the station, reaching Air Group 122 before anyone else. Had not Raskova herself told her chief of staff, Militsa Kazarinova, that Katya Budanova, Valya Gvozdikova, and Tamara Pamyatnykh would make great fighter pilots, and now Gvozdikova was being asked to pilot a bomber? Valya was "so upset she decided she did not want to fly anything". She refused to move out of the accommodation allocated to the fighter pilots, and was "prepared to ram the leading bomber pilot if she was moved". Passions were further inflamed when Raskova unhesitatingly selected Gvozdikova's friend from the Kherson flying school, Lilya Litvyak, even after it was discovered she had contrived to add 100 flying hours to her record in order to be assigned to Raskova – her real experience being barely enough to qualify her for inclusion in the night bomber regiment. When

Gvozdikova's behaviour came to Raskova's attention she just laughed. She respected women as stubborn as herself, and gave permission for Gvozdikova to stay with the fighter pilots.[57]

The girls from Zhenya Prokhorova's renowned aerobatic team were eagerly expected and were to provide the nucleus of the fighter regiment. They were very late for the test flights since Lera Khomyakova and other instructors from the Moscow Central Flying Club had to make their own way to Engels, which proved a very slow business. The club had been evacuated to Vladimirovka, a village near Stalingrad. The instructors had been allowed to take their families with them, and Lera had insisted on taking all her immediate family: her ill father, her mother, and her sister with her three small children. When they had transferred all the planes and evacuated their families, several of the instructors, including Lera, received papers drafting them to the front. Their families stayed in Vladimirovka, and from then until she was killed Lera wrote fifty letters, each beginning, "My dear family, whom I love so much".[58]

Reinforcements were arriving throughout November, but in addition a steady stream of young Komsomol girls who had completed courses at flying clubs and also those who had no training of any sort made their way, on their own initiative, to Raskova in the hope she would find them a place in the ranks of her little army. Most came from Saratov, a city only separated from Engels by the two-kilometre-wide expanse of the Volga.

Lena Lukina, a student at the Saratov Agricultural Institute, returned to the city after helping with the harvest to find that her college had been closed and its building now housed an evacuated war production factory. Her mother said officials had already been round to enlist her to dig trenches, but who wanted to dig trenches when people around her were doing far more interesting and heroic things? Boys she knew were going off to fight at the front, girls were going there as nurses. The quickest way to find out all that was happening was to talk to her friend Irina Dryagina, who was the Party secretary of her faculty. Irina was always in the thick of everything, knew how to shoot, tie bandages properly, and had even trained at the flying club herself. Irina's mother, an emotional Ukrainian woman, told her Irina was not at home. "She's run off to sign up with Raskova!" she said crossly.

Irina, hearing from friends at the flying club that Raskova was forming air regiments across the river, had impulsively set off for Engels. There was no bridge across the Volga but, already in November, people were crossing on the still thin ice. The guard at the flying school on the other side told Irina her documents were insufficient, so she had to go back over the ice to Saratov and from there back again to Engels. Raskova and her commissar Yeliseyeva did their best to persuade Irina and other students to return to their studies, but Irina was having none of it. She asked whether, if she could not be taken on as a pilot, she could at least be an armourer (a possibility she had heard about from girls in the queue). Yeliseyeva pointed out that Irina, as a Party member, would be just right for the post of commissar of the Night Bomber Squadron. Irina kept her head and retorted, "It is important for a commissar to fly!" Raskova laughed and promised that she would.

After hearing all this, Lena Lukina also went to find Raskova. If her mother had known the truth she would never have let her go. Already her father and brother were at the front, and Lena had little brothers and sisters at home. She was her mother's only help. Lena told her she would go and work on the garrison's farm and be part paid in vegetables, which even before the war had been in short supply for their poor family. Her mother agreed.

Lena was familiar with the flying school in Engels and had been to dances there with her friends. She was very jealous when she arrived to find Irina Dryagina already wearing a military greatcoat. Irina brought her to Raskova, who was reluctant to take her away from her family responsibilities, but here too Yeliseyeva intervened, pointing out that they needed a Komsomol administrator in the heavy bomber regiment. Like Irina, she was required to supply the right documentation, so Lena went back home across the ice, telling her mother as she was leaving that she would only be away for a week. After ten days had passed her mother guessed what was going on and went to see Irina's mother. "They're flying!" she exclaimed.

Lena's mother threw up her hands. Only a week ago her daughter had known not the first thing about flying. "Where are they flying?" she could only ask. "With Raskova, of course!" Irina's mother retorted.[59]

Olga Golubeva now also turned up in Engels. She was a talented, seventeen-year-old daredevil who dreamed of becoming an actress, despite the fact that she was no great beauty. Her vivacity and self-confidence more than made up for what she lacked in looks. Her priority was to get back to life in peacetime just as quickly as possible by defending her homeland, and she wanted to do that from the clouds.

She had already joined the war effort in the summer, completing a nursing course and applying to work on a hospital train heading for the front. Her mother cried and upbraided her father, "Why aren't you saying anything? You've let the girl get completely out of hand. Just look at the way she's behaving!" Her father, however, was a committed Communist who had fought in the Red Army back in the Civil War period, and only said to his young daughter, "Do what you think is right." He was a member of the mobilisation commission and would have had little difficulty ensuring that neither Olga nor her brothers ended up at the front, but Olga was sure that thought never crossed his mind.[60]

The young nurse enjoyed working in the hospital carriage. It had that unmistakable smell of trains and railway stations. The train had red crosses painted on the tops of the carriages and an old doctor told her the Germans would not bomb those crosses. He was wrong: they were bombed constantly.

On the first day they were bombed Olga met Sasha, a friend from her school in Siberia. He was a sergeant now, and was just about to tell her something when the train suddenly braked and stopped. Olga jumped out, shouting back to him, "Tell me about it afterwards, Sasha!" She wanted to look up at the aircraft in the sky and wish them luck, sure that they were Soviet planes. The aircraft, however, wheeled round and came back to bomb them, red crosses or no red crosses.

Olga had no idea how long the attack lasted. Through a blanket that muted all sound she clearly heard the ground cracking beneath her into a thousand tiny pieces. She heard people shouting, "Nu-urse!" Her colleagues were already rushing around helping the wounded but she stood there, rooted to the spot. Someone touched her on the shoulder and said, "Help us." She looked up and saw a middle-aged soldier was asking her to help a man writhing in agony. The injured man was screaming dreadfully and Olga found herself breaking out in a cold sweat. She leaned over him and started trying to bandage him but he would not lie still. Her hands were shaking and she was ashamed and in despair at doing everything so clumsily. She heard a gurgling in the wounded man's throat and he stopped thrashing about and lay still, as if her bandaging really had helped. She relaxed a little, but when the old soldier stood up and took off his cap Olga realised what had happened. She wailed out loud. "She's just a young girl, hasn't seen people die," one person said, but someone else yelled at her, "Shut it, will you?" The raid continued for some time longer, and when the German bombers finally left and Olga looked around, the station was unrecognisable: carriages were on fire, buildings collapsing, dead and wounded people were being dragged out of the rubble. Sasha was lying next to the train. His face was intact and for a moment Olga thought he was alive but, running over, she saw his legs were missing and he was dead. Wiping away her helpless tears with hands wet with blood, Olga kept repeating what she had said such a short time ago in a different life: "Tell me about it afterwards, Sasha."

The train continued on its way. Her chief, a fat man with a huge nose like the old witch Baba Yaga, had eyed Olga lustfully her first day on the train and said he would promote her to be the train's dietician. He summoned her one day to his compartment and told her a sob story about a daughter who was just like Olga only he did not know where she was now and his whole family had disappeared. As he told the tragic tale he caressed her hand before groping her leg. Olga fled and, for her insubordination, was demoted to the rank of orderly. She was not unduly upset.

The train made one trip after another. She was working in a wagon for the less seriously wounded, but this proved more trying than working with the severely injured. Those lay, "poor fellows, in their hammocks and were mostly silent".[61] None of them visited the other carriages or climbed down in their shorts at the stations to buy potatoes and vodka. The less seriously wounded, while they were in pain, grunted and groaned, but as soon as they recovered a little started telling tall tales, flirting with the nurses, and singing songs. They had not a care in the world, having left the horrors of the front behind, if only for a time, and with life at the rear to look forward to. They had paid for this good fortune with only a slight wound. Time would show, however, that their sense of relief was premature and that it was the seriously wounded who had the better prospect of surviving the war if, when their treatment was over, they were declared unfit for further military service and not returned to the front. They comprised a significant proportion of the few Soviet young men who survived the war. According to some sources, only 3 per cent of men born in 1923 made it beyond 1945.[62]

The less seriously wounded behaved uproariously and generally made such a racket that the whole wagon shook. "Comrades, it isn't decent to go out onto the platform in your underwear!" Olga shouted after them, but they only laughed. It was pointless to remind them that home-distilled vodka was bad for them. They only quietened down while Olga recited her favourite poetry to them.

Time passed and the immensity of Russia passed by the windows of the train, its fields and forests, its grey villages. She became inured to the hard work, the smell of unwashed bodies, urine and medicines, the groans of the wounded and the sleepless nights. She would probably have stayed doing that job until the war was over if she had not heard from a wounded pilot that Marina Raskova was recruiting women's regiments. That was where she ought to be! Her chance came when another nurse, Lida, who had flying experience, was sent to Raskova. Olga, obtaining leave to see her off, ran away. She never went back to the train.

By the time she arrived in Engels her travel warrant had expired. Raskova frowned, but Olga claimed to have deserted because of the unwelcome attentions of her boss on the train. That did the trick and Raskova, telling everyone to keep quiet about Olga's escape, took her on as an electrician. It was better than nothing and, for someone as tenacious as Olga Golubeva, it was only ever going to be the first step on her way to flying.

Dispatched from Baranov's 296 Fighter Regiment, Masha Dolina arrived at the Engels military school in a dreadful state of mind. "I felt I had literally been sent down from heaven to earth with my hands tied behind my back." She was in the very prepossessing uniform of a fighter pilot, wearing a dark blue greatcoat with light blue tabs and a light blue *pilotka* cap which really suited her. The girls marching in front of her on the parade ground, however, were wearing ungainly canvas boots and grey, ill-fitting greatcoats. Masha was terribly hurt. Who on earth had decided to pluck her, an experienced front-line pilot, from the thick of the action and plonk her down at a school desk with these greenhorns? Well, she was not going to put up with it. She would run away. She knew, of course, that under military law her act could be construed as desertion, but hoped that when she got back to Baranov's regiment he might be persuaded to hush it up. It seemed unlikely that, in the universal chaos prevailing at the time, anyone would be much bothered about what she had done.

She was out of luck, however, and was picked up by a patrol the instant she arrived at Engels railway station. An angry Raskova handed her over to the Political Section, who gave her a thorough dressing-down and threatened to have her court-martialled as a deserter. There was nothing for it. She put on a grey overcoat the wrong size for her petite figure and turned up in the classroom.

In the heavy bomber regiment, which Raskova decided to command herself, there were now two battle-hardened pilots who had been at the front in men's regiments, both of them dauntless, outgoing women with a mannish fearlessness. Nadezhda Fedutenko left her regiment after being wounded and, when she recovered, was sent to Raskova. She was unhappy about the transfer but, respectful of army discipline, kept her feelings to herself. Masha Dolina, however, remained conspicuously angry.

7

"No talking in the ranks!"

The wake-up call, "*Podyom!*", rang out long before the cold November sun rose over a frozen Volga. It was Olga Golubeva's most hated command.[63] She seemed only just to have got warm, only just to have fallen asleep when she heard "*Podyom!*". She snuggled into the pillow, but immediately jumped when the squadron adjutant bawled, "Do you need a special invitation?" Still half asleep, the girls reached out to the barely warm radiators on which they were drying wrappings of fluffy flannel which Commissar Rachkevich, who had been in the army for many years, had taught them to bind round their feet.

They were only now beginning to understand what being in the army was all about. Olga was not alone in being simply unable to see why it was necessary to march everywhere in line. They marched to their classes, to the canteen, to the aerodrome, and even to the bathhouse, from dawn until dark. At night they even heard the still strange commands in their dreams: "Dress right, dress! Atten-shun! About turn! No talking in the ranks!"

A lieutenant in his mid-thirties was in charge of drill practice. They called him their parade ground grandad. In their eyes he was really old. This ancient 35-year-old went down the rank "narrowing his beady, impudent eyes", poking the girls in the belly and shouting, "Straighten up!"[64] Grandad was universally loathed but most kept their loathing to themselves. Only a few dared let their feelings show. Intrepid Olga provoked him by coming on parade ostentatiously wearing felt winter boots instead of the regulation canvas boots. There was a spell of fearsomely cold weather and it would have seemed common sense for them all to be in felt boots, but their officers did not share this view. They believed dress regulations needed to be strictly observed on parade whatever the weather. Grandad imposed three extra fatigue duties on anyone wearing felt boots.

The mechanics in the night bomber regiment took an instant dislike to their chief mechanic, Sonya Ozerkova, a physically very fit martinet with a distinctly martial bearing. She came to the regiment from the Irkutsk Military College and she too got to work on enforcing strong discipline and a strict observance of the regulations. They were required to repeat her orders word for word, to report they had been performed, and to do so with unwavering formality. The mechanics, fresh from civilian life, considered her methods completely unnecessary, and detested Ozerkova for calling them out on drills at any time and whatever the weather, and for quizzing them endlessly about how they had carried out her orders. It was only when they reached the front that they understood the military logic that informed her prescriptions.

Girls trained at a flying club found it easier to adapt to this new environment than complete newcomers. They all had activities from early morning until late at night: navigation training, firearms training, parade ground training, equipment maintenance. In addition to all this the pilots, to their delight, at last started training flights.

The political commissars believed that constant indoctrination and supervision by the Party and Komsomol was imperative in a collective of women with an average age of twenty. They did not trust the girls in their care ever, under any circumstances. Not even on 7 November 1941, the anniversary of the October Revolution, when those serving in 122 Air Group were to take the military oath.

It was a wonderful, sunny day. The snow, "covering the fields and hills with a white veil",[65] glistened merrily in the sun, as if to add to the festivities. The day before, the girls had decorated the rooms and gone with bundles of clean underwear in their arms to the bathhouse. Then they worked into the night editing their first wall newspaper (handmade newssheets designed for display on walls or other prominent places), For the Motherland. Early in the morning, a band played in the main hall of the officers' club and Raskova made a speech. Taking the oath was an exceptionally important Soviet ritual, like Easter for Orthodox Christians, only even more momentous because it was taken only once in a lifetime. Many eyes were bright with tears and now, after taking the oath, they could consider themselves real soldiers. That evening, however, the girls from 122 Air Group were absent from the celebrations in that same hall. They had to sing and dance in the corridor behind a locked door, apart from the other service personnel in the garrison. They danced "not for joy but to dispel the sense of gloom which had overcome rather a lot of them" because of a decision by Yevdokia Rachkevich, the senior commissar, who felt the women she was responsible for should celebrate the anniversary separately from the garrison's men. It was a decision that stunned even her fellow political officers.

Komsomol Administrator Nina Ivakina was a colleague of Rachkevich, but found the decision to oblige 122 Air Group to celebrate the anniversary in the corridor bizarre. It was insulting that they were being kept "like nuns". Why were Komsomol members, who had volunteered to fight in the war, being treated like giddy adolescents incapable of looking after themselves? Ivakina believed her girls should be able in their free time "to interact with the Soviet people", i.e., men. She considered Rachkevich would do well to remember that "parents who try to control their little fledglings too strictly in these matters are more likely to end up with loose-living daughters".

Rachkevich did eventually relent, the girls were allowed into the hall to watch the show and dance during the interval. They went to bed "tired but happy".

Battalion Commissar Yevdokia Rachkevich was a colourful character. Small and stout, she looked ridiculous in uniform but could not imagine life without the army. Fleeing as a young girl during the Civil War from the Ukrainian nationalists led by Symon Petlyura, she found herself working at a Soviet frontier post in Moldavia, initially as a cleaner, laundress and nursing orderly. The young woman could barely read or write, but was eager to study. While there she completed a law course but, wanting to stay in the army, decided to carry on studying. She was keen to become a political instructor because she was fanatically devoted to the new regime, which had raised her from an illiterate farm girl into a person of substance.

Rachkevich sent a letter to the Military Political Academy in Moscow, but received a peremptory response stating: "We do not admit women." She wrote indignantly to Marshal Budyonny, the Commander-in-Chief of the Red Army, who intervened, and she was soon accepted, becoming the first woman to graduate from the Academy. The former cowherd stayed on as a postgraduate and wrote a dissertation. She decided, however, to defend it after the war was over and, when offered the position of commissar in a women's air unit, jumped at the opportunity. When she set off to Engels she said goodbye to her husband, for good as it turned out. After parting from Rachkevich he soon found a new, younger wife. With no children and no family, Rachkevich had only the girls entrusted to her care.

"A commissar is a father to his soldiers and I, as a female commissar, shall be your mumsy," she never tired of saying to the girls. She behaved accordingly, like a loving, fussing, not very bright mumsy and, just as the village women frightened their children by threatening them with the big bad wolf, so Rachkevich would threaten to write to Comrade Stalin, scaring the daylights out of whichever young woman she was currently finding fault with. The next day, having completely forgotten all her threats, Rachkevich would be back to calling the same girl "dearie" and discussing plans for the girl's future.[66]

If she noticed anything amiss in the dress or conduct of one of her charges, Rachkevich was likely to give the delinquent the kind of dressing-down only a Ukrainian woman is capable of, excoriating them "with vehement, passionate sincerity". If a girl exchanged even a few words with a man, Rachkevich would materialise instantly and put an end to any flirtation before it had begun. Behind her back all the girls in the regiments called her "Mumsy", but without affection. Because of her power as a political commissar the girls did not argue with her and obeyed her often wilful and eccentric instructions, but disliked her and tried to keep out of her way. It became clear in later years how completely devoted this rather dim woman was to her pilots and ground staff. When the war was over Rachkevich, by now getting on in years and in poor health, would spend her vacations going round the territories where they had served, not resting until she had found the crash site of every missing airwoman from her regiment.

Nina Ivakina instantly took against her superior political officer, but as time passed, she herself became increasingly persuaded that strict discipline was essential for Air Group 122. The newly recruited servicewomen would skitter into town to get their hair permed, and behave dismissively towards their officers and commissars. "They talked endless nonsense" and even "got themselves into affairs". The commissars were sometimes on the verge of despair. Only Raskova never doubted that her girls would become outstanding combatants. She had faith in them, and they had faith in her. Indeed, they were all "a little in love with her".[67] Raskova's motto was, "We can do anything!" and her pilots, navigators and mechanics believed they really could while they were under the command of someone like her.

8

"Stop flirting! There's a war on!"

Women's Fighter Regiment 586 was the first of the three regiments to be formed and, according to Nina Ivakina's notes, they felt ready for action by 8 December 1941. However, prospects of flying to the front seemed remote: "There seemed to be no end in sight to our classes." More seriously, they had no fighters. "There are rumours we shall be here until May because of a lack of aircraft. That is too bad," Ivakina wrote.

They already knew they would be receiving the Yakovlev Yak-1, the most advanced fighter available to the Russians then, but in the meantime, as they waited impatiently for their own planes, they carried on practising in the garrison's old trainer aircraft. After Vera Lomako left, Zhenya Prokhorova was acting commander, and they all believed she would be the one to lead them into combat. She was greatly respected, her authority was unquestioned, and at the same time she was a very likeable human being.

The future fighter pilots saw her as an ideal commander.

A large head and prominent chin out of proportion to her petite, slender body somewhat detracted from Zhenya's overall appearance, but to compensate she had wonderful straight hair "the deep golden colour of ripe rye," big green eyes and a lovely smile which dimpled her cheeks. She was about thirty and was a dazzlingly skilful pilot.[68] Another of the pilots, Valya Lisitsina, remembered first seeing her in the late 1930s. One hot July day Valya was training young would-be pilots at an aerodrome near Moscow when suddenly a Yakovlev UT-1 sports plane flew in from the south at low level. It circled above the airfield before making an elegant landing. Valya was curious to see who this new arrival was. Even she, an experienced instructor, would not have been confident flying a UT-1, which was a very temperamental sports aircraft flown only by first-rate pilots. A diminutive figure, "with the stoop of a professional pilot", climbed out of the cockpit. When the pilot came closer and took off his helmet, he turned out to be a she. Somebody standing next to Valya whispered that this was Zhenya Prokhorova, who had come to the aerodrome to rehearse the members of her aerobatic team before the Tushino Air Show. Now that she had encountered Zhenya again during the war, Valya was delighted to be serving under her command. All they now needed was planes to fly.

Zhenya Prokhorova had long been familiar with aircraft designed by Alexander Yakovlev. In 1935 she took part in the test flight from Leningrad to Moscow of his "No. 6" plane. Yakovlev's Yak-1 fighter, which the regiment was now so eagerly awaiting, was an exceptionally successful design, and became the outstanding Soviet fighter plane of World War II.[69] Yakovlev was superlatively talented, but is remembered by many as a cantankerous individual.[70] He was almost the only Soviet aircraft designer not to fall foul of the purges in the 1930s and 1940s. Like Raskova, Yakovlev enjoyed the trust of Stalin who, already in 1939, would summon him to the Kremlin to hear his opinion on various matters and on various people. Yakovlev recalled Stalin complaining to him at the time that he "did not know who to trust".[71] Going by the numerous prizes Yakovlev was awarded while his colleagues were being incarcerated in prison aircraft design centres, he was someone Stalin did trust. In 1940 Stalin made him deputy commissar for experimental aircraft design.

We can only speculate about how much harm Yakovlev did to his colleagues: it is certainly likely that he informed on them. The damage he did to many excellent projects inititated by other designers is, however, plain to see: he quashed a whole succession of new aircraft developed in other design offices before they could go into production. Yakovlev was afraid of competition, probably quite groundlessly. The Yak-1, replacing antediluvian Polikarpov I-16 fighters, was reliable, fast and manoeuvrable, and was hailed by the Russian pilots as a machine that would at last be a match for the German Messerschmitts.

The U-2s, which the night bomber regiment would be flying, were due to arrive at any moment, but 587 Regiment, the heavy bomber pilots, while their navigators were being trained, still had no idea which aircraft they would be supplied with. Immediately before the New Year, instructors flew in three old Sukhoi Su-2s for them to train on. Raskova, by now commander of 587 Heavy Bomber Regiment, "paced around these squat single-engine planes", sniffing.[72] They did not smell like other aircraft: the whiff of petrol was mixed with another strong, unfamiliar odour. "What's that smell?" She asked a mechanic. The boy grinned. "They run on castor oil. No problem in the winter, but we are going to sweat in the summer. When it spatters the cockpit you'll never get it off."

Quite apart from aesthetic considerations, Raskova found a number of other, more serious problems with the Su-2. It was slow and, if it caught fire, flared up like a match. Another major drawback of the aircraft, which was first tested in 1937 and immediately put into service at the front as a light bomber and for reconnaissance, was that, especially in winter, its nose tended to dip when landing and it could even flip right over, ending with its wheels in the air and the crew killed or injured. The women hated the Su-2s, which they knew were nicknamed "Bitches". They heard that the Su-2 was about to be taken out of production, but what aircraft would they be allocated then? Raskova, as usual, took matters into her own hands.

★

"Pilot Litvyak was absent without leave after lights out. She was absent for one hour and thirty minutes," Komsomol Administrator Nina Ivakina noted in her diary on 21 December 1941.[73] Litvyak's absence was suspiciously contemporaneous with the dance the garrison held on Saturday nights. Altogether, in the eyes of the authorities, Litvyak "behaved disgracefully". She answered back, was late, and broke the rules almost daily.

With her strong and wilful character she found it very difficult to submit to military discipline, but Lilya Litvyak was by no means the only girl behaving badly. Many of her new comrades who, until recently, had been wearing crêpe de chine dresses and dainty shoes, simply could not see why they should be unable to visit the hairdresser or go to the dances which were held for the garrison right next door in the main hall of the officers' club. On the first day, their chief of staff, Militsa Kazarinova, had prudently locked the door between the sports hall where the girls slept in two-tier bunks and the club hall where the dances and concerts were held. The girls, however, promptly scratched holes in the white paint obscuring the glass so they could watch the dancing. They all watched, but Lilya Litvyak was one of the first to gatecrash. She was punished, but that did not stop her going to the dances. Others followed her deplorable example.

Valya Krasnoshchyokova found she could resist the dances, but when pilot Klava Blinova invited her to decamp to the operetta, she agreed on the spot: she adored operetta. The genre had initially been considered bourgeois and frowned on in the new Soviet state, and it was only in the second half of the 1930s that it really found its way back. European operettas began to be staged, first and foremost "The Gypsy Princess" by Imre Kálmán and the operettas of Strauss ("The Gypsy Baron" was Lilya Litvyak's favourite); and the new Soviet operettas, mostly written by Isaak Dunaevsky: "Bridegrooms", "The Golden Valley" and so on. They were tremendously popular, and when Valya Krasnoshchyokova arrived in Moscow from Kaluga as a student she frequently rushed to see them, usually, as she was short of money, buying a ticket in the gods or for standing room only.

The company that turned up in Engels, needless to say, bore no comparison with the Musical Comedy Theatre in Moscow, but there was no alternative. Valya was well aware it would be a long time before she had another chance. In any case, she liked Klava Blinova, who was destined to become a fighter pilot. Klava was the youngest of the female pilots and, unlike many of the others, did not look down her nose at the mechanics. Some in the fighter regiment considered Lilya Litvyak the most beautiful, while others said Klava Nechaeva was. Valya, however, had no doubt that Klava Blinova was the best looking of them all. She had light hair, a sweet, young, rosy-cheeked face, and big eyes. Klava was fun, brave, sang beautifully, and was constantly laughing.

If Lilya Litvyak's unauthorised attendance at dances was reported by neighbours in the barracks informing on her, Valya and Klava were apprehended by Raskova herself who had seen them coming back. She gave them a talking to, then issued each with a reprimand and gave them extra duties: Klava was told she would carry out her fatigue at the aerodrome, but Valya was sent off to clean the barrack latrines.

In cold weather the latrines, a wooden hut with a hole in the floor, could only be cleaned using a crowbar. Chipping away the frozen excrement, Valya was quietly sobbing. She was upset at the punishment itself, but she was also ashamed because of what Raskova had said about such behaviour in wartime. Suddenly she heard a voice: "Don't cry, Valya. It's me." Klava had secretly come to help.[74]

In order to give them some compensation for placing the officers' club hall off-limits, the girls were allowed to listen to a gramophone. Klava Pankratova, another future fighter pilot, managed to get hold of a supply of records from the men, and in the girls' dormitory in the evening she would turn the handle of the primitive device with such tender care it was "as if she was afraid to trespass on the delicate melody of a Russian romance". Her friends would already be getting ready for lights-out and lying on their bunks in men's white shirts, but "with an expression of tender girlish emotion on their faces".[75]

While others only had extra fatigue duties meted out to them for being absent without leave, Lilya Litvyak was more severely punished. She had already been given additional work, so the authorities decided something heavier was needed. The next day the regiment was assembled and it was announced that she would be arraigned before a Red Army Comrades' Court.

Communal courts of this kind became ubiquitous in the 1930s. There were endless courts of workers, collective farmers, factories, labour brigades, and so on. They were informal and their purpose was less to punish delinquents than to re-educate them ideologically. The Red Army Courts, which later became known as "Officers' Courts of Honour" were to deal with cases like disorderly conduct, fighting, insulting behaviour, and pilfering among the soldiers of a particular unit. They played a major role during the war because military tribunals did not involve themselves in administrative or civil cases like this.

The following day the members of the court were nominated. Its session when it met on 24 December resembled a discussion rather than a court martial. Lilya did not take it very seriously. "She is not conscious of being at fault," Nina Ivakina noted in her diary.[76] Litvyak was issued a severe reprimand and warning, which had no effect on her behaviour whatsoever, and sent to the guardhouse. The "cooler" was just a shed on the airfield guarded by an armed sentry. To ease the tedium for the miscreant her friends, egged on by Klava Pankratova, provided her with the gramophone.

Young navigators and mechanics like Olga Golubeva could not take their eyes off Lilya. She was not, if you looked closely, any great beauty. In fact, she was quite plain. "You could have passed her in the street without noticing."[77] She was not tall, quite thin, and had a pointed nose, but she had a very elegant figure, a pleasing complexion, curls but, most importantly, a very lively expression, shining eyes and a winning smile. She did not give herself airs and made little distinction between senior officers, her fellow pilots, and the mechanics.

At the college in Engels, as everywhere else, Lilya Litvyak "was the centre of attention", especially after she started going to dances at the officers' club. She was a great dancer. Some girls were horrified and demanded she should "Stop flirting! There's a war on!" Lilya, unabashed, replied, "So what if there's a war on?" When someone asserted that any moment now she might start kissing boys, she retorted, "You're all plain weird! Wartime does not abolish kissing and love!" Olga Golubeva thought she had probably only said that to provoke the wet blankets amongst the girls.[78]

It was already New Year. There was a terrible frost on 31 December but the work of the aerodrome and in the classes continued as normal. That evening people brought out their party tricks among bunks draped with white sheets, and there was much singing and dancing. When finally everyone went to bed, many felt homesick and nostalgic for the peacetime life that was essential for properly celebrating the festival. Suddenly, Grandfather Frost appeared with a white beard and long grey locks to wish them all a Happy New Year. He even brought toys: horses on wheels, bunny rabbits and concertinas. The pilots and navigators, as Ivakina records in her diary, "jumped out of bed and, in their drawers and men's shirts as long as strait-jackets, swirled joyfully in a dance which to an outsider would have seemed insane".[79] Thus they welcomed in 1942.

The festivities had all been organised by the navigators, no doubt with the active involvement of Zhenya Rudneva, who from the unit's earliest days had been one of the group's leaders and an instigator of all kinds of events. In Nina Ivakina's opinion, 1942 would be "the graveyard of those fascist bastards, who have torn us from our peaceful labours, our homes and comforts". That was how all of them were thinking, despite the devastating defeats of 1941. The country's leaders had said the war would be over in 1942, so how could anyone doubt it? At the Red Army Parade on 7 November 1941 Stalin said, "In a few months more, half a year, perhaps a year at most, Hitler's Germany will collapse under the weight of its crimes."[80] If great, wise Stalin had said that, then how could events develop otherwise?

They had fun again thirteen days later on the traditional Russian New Year's Eve. Following ancient custom, the girls tried to foretell their future. Going back to the old ways, they became just young girls again, dreaming of love. The most popular fortune-telling method was to go outside and ask the first man they met what his name was. While doing so they had to look carefully at his face. Their destined bridegroom would assuredly have the same name and look similar. They also threw shoes out of the door to show the direction from which their intended would come, and dripped wax from a candle into water, to see what the lump of wax reminded them of. But if Lilya was speculating about her future bridegroom, she was not admitting it to her family. In a letter to her mother and brother, Yury, Lilya wrote only: "We come together to foretell what awaits us in our new life at war. There are so many interesting things ahead, so many surprises, chance twists and turns of fate."[81] Not sparing her mother's feelings, Lilya went on to explain the life she hoped was in store for her. Her words are full of the kind of youthful exuberance you would expect from a twenty-year-old. "What can be in store for me? Either something wonderful and magnificent, or everything might collapse in an instant into the ordinary routine of the civilian life which ordinary sinners live. Of course, what I want is to live, if only a little, but a wild, interesting life like in that tale told by Vasiliy Chapaev about the eagle and the raven. The hour will soon come when we shall soar on the wings of hawks, and the life we live will be very different."

Lilya was referring to a tale told by the Kalmyks, a nomadic people who roved the expanses of the Russian steppe, in which an eagle asks a raven, "Tell me, oh Raven, why is it you live 300 years in this world while I am allotted a meagre thirty-three?" The raven replies, "Sir, it is because you drink the blood of the living, while I feed on the flesh of the dead." The eagle decides to try it himself. They fly out, find a dead horse, and settle. The raven begins pecking and saying how good the carrion is, but the eagle pecks once, pecks again, but then flaps his wing in disgust and says, "No, Brother Raven, rather than feed for 300 years on the flesh of the dead I shall drink my fill of the blood of the living, and for the rest, God's will be done!"

This kind of thinking was typical of all the girls. "We were young and fearless. The fear came later," remembers one of those who survived.[82] For the present, they not only had little idea of what the profession of a wartime pilot involved, but also had virtually no information about what was really occurring on the front lines of the Great Patriotic War.

In political instruction classes for the Komsomol members in her care, Nina Ivakina did not tell them about the true situation on the fronts for the simple reason that she knew nothing about it. Neither did her superior, Yevdokia Rachkevich, or, indeed, Raskova herself. Only the top military authorities had a more or less complete picture of what was happening.

News of the retreat, which Sovinformbyuro bulletins usually presented as redeployment to a more advantageous position, and about which Nina Ivakina tried to speak as little as possible, did nevertheless reach the ranks in the form of disquieting rumours, scraps of official information, and hints in letters from home.[83] In units closer to the front, the girls could see for themselves how the war was going.

Anya Skorobogatova was on the retreat with demoralised Soviet troops. She had completed her two-month course in Rossosh, qualified as a radio operator, and had taken the oath. Her hopes of being posted to an aviation regiment were dashed when she was assigned to the specialist 65 Signals Battalion of the Southwestern Front. In mid-November 1941 Anya learned that the Germans had occupied Taganrog where her parents lived. Her father was a Party activist, and from what she had gleaned from the newspapers, the chances of survival under the Germans for him, her mother and younger brother were almost nil. Anya had a strong personality and had had a spartan communist upbringing, so she did not allow herself to be seen crying. Instead she went out into the steppe and wept there. It was a long time before she discovered that her family had been evacuated at the last moment from Taganrog. She lived with the anguish of believing they had perished but shed no more tears. It was as if she had wept them all that one time, into the icy wind.[84]

Her battalion's preparations to leave Rossosh were made to the rumble of artillery fire. They had been ordered to evacuate to Stalingrad, which would oblige them to cross the River Don. "Our retreat," Skorobogatova recalled, "was totally chaotic."[85] The Germans destroyed the main forces of the Southwestern Front in the Kiev encirclement, the largest in the whole of the Second World War. According to their figures, 665,000 people were taken prisoner and the total of Soviet casualties, killed or wounded, was over half a million.[86] Divisions whose full complement was almost 10,000 men had only a thousand left, the equivalent of an infantry battalion. The retreat was disorderly, units got mixed up, and it was not always clear where each unit was at any given time. Anya, like the battalion's other radio operators travelling with their radios in trucks, was ordered by the head of signals to halt when possible, open their radio transmitters and scan the airwaves.[87] They were to identify their own location and report it to headquarters. When she received the call sign, Anya was able to advise that they were close to Kotelnikovo, a small town about 200 kilometres from Stalingrad. When she next got in touch, she reported that they, along with a large column of soldiers, had been bombed but were now moving on.

The bombing was terrible. German Focke-Wulf Fw 189 spy planes were nicknamed "the Frame" because of their strange rectangular shape. When they spotted a large column of Soviet soldiers they radioed back to base to summon bombers. It was already evening. The Germans dropped flares and started their attack. There were instantly many dead and wounded. All around was commotion and terrible screaming. Soldiers when they saw Anya shouted, "Nurse, nurse! Help us to move the wounded."

Anya's course for radio operators had not taught her even the rudiments of first aid, but as there was no real nurse available she did her best to help. Together with the soldiers she carried those wounded who could be moved to the nearest hut. Inside, the woman who lived there tore up sheets and shirts to make bandages. There were twelve casualties, with every imaginable kind of wound. It was a horrific situation unlike any Anya had ever experienced. She, the woman and a soldier did what they could. They had to leave, but there was no way they could take the wounded along.

They were left in the hut to await the arrival of the Germans who, in all probability, finished them off.

It was late at night before Anya found her truck. Her colleagues shouted, "Thank God, she's alive!" when they saw her. Anya was terribly distressed by the thought that the wounded had been left behind in a village without protection or medical care. They tried to reassure her: "When our troops come by they will pick them up." It was only too clear, however, that there were no Soviet troops following. The Germans were right on their heels.

All the recruits in Raskova's unit remembered the winter of 1941–2 as exceptionally cold, with severe frosts and merciless blizzards. They were given very warm clothing: high flying-boots with fur stockings, fur-lined flying suits, fur-lined gloves, and mole-fur masks to cover their faces. Even that was hardly sufficient protection for someone flying at altitude in the depths of a harsh winter in the open cockpit of a U-2. They got terribly cold and despite the masks they'd been issued their faces were often frost-bitten. The navigators, who invariably had less flying experience than the pilots, would become nauseous until they were acclimatised to the freezing temperatures. If during a big freeze you grasped a metal component in an aircraft with your bare hand, you would leave pieces of frozen skin behind on the metal when you tried to pull it away, a wound that would take a long time to heal. Both the women piloting U-2s and their mechanics soon learned never to take their gloves off in the planes. There was, however, almost no complaining. "On 5 January I was in the air for ten minutes for the first time," Zhenya Rudneva noted. "I will not even attempt to describe the feeling because I know it is impossible. Back on the ground I felt I had just been born again. It was even better on 7 January: the plane did a corkscrew and performed a roll. I was tied in with a harness. The ground rocked and swayed and was suddenly above my head. Below me was blue sky with clouds in the distance. It occurred to me that you could turn a tumbler upside down without the water coming out of it. After the first flight, I saw the world differently. Sometimes I am horrified to think I might have lived my whole life without ever flying."[88]

At just this time Galya Dokutovich, too, began flying as a navigator and found it no less interesting than being the pilot. "Now I see how exciting being a navigator is!" she wrote. "When you have done a little flying you walk around in a dream and just want to get back up in the sky."[89] She was to be bitterly disappointed, however, because as she had not completed higher aviation training and thus did not possess the requisite flying experience, she was appointed the squadron's ground-based administrative adjutant.

The pilots and navigators of the night bomber regiment were divided into pairs, and the expressions "my navigator" and "my pilot" gained currency. Yevdokia Bershanskaya, who had been appointed commanding officer of their regiment, as an experienced pilot and instructor was well aware how important it was for the pilot and navigator to be temperamentally suited to each other. When flying they would have to function as a single unit. Together with chief of staff Irina Rakobolskaya, she thought long and hard when teaming them up. In most cases they got it right and there were almost no requests for a transfer to a different crew.

With the girls flying all the daylight hours, their mechanics were now run off their feet. The political instructors in the three women's regiments were also working tirelessly. In addition to such tasks as conducting classes on "The Red Army: Indomitable Sentinel of the Socialist State" and giving talks about Comrade Stalin, they had to devote much time to dealing with personal issues. There were endless squabbles among the women, which the commissars had to resolve. On the Russian Christmas Day, 7 January 1942, the full complement of 586 Fighter Regiment moved from the sports hall of the officers' club to the flying school's administrative building where conditions were much better. The command was pleased to have arranged for the whole regiment to be accommodated in one large hall. The pilots, however, surprised them and the political instructors by protesting that they did not want to live alongside their colleagues, the mechanics.

In the Soviet state equality was only ever really theoretical. The mechanics were used to putting up with receiving inferior rations and to being looked down on by the pilots. "What pilot would ever respect a non-pilot?"[90] Everybody was outraged, however, by the crude way they made their point. Klava Nechaeva, who as a card-carrying Communist should have been setting a good example, complained, for instance, that the mechanics' feet were at the head of her bed, which she considered intolerable.[91]

For their part, the mechanics were "more equal" than the engine maintenance technicians and were supposed to receive better nutrition. The fact that the plane crews and mechanics would have different rations became known almost as soon as they arrived in Engels. The logic was that the pilots were to rank as officers, and in the Soviet army, as in the Tsarist army, officers and rank-and-file soldiers were fed very differently. Now the technical staff was subdivided: mechanics were to be classed as non-commissioned officers, and accordingly better fed than the technicians and armourers. These then also protested. Nina Ivakina was horrified when some members of the Komsomol Committee sided with the rebels arguing that all the maintenance staff should receive equal rations. What made the situation even more fraught was that by this point in time there were serious shortages of everything from food to forks and spoons that affected everyone regardless of rank. Anyone dining in the privileged dining room for senior officers and political instructors would see them reduced to trying to eat "watery buckwheat porridge with their hands" because there was "nothing to eat and nothing to eat it with".[92] Even tea was unsweetened, and this dearth only served to heighten the impatience of everyone to go to the front where it was believed food was in far greater supply.

Almost every day Nina Ivakina had to referee squabbles and arguments. Komsomol Member Fyodorova quarrelled with Komsomol Member Sokolova and called her a pain in the ass. Both of them were weeping and wailing as the Komsomol administrator tried to adjudicate. Belyaeva, the commander of First Squadron, was reluctant to prepare a political indoctrination talk and had to be coerced into doing so. There was a division of authority between the officers: Raskova and Vera Lomako could not stand Commissar Kulikova and made little attempt to hide it. Ivakina, of course, informed Kulikova about this. Ivakina herself quarrelled with Kasatkina, the Communist Party administrator, and told her she had a foul mouth. Even the Party and Komsomol administrators within the squadrons struggled to get on.

The Air Division commissar, sent by the Political Department, was constantly harassing political instructors in the regiments, reading them directives and telling them how to conduct political work in different situations. Ivakina was surprised to learn from him that "senior military figures" on the courses for commissars got up to no less mischief than her girls. They were not averse to leaving their units without permission to go to the dances at the officers' club. Indeed Ivakina discovered that such behaviour was perfectly normal, and that it was only in Raskova's regiments that the commissars, unlike their counterparts elsewhere, believed they could eradicate such disorderly conduct. The methods Ivakina and her colleagues used to enforce discipline and root out sedition were nothing out of the ordinary for that time. Nina Ivakina wrote approvingly in her diary about a letter Valya Krasnoshchyokova had received from a school friend, an eighteen-year-old boy who lost an eye at the front. Ivakina judged the letter "very mature".[93] Valya had not given her the letter to read, and would have been surprised to know it was being read by anyone other than herself.[94]

In Stalin's Russia, it was made clear to political instructors that there was nothing shameful about secretly reading the letters and rummaging through the belongings of those for whom they were responsible. "Our country is fighting enemies, internal and external; our enemies are strong, which is why it is important to know what people are thinking and feeling. We need to have in our possession all the information we can obtain."

Party and Komsomol administrators were usually sociable individuals who got on well with everyone. One of their methods was to try periodically to talk heart-to-heart with their charges. Surreptitiously they would make themselves liked, bring people round to talking frankly, and then ask them about their friends. Valya Krasnoshchyokova remembered what her wise grandmother had told her: "The sneak is the first to feel the lash." She did not dish dirt or tell tales about anyone, but there were plenty of others who did, often quite unaware of the danger to which they were exposing their friends.

In a letter dated 13 January 1942, Lilya Litvyak wrote to her mother and brother Yury that she was pleased to say all the little difficulties that had been plaguing her had been "smoothed over by grateful superiors. In fact, you could say I am rather in favour at the moment." Even those who kept an unfriendly eye on her, and there were plenty of them, had to admit after the start of training flights that Litvyak was a very good pilot, and the most proficient of all at shooting.

On 7 January, when the pilots practised firing at oversized windsocks dragged behind a tow plane, Ivakina noted in her diary that they had not yet learned how to shoot. Masha Kuznetsova, Klava Blinova and many others "failed to cope with the task".[95] According to Ivakina, only Litvyak acquitted herself well. "She has the ability to achieve great things, but only makes the effort when she wants to get someone to like her." Ivakina's guarded attitude to Litvyak remained unchanged by her good showing in combat training. She vehemently disagreed with those political instructors who, like the squadron's Communist Party administrator, Tanya Govoryako, spoke up for Litvyak. Ivakina felt she could not lower her guard, because she was dealing with someone who was "just too full of herself". Litvyak, having had her various disciplinary penalties reduced, continued to break the rules and went to dances without permission. That was the least of it. Soon Ivakina was informing her diary, "We have produced a right swanky, flirtatious aviatrix."

"Cadet Litvyak, two steps forward!" Raskova ordered. Only at this point did the line-up of over a hundred cadets of the Fighter Regiment, pilots, mechanics, armourers and technicians, notice that Lilya Litvyak's winter flying suit was now sporting a fluffy white collar. The day before they had all been issued with winter uniforms, including warm flying suits with ugly brown lambskin collars. Lilya, dissatisfied with their appearance, had come up with a solution. She had ripped the white fur off the warm stockings they wore inside their flying boots and stitched it onto the collar. She loved white, and it suited her.

It had not occurred to her that it might be against regulations to alter military uniform. At home if she had a dress which she felt did not quite suit her, she would sit down at her beloved sewing machine and alter it on the spot.

Before the revolution, her mother had been a milliner, and it is possible even owned a hat shop. She was a great seamstress, and taught Lilya how to sew. Her daughter inherited a rare talent for creating a handsome outfit out of nothing. After her father walked out, her mother was in dire straits, but Lilya's dresses always had pretty bows and her coats had big fur collars. Lilya made lovely scarves for herself and was the envy of the girls in their courtyard, where she was always the best attired.

Most of Lilya's contemporaries had been poorly dressed until the late thirties when the situation began to change: there were fashion magazines and citizens were even encouraged to wear better, more chic clothes. There was a vogue for crêpe de chine dresses and stylish hairdos. The wives of Party and Soviet officials no longer wore military-style tunics and red scarves, but bought their outfits in exclusive stores open only to the elite. It was more difficult for other women to buy these beautiful outfits, and in any case they could not afford them. Instead, obtaining a warrant to buy material, they made their own dresses. If they were poor, like Lilya's family, they fell back on clothing left over from more prosperous times, which they magically transformed. Thanks to her mother's and her own dress-making skills, Lilya was accustomed to turning heads.

Military personnel, however, were expected to wear uniform, especially those who had only been cadets for a little over a month. Raskova called Lilya forward and asked when she had sewn on her new collar. Lilya told her she had done so the night before, and Raskova sent her off under arrest to the guardhouse to sew the white fur back onto the stockings and the lambskin collar back onto her flying suit.

There was widespread horror at Lilya's conduct. Faina Pleshivtseva, a tall, sport-loving mechanic, looked at Lilya disapprovingly and wondered how, with a brutal war going on, this blonde bombshell could be thinking about something as frivolous as a fur collar. What sort of pilot would such a person ever make?[96] Nina Ivakina found the episode highly revealing. She had seen immediately she arrived in Engels that Litvyak would need to be worked on. First someone told her Litvyak had exaggerated the number of hours she had flown. Then, when Ivakina started making discreet enquiries, she found that some of the other pilots had a far from flattering opinion of her. Ivakina decided she ought to investigate Litvyak's social antecedents in more detail, which boded ill for Lilya. It would have been a relatively simple matter for her to discover that Lilya's father had been arrested in the 1937 purges, though if she did find that out, this damaging revelation was evidently mitigated by the fact that he had abandoned his family long before it happened.

Lilya's act split the regiment. Most condemned her, but Komsomol Administrator Ivakina was outraged that Litvyak's friends Klava Pankratova and Valya Lisitsina had not only failed to stop her, but had actively "helped her and then merrily accompanied Litvyak in her modified apparel to the airfield".[97] Even after her sojourn in the guardhouse Lilya continued to spend much time arranging her blonde curls (which some said she bleached with peroxide) and wore her Samurai sleeveless summer jacket, fetchingly turned inside-out to show off its own white fur.[98]

9

"An aircraft you could use to fight"

The Fighter Regiment received its Yaks in late January 1942. On the day the aircraft were to be delivered everyone ran to the windows the instant they woke to see whether the weather was suitable for flying. It was bright and sunny and could not have been better. The snow on the aerodrome sparkled so dazzlingly it hurt their eyes, but they all looked up squinting into the sky and waited. They heard the long-awaited roar of engines around midday and were breathless when the Yaks appeared.

On 28 January, Nina Ivakina wrote that the first Yak-1 to be delivered was "a sign of spring . . . It was a little aeroplane as white as snow and equipped with skis, two rapid-fire machine guns and a cannon." Ivakina was surprised how awestruck the pilots were at the sight of it, and how impatient they were to see who would receive this gift from the gods.[99] Everybody abandoned what they were doing and gathered in a "heaving crush" at the aerodrome. Very soon the rest of the Yaks were flown over from the Saratov Aviation Plant on the other side of the Volga. When the order was received, "Prepare to receive equipment," the mechanics rushed to check their tools yet again and to check and re-check the readiness of their aircraft stands, to repeat the rules for receiving the planes and escorting them there.

The girls were ecstatic: these Yaks too were in white winter camouflage and on skis. In fact they were the only white planes they flew during the war, which is why they all remembered so vividly those first planes that flew in on that sunny winter's day. White camouflage was soon abandoned – it was a waste of time to repaint the planes twice a year – and once it became clear that replacing wheels with skis in wintertime was impractical, all planes were fitted only with wheels. Saninsky, the unit's chief mechanic, kept up an endless stream of banter to counter the other mechanics' fatigue, and made them work all day in the freezing cold. By evening the aircraft were ready.

Other fighting units that received Yaks from the Saratov Plant, recently re-tooled to produce aircraft instead of combine harvesters, could not believe their luck. The I-16 aircraft in which they had been fighting up till then, nicknamed "the Donkey", was "a small, poorly armed aircraft, and slow".[100] Its weaponry consisted of a single machine gun that proved inadequate in combat. "You would press the firing button and, before you knew it, were out of ammunition." When the Yaks were delivered to 296 Fighter Regiment, to which Masha Dolina so longed to return, its pilots immediately appreciated that this was a qualitatively new aircraft: it had an outstanding specification and serious armaments with its machine guns,

1. Marina Raskova.

2. Marina Raskova, Polina Osipenko and Valentina Grizodubova, 1938.

3. Lilya, pre-war.

4. Young Lilya.

5. Galya Dokutovich and
Polina Gelman before the war.

6. Another picture taken before the German invasion. Lilya with her typical
expression, looking both proud and cheeky at the same time, with her male
trainees, who are exchanging grins.

7. Katya Budanova and male trainees, pre-war.

8. Klava Nechaeva training a male cadet; pre-war photo.

9. Zhenya Prokhorova and her team at an air parade in Tushino.

10. Anna Yegorova with other Komsomol members, construction of the Metro.

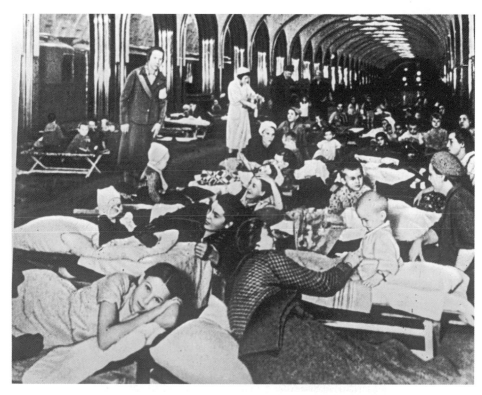

11. Women and children in the underground hall of Mayakovskaya Metro station during an air raid in Moscow, 1941.

12. Volunteers enlist in the national militia in Moscow, 1941.

13. Masha Kuznetsova.

14. Raisa Surnachevskaya, Katya Budanova and Olga Shakhova.
Taken in Engels in either 1941 or the early part of 1942.

15. Anna Yegorova being briefed next to her U-2, 1941.

16. Unidentified, Katya Budanova and Zhenya Prokhorova, Engels.

cannon, and six rocket-propelled missiles. They found landing on skis tricky at first because "there were no brakes", but at last they had "an aircraft you could use to fight".[101]

On 29 January Lilya Litvyak wrote to her mother that she had finally flown solo in a Yak, a day she had been looking forward to for months. "I am now a fully fledged fighter pilot," she wrote.[102] She was particularly pleased that her training period, before she was allowed to fly a Yak without an instructor on board, had been minimal. The real training, when they would learn about flying at high altitude, aerobatics, and air combat, was yet to come.

The pilots also started studying fighter tactics and photo reconnaissance. They now each had their own plane, which the mechanics polished until they were gleaming. As before they all got up at 0600 hours, and flew from 0900 to 1700 hours. The only drawback was that, as a result, they had a huge gap between their early breakfast and the chance to eat again at 1800 hours. Even pilots were now sometimes being underfed. "We get 20 grams of butter once every five days and now, for the first time, we only get one egg," Lera Khomyakova wrote home. "I leave the canteen still hungry."[103] The mechanics, who got less than pilots, would try not to eat their bread at lunchtime and take it out with them to the aircraft. When the hunger became too much, they would take it out and gnaw it, frozen hard by the cold, and feel better.

On the same day that Lilya Litvyak was writing about her first solo flight in a Yak, Nina Ivakina heard at a closed meeting that there were plans to send them to the front in February. For the time being this was to be kept secret. The intention was to send the night bomber regiment, which would be flying U-2s, before that, since training them was a simpler matter.

On the day mobilisation of the night bomber regiment was announced, the instructor teaching the navigators Morse code was in high spirits. On his key he tapped out various humorous sentences, and now and then laughter rippled through the class. He suddenly started tapping away faster, at a speed few could keep up with. "The order has come to mobilise the night bomber regiment. If you have understood this, you are free to leave the classroom quietly."[104] Several girls got up and went out with a secretive smile while the rest, flustered, looked on. When everyone found out, it was as if the girls had sprouted wings. "In no time now we'll be going to the front!"

The long-awaited U-2 light bomber aircraft were delivered in early February. They were exactly the same as the old ones the girls had trained on: light, slow-moving, their wings covered with fabric. No parachutes were issued. In the view of the authorities, and of the crews themselves, if this type of aircraft suffered engine failure there should be no problem gliding it down to land, so no provision needed to be made for bailing out. The fact that the plane was made of plywood and percale cotton fabric, burned like tinder if it caught fire, and that the crew might burn to death before they could land, seemed not to occur to anybody. Sometimes U-2 pilots were told that, since they would be flying behind the front line, it would better to die in their aircraft than land and be taken prisoner by the Gemans. It was commonly held that death was preferable to German captivity, the horrors of which were written about at length in the newspapers. Most, however, gave no thought to the possibility of captivity or death. At twenty you do not think about such things, even in wartime.

Girls like Galya Dokutovich, who combined an administrative position with flying, were not given a fixed partner. The idea was that they would fly in the time left over from their administrative duties, but there was little of that, and so they were assigned to pilots who, for whatever reason, were temporarily short of a navigator. Galya found this very upsetting: she really wanted to fly. "I have a problem," she jotted in her diary. "I have been appointed squadron adjutant. I suspect that means I can forget flying."[105] Sitting every day on the training courses of the headquarters staff group that were supposed to make them "fearfully clever", Galya envied those who instead were flying in the heavens. She greatly appreciated her infrequent training flights, especially the more testing ones that took place at night. On 5 February 1942 she wrote, "It was funny how elated we were yesterday when we came into the canteen after our night flights. Red-faced, our hair all over the place, our eyes bloodshot, we turned up in the morning still in our flying suits and boots. We sat there eating our meal, and Zhenya Zhigulenko's head kept leaning over onto Vera Belik's shoulder, her eyes closing completely."

The night bomber navigators had not only to find their way to the target at night and get their aircraft back to base; it was also their job to drop bombs accurately on the target. After they were delivered, the quiet, peaceable little U-2s were converted into bombers in the simplest imaginable manner. An improved version, specifically adapted for carrying a bomb payload, began coming into service only in 1943. Until then, bombs were slung under the wings with rudimentary attachments, and the small flare bombs used to illuminate a target were carried like luggage in the navigators' laps. The planes could carry a payload of 200–300 kilograms of bombs. Galya wrote in her diary that, as soon as they had familiarised themselves with "the equipment", they would be sent to the front. Major Bershanskaya was expecting at any moment to fly to Moscow to be given the order.

The pilots of 587 Heavy Bomber Regiment envied the fighter and night bomber crews: they were still waiting for their planes, and training in the meantime on the "bitchy" Su-2s. Their navigators were being trained on the huge Tupolev TB-3 bomber, which they were all loaded onto together. Before the first flight they timidly approached the huge aircraft and stared in perplexity at the parachutes dumped under the wing. "Don parachutes," the instructor ordered, but nobody knew how to do that. Little Tonya Pugachyova, nevertheless, confidently took one and started putting it on. The parachutes were intended for men, with the result that the shoulder straps hung down to Tonya's legs, which she slipped through them. The male bomber crew roared with laughter, but the instructor was unabashed, told the men to behave, took Tonya's parachute and explained to the girls how to put it on.[106]

The planes they finally got their hands on were the most up-to-date available at that time, thanks to Raskova. She had flown to Moscow to see the People's Commissar of the Aviation Industry, Alexey Shakhurin, whom she knew well. When asked the purpose of her visit, Raskova replied that she had come to ask him to supply her regiment with the latest Petlyakov Pe-2 dive-bombers. Shakhurin almost laughed in her face: "Those are a bit different from your U-2s!" he exclaimed.[107] Production of the twin-engined Pe-2 ground attack bomber had begun even before the outbreak of war, but in 1942 very few units were yet equipped with them.

Its designer, Vladimir Petlyakov, designed the aircraft in prison, having been found guilty in 1937 of the fanciful charge of attempting to establish a Russian fascist party. Initially the Pe-2 was to be developed as a fighter, but when it became evident that a dive-bomber was more urgently needed, the fighter was rapidly converted. The country's leaders were pleased with the result and rewarded the designer with a Stalin Prize. They even let him out of jail. This cutting-edge dive-bomber had a payload of one and a half tons of bombs, a top speed of 540 kilometres an hour, and could fly at high altitude. It could also dive at an angle of 50–60 degrees, enabling more accurate placement of its bombs. Moreover, no other aircraft had an undercarriage as robust as the Pe-2.

Needless to say, like all aircraft, it had its disadvantages, and unfortunately these were major. Fundamentally it was an extremely difficult plane to handle. It could only land at high speed, which was dangerous. The precise angle at which the plane landed was also crucial: the slightest mistake could prove fatal. This was said to have been the cause of Petlyakov's death in an air crash in 1942 when he was flying to Moscow in his own plane. He was buried in a cemetery near Kazan close to where the aircraft crashed, and a chiselled inscription appeared shortly afterwards on his stone monument. It read, "Thank you for the undercarriage, but the flight characteristics you've experienced for yourself."[108] This rueful inscription was clearly made by someone with inside knowledge.

Nevertheless, nothing Raskova heard about the difficulties of flying this new aircraft discouraged her. Unlike raw graduates from flying school who were sent to the front with very little experience (usually less than

100 hours) the pilots in her regiment had thousands of hours in the air, which meant that retraining them to fly even this trickiest of planes was a more straightforward matter. Raskova did not back down, and Shakhurin succumbed to the insistent arguments of this heroic aviatrix. He promised to let her regiment have the Pe-2 even ahead of those front-line regiments which were in desperate need of it.

The news that they would be required to master this problematical plane was not met with great enthusiasm in 587 Regiment. Even the squadron leaders were disconcerted by the prospect of training their crews to fly the huge Pe-2 at short notice. Raskova urged them not to be disheartened, and as soon as the Pe-2s arrived joined the training classes herself. For her it was even more difficult than for others because of her relatively modest flying experience.

Raskova's regiment tamed the capricious aircraft and came to love it. They soon called it their little *Peshka* (Pawn) and their Swallow. The regiment did not suffer a single fatality during the training, unlike the neighbouring reserve regiment where cadets straight out of flying school, some with 100 hours in the air but some with only twenty, were grappling with the complexities of the Pe-2. Accidents occurred because pilots simply could not master the controls. There was a regulation that, if there was a crash, flying would be abandoned for the day but, in the face of so many fatal accidents, the regulation had to be repealed and flying continued even if one their friends had just been killed.

10

"You ask how we drop bombs?"

On 18 February, Komsomol Administrator Ivakina noted in her diary that she and Party Administrator Klava Kasatkina had "found" some pages in the diary of Nina Slovokhotova, the regiment's chief of staff, and a letter to her sister. She had written "a lot of muck" in them about the regiment and there were "outrageous things said about the officers, the other ranks, and regimental matters".[109] Ivakina and Kasatkina passed both the diary and the letter to "the *competent authorities*" (Ivakina's italics), fully aware of how dire the consequences might be for Slovokhotova.

Most Soviet citizens, however, carried on believing that to read other people's diaries and letters was beneath contempt. Keeping a diary was considered beneficial for developing your personality and was widely practised. They were not, needless to say, intended to be read by anybody else.

Those who found themselves at the front usually had to give up diary writing. There was no official ban on it, but in almost every unit the political instructors and officers would explain to their subordinates that a diary could be damaging if it fell into enemy hands. In reality, the Germans were not the only enemy; it could equally well prove to be the person immediately next to you.

In 1942 Daniil Fibikh, a war correspondent, made a fateful entry in his diary about the commander of the army in which he was embedded: "Our little army commander readily spills Soviet blood." Shortly afterwards, unaware that anything was amiss, he was summoned to see the commander in question.[110] Besides the commander there were a number of N.K.V.D. officers in attendance. A summary closed court martial was held at which the diary was the primary exhibit, and provided sufficient grounds for him to be dispatched for many years to Stalin's labour camps. Only later did Fibikh come to realise that this violation of his privacy and the denunciation that followed were common practice at the time.

"Just as soon as I want to get something clear or query something someone barks at me, 'As you were!' Where do they find such narrow-minded disciplinarians? They do not see us as human beings," Olga Golubeva wrote in her diary.[111] She had always loved writing and now, finding herself in the army, could not resist writing about this new life that was so different from her old existence, and about all the impressions with which she was brimming. Before long, however, her diary, "accidentally" read by someone else and soon in the hands of many others with the power to decide her fate, brought her "a whole lot of trouble". It goes without saying that there was nothing accidental about its being read. One or other of the colleagues with whom Olga would soon be risking her life at the front had said "Yes" when asked by a political instructor to spy on her friends. People did this for a variety of reasons. Someone whose relatives had been arrested might fear for themselves. Another might collaborate for ideological reasons. They were, after all, only twenty years old. The same newspapers that wrote of records broken and the all-conquering power of socialism, of heroic pilots and Stakhanovites who achieved exceptional productivity, also called for vigilance, denunciation of the wiles of saboteurs, spies and wreckers. How could you not believe them when they were printing the confessions of enemies of the people, uncovering arsonists who set fire to the grain of collective farms, slaughtered livestock, and blew up factories?[112] Most believed, trusting the authorities even when an old, ailing German teacher was arrested as a spy; even when it was claimed that a polite, intellectual friend of the family had been unmasked as a dangerous Trotskyite.

If a political instructor, a person older and more experienced than you, endowed with authority, gave you a lecture on the need for vigilance, you might involuntarily find yourself beginning to believe that the girl in the bunk next to yours, a patriotic member of the Komsomol with whom you shared a blanket, might be a covert enemy. And if you were asked in the name of revolutionary vigilance to find and look through your friend's diary, what right would you have to refuse?

The political instructors believed, mistakenly, that they themselves could keep a diary without any problem, as there was no one to check up on them. Komsomol Administrator Nina Ivakina, for example, confident that nobody would read her diary, wrote incessantly, describing in detail the work she was doing and her other experiences. With the arrival in mid-January 1942 of a new cohort of Komsomol members from Saratov her work became even more demanding.

When it became evident that Engels could not supply the needs of her three regiments for technical staff, Raskova turned to the Saratov Komsomol

Committee. The girls, mostly students but also some factory workers, rushed to her aid. From early morning the narrow corridor was crowded with applicants queueing to be interviewed. All eyes were on the door behind which the interview panel was in session. As the candidates came out they were mobbed by eager questioners. The girls were very young and many just did not look mature enough to serve in the army. "What are you thinking of, little one? This is not a kindergarten," Commissar Rachkevich said to one of them.[113] Students from the flying clubs appeared confident, intimidated only by Raskova who was instantly recognisable. "She had a high forehead, smooth dark hair parted in the middle, and that gold star on her chest." She looked closely at the girls, asking a lot of questions about their education, their family and work, trying to figure out whether they were suitable to be part of her unit. Her steady, benevolent voice gave them confidence. Roughly half the girls were taken on.

The Komsomol members, mainly students from a number of colleges in Saratov, were accommodated in one large room, which became very noisy and crowded. On the whole they did well, even almost illiterate Masha Makarova who made up for her lack of education because, having worked as a truck and tractor driver, she instantly grasped what was what in the engine of a Yak. The new girls brought new headaches in terms of discipline. They would run away from the airfield to warm themselves, be late for roll call, bring kittens back to the barracks, and flirt enthusiastically with the men in the garrison.

Fedotova, a Komsomol member, was caught by the garrison guards on stairs near the attic in the company of a lieutenant who "fled ignominiously".[114] The dishevelled Fedotova gave a false name and regiment, but pilot Malkova and mechanic Favorskaya of the Fighter Regiment, who witnessed the incident, considered it their duty, blushing, to obtain all the details of her offence from the guard and pass them on to the competent authorities, in this case Ivakina and her superiors.

Donetskaya, who was not a Komsomol member, was often nowhere to be found on the aerodrome, ignored orders, and then committed an act so terrible that Ivakina could not bring herself to write it down in her diary and veterans of the regiment refused to talk about it even years later. Her misconduct was so grave that she was escorted away from the regiment under guard. There was great controversy over how to deal with girls like Fedotova and Donetskaya at the regiment's Communist Party Meeting. Mechanic Osipova said the Red Army was a home from home and that it had a responsibility to re-educate miscreants, but many others felt that, with a war on, they should waste no time on the likes of Donetskaya, and the sooner they were kicked out of the regiment and ceased to damage its reputation the better.[115] The political instructors thought there were few bad eggs in the regiment, not least because everybody was so busy working from early morning until late at night that they had little time to get up to any mischief. Their observations suggested that such "squalid affairs" were mostly confined to girls doing administrative and office work. They had been secretaries of government bigwigs in the past and were continuing to behave as frivolously as they had in civilian life. The instructors felt it was important to deal severely with individuals such as Fedotova and Donetskaya, but the situation was complicated by the fact that even the pilots, in theory the most mature and educated people in the regiments, often showed a woeful lack of political consciousness in the way they conducted themselves.

The ground would be invisible, lost in the murk below. The horizon too would have been erased. "We needed a special knack, a special flair to work out where we were from places where the darkness seemed blacker, faint outlines, and paler areas. Sometimes a stray light could tell us a great deal and act as a life-saving lighthouse in the ocean of darkness," one of Bershanskaya's pilots said of flying at night.[116] It is difficult to gain a real sense from descriptions of just what night flying with rudimentary instruments was like. Only if you had experienced it yourself could you really understand the highly specialised skills it demanded. The pilots and navigators of the night bomber regiment learned to see in the dark and totally restructured their lives around living at night.

Aircraft designer Nikolai Polikarpov had suddenly had the bright idea of using U-2 trainer aircraft as light night-bombers, and this proved amazingly successful. His aircraft (which were renamed the Polikarpov Po-2 in his honour after his death in 1944) could carry a payload of 200–300 kilograms of light bombs and, although they could inflict only relatively minor damage on the enemy (heavy bombers carried a payload dozens of times greater), they nevertheless served a very important purpose. "They carried out bombing missions at low altitude, particularly at night, in order to harass the enemy, to deprive him of sleep and rest, to wear him down, destroy his aircraft on his own airfields, his fuel depots, his munitions and food supplies, disrupting transport movements, hindering the work of his headquarters and such like."[117] The Germans really hated them.

The night bomber regiment switched to living its strange, wearing nocturnal life immediately the new aircraft were delivered, and its routine remained unaltered until the end of the war. Upon returning at dawn from their night-time missions, the pilots and navigators had breakfast in the canteen and went straight to bed. Of course, they did not get enough sleep: the sounds of the world awakening around them saw to that. When exactly the mechanics and armourers slept is unclear. They had to wait up to service their aircraft all night and then to repair them during the day. It was possible to snatch a few hours of sleep at the dormitory and the odd hour in warmer weather under the wing of the aircraft, but the ground-crew remained constantly tired and hungry.

Training consisted of following a prearranged route at night, and flying over the parade ground for night bombing practice. They worked on the precision of their bombing by first dropping a "chandelier", an aerial flare bomb, and then trying to hit it with a concrete training bomb. The flight took about an hour, which was as long as the fuel lasted.

As soon as a U-2 landed it was immediately refuelled, armed, and was again ready to fly. Every night until dawn Major Bershanskaya was at the start to see off the little planes setting out one by one into the night, and she was there to meet them when they landed at an area marked out by a glowing letter "T". She hid her fears for her cadets behind a barrier of severity and a stern, impassive expression.

Bershanskaya herself had many thousands of hours of flying experience, both daytime and night-time, and was used to flying blind by instruments. At the Bataisk Aviation College she had been the commander of a flight of women pilots. She worked there for some years as an instructor, later becoming a pilot on civil airlines. Her path to becoming a pilot had been as thorny as those of most of her cadets. Bershanskaya was twenty-eight years old in 1941 and had grown up in the terrible era of the Russian Civil War. Once as a little girl she had to sit all night next to the corpse of her mother, comforting her little brother. They were lucky that, a few days later, her uncle appeared and took them back to his family where they grew up in great hardship but surrounded by love. One day when the little girl was running around the school playground with other children she heard a high-pitched young voice shout, "Look, it's an aeroplane!" The plane flew over the village, and began to descend precipitately. When the children, completely out of breath, reached the aircraft, a young freckled boy who looked exactly like any villager was standing next to it, stretching his stiff legs, squatting and jumping up and down. As she gazed at him, the young Yevdokia suddenly realised that the mystery of flight was open even for completely ordinary people. She decided there and then that she too would be a pilot. There was no talking her out of it. Yevdokia graduated from a flying club, then the Bataisk Aviation College.

Raskova had long been acquainted with Bershanskaya, and she was one of the first women to be invited to join 122 Air Group. Needless to say, when she turned up Bershanskaya demanded to be retrained as a fighter pilot, and was upset to be told she would be in command of the night bomber regiment. She would have much preferred to be a fighter pilot, but when she received the order she set to work without protest. Her little son from a failed marriage to a pilot called Bershansky stayed in the rear with his grandmother. By the end of the war she was married to Bocharov, the colonel in charge of a U-2 regiment alongside which the women's night-bomber regiment spent the entire war.

Bershanskaya was not the only person meeting the planes and debriefing the crew after they landed on that glowing letter "T". She was accompanied by Irina Rakobolskaya, who had been appointed her chief of staff, a slender, brown-eyed, dark-haired woman of average height. For the pilots and navigators she was in quite a different category from Major Bershanskaya, who seemed to them to be much older than they were, a professional aviator and a real officer, an unfathomable, remote figure who inspired respect and humility. Irina was simply a friend who had been elevated to officer rank. Hardly any time ago she had been a student at the Mechanics and Mathematics Faculty of Moscow University. Unlike Bershanskaya, Commissar Rachkevich, or the regiment's chief engineer, Ozerkova, who were superiors and whom they tried to steer clear of, Irina, although an officer, was one of them, with the same intellectual interests and the same love of books, as the other ex-students. In the barracks they called her Irina, in a formal setting "Comrade Lieutenant". Irina, a girl with a remarkable intellect that shone through in her mischievous brown eyes, was the link connecting the regiment's officers to everybody else.[118]

Irina Rakobolskaya was perplexed about how best to build a relationship with her regimental commander, who was older and had a background very different from this former Moscow University student.[119] Irina had to write out all the speeches for her to deliver at various gatherings, and Bershanskaya would read them, never taking her eyes off the text. Irina never felt close to Bershanskaya, who seemed to be made of sterner stuff, but for some reason her superior chose her as a confidante, unilaterally deciding that Irina was the person closest to her in the regiment. She would share many personal details which Irina really had no wish to know. Yevdokia would talk to her about her son, and even share intimate details about life with her pilot husband, wholly unconcerned that Irina was still a virgin and often had no idea what she was talking about. As time passed, however, Irina came increasingly to like Yevdokia Bershanskaya. She admired her determination and decency, her reliability, the fact that she was an excellent pilot, her austere but tireless concern for those in her care, and her ability to keep on learning and developing. Without Irina's noticing, no doubt because they were together all the time, Bershanskaya raised her level of education. By the end of the war she was writing her own speeches.

"You ask how we drop bombs?" Zhenya Rudneva wrote to a friend in Moscow. "You point your plane at the target and press the bomb release catch. The bomb is released and lands on the heads of the damnable Germans. God, how I hate them!"[120]

It was only now that she told her parents she was in an airborne unit and about to be sent to the front. "My dear father," she wrote, "so much effort, money and, most importantly of all, knowledge have been invested in me that I and the others are of considerable value to the front. I will be sure to come back home to you after the war but, if anything happens, the Germans will pay dearly for my life, because I have outstanding technology at my disposal." Zhenya was awkward, slow moving and looked ridiculous in military uniform, but was already the regiment's chief navigator. She had come a very long way. Early on in their training in Engels they were told that every item of a navigator's equipment must be tied down so as not to blow away. The following day Zhenya appeared festooned with all the appurtenances of her profession neatly tied to the buttons on her uniform. She was subjected to good-natured laughter but, obsessed with mastering her job to perfection, paid no attention. "I feel I am doing the only right thing," she wrote to her family. "I am doing what it is my duty to do." [121] She was constantly working on self-improvement, but continued to struggle to get into the cockpit quickly. Her pilot, Dina Nikulina, did not spare her feelings and coached her at great length, obliging Zhenya to climb in and out of the plane over and over again in her hot, bulky flying suit and fur boots. Others felt this was almost humiliating, but Zhenya was invariably grateful for the lesson. "I really do like flying with Dina most of all, because now I know I am competent, and that it is safe for people to fly with me. Dina is the only person who points out my mistakes. Every time I fly with her I learn something new." [122] In any theory class, after the instructor had finished and asked whether there were any questions, Zhenya could be relied on to pipe up, "What is this formula for? How is it derived?" The instructor would have to think about it and explain how it was arrived at, venturing into the realms of higher mathematics. Not a day passed when Zhenya did not ask "Why?" She wanted to know everything. That was how she believed in studying, certain that all the theory and practice would soon prove useful on the front line.

II

"It's simply wonderful! Imagine the speed!"

Major Tamara Kazarinova was posted to 586 Fighter Regiment at the end of February 1942. Like her sister, Militsa, the chief of staff of Raskova's heavy bomber regiment, she was a career army pilot whom Raskova had known since before the war. Nobody warned the regiment she was coming; Kazarinova's arrival was an unpleasant surprise. For all Zhenya Prokhorova's popularity, the senior staff had never contemplated appointing her as commander. She was a brilliant pilot, but a sportswoman rather than a soldier and, most importantly, she was not a member of the Communist Party. That meant that whatever the circumstances, she had no prospect of ever rising higher than squadron leader. Bershanskaya, the commander of the night bomber regiment, had a civil aviation background and, unlike Zhenya, had graduated from a flying college, where she had been in command of a special women's unit. But, most importantly, she was a longstanding Party member. Raskova, in command of the heavy bomber regiment, owed her army career to her service in the N.K.V.D. and record-breaking flights. As regards Major Tamara Kazarinova, she had an Order of Lenin, the second most prestigious Soviet medal after Hero of the Soviet Union, pinned to her chest. She had been awarded it in 1937, in a war the Soviet regime was waging against its own people, who were being dispatched in their hundreds of thousands to the Gulag.

For all that, initially Tamara Kazarinova made a favourable impression.

"She is a likeable and intelligent woman, clearly a strong-willed commander who will really teach us how to work instead of playing at soldiers," was Nina Ivakina's assessment.[123] Kazarinova spoke well and had an educated accent. She had a handsome if impassive face and her military uniform fitted her faultlessly. That was how she first struck Alexander Gridnev, who could never have imagined that within a few months he would replace her as commander of a female fighter regiment. "A woman still young, with good deportment, shorter than average, a bit stocky. A frank expression and inflamed eyes with a hint of sadness. You detect independence of spirit and self-assertiveness in the way she looks at you and her general manner. When someone asked, not without irony, whether women pilots need assistance to fly a fighter plane, she froze them out and did not reply."[124]

What really was surprising was that Kazarinova turned up in the fighter regiment with a walking stick and limping: she had broken her leg. It would never have occurred to most people that a person in that condition could be appointed to command a military unit shortly due to leave for the front. The only possible explanation seemed to be that she was expected to recover from her injury very quickly, and that in the meantime it would not prevent her from carrying out her duties. Everyone was eager to see what kind of "signature" she would have as a pilot when she started flying, and to improve their own skills by flying as a wingmate to a highly professional fighter regiment commander. The only way such an officer could establish their authority was by demonstrating their flying skills, firing at targets, and taking part in practice dogfights with other pilots. Weeks passed, however, and Tamara Kazarinova showed no inclination to climb into the cockpit.

"It's simply wonderful! Imagine the speed!" Lilya wrote home to her mother.[125] The fighter pilots were now fully familiar with their planes and were given permission to fly solo training flights in "the zone", a defined airspace where pilots customarily awaited their turn to come in to land or make their approach to the airfield. Lilya boasted she had flown at an altitude of 5,000 metres without oxygen, a risky experiment she probably undertook without permission – which would have been entirely in character. At high altitudes the air is so thin that, without supplementary oxygen, pilots are liable to behave erratically. She wrote enthusiastically that, "for the first time I felt what it is like to fly without the wheels down." Never one to spare her mother, she added that she had several times got into a spin, but had finally learned how to bank steeply. They were now training in earnest, not only practising firing their weaponry, but also engaging in aerobatics and, of course, dogfights.

There was no shortage of fuel and the fighter pilots trained from morning to night, growing increasingly confident in their high-speed aircraft. "How our girls can fly!" Ivakina wrote. "Even those men who used to say we would only make a mess of everything today look up at our pilots in silent admiration."

They had no time now for the blandishments of the officers' club and were only able to meet up with the pilots they were friendly with in the canteen. All the same, as Lilya admitted in a letter, "the truth is that before we go there the girls spend half an hour powdering their faces."[126]

In fact, only a small proportion of airwomen did actually powder their faces. Most girls had never used cosmetics. Powder, lipstick and eye shadow were on sale in big cities, but few women could afford them. If you lived in a small town or in the countryside, they were not even on offer. Women made artless cosmetics themselves and, if they were going to a dance, might shade their eyebrows with burnt cork, or make lipstick by grating the lead of a red pencil and mixing it with fat.

Mascara, if you were lucky enough to have it, came in the form of a hard paste in a rectangular box. Before applying it, you needed to spit on it and give it a good stir with the brush. But quite apart from the absence of mascara and lipstick, in the 1940s there was no toothpaste or toilet paper in the U.S.S.R., and shampoo was yet to be heard of. They only appeared in Soviet shops in the 1960s.

With or without make-up, the girls always wanted to look pretty, even in war. Katya Peredera, a sniper who in 1943 was positioned along with the rest of her squad in quarries near Kerch, remembers using precious water that she would gladly have drunk to wash her face. "What are you doing that for? There is hardly any light here," her friend, dark-eyed Zhenya Makeyeva, teased her.[127] Their underground shelters were lit with dim lamps fashioned from shell cases. Nevertheless, Katya, Zhenya and the other girls in their squad did everything they could, in conditions where they could wash neither themselves nor their clothes, to remain attractive. They worried that they might not be invited to dance when parties were held, by the light of makeshift lamps and to the music of an accordion, in one of the more cavernous caves. They had never seen face cream and were delighted to find a battered tin of Nivea in an abandoned German trench. The smell was wonderful! They all rubbed in a tiny amount and eked it out for ages.

Lilya, as a Muscovite sophisticate, knew more about make-up than her virginal friends, but did not overdo it. She was proud, for example, that she did not yet need to use powder. However, although her hair was naturally light brown, Lilya thought she looked better as a blonde.[128]

There were some girls in Raskova's care who, granted leave to go into the city, had their hair permed. This gave rise to much controversy, many taking the view that, like flirting, it was inappropriate in wartime. Of course, after six months in the army their ideas about many things had changed. Irina Rakobolskaya, as chief of staff of the night bombers, now took a different view from the one she had held during their first days in Engels. Then, at the very outset of their military careers, they had walked into the canteen accompanied by Bobik, a black dog that barked at every man they saw. One time the girls from Moscow University had met some of their former fellow students, and after lunch went off chatting with them instead of marching out in the line with the others. Irina and other comrades found that unacceptable. The offenders were told they had disgraced their university. They burst into tears and promised never to do it again.

The view then, Irina recalls, was that the war would soon be over and they should get through it by renouncing everything personal.[129] As the months passed, however, they came to see that "the war *was* their life, and that there was nothing wrong about talking to a man". Some, however, were less flexible, among them Galya Dokutovich. She fumed indignantly to her diary, "I am outraged!" The occasion of her ire was girls from her regiment having a perm. "All three of them have had permanent waving. There is no place in the army for the likes of these. These are not our Soviet girls, worthy of taking their place at the front . . . I do not care if they are offended. Before you know it they will be putting on lipstick, darkening their eyebrows, and gluing on beauty spots. After that they will only be fit to be sent to . . . well, I do not know where they could be sent to. To the Institute of Foreign Languages, perhaps, or some marriage market!"[130]

Many found Galya unreasonably hard, both on herself and on others. Even when her best friend, Polina Gelman, was going through a difficult time, she at first evoked Galya's disapproval and only later her sympathy. Galya told her she should never have come to the front. When Polina accused Galya of being rude and unkind, she admitted that in many ways her friend was right. But then, what times these were! And was she any less demanding of herself than of others? In Galya's opinion, only people like herself were fit for this kind of unforgiving existence.

Lilya Litvyak was always independently minded and took condemnation by other comrades in her stride. She had, in any case, many friends. Her personal appearance was as important to her as being a pilot. Lilya was upset that she had not thought to bring an attractive blue tunic from home, probably her flying club uniform.[131] She also complained to her mother about her boots: they were too big, and one was shorter than the other. Hearing that the regiment's chief engineer and the commissars periodically flew to Moscow, Lilya asked her mother to make up a parcel for her of a white helmet of stout material which would wash well, socks, gloves, and linen or silk handkerchiefs. In short, she closely resembled the kind of girl who, in Galya Dokutovich's opinion, was fit only for "some marriage market". On every training flight, however, she disproved Dokutovich's claim that women who took so much interest in their appearance had no place at the front. In reply to her brother, Yury, who wrote to tell his sister how proud he was of her, Lilya wrote that she had not yet done anything to deserve that distinction. She had not finished her training nor won any victories over the enemy. She had, however, a good idea of what the job of a fighter pilot involved and was sure she would cope with it "admirably". She was in a great mood, her training was interesting, and she was even being decently fed. Her only anxiety was for her family.

Lilya's mother's letters to her daughter which, in violation of military secrecy, she naively addressed to Pilot Litvyak, included little about how she and Yury were getting on. Lilya demanded that she should write more often and in greater detail, suspecting that life for her mother, which had not been easy before the war, was now very hard. Moscow was no longer in danger, the Germans having been driven back by the counter-attack that started on 5 December 1941 (the first, and to date only, significant Soviet victory). Now, in early March 1942, the fighting was some 200 kilometres away from the capital in the vicinity of Vyazma. However, the initial nation-wide euphoria at the rolling back of the immediate threat to Moscow had given way to fatigue and depression. Mere existence had become a struggle.[132]

12

"A whole lifetime older"

Orders for the fighter and night bomber regiments to begin active service arrived simultaneously. Both were brought from Moscow by Raskova on 7 March, the day before International Women's Day, which was celebrated enthusiastically in the Soviet Union.

Sending her mother greetings on "this day that proclaims the strength and power of Soviet woman", Lilya Litvyak told her that on this "joyful day the major has brought us wonderful news from Moscow".[133] For Lilya the news was all the more wonderful because the fighter regiment was being sent to defend her home town, Moscow. "We have the happy duty and honour all fighter pilots dream of. We did not even dare to hope that the Party and government would entrust to us the defence of our glorious capital city. Very soon we will be near Moscow on our unconquerable wings, and if we do not see each other, our closeness will be some consolation for how much I miss you."

Raskova read out the order in the familiar hall of the officers' club. She wished them all a happy International Women's Day tomorrow, and announced that the U-2 night-bomber regiment would fly to the Western Front in one week's time, on 14 March, as part of the effort to build on the successful counter-attack which had driven the Germans back from Moscow. The fighter regiment, she added, would follow shortly after. The girls leapt to their feet, applauding. Katya Budanova spoke very eloquently after Raskova, saying that the fearsome wings of her plane would protect the heart of the Motherland. She too was thrilled to be defending Moscow. Katya's mother and her little niece were living in their home village of Konoplyanka under German occupation, but in Moscow there lived her sister, her friends from the factory, and the Young Pioneers on whose upbringing she had lavished so much care before the war. For the girls who were Muscovites, defending Moscow meant protecting their home town as well as the capital, but for the others too this was the most important combat mission they could be entrusted with. Moscow was the heart of the U.S.S.R., the city that, even in the moment of utmost peril, Stalin had not abandoned. As far as they were concerned, Moscow, the U.S.S.R., and Comrade Stalin were an indivisible trinity.

Lilya wrote to her mother that they would be leaving Engels very soon now, "apparently before the snow melts", and of course she was jealous of the night bombers who had only a couple more days to cool their heels in Engels.

March 14 was not, however, to be the day of departure for the Night Witches, as the Germans were to call them. Major Bershanskaya recalled that initially the weather on the evening of 9 March was entirely favourable for training flights. "The crews set off along their designated routes to drop their concrete bombs on the parade ground. Soon, however, the wind picked up and it started to snow. The horizon disappeared and even the lights marking the aerodrome vanished. It was like flying through milk. We could not see anything beyond the instruments in the cockpit." [134] Bershanskaya's experience and familiarity with the route helped her get back to the airfield, but her students had as yet very little experience of night flying.

Pilots know how dangerous it is to encounter snow, especially in a U-2 that is virtually unequipped for flying blind. They know too how serious it is to become disorientated. The pilot loses awareness of how the plane is flying and, worse still, can become subject to delusions. She may begin to think she is veering right and try to correct that when in fact she is banking left, so that the action taken only exacerbates the situation and the plane spirals to the ground. These false perceptions can be so strong that the pilot ceases to believe the readings on the instrument panel. It is perhaps the worst thing that can happen to a pilot during a flight.

Even today, small recreational aircraft, unlike airliners that can fly blind on their instruments, do not take to the air in bad weather. In a U-2, which had only the most basic kind of instruments, it was only too easy to come to grief in unfavourable conditions. If you were caught in a sudden storm, the only solution was immediately to turn 180 degrees and fly back to your airfield, monitoring your altitude, speed and direction from the instruments and working out (one of the tasks of the navigator) how long it would take for you to be over the airfield (assuming you were on course), descend and circle over where you believed the airfield to be, and try to make out any familiar features on the ground. If that did not work, you needed to continue to circle, changing the radius and looking for the airfield. If you could not see anything and were running low on fuel (which you calculated by the amount of time you had been in the air), you needed to make a precautionary crash landing, which in bad weather and in the dark, was terribly dangerous. As you descended, trying to see the ground, you were in danger of crashing into the high bank of a river or a ravine, or into trees. Even if you succeeded in landing the plane, the wheels might hit a pothole and the aircraft overturn. Anyone who found themselves flying a U-2 at night in bad weather was lucky to escape with their life.

That night a heavy snowfall hid the earth and sky, everything was flickering before their eyes in a whirl of snow. "Lights on the ground twinkling through the heavy wall of snow began to seem like distant stars, while the real stars began to seem like lights on the road." Three of the crews failed to return. Before dawn a terrible phone call came through: "There has been an accident. Prepare a room where the bodies can be laid." Four girls had died: Lilya Tormosina and her navigator Nadya Komogortseva, Anya Malakhova and Marina Vinogradova. Only a few hours previously, getting ready for the flight, Lilya had joked with Nadya Komogortseva, "Navigator, I'm giving you a chocolate, only make sure you hit at least one of the lights today! If you can put all three of them out, I'll give you two more."[135] Miraculously the crew from the third missing U-2 survived. Their plane crashed, but they climbed out of the wreckage almost unscathed.

On the night of 9 March the possibility of dying while on a night mission ceased to be an abstraction and became a reality. Four open coffins were placed side by side in the hall where the girls had so enjoyed dancing. Despite their crushed faces, broken limbs and twisted backs, the pilots and navigators were still recognisable. Many remember that Lilya Tormosina's face was just as pretty in death as it had been in life, except that it had lost its rosy glow.

Nina Ivakina wrote that these senseless deaths left them all dreadfully sad.[136] Everybody was crying. "We tenderly put the coffins with our friends, who only yesterday had been so full of fun and laughter, on the truck and to the strains of the 'Funeral March' slowly accompanied our dear young falcons on their last journey, to the graveyard."

Raskova organised every detail of the funeral herself. She "carefully laid flowers in the coffins, positioned the lids on them, and was the first to throw a parting handful of earth into the graves". At the meeting at the graveyard her words of farewell were deeply sincere. "Sleep, dear friends, in peace. We shall fulfil your dreams." Raskova was a woman of many talents, and every word resonated in the hearts of those assembled.

"The pilots are depressed," Ivakina noted a few days later. "They have been very upset by the death of the girls. The U-2 regiment is not leaving for the front."[137] That had been cancelled in view of the disaster, the position evidently being taken that the night bomber regiment was not yet psychologically ready for the front, or that they needed more training. Their departure was postponed indefinitely.

Dusya Pasko, a navigator in the night bomber regiment, was one of the first to hear that not all the missing crews would be returning, and from an unexpected quarter. She had grown up in a large rural family with three sisters and six brothers. All the brothers were at the front, but from their infrequent letters home it was difficult to tell where. One can only imagine her surprise when she was called to the garrison's security entrance on the morning of 10 March to find her brother Stepan waiting for her. She closed her eyes, thinking she must be imagining things, but when she opened them there was Stepan standing right next to her.[138] He had graduated from a military college in Alma-Ata, was now the commander of a machine-gun company, and was on his way to the front with his men. Dusya did not even find out where he was going because, as her senior, he did most of the talking. He wanted to know everything about his sister's work and life. "You have a really hard, dangerous job, then, with this flying?" he kept asking. Not knowing why he was so worried, Dusya assured him that everything was fine and there was nothing to worry about. Finally, with a rueful smile, Stepan told her that he had had to conduct a meeting at dawn about the death of some girls from her regiment. They had crashed near the road along which Stepan's unit was marching and he had seen the accident. After that it was useless for Dusya to continue telling her brother how safe she was going to be at the front. Dusya came back from the war as a Hero of the Soviet Union without a scratch, but never saw Stepan again. He was killed in the Ukraine.

Galya Dokutovich had thought before about the possibility that she might die in the war, but had not been frightened. She imagined she would surely die a fine, heroic death in a crashing plane but now, after these first funerals of her comrades, "a whole lifetime older", she smiled wryly at those childish ideas, and at those of her friends who still clung to such fantasies.

On 13 March, still hardly able to believe that her "dear, honest friends" had been taken from them, she confided to her diary that their deaths had been the result of overconfidence; that they were all imagining they were marvellous pilots when that was far from being true. After the disaster she felt her comrades were suffering a drastic loss of faith in their flying skills, and specifically their ability to maintain their orientation when conditions were tough. What could she do to restore their confidence? Galya felt she should be sent out with a pilot on an equally dark night with poor visibility to fly a route and drop practice bombs, and that any pilots and navigators still suffering from self-doubt should be fully informed about it. But the exigencies of war took over, and this never took place.

The single Air Group 122 created by Marina Raskova no longer existed. All three regiments were still based in Engels, and old friends, if no longer living under the same roof, ran into each other in the canteen and on the airfield. They were, however, no longer all members of the same team. Coming over to one of the other regiments for an evening of home-made entertainment, the girls of 586 Fighter Regiment "seemed awkward, and there was no longer that sense of rapport which we had felt before the separate regiments were established".[139] How that had come about no one was sure. Perhaps it was just that now they were living and working apart and had different aspirations for the future. Ivakina supposed the cooling of relations was inevitable, but many of them were saddened by it. Air Group 122, which so recently had meant everything to them, was already history.

13

"See that? Your planes have proved themselves"

586 Fighter Regiment was the first to leave Engels, on 9 April 1942. On the way to Moscow they needed a "change of footwear", from skis to wheels at the transit airfield of Razboyshchina. Alas, there were no wheels, and they found themselves stuck for ages at this godforsaken airport, which fully lived up to its baleful name.* "It was a ghastly little garrison," Nina Ivakina observed. In the middle of the airfield she noticed "a lake of oil and petrol, on the banks of which defunct vehicles were rusting. Piles of shit everywhere. All sorts of unspeakable stuff dripping from the canteen ceiling straight onto the plates."[140]

There was no radio, and no water or electricity either. After the passable amenities in Engels, the conditions in Razboyshchina struck many of them as totally intolerable. The huts in which they were all accommodated were very small and the food was terrible. Nina Ivakina once again found herself under fire from the mechanics. They were outraged both by the bad food and now also, more than ever, by the glaringly obvious difference in rations between commanders and other ranks. "The top dogs are sitting pretty while we are on starvation rations!" Sonya Tishurova complained indignantly, urging her friends to boycott the canteen.[141] It seemed to Administrator Ivakina that soup and porridge and two-thirds of a kilo of bread a day were what Red Army soldiers should expect, and not at all bad considering there was a war on. She, of course, was on commander's rations, which included sausage, cheese and butter.

Weeks passed with no sign of the wheels. Ivakina recorded that the girls "sang and played" to pass the time. They had no real work and Katya Budanova, with nothing better to do, decided to improve her regiment's amenities by building a toilet. Nina Ivakina documented the date the project was completed, noting, "The pilots have constructed a delightful

---

* The name of the settlement, Razboyshchina, is derived from the Russian words *razboynik* (robber, bandit, highwayman), or *razboy* (robbery, plunder).

little wooden convenience with a waiting room, etc., etc." It "is only faith that stops it from falling down", but it was entwined with twigs like a romantic bower, and it had been cleverly designed. A notice proclaimed: "12 April 1942. Chief Engineer: Budanova. Chief Designer: Khomyakova. Planks pilfered by: Everyone."[142]

While airwomen who had regularly flown in the Tushino air shows were constructing a wooden toilet in Razboyshchina, the contribution Soviet aviators, including those in the fighter regiments, were making to the war effort was far from satisfactory. The newspapers of the time, and indeed the histories written in the U.S.S.R. after the war, praised the selfless courage of Soviet pilots, their immense skill, and determination to vanquish the enemy at all times and in all circumstances. But the reality is that, in 1941 and the first half of 1942, Soviet fighters by and large shied away from combat. In his memoirs, Air Marshal Alexander Novikov, the former commander of the Soviet Air Force, celebrated the "fantastic fortitude of Soviet pilots".[143] Accounts by German front-line pilots suggest, however, that: "At the beginning of the war, Soviet fighters posed no threat to German bomber formations, and often avoided combat with them."[144] German planes were so much more technically advanced and German pilots so much better trained, that Soviet pilots believed it was impossible to beat them. Moreover, the Soviets, at least at the beginning of the war, were also heavily outnumbered. Although there was never a word about it in the newspapers, when Soviet fighter forces did engage the Luftwaffe they invariably suffered catastrophic defeats. Pilots were often shot down on their very first sortie, and the losses meant heavy bombers and ground-attack aircraft often had to fly without fighter escort.

This was known only to those at or close to the front. In summer 1941 Konstantin Simonov returned to Moscow from Byelorussia, where he had watched the Luftwaffe shoot down in flames six huge unescorted TB-3 bombers in ten minutes. He could not talk about this even to those closest to him. They had no idea what was going on, but Simonov could compare the real situation at the front with its coverage in the newspapers. He comments that, "Anyone reading what the newspapers were printing about the war in the air would have come to highly unrealistic conclusions."[145] Simonov could not tell even his mother what he had seen in the skies above the Bobruisk Highway. "She was still living with a pre-war faith" in the unprecedented might of the Soviet Army. His opinion was that, at the beginning of the war, the Soviet Air Force was in the worst situation of any branch of the armed services.

In 1941, the ramming of enemy aircraft featured extensively in Soviet propaganda. If pilots were unable to outfight the enemy, they could at least use a Soviet plane to destroy a superior German one, usually at the cost of their own lives. Human life was cheap. Those who rammed Luftwaffe aircraft, of whom Victor Talalikhin was one of the first, became heroes, usually posthumously. The propaganda machine made heroes even of those who accidentally flew into German aircraft after losing control of their own.

Soviet aerial combat tactics only began to change in 1942, and the momentum came not from the Air Force command and theorists, but from the pilots themselves, who learned from their own experience and also, to a large extent, from observing the Germans.

Aware of how obsolete the Soviet aircraft were, Air Force commanders pinned their hopes on the new Yaks, but these had teething problems. In late February or early March 1942, their designer, Alexander Yakovlev, was summoned to explain himself to Stalin. He had always enjoyed the Leader's favour, but now was a frightened man. Stalin asked menacingly, "I have received information that the Yaks readily burn in aerial combat with the Hitlerites. Would it not be an error to embark on extensive mass production of these fighters?"[146]

Soviet newspapers clutched at every successful mission of "Stalin's Falcons", a favourite cliché of the time that was even adopted as the title of the Air Force newspaper. In early March 1942, seven pilots from 296 Fighter Regiment, led by Squadron Leader Boris Yeremin, really did win a dazzling victory over a numerically superior group of German planes. It was in all the newspapers, with the entire front page of Pravda devoted to the battle and those who had taken part in it. Although she had come to love her Pe-2 and Marina Raskova's regiment, Masha Dolina nevertheless felt a pang of regret that Nikolai Baranov had not been able to keep her on. Here is an excerpt from *Pravda*:

> Our valiant heroes, turning in combat formation, flew at the Messerschmitts. In the skies engines scream, machine guns rattle, cannons roar. One sweep follows another. This is war! The combat becomes increasingly ferocious. Our skilful pilots strike with precision again and again. The enemy is annihilated, and one after another four enemy aircraft crash to the ground.[147]

And so on. There is no skimping on banal bombast, but the battle was a real enough victory. Boris Yeremin, almost the only one of its participants to survive the war, remembered it vividly, despite subsequently fighting in dozens of others.[148] He recalled that this was one of the first missions his regiment had flown in the new Yak-1 fighters after being retrained from the earlier I-16. He was a 29-year-old captain and set out with burly, blond Alexey Salomatin, a talented and courageous pilot, as his wingman or "slave". There were two other pairs and the regimental navigator, Ivan Zapryagaev: a total of seven aircraft. Near the front line they spotted a large formation of German bombers with a Messerschmitt escort.

Yeremin was already an experienced fighter pilot, having fought in air battles over Lake Khasan during the border conflict with Japan in 1938. He had been at the front since the beginning of the war. Taking them to higher altitude, he lined his fighters up. The attack started well and they split into the pairs, immediately shooting down four aircraft. In the close-quarter aerial combat aircraft and fiery tracer bullets flashed past, and they could not be certain they were not shooting at their own people. The Germans, however, decided to retreat, one group heading north and the other west. Yeremin's pilots pursued them and shot down three more aircraft. Having used up all their ammunition, it was time to return to base. Yeremin had to call the group together by dipping his wings: it was another year before they got radios.

Salomatin's fighter had "a decidedly strange look to it". On closer inspection, Yeremin noticed that the cockpit canopy, which shelters the pilot from the airstream, had been shot off. Salomatin was crouching forward in order not to be blown out of the plane and "was not looking happy". Ivan Skotnoy's plane was trailing a plume of white steam because his radiator had been punctured. Incredibly, however, the full complement of six pilots in Yeremin's group formed up behind him. They were all alive, and what emotion they were feeling at having scored the first victory in this war! They flew back to the airfield and gave a victory salute. They landed and people ran to congratulate them, shouting and yelling, "Victory! Victory!" The chief of staff and Regimental Commander Baranov came running out. What happened? How? How many planes had they shot down?

Their report delighted the high command and made its way right to the top. Stalin telephoned Yakovlev and said, "See that? Your planes have proved themselves."[149] The Air Force commander of the Southwestern Front was ordered to meet the pilots, establish all the circumstances, and reward them accordingly. There were phone calls, endless questions, journalists arrived, medals were awarded. More important than all that, however, was that everybody now knew that the Germans could be beaten. For Yeremin and his men, 9 March 1942 was the turning point of the war.

Vasiliy Grossman spent two days with the pilots and recorded in detail everything they told him about themselves and the battle. He noted who had shot down what, recorded what Yeremin had to say about such tactics as making sure they kept in pairs, and wrote down their disparaging remarks about German aircraft. "The Messer looks like a pike," "I saw straight away it was a Junkers Ju 87: its legs stuck out and it had a yellow nose". He asked the pilots what they thought about ramming enemy aircraft. Alexey Salomatin considered it heroism, but the others disagreed. Crashing your own plane in order to destroy a German one was the easiest thing in the world, with nothing heroic about it. Heroism was shooting down more than one enemy plane and living to fight another day. These pilots knew how to fight, and there was no need to sacrifice themselves and their planes by ramming a German.[150]

Each spoke briefly about themselves, but were keener to talk about their friend Demidov, who had just been killed and whom they had all liked. "Wetting" their medals, they first drank a toast to Stalin, and then to Demidov, who "lived in Sushchevsky Val in Moscow and was studying to become an actor". Demidov "loved singing and flying". He was a couple of years older than Salomatin and the others and had been like an elder brother to them. When they were flying he was constantly checking they were all right and making sure no one got left behind. Commander Nikolai Baranov was crying as he pinned on their medals, remembering Demidov.

Those young fighter pilots, with whom Grossman spent only a short time, made such an impression that when, a few years later, he was working on his novel *Life and Fate*, he used their names and personalities for the characters in his novel: a place in it was even found for Demidov. But by this time, of the seven young fighter pilots, only their leader, Boris Yeremin, and Alexander Martynov were still alive.

14

"Nails should be made out of people like these"

After several hungry weeks of idleness 586 Fighter Regiment finally got the order to move, but it came as an unpleasant shock. "Everybody is devastated, and how could they not be?" Nina Ivakina asked.[151] For a moment she saw her wards as children who had had their favourite toy taken away from them. Their move to Moscow, they were told, was now some time in the future and for the present they would have to show their mettle protecting Saratov from any German bombers that might chance to appear over it. Although Saratov was home to a number of important facilities, it was well in the rear and had not so far suffered any bombing raids. The women pilots felt this order could mean only one thing: they were not trusted to do anything more serious. They had no option, however. An order was an order. They started preparing for the flight to Anisovka airfield from which they would perform their air defence duties.

It was a role that would have been seen as enviable by some fighter pilots in the Second World War. Taking to the air to protect strategically important sites in the rear required pilots to lie in wait for German bombers and their fighter escorts. There were risks, of course, but they bore no comparison with the casualty rate of fighter pilots at the front. In air defence they would shoot down fewer enemy aircraft and receive fewer medals, but they had a better chance of surviving. However, if many male pilots dreamed of sitting out the war in that manner, the women of 586 Fighter Regiment saw it as a humiliating option.

They flew "up to the Anisovka Front", as Nina Ivakina noted sarcastically, on 14 May. She went on, "Morale among the pilots is at rock bottom. This is the rear."[152] All around, the peaceful steppe was covered in spring flowers. In the orchards of the village that had sprung up around a railway junction the blossom was falling. The airfield was excellent, with a large landing area. Ivakina immediately organised a volleyball court, but the murmurs of discontent among the pilots were growing. They did not like not being sent to the front; they did not like the food served in the canteen, which was based on rear rather than front-line ration norms; and they did not like Tamara Kazarinova, the non-flying commander of their regiment who continued to give them a hard time. "Kazarinova says we are not ready yet," Lera Khomyakova wrote to her family. "Everything has changed," she continued. "Kazarinova does not get on with Raskova."[153] Needless to say, not getting on with their adored Raskova did nothing to enhance the popularity of their regiment's commander.

Nina Ivakina, who meticulously documented the conflict in her diary, noted that people were in such a bad mood that Second Squadron's leader Zhenya Prokhorova was giving her pilots permission to fly without Kazarinova's authorisation.[154] Komsomol Administrator Ivakina's principal informant about the mood among the pilots (which she probably reported straight to Tamara Kazarinova and the regiment's political commissar) was the chief navigator, Zuleikha Seydmamedova. It was she who told

Ivakina the Second Squadron pilots had written a letter to Stalin that they would ask Raskova to forward. The pilots complained that the conclusion of their combat training was being artificially delayed and that it was quite wrong that there should be so little confidence shown in them when they all had around 2,000 flying hours. Seydmamedova also passed on to Ivakina the nugget of information that pilots had been heard to remark it would be a good thing if "that lame witch" died in a crash, only it would be a shame to lose the plane. "After extensive surveillance", Ivakina established that the person giving voice to these resentments was Lieutenant Lera Khomyakova.

With exuberant youthful overstatement, pilots Klava Blinova and Olga Golysheva openly expressed a widely held view: "We hate the commander. She is a coward!" It had become clear to everyone that it was not Kazarinova's limp that kept her from going near the Yaks. She was perfectly well able to pilot the old, primitive fighter planes but had not previously encountered the Yak and saw no reason to learn to fly it now.

The commanders of the other two women's regiments well understood how essential it was for them to fly alongside their pilots. Yevdokia Rachkevich held that even as commissar of the night bomber regiment she had to be competent to fly. In Engels she made time to learn, if not as a pilot, then at least as a navigator. Overcoming the air sickness which constantly plagued her, she flew whenever she was allowed to. Raskova herself, although trained as a navigator, had long ago decided she had no moral right to command the heavy bomber regiment without herself being able to pilot the capricious Pe-2 dive-bomber.

Raskova had comparatively few flying hours to her name, but she was fearless, talented, and tenacious. She studied alongside the others, whose flying experience was dozens of times greater than her own, and showed on her first solo flight in a heavy bomber that she had assimilated the theory well. No sooner had she taken off than white smoke began streaming from one engine, which then failed. The pilots watching from the ground were desperately worried. Masha Dolina crushed her fists together. How would the relatively inexperienced Raskova get out of such a dangerous situation? "God, just help her to maintain speed!" Komsomol activist Dolina prayed to the Almighty, and in that she was not alone.[155]

As if in answer to their prayers, Raskova did the right thing by immediately preparing to land and, without veering off course, did so perfectly, not on the fuselage but with the undercarriage down which, with only one engine, was much more difficult. When Masha and her friends, overcome with joy, ran to the plane, Raskova climbed out of the cockpit and gave them her usual calm smile. "Masha, stop gaping or a bird will fly into your mouth," Masha's friend nudged her. As she gazed in admiration at Ras-kova, Masha was reminded of Nikolai Tikhonov's lines, "Nails should be made out of people like these; the world would not know any stronger."

The fighter pilots believed relations between Raskova and Tamara Kazarinova were strained over precisely this issue; Raskova would never have allowed herself to be in Kazarinova's flightless situation. Like them, she must surely have interpreted the commander's behaviour as cowardice, and she had no time for cowards. The pilots of 586 Fighter Regiment blamed Tamara Kazarinova for their having been shunted off into air defence. It was galling that far less experienced male fighter pilots were being sent to fight at the front. How could a regiment with a commander like her be taken seriously by anyone?

The conflict intensified with every passing day, escalating into open revolt. During the war this kind of situation was not uncommon on the front line. Unpopular commanders of reconnaissance units were often found shot in the back, but in an air regiment in the rear such mutiny was unheard of. The Majorette, as they contemptuously called her, tried to bring her subordinates to heel by intimidation but proved no match for her pilots. Fuel was added to the fire by the fact that 588 Night Bomber Regiment had already gone off to fight.

In late May 1942, the night bombers had circled in farewell over Engels aerodrome. Ahead flew Raskova, who had decided to lead them to the Southwestern Front and then return to her own heavy bomber regiment in Engels. The Saratov Young Communists gave the girls an accordion as a parting gift, of which the redoubtable mechanic Nina Danilova immediately took charge. For the rest of the war it raised the spirits of her comrades and herself alike.

This was the day they had dreamed of and prepared for, but they did not manage to fly all the way to their destination in graceful formation. Mistaking the Soviet fighters that joined them after they had passed Stalingrad to provide them with air cover for enemy aircraft, the girls panicked and scattered. It took them a long time to live that down. Raskova was annoyed but, with her usual ability to present setbacks in a favourable light, wrote to Militsa Kazarinova, "We flew from Stalingrad with an escort of I-153 'Seagull' fighters. They accompanied us for a long time because the Yaks were playing against Messers above the clouds. I had to drag everybody along at treetop height. In addition there was a headwind and terrible turbulence. People found it very trying. Before we reached Morozovskaya we met up with the Seagulls again and they covered our landing."[156] Raskova went on to say that the girls had changed out of all recognition. "They have suddenly become real servicewomen, which is more than could be said of them in Engels." After seeing the night bombers safely settled she intended, she said, to fly on to Moscow for a day or two to see her daughter and mother.

Raskova gave a moving farewell speech to her wards, hoping they would win many medals and become a guards regiment.[157] She told them they must show that women can fight as well as men, "and then in our country women too will be welcomed into the army."[158] Her students, as always, hung on every word. None of the night bombers would see her again, but for most of them she remained a guiding light for the rest of their lives, in war and in peace. Many years later, when they had made the transition from recklessly brave girls in uniform to ordinary Soviet women, when they faced some major task or challenge they would recall Raskova's words, "We can do anything." They adopted that as their motto.

The commander of 4 Air Army, forty-year-old General Konstantin

Vershinin, received Yevdokia Bershanskaya courteously and questioned her about her airwomen. He was particularly anxious to know whether they could fly in the glare of searchlights, and whether they knew how to land using only navigation lights, without turning on their landing lights. This meant the ground was not visible until the last moment and the plane's instruments had to be particularly closely monitored. They did know how to land in that manner, but had no experience of flying in the blinding beam of searchlights. Only too soon they were to run the gauntlet of these disorientating conditions that lit their little planes brightly and made them highly vulnerable to German anti-aircraft batteries and night fighters.

Vershinin handed 588 Night Bomber Regiment over to Colonel Popov's air division, where their U-2s were desperately needed. Popov, however, was far from pleased to learn he was receiving a women's regiment. "What have we done to deserve this? Why are we being sent reinforcements of this variety?" he asked.[159] When he arrived to inspect the regiment, Popov first taciturnly strode from one plane to the next, and was hard pressed not to laugh out loud when a girl sentry moved her rifle from her right to left hand to greet him. When introduced to Raskova and Bershanskaya, Popov was "silent and unsmiling". "Well, Comrade Colonel, do we have a sale?" Raskova asked breezily. Popov paused meaningfully before replying, "It's a deal." He had little choice.

Popov's division was providing support to the Soviet troops defending the remnant of the Ukraine that was yet to fall under German occupation. Again, as in Engels, for as far as the eye could see there stretched the steppe which Galya Dokutovich found so boring by comparison with the lush forests and green fields of Byelorussia. Here, in the Donetsk coal-basin in the vicinity of Voroshilovgrad, the scenery consisted of vast flat expanses separated by strips of tall poplars or gullies, muddy fishponds, and little villages with small white houses. The only raised land was oddly shaped mounds scattered here and there, slag heaps from the mines. It was late May, however, and even such unpromising scenery was pretty. In the village of Trud Gornyaka near Krasnodon, which was the first stop on their journeyings along the front line, the daisies flowered in the grass and the birds were singing. The girls were billeted in cottages and issued dazzlingly white bedlinen. They found it difficult to believe that the front line was only thirty kilometres away at the River Mius. The night bomber regiment stayed in Trud Gornyaka only briefly. Soviet troops were in retreat. The repulse of the Germans from Moscow was the only major military success of 1941 or the first half of 1942. The second year of the war was no less terrible than the first.

The first military mission the women's night bomber regiment were given was to harass the German units advancing on Rostov-on-Don. The Germans had taken the city on 21 November 1941. A week later, the Red Army was able, albeit at a heavy cost, to recapture it because the Germans did not have enough troops to retain it. The enemy army had holed up for the winter on a fortified line along the River Mius, and in the spring re-launched their offensive with fresh forces. By retaking Rostov-on-Don the Germans would not only have opened up the prospect of continuing through the Caucasus to the oil reserves of Baku, on which the U.S.S.R. depended, but would also be in a position to capture Stalingrad, a major transport hub and the centre of the U.S.S.R.'s military production. Fighting on the Southern Front resumed with renewed ferocity.

The 588 Night Bomber Regiment were tasked with attacking the German ammunition and fuel dumps, vehicles and ground troops. Those German soldiers they could not kill had to be demoralised and deprived of sleep by night-time bombing. Arriving in the mining town of Krasnodon not far from Trud Gornyaka, the girls were amazed at how remote from the front line it felt. The Germans had come close to Krasnodon but been driven back, and now the local people seemed completely unaware that the situation might recur with a very different outcome. Only a few days earlier Galya Dokutovich, still indignant about flirts in uniform, had written in imitation of Pushkin:

> While one girl in the washroom splashes,
> Galya Korsun paints her lashes.

Behind, Gorelkina at speed
Attends her physiog's every need.[160]

Now everything had changed, and instead she was indignant that their staging airfield was so far from the front line. She also felt their first combat missions were little more than dummy runs, a suspicion shared by the other pilots and navigators. Nobody was firing at them when they were over the targets. They had a sense that they were not trusted and were being fobbed off with missions to soft targets, which were little different from training flights.

Three hundred miles north-west of Rostov-on-Don, Anna Yegorova, who as yet had no inkling of the existence of Raskova's all-women regiments, was flying out to armies retreating from Kharkov who would soon be surrounded by the Germans. The disastrous Kharkov operation, intended as a strategic offensive to recapture the city that had surrendered the previous October, resulted in complete encirclement and the almost total destruction of the Soviet forces, trapped ultimately in a fifteen-square-kilometre patch of land. In late May, the Soviet armies attempted to break out of the encirclement and the German General Lantz later recalled horrifying attacks by massive numbers of Soviet infantry. Ninety per cent of the Soviet troops in the encirclement were killed or disappeared along with their generals. These included the deputy commander of the South-western Front.

On the morning of 20 May, flying to the town of Izyum with a secret package for 9 Army headquarters, Anna looked down to see troops retreating along the roads or through the fields. In the valley of the River Seversky Donets and at Izyum everything was in flames. There were dogfights in the sky. Anna's plane was attacked by a German fighter and set on fire. She landed the burning aircraft in a field of maize, tore off her smouldering overalls, and ran to the woods, under fire from the pursuing German pilot. The Messerschmitt finally flew off and Anna just wanted to lie down on the grass, close her eyes and forget everything. The new leaves were breaking through on the trees and she suddenly felt a tremendous urge to live. She had never been afraid of dying, but now felt how wrong it would be to die in springtime. The plane had burned to ashes, together with the bag of mail and a raglan coat that had been her pride and joy. How was she now to deliver the secret package? Her only option was to follow a telephone cable, laid on the tree branches, in the hope that it would lead to a command post of some sort. Almost immediately she came upon two soldiers coiling up the wire. When she asked where the command post was they shouted, without stopping what they were doing, "What do you mean command post? The Germans are there!" Everywhere isolated soldiers and groups of soldiers were retreating. Anna ran to the road, but found it empty. A truck careered past, ignoring her signals. Then an M-1 saloon, which she assumed was carrying some top brass, also rushed past totally ignoring her. Anna pulled out her pistol and fired in the air. The driver immediately reversed, jumped out of the car, boldly disarmed her and twisted her arms behind her back. When he delved into her breast pocket for her I.D., Anna sank her teeth into his arm. There is no knowing what might have happened next, had not a well-fed general emerged rather cumbersomely from the car and started questioning Anna, who still had her arms pinioned, as to who she was and why she was behaving so badly.

Anna, beside herself with resentment and pain from her burns and twisted arms, shouted, "Who the hell are you?" She asked for her arms to be released and pulled out a rather impressive card that requested all military units and organisations to render the bearer every assistance.

The fat general immediately became polite and asked where she needed to go. He seated Anna in the car to take her to 9 Army headquarters and asked how she came to be so badly burned. While she was telling him, Anna burst into tears. Her hands were hurting as the captain had stripped the skin off them.

"Don't cry, my dear," the general comforted her. "The tears will only make your face smart too."

Three hours later they found the army headquarters, Anna handed over the package, and went to the medical unit where she finally had ointment put on her face and her hands bandaged. She returned to her squadron, where they had almost given up hoping for her return.

15

Poetry and Prose

The Soviet armies were pulling out and Yevdokia Bershanskaya's night bomber regiment was constantly flying to airfields deeper and deeper in the Soviet interior, airfields that by now often proved to be off the edge of their maps. The mood was sombre and they were exhausted. Zhenya Rudneva did what she could to raise their spirits, and her own.

One rainy evening when they had all gathered at the command post waiting for the weather scout to arrive, Zhenya pulled a tattered book out of her map case. It was *How the Steel Was Tempered* by the blind and paralysed Nikolai Ostrovsky. Quietly, she began to read. At first no one paid attention, but one by one the girls moved closer to hear the story of Pavel Korchagin. First published as a serial between 1932 and 1934, this novel about a fearless revolutionary determined to serve Bolshevism against all odds was the Soviet Gospel.

Soviet culture, aspiring to transfigure society, space, and even time, conditioned the popular consciousness to expect that all sorts of transformations would be needed if the new state and the new Soviet human being were to emerge. Calendars were changed, streets and institutions, even cities (and after the Second World War entire countries) renamed. The goal was "electrification of the whole country", and there was a move to mass production of standardised apartment blocks. The ideal Soviet citizen, depicted in new books, paintings and films, seemed the man of the future, even though he had much in common with the ideals of antiquity. He was healthy in mind and body, uncompromising and fearless, ruthless towards his enemies, and devoted heart and soul to his state, which he valued more than his own life.

As a rule, books written at that time in the genre of socialist realism were remarkable for the absence of everyday, physiological, or intimate detail. You would never find out from reading them what kind of beds Soviet people slept in, what they drank, or how they kept their clothes clean. They became more and more lifeless and abstract, providing a mould into which whatever ideological content was required at a particular time could be poured. *How the Steel Was Tempered* was different. Hearing tales of how Pavel emerged victorious from seemingly the most hopeless situations, the young pilots forgot their tiredness and anxieties. When Junkers appeared and somebody shouted "Air raid!" nobody moved from where they were sitting.

In addition to Pavel Korchagin, Zhenya Rudneva invariably carried in her map case a slim volume of poetry that she was constantly reading to herself. One time, however, to cheer up her friends, she read the lines:

> If all the heavenly host should call,
> "Abandon Rus and live in Eden!"
> I will say, "What need I Eden
> When my Motherland is all?"

Seeing how warmly they reacted, she started reading to them from that collection, occasionally at first, and then more often. Her friends copied poems into their notebooks, which nearly all of them had, and learned them by heart. The poet was Sergey Yesenin.

One of the most gifted Russian poets of his time, the blue-eyed, golden-haired son of a peasant had a captivating, typical Russian face. Yesenin's poems praised the beauty of the Russian countryside, love, and his own poetic, youthful self. But he also spoke of the dark sufferings of the human soul, inner turmoil, and vodka. After he hanged himself in a fit of depression in Leningrad in 1925 his poetry was effectively, if unofficially, banned in the Soviet Union for many years.

What happens when you ignore such a ban was discovered at terrible cost by the family of Olga Golubeva. Her father, an old Bolshevik, came from a peasant family but always longed to be educated and was a great book-lover. In their large home library, though, there was no volume of Yesenin. In the campaign against him and his work in the aftermath of his suicide, he was branded a decadent poet inimical to the changes taking place in the country. His poetry ceased to be published. Nikolai Bukharin's article, "Hostile Notes", in *Pravda* put an end to all prospect of that.

"In ideological terms", Bukharin fumed, "Yesenin represents the most negative aspects of rural Russia and its so-called 'national character': brawls, a hopeless lack of personal discipline, and exaltation of retrograde forms of culture in general."[161] Yesenin's widow, Tolstoy's granddaughter, Sofia Andreyevna Tolstaya, and former lover, Nadezhda Volpin, who were both bringing up children by him, had an interest both in seeing Yesenin's poetry published and in getting some royalty income from it. All their efforts were in vain. In every editorial office they visited, they were given to understand that there was a covert ban from the top on publication of Yesenin. In 1933, a selection of his poetry was published in a print-run of 10,200 copies, but no further editions followed.

Despite this, he was not forgotten, and his poems circulated throughout the land in numerous handwritten copies. Even these proto-*samizdat* editions were persecuted. When Olga Golubeva's elder sister and her friend were found to have an album of his poems (probably discovered "by chance" by an informing schoolmate) there was a terrible scandal at their school. The girls, who were only fifteen years old, were subjected to constant harassment at all manner of meetings and turned into outcasts. Young and vulnerable, they could see no way out. They took Olga's father's revolver and shot themselves.[162]

Among all the charges thrown at the dead poet by Soviet writers and political figures, one was indisputably justified: that by taking his life he introduced a terrible fashion among young women in Russia for committing suicide. What, after all, could be more romantic than to die in the same way as Russia's most adored poet?

Apparently with the assistance of Mikhail Kalinin, Chairman of the

Presidium of the Supreme Soviet (equivalent to the Soviet President), the collection of poetry Zhenya Rudneva carried with her was published just before the war, in 1940. Few poems could have better met the needs of these young women, longing for love and mourning their friends.

> Farewell, my dearest friend.
> Know you are safe here in my heart.
> I pledge by this predestined end
> We shall not always be apart.

Yesenin wrote this, his last poem, in his own blood. It was much discussed and censured for its supposedly decadent overtones, but young hearts responded to its poignancy and sadness.

His beautiful earlier poems were also about love and parting:

Do not stray nor crush the fronds of love-lies-bleeding, seek no trace . . .

or

> Perhaps the avalanche of fate
> will notice us,
> reward our love
> with a nightingale's song.
> Foolish heart, why beat you so?

16

"But we'll beat them. We just have to not go soft"

"Rostov and Bataisk are being bombed constantly in the mornings, evenings and at night. Those bastards!" Galya Dokutovich noted on 16 July. "The Germans are on the attack again," she wrote the following day. "They have advanced from Izyum to Voroshilovgrad and on to Lisichansk,

Millerovo and Morozovskaya."[163] Soviet troops were retreating from Rostov.

Alexander Fedyayev, a very young soldier when he retreated from Rostov with his unit, always found his eyes filling with tears when he recalled 1942. "The Nazi tanks were furiously pressing in on the city, and all our infantry had against them were rifles." He could never forget the moment he and his friends were marching past a group of girls aged about fifteen. "They were all crying. They had already experienced one Nazi occupation and now a second was coming. Our soldiers were so shamefaced, because we had not the strength to protect them."[164]

In the south of Russia, between the two great rivers of the Don and the Volga and as far as the Sea of Azov, there is another sea, pale green and rippling in May, parched and yellow in July – the boundless steppe. In the feather grass and sagebrush (and little else grows in these semi-arid lands) the hares and antelope hide from wolves. Once the Nogai nomads, clad in fur and high leather boots, herded here huge numbers of horses and camels, cows and sheep. After them came another tribe, the Kalmyks, a stocky people with narrow eyes and broad, flat faces. Then the Don Cossacks, brave warriors, explorers, famed for their hospitality, their singers and storytellers. For centuries, indeed millennia, invaders crossed the steppe on their way to the shores of the Sea of Azov and the Black Sea, intent on conquering the Caucasus: Scythians, the Tatar-Mongols, Russians. Finally in 1942, driving their armoured columns over the steppe, Hitler's troops advanced on the Caucasus. That summer you could see only too clearly from the air numerous black stripes of freshly-dug trenches and anti-tank ditches scarring the ocean of the steppe in an attempt to halt the German offensive against Rostov-on-Don.

By June 1942, the Soviet Southern Front had been weakened by the failure of the Kharkov spring offensive. On 28 June, General Hoth's tank army managed to break through between Kursk and Kharkov and to advance rapidly towards the River Don. On 3 July, the Germans captured Voronezh and Soviet troops commanded by Marshal Timoshenko, defending the route to Rostov, found themselves under threat of encirclement from the north.

The German tanks advanced 200 kilometres in ten days, rapidly moving southwards between the Rivers Donets and Don. Timoshenko lost 200,000 men taken prisoner alone. The armies of the Southern Front and 4 Air Army providing them with air cover were badly mauled.

Yevdokia Bershanskaya's night bomber regiment, meanwhile, moved from airfield to airfield, following the flow of the retreating Soviet troops, but their morale remained high. Their own combat operations went well, with no new casualties. Zhenya Rudneva taught the navigators how to find their bearings in the steppe. It was no easy matter to find your way in a featureless landscape, particularly at night. The important thing was to find a fixed point, a road or railway, a village church, a grove of trees, a stream. On a clear night, of course, the stars and moon could help the navigator, and who better to describe them than Zhenya, the future astronomer? For her, the stars and constellations were familiar friends, and she enjoyed pointing them out to her pilot as they returned from a target. She would tell the legends of the stars to the rest of them on rainy evenings when they could not fly.

You cannot continuously live with the knowledge that you are risking your life every day, and that every sortie may be your last. You get used even to mortal danger as time goes by. "The situation at the front is different from our work in the classroom only in that sometimes you have anti-aircraft guns firing at you," Zhenya wrote to her parents. "Just like you, I well remember the bombing of Moscow. It was really very difficult to shoot a plane down. If anything does happen, though, what of it? You will be proud that your daughter was an airwoman. Being up in the air really is such a joy!"[165]

As the regiment's chief navigator, Zhenya Rudneva was not supposed to fly often but instead to supervise the pilots and navigators immediately prior to take-off. In fact she was constantly flying, excusing herself by arguing that she needed to know the personal qualities of every pilot in the regiment. She would often take a navigator out of the cockpit and navigate herself. These were days and, for the night bombers, nights of intense activity.

Katya Ryabova, Galya Dokutovich's pilot, was ill and Galya was flying with Nadya Popova, a slim, very beautiful, blue-eyed blonde. Galya liked flying with her because she was positive, flew confidently, and somehow was "very relaxed".[166] One night they succeeded in blowing up what was probably an ammunition dump, because the explosions down below were very powerful. They felt like birthday girls. Despite the fact that she was getting to fly a lot (the situation was so desperate that everybody was allowed into the air), despite the successful bombing and the posies that the armourer Anya would put in her cockpit, Galya sometimes felt she was living a nightmare. How had the Germans managed to advance so far?

From Olginskaya, where the night bomber regiment was now stationed, they could clearly see the German planes going to bomb Rostov, and even the bombs raining down from the aircraft. It was obvious the city would soon be abandoned, although for the time being no one was talking about it. The village people sat on benches outside their houses and looked towards Rostov. The old men talked quietly to each other, filling their pipes. The old women exclaimed and threw up their hands, but carried on selling their wares and cracking sunflower seeds. While they had the Army in the village they were sure nothing bad could happen.

When the regiment left, though, they stood silently at their gates, watching the aircraft moving out one after the other to a green field outside the village. The planes moved slowly and the girls just wanted to get away as quickly as they could, not to have to see that silent reproach, "those white headscarves of the women and the drooping moustaches of the old men".[167]

It seemed at the time to Olga Golubeva that the earth had tilted and everything that could move was slowly sliding towards the east. Number-less people who dared not stop were walking along the highway, the dusty back roads, and newly trodden trails through the unharvested fields of grain. Women carried children "in arms numb from the strain; old women were bent under the weight of the bundles they were carrying; crying children ran to catch up with their mothers or, worn out, fell behind and got lost in the flood of people." They all walked on, worn down by their own and others' grief, by hunger, and a terrible sense of humiliation. Had they not been assured for years past that the war, if it broke out, would be short and victorious and the enemy would be beaten on his own territory? "Those who come to us with the sword, shall die by the sword!" No one had warned them they would have to leave behind everything they had gained at such cost and flee headlong from the enemy. Among the stream of refugees, farm carts trundled and unfed and unmilked cows lowed plaintively, cars crawled, and obedient, impassive horses pulled artillery pieces. Behind this motley procession soldiers straggled in tunics wet with sweat. They walked in silence, their eyes downcast.[168]

Olga had been sent with the chief engineer of her squadron to Rostov to collect new engines, but they arrived to find the storage facility had been destroyed by a heavy bombing raid that threatened to trap Golubeva and her companion too. They had to get out fast and escaped the burning city in a truck complete with driver. On the road and by the roadside, clinging to the verges, moved a steady stream of retreating troops with artillery, cars, carts, kitchens and infantry. Refugees stumbled along, the wounded from bombed-out hospitals and hospital trains hobbled on. The wounded raised their crutches, signalled with their arms, begging for a lift, but their driver did not stop. Olga could see there was no room in the truck and that they could pick up one wounded man only by leaving behind aircraft parts. She wept bitterly and urged the driver to take the wounded man instead of her. The veteran sergeant behind the wheel told her, not without a measure of sympathy, to pack it in. He added, "Looks like we've been caught with our pants down the way these fascists are screwing us. But we'll beat them. We just have to not go soft."[169]

A German plane appeared in the sky and the driver turned off under roadside trees. Running away from the truck "with somehow unbelievably long strides", Olga stumbled over a dead woman and saw next to her a squawling, lacy parcel. Still very young, she had no idea how to calm a baby and in desperation called uselessly for help to her mother, before looking on as the hard-bitten truck driver scooped up the tiny child and hugged it to him. Who knows if that little girl survived the war, and if she did, what kind of life she had?

Olga Golubeva escaped back to her unit from near encirclement, but Sonya Ozerkova, the chief engineer in her regiment, was less fortunate. A regular servicewoman, intellectual, strict, she never allowed herself any show of familiarity towards her subordinates. Initially Sonya made herself unpopular in the regiment, where she was seen as too dry, but later came to be appreciated and admired. She worked well and knew her trade. She was demanding towards the mechanics, but cared deeply about them and took a lot of trouble over their welfare.

During one of their periodic emergency moves to a new airfield caused by the approach of German tanks, the regiment departed, leaving behind Sonya and Glafira Kashirina, a mechanic, with a damaged plane. When it became clear that the plane could not be quickly patched up they, following instructions, set fire to it and walked off the airfield.

After trekking all day along a road clogged with troops and refugees, the women spent the night in a haystack. Sonya woke up in the morning aware that someone was staring at her. A woman beside the haystack asked, "Are you lassies with the Army? You'd better get rid of those uniforms."[170] The woman warned them that German tanks had already gone by, although there were no Germans at the farm just then. She took the airwomen to her home and gave them food and some peasant clothes: long skirts and light-coloured shawls. They left, short stocky Sonya and sylph-like Glafira, who was not physically strong and found the long slog more difficult by the day.

They encountered two German motorcyclists on the road. One was busy repairing his motorcycle and the other pointed at their bundles, where, he was guessing, there would be food. Glafira was distraught, and began very slowly to untie her load, at the bottom of which was a gun. While this was going on, Sonya pulled out her own pistol, shot the German, ran over to the other one and shot him twice at point-blank range. The women dashed into the bushes and ran away as fast as they could.

It was three weeks before they saw any Soviet soldiers. Glafira by then was in a very bad state. When they realised she had typhus, Sonya took her to a hospital and got a lift back to her regiment from a passing car. She saw the landing lights of the U-2s when she was still far away and thought they seemed wonderfully pretty. When they arrived, Sonya jumped out of the car and ran to her friends. It was all over.

In fact, however, her real trial was just about to begin. The regiment had an agent of Soviet military counter-intelligence, S.M.E.R.S.h., attached to it and he prevented Sonya from returning to work. She found herself being summoned to the Special Department of the division and questioned in detail, or rather, interrogated, as to how she had escaped the encirclement. Ozerkova had some experience of life and knew plenty about the pre-war purges. She realised she was in a very dangerous situation.

In the Soviet Union anyone who had been captured, or even just spent time in occupied territory, carried the stigma for the rest of their life, and even after death. Until the end of the Soviet state the questionnaires of personnel departments included the question, "Were you or any of your relatives in occupied territory?" Soldiers who managed to break out of encirclement or escaped from captivity might be beside themselves with joy to have finally made it back to their own side and eager to get back to fighting the Germans, only to find that, unbelievably, the Special Department agents were demanding in the course of interrogation that they should confess to having been recruited by the Germans. Particularly in the case of officers, if it was decided they were traitors the Military Tribunal could sentence them to be shot, or stripped of their rank and sent to a penal battalion. In such a battalion it was possible to "redeem your guilt" with blood and regain the rank of officer, but for that you had first to survive. They were thrown into the most hopeless situations and most of those in a penal battalion died in their first battle.

Even people who before the war supposed there was no smoke without fire, that if someone was innocent they would not have been arrested, could not believe that soldiers in their unit who managed to return from encirclement could be traitors. It simply did not make sense. The only exception to this treatment would be if the soldiers had returned to a unit that was in the thick of the fighting and in desperate need of some more cannon fodder. Only then would S.M.E.R.S.h. decide that they had other things to do, leaving them to shed their blood on equal terms with everyone else.

Quite how hopeless her situation was, Sonya realised only after several days of interrogation. Not only had she been in occupied territory where she might have been recruited by the Germans but, far worse, fearing she would be captured, she had destroyed her Party membership card. She was well aware that at that time the Party card was valued more highly than a human life, but at the time she had been confident the Party would forgive her in view of the circumstances. Now, as she was repeatedly asked about the circumstances in which she lost it, she knew it was equally impossible to lie or tell the truth. Suddenly she herself was not sure whether or not she had done the right thing, and submissively awaited her fate.

Sonya was sent before the Military Tribunal. She was expecting a serious punishment, but was shocked when she heard she was to be shot. She was stripped of her epaulettes, her head was shaved, and she was taken to await execution. She was saved by the commissar of her battalion, who found out quite by chance what was going on when the driver he was with mentioned that: "The chief engineer of the women's night bomber regiment has been sentenced to be shot." [171] The commissar had heard nothing about it and immediately sent a coded message to the Air Force headquarters of the front, which ordered a stay of execution while the case was reviewed. Sonya Ozerkova was acquitted, and reappeared shortly afterwards in the regiment, bald as a coot and with a fixed, stony expression on her face. She would not speak about her experiences, and only after the war admitted to a comrade from the regiment, "If I am walking down the street and someone gives me a fixed stare, I shudder and my heart starts pounding."

Sonya Ozerkova was not the first and would not be the last of Raskova's wards to come to the attention of S.M.E.R.S.h., a powerful institution that trapped real traitors, but also unmasked as spies completely innocent people, in the best traditions of the Stalinist regime.

17

"What a misfortune, what a useless death"

For the women's 586 Fighter Regiment, the hot summer months in the steppe had been passing with monotonous spells on duty when suddenly the regiment suffered its first, dreadfully absurd fatality. It lost one of its best pilots, the beautiful, elegant, feminine Lina Smirnova. Before the war Lina had been a teacher. She wrote poetry and was more sensitive than the others: Smirnova took criticism very hard and, conversely, if she was praised, was childishly pleased.[172] By common consent, the catastrophe stemmed from bullying by Squadron Leader Belyaeva. Belyaeva disparaged other pilots in her squadron and they, like the technical staff, feared and disliked her. But Smirnova proved fatally susceptible.

On 21 July four Yaks, piloted by Budanova, Smirnova, Litvyak and Masha Kuznetsova had been sent to escort a VIP in a Douglas transport aircraft. "We waited and waited but there was no sign of the Douglas," Kuznetsova recalled.[173] Then they received new orders: Budanova and Lina Smirnova were to catch up with the transport plane, which had passed them by, and accompany it to Penza. Budanova and Smirnova immediately took off. It was not an uncommon situation, but this was no easy task. "Usually you can see who you are supposed to be protecting, but here we had first to catch up with them."[174] Unfortunately, they flew in the wrong direction and blundered around pointlessly. The first Yaks had only enough fuel to fly for an hour and a half, so their first priority was soon not to locate the Douglas but to land their planes safely. If they could not find an airfield before the fuel ran out, they would be forced to crash-land wherever they could, right there in the steppe. When crash-landing on unprepared ground, the official instructions were that the pilot must land on the fuselage, without lowering the undercarriage. This would inevitably damage the propeller and, if the engine had not been turned off before landing, it too would be damaged. However, landing on the wheels was much more dangerous in these circumstances, both for the aircraft and for the pilot, who could be killed.

Lina Smirnova was flying Belyaeva's plane, so she was particularly anxious. Relations between Belyaeva, who was very strict with all her subordinates, and Smirnova were poor. On one mission when Belyaeva was leading Smirnova, they lost each other. The general consensus was that ever since then she had been persecuting Smirnova, telling everyone she was a useless pilot. To wreck Belyaeva's plane would have been the ultimate disaster for Smirnova.

Compounding Smirnova's fear of Belyaeva was the close, almost affectionate relationship that the pilots had formed with their fighting machines. It had "something of the cavalryman's attitude to his horse: the technology was seen almost as a living thing, and if there was the slightest chance of saving it, even at the risk of their own lives, people tried".[175] Who could bring themselves to wilfully damage one of the new Yaks, the long-awaited, most advanced aircraft of their time?

The young take risks. Both pilots decided to play roulette by landing their planes on their wheels. In the steppe the grass was half a metre high, making it very difficult to judge the critical moment of landing or even to see whether there were obstacles below. The ground proved very uneven but Budanova nevertheless landed successfully. Lina was less lucky. Her plane slewed round at high speed. Evidently one wheel hit a pothole or a bump, the Yak slithered to one side, hit the ground again with its wing and tail, and returned to a normal position. Miraculously, Smirnova survived unscathed and the plane was almost intact, with only its propeller bent. Despite this good fortune, the young pilot went to pieces. She climbed out of the plane, saw it was damaged, tore up her ID, wrote a note, and shot herself in the head.[176]

Nina Ivakina believed this "crazy, unjustifiable decision" had not been taken on the spur of the moment because it was carried out so purposefully. "It seems to me that she had been moving in this direction for a long time because of the utterly wretched atmosphere in their squadron caused by Commander Belyaeva."[177] Ivakina's opinion was shared by almost everyone. If few people had much time for Belyaeva before, now she was treated with outright hostility.

Saninsky, the unit's chief technician, came to the site with mechanic Nina Shebalina. They loaded Belyaeva's plane onto a truck and it was repaired in the regimental workshops without too much difficulty. Nina Shebalina could not believe that the life of this dear person had ended. She was "a young, beautiful, charming girl. What a misfortune. What a useless death."[178]

Her note about Lina Smirnova's suicide was the last entry Nina Ivakina made in her diary as a Komsomol administrator. She remained at the front until 1944, but in autumn 1942, when the post of commissar in the Red Army was abolished, became the Party administrator of a men's parachute battalion.

In the autumn of 1942, Zhukov and Konev had as great a loathing of the commissars as everyone else in the Army. The generals exploited the fact that the Red Army had suffered heavy losses of officers, who now desperately needed replacing, to persuade Stalin to get rid of these political supervisors. Zhukov, who in private called them "snoops", once exploded, "What use are they to me? Teaching soldiers to shout 'Hurrah'? They can work that out for themselves! They are no use at the front whatsoever. How long do we have to put up with this? Can we really not trust our own officers?"[179] After the intervention of Zhukov and Konev, Stalin sounded out the opinion of others and decided to follow their recommendations. Commissars were transformed into political advisers, who retained their responsibility for supervising army morale and indoctrination but also lost the power of deputising for a commander in his absence. They were now "less able to get in the way".[180] Blocking detachments of the N.K.V.D. still shot on sight anyone retreating without orders. S.M.E.R.S.h., set up to catch spies, suspected everybody without exception of being an enemy of the Soviet state, but with the demise of the commissars, it was generally agreed, you could breathe a bit more freely at the front.

18

"Not one step back"

The loss of Rostov demoralised everyone, from the rank-and-file soldier to the Supreme Commander-in-Chief, Comrade Stalin. If the Germans crossed the Don, all the fronts would be in serious jeopardy.[181] Within a couple of days the Germans did just that, and began a rapid advance towards the Caucasus and Stalingrad. Stalin decided they must be stopped at all costs. If his soldiers did not want to fight to the death, they must be forced to do so at gunpoint.

On 28 July 1942, after the fall of Rostov, Stalin's Order No. 227, known as the "Not one step back" order, was read out to the troops of the Southern Front.

> Battles are taking place in the Voronezh area, on the Don, and in the south at the gates of the North Caucasus. The German invaders are rushing to Stalingrad, the Volga, and want at all costs to capture the Kuban and the North Caucasus with their oil and grain resources. The enemy has captured Voroshilovgrad, Starobelsk, Rossosh, Kupyansk, Valuiki, Novocherkassk, and Rostov-on-Don. Some of the troops of the Southern Front, following alarmists, abandoned Rostov and Novocherkassk without serious resistance and without orders from Moscow, bringing shame on their banners. The population of our country, which regards the Red Army with love and respect, is becoming disenchanted with it, losing faith in the Red Army, and many are cursing the Red Army for surrendering our people to the yoke of the German oppressors while itself drifting away to the east.[182]

In short, the troops of the Southern Front had abandoned the Don and were fleeing shamefully. The situation in the south of the Soviet Union was alarming. Retreating without orders would be regarded as treason.[183] This order was not published in the press, but "Not one step back" very soon became the dominant slogan in the newspapers in the summer of 1942, and editorials spread it among the masses.

The order was read to the servicewomen of 588 Night Bomber Regiment by their chief of staff, Irina Rakobolskaya. The previous night they had been forced to flee the farmstead at which they had only just arrived because German tanks were approaching. They had to leave so quickly they did not even have maps of the new district. "The site at which we are to land is off the map," Zhenya Rudneva told the navigators.

By dawn they were at their new location where, ravenously hungry, they fell upon the unripe watermelons in the fields. The villagers were only too happy. Soon the Germans would arrive, so it was better for their fruit to be eaten by their own side. The regiment washed in watermelon juice because there was no water. Raising clouds of dust with their planes on the village street, the pilots concealed them close to houses and trees. Suddenly they were called on parade and heard those terrible words from Rakobolskaya.[184]

They could not get their heads round the dreadful things that were happening and the words of the order from the Supreme Commander-in-Chief that they were hearing. It was obvious that in these southern steppes there was nowhere to dig in, nothing to provide support. What would happen? When Rakobolskaya finished, the girls stood for a long time in total silence. Tired and hungry, they wept, because they too were troops of the Southern Front.

Their regiment had not yet suffered heavy losses, but neighbouring bomber and fighter regiments had been reduced to a half, a third, or even less of their complement of men and aircraft. One day when the weather ruled out flying and a storm was gathering, the girls were preparing to go to bed in a large former stable when the regiment's Party administrator arrived. "Let us go to bury pilots from our neighbouring regiment. They have almost no one left."[185] They learned that the day before a Messerschmitt had shot down two pilots of a male U-2 regiment. The girls went off to the funeral. It was already quite dark and the thunderstorm began.

It was raining and lightning lit up the road. The cart with the coffins kept getting stuck in the mud. They hauled it out and dragged it onwards. Their silence was broken by the voice of Runt, the Party administrator, for whom the Party membership card was sacred: "Comrades, make sure you keep your Komsomol and Party cards dry." The girls were already soaked to the skin, with water dripping from their sodden field caps onto their hair and noses and squelching in their boots.

None of them knew the dead pilots or remembered their names. In the dark they accompanied the cart with the coffins to the village graveyard and, while the grave was being dug, stood in the rain sinking into the churned-up clay. It struck many of them as peculiar that the deaths of these unknown pilots hardly affected them at all.

As Galya Dokutovich noted, it was "strange that here the death of comrades-in-arms was less painful than it had been in Engels. Each of us knew the same might happen to her and was prepared for that." [186]

Anna Yegorova listened to Order No. 227 in the heavily battle-scarred 4 Air Army of General Konstantin Vershinin, which was retreating with the Southern Front. They now had orders to fight to the death, but what they did not have was any resources. Having flown yet again to a new location, the U-2 pilots had lost their ground support. They no longer had a staff headquarters, a canteen, or any fuel. Where were these to be found?

They were fed that day by an elderly woman who, when she saw them landing, came out from the village. She said hello, looked closely at Anna and her comrades, and said, "Do you have any food of your own?" They did not answer; the exhausted, hungry look on their faces spoke for itself. The woman said that just that day she had made a cauldron of borshch, "As if I knew you would fly here." She told them her own son was a pilot, but she had long had no letters from him. Perhaps somewhere some kind person was feeding him. [187] After their meal with this generous lady, who stayed with them, wiping away tears with the hem of her loose cardigan, the pilots decided to drain the petrol from all the planes in order to fuel one and send it off in search of ground support. As the most experienced, Anna was entrusted with this mission. Again, the ground below was shrouded in smoke, houses were burning, fields untended. An endless stream of refugees was walking or riding on carts. People were dragging bundles and leading cows on a harness. It was a painful sight, made all the more so because there was nothing she could do to help them.

An immense flood of refugees was trying to cross the Don in the direction of Stalingrad. It was by no means certain they would have time to get across before the Germans arrived, or that they would not die during the crossing. The Don crossing points were like a scene from hell. Troops were waiting their turn to cross the Don with their equipment and wounded. Peasant families were waiting with their livestock, tractors and carts laden with household goods, and with children sitting on top. The roads leading to crossings were terribly congested with this flood of humanity. People crossed the Don mostly at night, because during the day they were bombed. "There were almost no planes with red stars on their wings" and the Germans terrorised soldiers and civilians alike with impunity, first bombing, then strafing them from low altitude.

Anya Skorobogatova, as a radio operator with the Signals Battalion of the Southern Front, worked from a radio mounted on a truck. She was there among the military personnel who were trying not to make eye contact with the civilians waiting their turn to cross the Don. Skorobogatova had already seen a lot in the war, but the never-ending nightmare of the bombing of the river crossing stayed with her for many years. What was happening was too dreadful. Her memory retained only episodes. There was a general standing at the crossing and bawling obscenities at Anya: "Where are you going? Lie down! What are you standing for?" And then to somebody else: "Where do you think you're going? As you were! Put this truck on first, it's a radio station."[188] Anya, completely bewildered, had no idea what she was supposed to do. During that bombing she saw Germans clearly for the first time, or more precisely, German planes with crosses. When they dive-bombed she heard the screaming of their sirens. Only later, when she was a seasoned servicewoman, did she learn they were Junkers Ju 87 "Stuka" bombers. In time, she would get used to bombs, but for now, distinctly seeing them separate from the aircraft and head downwards, she felt that every one was hurtling directly at her. Every time she hit the ground she wished it would swallow her up, she so wanted to become invisible. German Messerschmitt fighters darted above, protecting their bombers, and there was not a Soviet fighter to be seen. They would probably not have been much help if they had appeared. A German bomber pilot recalled, "We had long been aware that the morale of Soviet fighter pilots was unsatisfactory. Only a few select units were an exception to that."[189]

Anna Yegorova and her communications comrades flying their U-2s in broad daylight were constantly in the air, couriering orders and reconnoitring the location of Soviet and enemy troops. Their airfields, or rather, open fields equipped to support the undemanding U-2s, were constantly changing, moving further and further towards the Don, and then towards the Volga. There was nowhere for them to rest. There was nowhere and no time for them to eat either, and often no food anyway. A meal cooked at the old airfield would be sent on to the new one or might disappear altogether. They slept where they could: in the cockpit, on a cover under a wing, on the grass, or in an abandoned peasant hut. At any time of the day and night they might be woken with the shout, "Scramble!"[190] Reconnoitring the disposition of units on the front line was extremely dangerous. The Germans might already be in a village to which a slow, unarmed U-2 was sent. Anya's comrades, for example, came under fire in just this way. Realising something was wrong with his navigator in the second cockpit, the pilot landed at the first opportunity to help him but found it was too late. In a daze the pilot took off his leather jacket, rolled it up and, weeping silently, tried to tuck it under his friend's head to make him more comfortable.

The death of someone with whom you have risked your life, with whom you have completely merged as together you flew your little cardboard plane under fire, was a terrible trauma for the U-2 pilots and navigators. "Why her and not me? She has died, so now I must live for her." Their dead friend was with them for life, present in it every day, never growing old, always twenty. For a pilot who lost their navigator, for a sniper who lost their partner, this was the most terrible wound they could suffer in the war. The pain dulled with the passing years, but a terrible sense of guilt remained.

For Anna the most dreadful memory of the war was a three-year-old orphan who, dirty, famished, and covered in raw grazes, attached himself to her and her comrades near Novocherkassk, unable to say anything more than his name, "Ilyusha", and "Mama". He called constantly for his mother but, as the soldiers told Anna, his mother was dead. The little boy was no longer capable of crying and just sobbed quietly. Anna's heart was breaking. They needed to fly on but Ilyusha clung to her neck and would not let go. What could she do? How could she abandon this defenceless toddler, the most unfortunate of the victims of war, a little child who had lost his mother?

Anna decided to take Ilyusha with her. "Are you out of your mind?" her fellow pilots yelled. "What help can you give him? Do you even know where we will be stopping next? What will happen to him if you get killed?"[191]

They had to leave. Crying, hugging the little child to her, Anna rushed to the village, and fate suddenly relented. They came upon an old lady with a walking stick who looked at the child with rheumy eyes and suddenly cried out, "Ilyusha, my little grandson!"

Anna quickly passed the child over and ran to her plane. She suddenly felt "such unendurable pain for everything – for orphaned Ilyusha – how many orphans like him there were on the war-torn roads – and for the wasted years which were passing, and for myself." She so loved children, and so much longed to have her own, big family.[192]

Anna's thoughts often turned to a boy called Victor Kutov she had worked with while building the Moscow Metro. They went out on dates. "Do you love me?" he had asked, and Anna had laughed. "Of course not! What are you thinking of!" That, however, was not the reply her eyes were giving. "Yes you do! Yes you do!" Victor shouted and whirled her round, holding her hands tightly.

Victor was now fighting somewhere on the Northwestern Front and it was five months since she had last heard from him. Brooding over this, Anna asked herself again and again, "Is he alive?" She comforted herself with the thought that the army postal service left much to be desired and his letters might just not have been delivered to her. She cursed herself now for never having told him that, yes, of course, she loved him.

Nobody wrote at the time or later about the heroism of the defenders of Rostov, so many of whom perished in the rapid German advance on the city. The second capture by the Germans of Rostov was not seen as one of the glorious episodes of the war. It was fifty years before any mention was made of the death in the city's outskirts of an entire anti-aircraft battery operated by young girls.

With the lightning advance of the Germans on Soviet cities, it often happened that there was no time to evacuate anti-aircraft batteries, which found themselves firing not at planes but at tanks. Three Battery of 1 Battalion of 734 Anti-Aircraft and Artillery Regiment was formed from Rostov girls who were members of the Komsomol. Most were aged seventeen to nineteen. While the Germans were advancing on the city their planes bombed Rostov for several days. It is believed that every twenty-four hours they made some 1,200 sorties. About 100 young girls servicing the guns of the battery were continuously bringing shells, loading the guns, firing them, and resting only when their guns overheated. On 21 July, after several hours of continuous bombing, there was a sudden silence. Not realising that this was a stillness preceding the assault on the city, or perhaps so exhausted that they no longer cared, the entire battery fell asleep in the foxholes next to their guns. Many did not even hear the roar of the German tanks advancing on them. It was all over very quickly. Only a few girls woke up in time to turn their anti-aircraft guns on the tanks of the 5th S.S. Viking Division. They managed to knock out two tanks: the rest crushed the battery together with its defenders.[193]

It has been claimed that the Germans were dismayed when they realised the battery they had totally destroyed had been operated solely by young girls, and that they ordered local old men and women to collect and bury the bodies. It is said too that they made a cross of forage caps on the mound of the mass grave.

19

"We can do anything, we never surrender"

By cutting through the Salsk–Stalingrad railway and occupying both banks of the Volga, the Germans would have been able to completely sever communications between the Caucasus and European Russia.

In those days, or rather nights, in the steppe around Salsk the women's night bomber regiment targeted the crossings the Germans had constructed over the Don, and dropped their small bombs on German motorised units on the roads. At night fires could be seen in many places from the air, and during one daytime sortie Olga Golubeva saw the charred ruins of a small town and surrounding villages: it bore an uncanny resemblance to a graveyard.

The theatre of operations of the night bomber regiment was changing almost daily, following the constantly moving front line. One time, when they were bombing during the night from an airfield six kilometres from Tselina Station, Popov, the divisional commander himself, flew in to order them to move on urgently: the station was already occupied by the Germans. There was no transports for the mechanics and armourers and no room for them either in the planes or vehicles. They slogged eighty kilometres on foot and were saved from encirclement only by a miracle.

The moral and physical strain was terrible. They often got no sleep for days at a time. At night they were working, and during the day their situation prevented it. Constantly retreating to new airfields, the regiment bombed German troops advancing across the steppe to Salsk and, after Salsk was captured, towards the Caucasus.

Galya Dokutovich got to fly, although not as often as she would have liked. She was one of the few people on whom the terrible burden of the last few days seemed not to have taken its toll. As she wrote in a letter:

Although outwardly the war has left its imprint on me, inwardly little has changed. I am still the little girl I always was. In the rear most people may imagine that out here on the front line something terrifically heroic happens every day, and that the people here are not just people, but somehow special. That is nonsense! Everything is very straightforward. Routine wartime work. Perhaps we've just got used to everything, the bad weather, the searchlights, the anti-aircraft guns, and to nights so dark you can see neither the sky nor the stars, when it is so dark that not only flying but even walking on the ground is difficult.

I have contradictory thoughts. Sometimes I think the war and everything I am seeing now will soon be over and then I shall remember it like a half-forgotten dream. You do feel that here you see more clearly what the human heart is capable of. Maybe that is why life right now seems more vivid and expansive. You pay more dearly for everything.[194]

Galya, with her exceptional willpower, believed in achieving goals even in the most unpromising conditions. Now, when all hell was let loose on the ground and in the air, she kept asking Irina Dryagina to let her take the controls. She wanted to learn no matter what, and Irina, with whom Galya enjoyed flying more than anything, always allowed her to. Galya was already competent at piloting the U-2 in the air, and now she wanted to learn to take off.

The day and night of 25 July 1942 had some very unpleasant surprises in store for them both. During the day the regiment was again moved to another airfield, and Dryagina allowed Galya to fly. No sooner had the plane left the ground, taking off from a narrow airstrip beside trees, than a truck appeared out of the woods. The plane was still very low and its wheels snagged the top of the truck's cab. This potentially disastrous collision ended happily, however, and they only damaged a wheel. They completed the flight and were unharmed even when the plane, with its damaged wheel, damaged its propeller too on landing. This, however, was not the end of their troubles. They could hardly fly a combat mission that night with a damaged plane and, while waiting for a replacement, Galya lay down to rest in the tall grass at the edge of the airfield. The driver of a refuelling truck that was going around the airfield did not see her in the grass and ran his heavy vehicle straight over her.

She had survived being shelled by German anti-aircraft guns without a scratch, had escaped from a potentially fatal collision, only then to fall asleep in the grass and be run over by a refuelling truck. When Irina Rakobolskaya leaned over the stretcher on which Galya was lying, her face contorted with pain, Galya's grey lips whispered, "Irina, promise me . . . when I come back, I'll get to fly."[195] Irina swore she would. She probably felt she could promise Galya almost anything at that moment. Galya's spine was broken and her legs injured. There was no guarantee she was going to survive or, if she did, that she would ever walk again. The possibility that Galya might be able to return even to a desk job in the Air Force seemed wildly optimistic. Galya was taken to hospital in a serious condition and evacuated far to the rear. The next entry in her diary was made on 6 August in a hospital at Makhachkala on the Caspian Sea.

"At first I had to lie flat on my back, and even now I am not allowed to move. The Germans are in Armavir. When will this horrible nightmare end?" She could not get Pushkin's lines out of her head, "Comrade, believe that it will rise, the star of happiness sublime." Her spine was terribly painful. "My right hip hurts too. My legs are splayed out." Galya Dokutovich would not have been herself, however, if she had not been doing everything conceivable to return to duty. On that same day she recorded that she had tried, with the help of two nurses, to stand on her own two feet. Her head had been spinning, and when she lay down again "I felt as if I had done a hard day's work and was dog tired." Soon, however, she was up again and shuffling around on crutches. What a long, exhausting distance thirty metres had become for her![196]

Days, weeks and months passed in hospital and she gradually recovered her mobility, but the severe pain continued. "Galya, you are a maidenly incarnation of Pavel Korchagin," Irina Dryagina told her, and she now reread *How the Steel Was Tempered*, taking strength from the incurably ill hero of Ostrovsky's novel. Galya, whose hero was Ethel Lilian Voynich's Gadfly, wanted no one to see how ill she was. She was ashamed when she fainted in public, ashamed when she wept from the pain. "Yesterday I gave in. I cried. Why? Because of the pain! I am ashamed, ashamed of my lack of self-control, of my weakness in not managing to hide it." She compared herself with the Gadfly and excoriated herself for not being as strong, ignoring the fact that the Gadfly was the fictional creation of an over-the-top Irish writer.

Slowly convalescing, spending a lot of time on her hospital bed, Galya recollected and analysed her childhood and adolescence in detail, trying to decide what kind of person she was, and reflecting on love. It was probably her last such opportunity for contemplation. The seven months of life remaining to her after discharge from hospital passed in a mad whirl of night flying, with short periods of rest during the day. Her reflections were put down on paper in her neat handwriting during the long months of illness in the hospital.

When she was twelve, Galya Dokutovich moved from the countryside to school in Gomel. She loved the new life: the Young Pioneer patrols, the physical education. Galya was passionately interested in physics, but then became fascinated by literature, and at the Literary Society found her best friend, from whom she never parted – little, blue-eyed Polina Gelman. Along with literature, Galya loved gymnastics, because Soviet people had to be perfect in mind and body. No one was ever so much as a minute late for the Pioneer meetings that took over her life. Her next passion was the Komsomol, which she joined just after Polina.

The thirties were a time for young people. Collectivisation, industrialisation, great construction projects, education accessible to everyone, records being broken in every sphere of life, the superiority of the new Soviet person above all others (admittedly they had never seen any others).

During collectivisation the peasantry were destroyed as a class. The industrialisation and great construction projects were driven through not least by exploiting the unpaid labour of millions of prisoners caught up by the monstrous juggernaut of repression, but only those directly affected knew about that. On the surface there was just tremendous energy, dynamism and high hopes, and the young tend not to look too far beneath the surface.

Galya was a girl of her time. When, again in the footsteps of Polina Gelman, she joined a flying club, she found another, more serious passion – aviation. Thinking about love, Galya wondered why, in her twenty-two years, she had never experienced it. "What is this, strength of character or emotional frigidity?" She reminded herself that she must, and would, be strong above all else. "They say sincerity and directness are a mistake. Too bad. These are my principles, and you do not compromise your principles."[197]

Her main principle came, however, from her role model, Raskova. "We can do anything. We never surrender." For now, her first priority must be to recover, to regain her mobility, and by hook or by crook get back to her regiment where she knew she was very much needed.

20

"Falling like vultures"

Having crossed the Don in July 1942, by August the Wehrmacht had reached the Volga. Young medical orderly Leonid Fialkovsky, making for Stalingrad with a tank unit, remembers an old repair technician sending them on their way with these words: "I feel sorry for you lads. You're healthy, intelligent, and what is waiting for you there? Look how far the enemy has come, and no one is going to stop him. The news service can barely keep up with him. He's at the gates of Moscow, right? He's starving Leningrad out – how much longer can people hold out there? The Baltic states are under enemy control, Byelorussia, the Ukraine, Crimea. He's taken Voronezh and Rostov. He's helping himself to all of Russia. What does the future hold for all of us?"[198]

Their sergeant turned on him. "Listen, you, are you spreading counter-revolution?" The old man replied simply, "What sort of counterrevolutionary do I look like, sonny? It breaks my heart." Fialkovsky and his companions did not take up the topic, but they were all thinking the same as the old man. How could the Germans have come so far and where would it all end? They were on their way now to Stalingrad.

Hitler considered it imperative to take Stalingrad. He wanted to block traffic along the Volga, the artery connecting the centre of Russia with the south of the U.S.S.R., including the Caucasus and Transcaucasia. There were major military factories in Stalingrad. Some had been evacuated eastwards but others were still in the city. Finally, capturing the city that bore the name of Stalin would be a great propaganda victory (just as defending it became an important propaganda achievement for the Soviet side).

Beginning their offensive in mid-July, the Germans encountered fierce Russian resistance. After three weeks they had advanced only 60–80 kilometres, but by reinforcing the attacking Sixth Army, they eventually succeeded in encircling three Soviet divisions and reaching the Don. Soon the Red Army was pushed back to the other side of the Don, but there, in a great bend in the river, the Germans were held for a long time, halted by stubborn Soviet resistance. Stalin's Order No. 227 was having the desired effect.

Yeremin, who was then a major, remembered those days as the worst in the war.[199] Like other air units, 296 Fighter Regiment was constantly being forced to move to new airfields: Svatovo, Novopskov, Rossosh, closer and closer to Stalingrad. These redeployments were usually combined with combat missions to protect retreating Soviet troops and river crossings, and to attack German ground troops. "Extremely urgent" departures, when they evacuated under attack, became more frequent. They were flying from dawn to dusk in hot, dry weather, with the sky cloudless. There were almost no days when the conditions made flying impossible.

The short summer night would come, "Weary to the point of exhaustion," the pilots would fall asleep, but the few hours of darkness were too little for them to recover properly. With the dawn a new, infinitely long day of intolerable stress began. Not infrequently, Yeremin woke up feeling anxious and received orders from Nikolai Baranov to withdraw part of his regiment ahead of advancing German tanks. Baranov would follow with the rest of the regiment. Taking off at the head of his group, Yeremin would see Baranov vigorously waving at him, as if to say, "Go on, go on. Move it!"

As they retreated towards Stalingrad, 296 Regiment often found themselves based in windswept fields with stunted vegetation and no shelter from the sandy dust. For many of the young pilots thrown against the enemy above the city, their first battle was also their last. Totally inexperienced, they lost all sense of orientation in the murderous carousel of a dogfight, trying only not to lose track of their lead aircraft. Such novices were an easy target for experienced enemy pilots, who were concentrated in the sky above Stalingrad, the most important sector of the German advance. On one occasion, when much of Baranov's regiment was refuelling and taking on ammunition, two-dozen Messerschmitts suddenly appeared and attacked the airfield. They caused a great deal of damage, setting fire to many planes and cratering the landing strip to make it unusable. They also dropped numerous "frogs", small anti-personnel mines which, if you stood on them, jumped up and exploded.[200]

At dawn the next day, the surviving aircraft flew onto an airstrip 15–20 kilometres south of Stalingrad. From here they again gave protection to the river crossings in the vicinity of Kalach and provided cover for Pe-2s bombing German tanks that had broken through. By this time the Germans were only fifty kilometres from the city and the fighter regiment was transferred to an airport located in Stalingrad itself. This was still known as the "School Airfield", doubtless because it had been used to train cadets from Stalingrad flying school. The regiment was accommodated in the houses of residents who had fled the city. They spent the short nights in beds with decorative nickel-plated orbs, in rooms with old-fashioned chests of drawers ornamented with miniature elephants, the very epitome of domestic comfort and wellbeing. They could imagine no greater contrast with the destruction and chaos close to Stalingrad, and indeed in Stalingrad itself, because German bombers were already pounding the city. The scale of the air raids increased day by day until finally, on 23 August, it reached its terrible climax.

In the short history of Stalin's city there has been no worse day than 23 August 1942. From dawn, Baranov's regiment, as on the preceding days, set out on combat missions. Hundreds of German bombers appeared over Stalingrad just as Baranov and many of his pilots had returned from their last sortie. About a dozen bombers hit the School Airfield and surrounding area. As he ran with Alexey Salomatin back towards his fighter, Yeremin noted that, in the midst of all the explosions, turmoil and chaos, seconds seemed to last an eternity. It was going to be difficult to take off from the airfield, but was not yet impossible. If a few more bombs were dropped, the place would become a deathtrap. Baranov gave orders to repulse the raiders and, joining Yeremin and Salomatin as they scrambled, Squadron Leader Balashov asked him with his customary imperturbability whether he had remembered to bring along his *trantishki*. This was the name he had given the overnight bag in which Yeremin kept all his front-line belongings – photographs, shaving kit, toiletries. He always had it with him, ready for their next move onwards. It was already only too obvious that they would have to move to another airfield, the only question was, which one?[201]

Needless to say, Yeremin had the bag with him, and Vladimir Balashov grinned as he gave him a cheery wave. Half an hour later Yeremin was looking at the dead body of his friend. When Balashov's plane was shot down, it caught fire and exploded, hurling him out of the cockpit so that, unusually, the body was not charred. Yeremin looked at his friend's "fair, curly hair", and bade him a last farewell.[202]

The German high command's plan for the assault on Stalingrad by the 6th Field Army under General Friedrich Paulus envisaged an air strike of unprecedented savagery. At 1718 hours on 23 August the command post of the Municipal Defence Committee was notified that observation posts of the Air Surveillance, Warning and Communication troops had reported a large formation of German bombers flying towards Stalingrad. They would be over the city in just five minutes' time. Hearing the air-raid sirens and the emergency hooting of locomotives, the citizens of Stalingrad, already accustomed to air raids, turned to look west, but there the sky was clear. The roar of approaching aircraft was soon heard coming from the east: the Luftwaffe had outwitted the city's anti-aircraft defences by approaching from the other direction.

The bombers were flying slowly, weighed down by their deadly cargo. The anti-aircraft guns belatedly opened fire and a moment later "the entire sky was filled with ragged black tufts of explosions. Those watching the scene saw anti-aircraft artillery fire so dense that sometimes the aircraft disappeared in the blurred bouquets of the explosions. Nevertheless, they appeared again through the smoke and, without breaking formation or deviating from their battle plan, they inexorably moved towards the city centre."[203]

The first wave of German bombing took out most of Stalingrad's anti-aircraft guns. After the "Frame", the universally hated German spy plane, had established the position of the anti-aircraft batteries, they had been bombed systematically. Eighteen-year-old Natasha Sholokh was at the battery of the first battalion of 1083 Anti-Aircraft Artillery Regiment, stationed in the village of Krasnaya Sloboda on the left bank of the Volga near the central crossing. From her position in a trench some 200 metres from the battery she saw "a whole suite" of German bombers moving in on the crossing. Suddenly a Stuka broke away from them and started to dive – it seemed to Natasha, straight at her. In horror she darted around her earthen shelter, finally grabbing a huge tumbleweed bush. She crouched down, covering herself with it and somehow convinced herself later that the bush had saved her life. Running to the headquarters of her battalion, Natasha found a terrible sight. Almost everyone had been killed: the drivers, radio operators, telephonists, cooks, and observers. There had been a direct hit on the operations dugout housing the battalion headquarters, killing the commander, Captain Alexeyev, the chief of staff, and the commander of the operations squad. The commissar had suffered concussion and been blinded. Many of the girls operating the guns had been wounded rather than killed but there was nobody to tend them: Galya, the military nurse, had lost a leg and was wounded in the stomach. She died there. When they had dropped their bombs, the German pilots machine-gunned the girls in observation towers.[204]

The ceaseless bombing and constant air battles, in which many Soviet pilots did what they could to defend Stalingrad and support the Red Army units defending it, continued through the days which followed. Vladimir Lavrinenkov, a pilot with 4 Fighter Regiment, was lucky to survive these terrible battles. He recalled the sky literally swarming with enemy aircraft. It was clear that the Germans intended to wipe the city off the map. "We knew that nearby pilots of neighbouring regiments were in action, but nevertheless saw only enemy aircraft in front of us, and on the ground nothing but fires," Lavrinenkov remembered. He fought in the war from July 1941 until its end and was twice awarded the honour of Hero of the Soviet Union.

Looking up at the sky from the left bank of the Volga, Natasha Yuryina, a driver for an air unit, counted planes as they crashed. "Over the city on the other bank was a continuous haze from the fires, pink and black clouds of dust, an incessant roar. Above literally every one of the crossings there was a swarm of planes. If you did not know that these were two deadly enemies locked in battle, if you had not seen the crimson stars on the wings of our fighters and the swastikas on the Junkers, if it were not for the fountains of water where bombs had dropped, and the direct hits to the right and left of us . . . If it were not for all that, you might have thought the pilots were playing some exhilarating game in the air, hurling their planes skywards, then falling like vultures, chasing each others' tails, pursuing, circling. You could not take your eyes off it, and all the while your heart was pounding with fear for our pilots!"[205]

Stalingrad was ablaze. The oil storage tanks were in flames. Dense black smoke rose high in the sky, creeping southwards along the bank of the river. The shrieking of bombs and the boom of explosions were joined by the wailing of factory sirens and the hooting of ships on the Volga. "There was no respite, neither on the ground nor in the skies."[206]

Even at Stalingrad, the pilots of 296 Fighter Regiment had borshch and meat in the canteen, but they "had no appetite. Our lips were glued together by the heat."[207] Between sorties they wanted only to drink water or eat the watermelons so abundant at that time of year on the east side of the Volga. They were depressed and under constant strain. The regiment's veterans, Salomatin, Martynov, Yeremin, Commander Baranov himself, felt close to disintegration. Young pilots were being killed before they could gain experience. Ever fewer people remained of those they had fought alongside at the beginning of the war in 1941. They had neither the energy nor the desire to talk in their brief moments of rest. In the dugouts in the steppe at the Leninsk airfield, bunks were built and covered with straw and a tarpaulin. They would lie down but could not sleep. There were laconic exchanges. "The engine's burning oil. It isn't flowing properly." "Have you noticed the Messers are attacking in succession again? They're probably training up new pilots." "Hell, I could do with a dip in the river right now." "Go to sleep. We'll be off again soon," a comrade would reply. When the previous shift of pilots returned, Salomatin and his companions would get up without a word, take their map cases and headsets off the nails, and go out for their next mission, which might just possibly be their last.

Sitting next to Alexander Martynov, Boris Yeremin was silent, supposing his comrade must also have been harbouring gloomy thoughts. If he was, Alexander would never have shown it. He turned to Yeremin and asked with evident concern, "Not too chilly in here for you I hope, Boris?" "That is one cheery, indestructible sod," Yeremin thought. They were flying four or five sorties a day, putting their lives on the line every time, and still he could joke. Someone as reassuring as that was worth their weight in gold to the regiment.

One incident from this time lodged in Yeremin's memory. It disturbed him deeply even among the welter of other, no less traumatic events. When the father of one of the young pilots was notified of his son's death, he somehow found his way to Baranov's regiment. Baranov delegated Yeremin to tell him all he could about his son's short time with them, although there could be little to tell about a boy who "lived only a few days in the regiment, eagerly anticipating combat, only to be killed on his first or second sortie".[208]

Yeremin assembled other young pilots who had known the dead youth, and they talked at length to his father. Yeremin thought the man was beginning to "understand the reality of war on the Stalingrad Front, which it was impossible to explain to someone who had not experienced it". Suddenly, however, the man said, "Where is my son's grave? Take me there. I want to spend some time with him." Yeremin was silent, a lump in his throat. The father had understood nothing. What graves did he suppose there were at Stalingrad? The friends of Yeremin or Salomatin who were shot down fell into the Volga or the smouldering ruins of the city. Yeremin tried to change the subject and started talking about companions of his who had died in 1941. It dawned on the father of the dead boy that he had no grave. The man looked down at the ground and clutched his head, crying.[209]

21

"Blazing away in all directions"

Between 23 and 31 August 1942, 8 Air Army lost more than 200 aircraft in defending Stalingrad. By the beginning of September they had only 192 left, including many in need of repair.[210]

In September, Lieutenant General Timofey Khryukin, the commander of 8 Air Army was sleeping only two or three hours a day. He was just thirty-two years old. The Supreme High Command ordered him to attack the Germans using all the means at his disposal, bringing in all available aircraft, but the order could not be fulfilled. He was already using every plane he had and there were no more.

Red Star, Pravda and Stalin's Falcons published articles about the victories of Soviet tanks, artillery and aircraft, as always concealing the gravity of the actual situation. They wrote about the ace pilots making a name for themselves in the Stalingrad fighting.

To the women's fighter regiment it seemed that, a few hundred kilometres away on another stretch of the Volga, male fighter pilots, their peers, were covering themselves in glory, while their women's regiment was not taking part in anything! 586 Fighter Regiment, which consisted of the Soviet Union's best women pilots (with the exception, as they noted bitterly, of Majorette Kazarinova), was still stuck out at Anisovka airfield in the tranquil steppe surrounded by the fragrance of herbs and the singing of the larks.

"In these times of great trial we find ourselves taking a holiday, when our exhausted fraternal regiments could be resting here instead," Lilya wrote to her mother.[211] They were still responsible for the air defence of Saratov, and still nothing was happening. Lilya was becoming inured to being on duty, sitting in a plane waiting for the order to take off, in rain and the heat of the sun, strapped into the cockpit in a sweaty flying suit. Having nothing to do made her all the more homesick for their old life. "Dear Mum," Lilya wrote during one such spell, "I often dream that you and I are going somewhere in a hurry, perhaps to visit friends or to the theatre, and we are so dressed up, so happy, and I see you young and chirpy. I feel so good and don't know why. God grant that it comes true."[212] Although Lilya was a Komsomol member she believed in dreams and fortune telling. "My dreams have always been very accurate," she wrote.

Lilya missed not only her mother and her brother Yury, but also her father whom she had hardly seen after he left his family and who had disappeared without trace in the 1937 purges. She did not even know if he was still alive. "I am on duty today," she wrote in another letter. "I got up at two in the morning and have been at my plane all day. In front of me I see the steppe, the airfield. To my right a train is going to Moscow. Everything feels so sad and lonely. Yury, if you can, send me a photo of Dad."[213]

The mechanics and armourers helped to brighten up the pilots' long hours on duty as they sat waiting for the order to take to the sky. The pilots would invite them to sit on the wing and chat. The squadron leaders disapproved, especially Lilya's commander, Belyaeva, but Lilya did not care. She would beckon Valya Krasnoshchyokova, who was an armourer, over to her plane and they would talk about all the things they had in common: Moscow, where Lilya lived and Valya had been a student; the books they had read before the war; and the theatres they both loved, especially the operetta. "I am the Gypsy Baron and I love a gypsy girl!" they would even sing together.[214] Valya had read much more widely than Lilya, who loved to talk with her about such matters. Valya liked Lilya. She was a good pilot, very pretty, a flirt, but also fun, easy-going, and not stand-offish towards those who were not pilots. "The blue bloods and the plebs" as they said jokingly in Raskova's units.

Katya Budanova behaved differently. She was coarser and much less educated than Lilya. A simple country girl who had gone to work in a factory, she never forgot to make clear her superiority over the mechanics and armourers. Her lively personality redeemed her, however. She had a rough wit, was resourceful in every situation, and so reliable that she could be forgiven her snobbishness. When Valya remembered Katya in later years it struck her that she had no need to bleach her hair, use lipstick or dress in anything special to be noticed. She was just invariably a brighter presence than everyone else.

By 1 September, according to its official historians, the entire 8 Air Army had at its disposal only ninety-seven serviceable fighters, many of which were obsolete and totally unfit for combat with German planes. They included the Il-15, manufactured in the 1930s and so accident-prone it was familiarly known as "the Flying Coffin". Bombers had to fly without fighter escort because all the fighters were attacking German bombers. Khryukin managed to elicit an order requiring all Yak-1s produced by the Saratov Aviation Plant to be transferred within two weeks to 8 Air Army. On 6 September Levin, the factory manager, was phoned by Stalin personally to find out how many aircraft he had, to order him to increase production, and to tell him to send all completed aircraft as a matter of urgency to the Stalingrad Front.[215] It is no surprise, then, that the First Squadron of the women's 586 Fighter Regiment was transferred to the male regiments defending Stalingrad. They had no fewer than eight new aircraft, almost one-tenth of the total number of fighter planes in 8 Air Army. Their official task, under an order signed by General Osipenko, commander of the anti-aircraft division, was to combat German reconnaissance aircraft.

News of the transfer had the eight pilots and their ground support staff jumping for joy. Most people agreed that their commander, Tamara Kazarinova, was only too glad to be rid of half of them. There are suggestions that the transfer of the regiment's First Squadron was at her request in order to prevent, or even quell, mutiny in the regiment.[216] Alexander Gridnev, who subsequently replaced Kazarinova, wrote in his memoirs that she asked Osipenko, with whom she was on friendly terms, to arrange it.[217] Osipenko was regarded as a neurotic tyrant who had no qualms about sending pilots to almost certain death, and would have had no problem satisfying her request.[218]

The order was announced by Raskova, who flew in specially from Engels to Anisovka.[219] She informed the regiment drawn up in front of her that a very grave situation had developed at Stalingrad. The Germans had air superiority and volunteers were needed from the fighter regiment to serve there temporarily. As once before at the Pedagogical Institute when Valya Krasnoshchyokova had decided to go to war they heard the call, "Volunteers take one step forward." Valya stepped forward without hesitation, as did all the other girls. Not all of them were heroically inclined, and certainly among the mechanics there were some who had no great desire to rush into battle, but in the circumstances not to volunteer would have been to lose face in front of your comrades. It could even have been dangerous, as the Special Department's officer would instantly have noted you as a potential deserter. Commissar Olga Kulikova selected the technical personnel to be sent to Stalingrad. As for the pilots, the eight women fighter pilots of First Squadron were divided into two flights and sent to different air regiments: Klava Nechaeva's flight to 434, and Raisa Belyaeva's to 437 Regiment. The pilots were jubilant at the realisation of their dreams at last. The mechanics were pleased too, feeling that their backbreaking toil, which the officers and pilots took for granted, would be a good deal more useful at the front line than in Saratov. "The fighter pilots wanted just one thing: to take part in real combat. Their elation was indescribable."[220] They would fight on equal terms with men and finally be able to make full use of the flying skills they had acquired in peace and wartime. After nearly a year in the Army, "We still imagined war the way we had read about the Civil War in our schoolbooks, whizzing around on a machine-gun carriage blazing away in all directions!" Klava Blinova recalled many years later.[221] And what could be more wonderful than to defend the skies of your Motherland from its sworn enemies at the controls of a Yakovlev fighter. This was an aircraft which was obedient to their will, with which they almost could be said to fuse in combat, and in which they could fight toe to toe with even this most terrible of enemies.

The girls of the Second Squadron under Zhenya Prokhorova were envious, fearing, not without reason, that they might be missing their last chance of taking part in front-line combat. Flight Sergeant Anya Demchenko, a brilliant but reckless pilot, a bully and a garbage mouth who was famous for having thrown her plane into a six-spin manoeuvre at training when the maximum was supposed to be four, even flew to Stalingrad a few days after the departure of the First Squadron without permission. As far as we know, her insubordination went unpunished.

Before their departure, the regiment was assembled for parade and "stood motionless and in solemn silence on the sun-scorched grass. The order was read out. Everyone was conscious that within a couple of minutes First Squadron would be heading out to where the fate of our Motherland was being decided."[222] Of the eight pilots who left that day, five were to die and one would be captured.

As they took off on 10 September for Stalingrad, the First Squadron's pilots had little idea of what was actually happening there, on the ground and in the sky. The newspapers were writing about how magnificently Soviet pilots were fighting in the air above Stalingrad, but gave little idea of the scale of the catastrophe that had struck the city. Although some of the regiment's pilots had flown a sortie near Stalingrad a few days previously, taking their bearings in the steppe at night from the burning city, they had not flown over Stalingrad itself, and those in the regiment had no idea that it had been reduced to smouldering ruins.

Two Tupolev ANT-40 high-speed bombers were sent to collect the mechanics. The planes had not been modified to carry passengers – travelling in comfort would have to wait until after the war.[223] The girls were loaded into the bomb bays and the aircraft took off. It was completely dark inside, and many of the girls began to suffer from airsickness. Valya Krasnoshchyokova and Nina Shebalina held out, but many vomited. The plane suddenly landed at an airfield, after having come under fire. "We landed, the bays were opened and out we fell. Some girls were prostrate, such was the state we were in," Nina Shebalina recalled. They had no time to relax, however. A cursing soldier ran up to tell them the airport had just been bombed and was covered in the lethal frog anti-personnel mines. The enemy was very close and the airfield was also under German artillery bombardment. This was the first time the girls had experienced shelling and bombing and they were scared out of their wits. Mechanics at the airfield rushed over, pushed them into foxholes and covered them with their own bodies, lying with them until everything had quietened down. Nina Shebalina was surprised none of them were killed. "We quickly got up and flew on. Our plane landed at one airfield, and the other at a different one."

After leaving their regiment, Belyaeva's flight landed near Stalingrad and the Volga in the village of Upper Akhtuba. Just as in the case of the mechanics, it was found that while they had been in the air the Germans had moved much closer. Almost the entire airfield had been evacuated and there were no other aircraft there. A mechanic ran up and urged them to fly on immediately, warning that the area was being directly targeted by artillery. No sooner had he warned them than shells began exploding nearby. Belyaeva and her flight were directed now to the same airfield as Klava Nechaeva at Middle Akhtuba, twenty kilometres from Stalingrad but on the opposite, left bank of the Volga.[224]

In this "little clapboard town", as Vasiliy Grossman, who was also there in autumn 1942, described it, people were gathering the harvest in the orchards and digging up the potatoes.[225] Autumn flowers were blooming in front gardens. Stalingrad was quite far away and heard as a rumble in the distance. It was only when, a few days later, the regiment moved up to a forward staging airfield close to the Volga and the city that they heard the cacophony and saw for themselves the catastrophe that had befallen Stalingrad. Burning barges floated down the Volga and they heard the gunfire and explosions. The air was full of fumes from an immense conflagration.

Nina Shebalina remembered how amazed the male pilots of 437 Regiment were when they first caught sight of Belyaeva's flight at their airfield. "They stared at them unable to believe their eyes." Until then they had not only never seen a woman fighter pilot but had not even heard of their existence. One said sadly, "You will all be killed. You are all still so young." Another said with a sneer, "You are not in Alma-Ata now, you know."[226] The capital of Kazakhstan was pictured during the war as a paradise far from the fighting, full of fruit and sunlight and nestling among the mountains. The girls tried to look confident, although they now realised they would soon be in the thick of the fighting, and it would be difficult for any of them to hide their fear and exhaustion. "Everyone had been so pleased to be flying to the front, but having arrived it was fairly terrifying," Nina Shebalina recalled.

Unlike his pilots, the discreet Maxim Khvostikov, commander of 437 Regiment, refrained from publicly expressing puzzlement at being sent women as reinforcements. The regiment, which he had formed personally, had been fighting at the Stalingrad Front from 19 August, and by mid-September had lost most of its aircraft and pilots. The regimental archive indicates that from the beginning of fighting on 11 September ten or eleven aircraft had been lost and very few of the regiment's pilots had survived.[227]

Khvostikov, a professional military airman since the early 1930s, still had a number of experienced pilots, such as Yevgeny Dranishchev, in his regiment but the new male pilots he was sent had far fewer flying hours than those in the women's flight.[228] There was no question but that the girls would take part in the fighting from the moment they arrived. Khvostikov had no option.

The situation in 434 Regiment, to which Klava Nechaeva's flight had been transferred, was somewhat different. The regiment had been in the region only since the beginning of September and, although it had lost a number of aircraft, it was not short of pilots. Accordingly the commander, the already much decorated 22-year-old Major Ivan Kleshchev, had no wish to send girls into battle. He openly expressed his attitude to the new reinforcements: "It pains me and makes me ashamed to see women in war. It is as if we men cannot protect you from this unwomanly work. Besides, you'll keep crying." Klava Blinova replied cheerfully, "Well, if we do cry, please just ignore it."[229]

Unlike his female reinforcements, Major Kleshchev, commander of 434 Regiment, although not yet twenty-three had first-hand experience of war. He had been in dogfights when flying with the best pilots of the Soviet Air Force during the 1938–9 border conflict with Japan, and had been at the front in this war for the best part of a year. The Air Force was the pre-eminent armed service, and within it he was one of an elite of young but already battle-hardened and decorated commanders. He had shot down sixteen enemy aircraft on his own account, and another twenty-four jointly with other pilots.[230] He had recently received the Soviet Union's highest award, the Gold Star, a distinction awarded only to those who were already Heroes of the Soviet Union. He lost his star on 19 September when he bailed out of a burning plane during a dogfight and, after being discharged from hospital, was given a replacement in the Kremlin.

It may seem surprising today that one of the most beautiful women in the U.S.S.R. could lose her head over a simple lad from a peasant family, even one with the Gold Star on his chest. In those years, however, the celebrity and social status of a pilot was comparable to that of today's top footballers. When, on 3 September 1942, 434 Regiment left for the front from Lyubertsy, the town outside Moscow where it was based, youthful Commander Ivan Kleshchev was seen on his way by Zoya Fyodorova, a famous film star. She often reminisced in later years about the young pilot she had loved, and who died tragically so soon afterwards.[231]

Stalin's elder son, Yakov Dzhugashvili, was a gunner, but his younger son Vasiliy, a weedy, difficult boy, would settle for nothing less than a career as a pilot. In the 1930s there was no more popular profession in the U.S.S.R.

Colonel Vasiliy Stalin was the same age as many of this book's heroes: in 1942 he was twenty-one. Unsurprisingly for someone with that name, he enjoyed a meteoric rise in his career in the Air Force Inspectorate. His companions recall that, although he had his father's face and small stature, his personality was completely unlike that of Stalin.[232] He was cocky and pushy, and most of those who knew him describe him as a weak, tetchy individual. For all that, he was also generous in material and emotional terms and, unlike his father, neither devious nor vindictive. "Vasiliy would give you the shirt off his back," they said of him. He responded if asked for help. Vasiliy Stalin saved many pilots from the purges instituted by his father.

His behaviour was famously unsubtle. He had a sense of humour, as did Stalin, had no complexes or inhibitions, and did exactly as he pleased even when a cadet at the Kacha Aviation Academy. Speeding round hairpin bends on a road in the Crimea with the academy's chief of staff, he ended up in the ditch. The incident came to the attention of his father, who punished the rector of the academy for having allowed his son so much leeway. His fellow students also remembered that, receiving a handwritten letter from his father, he was apt to open it in the smoking room and comment on it aloud, approvingly or otherwise. He did nevertheless become a highly professional pilot.

Arriving at the Air Force Inspectorate in 1941 with the rank of captain, Vasiliy Stalin had by 1942 risen to the rank of colonel and was in overall command of the institution. When the Air Force high command decided to form a number of fighter regiments which would bring together the U.S.S.R.'s most outstanding pilots, to be deployed on the most critical stretches of the front and ensure Soviet air superiority, Vasiliy took personal charge of one. An ace who had known him as a fellow student at the academy recalled, "Colonel Stalin was capable of taking decisions quickly and getting them implemented quickly." He had no need to co-ordinate every last detail with numerous different offices. For some reason, 434 Fighter Regiment caught his eye. After the battles for Leningrad it was very short of planes and pilots and Colonel Stalin undertook to make it an exemplary unit, highly mobile and effective.

Unlike most fighter regiments, in which between one third and one-half of the pilots were young and inexperienced, 434 Regiment's pilots were almost all combat veterans. Two exceptions were the sons of People's Commissar of the Food Industry Anastas Mikoyan, who was also a member of the State Defence Committee. Stepan and Vladimir Mikoyan had just graduated from military college but Vasiliy Stalin knew them well and decided to take them into his regiment and under his protection. The other exceptions were the four young girls of Klava Nechaeva's flight.

The re-formed fighter regiment was greatly needed by 8 Air Army, especially in September 1942. The Soviet air forces in the skies were under ever greater pressure at a time when they were desperately short of both pilots and machines. More and more fresh troops were arriving in the city and having to cross from the left bank of the Volga under fire. Sub-jected to constant bombing, barges that were not sunk brought back the wounded. On the ground, the eyes of thousands of Red Army soldiers in trenches were searching the sky for "our hawks", their only hope of deliverance.

Kotluban Station changed hands repeatedly. It was provided with air cover by 434 Regiment, flying from the airfield in Middle Akhtuba. This small town in which Klava Nechaeva spent her last days, went down in history as the place where General Rodimtsev awaited ammunition and weapons before his historic crossing of the Volga to defend Stalingrad on 14 September. Girls from Nechaeva's flight and their support staff, billeted in the homes of local people, were getting accustomed to living among men. Klava, who was twenty-six, often borrowed a basin from a neighbour to wash her clothes. The woman later recalled her as "a very sweet, modest girl".[233] The male pilots of 434 Regiment remembered her as the prettiest of the four women who joined them.

The young pilots who had not yet been under fire or lost friends in battle were greatly excited by the appearance among them of the girls and their flock of support staff. They too had heard nothing of women's regiments. Stepan Mikoyan recalled that everyone was "very interested to find out more about these women pilots".[234] It seems not to have worried them that this might be no place for girls, who might get killed, as indeed they did not think about the possibility that they themselves might die. With the arrival of the girls, the men started shaving more regularly and swearing less.[235] Major Kleshchev need not have been so concerned that the presence of girl pilots would distract his men from their military duties. Their effect was to make the men more focused and serious.

Of the four pilots, Klava Nechaeva was best remembered in the regiment, both because she was pretty and because she was the first to be killed. She wore a forage cap, from which a lock of curly fair hair always escaped to fall over her forehead. Within a few days of her arrival two men had already fallen in love with her, eighteen-year-old Vladimir Mikoyan, youngest son of the People's Commissar for Foreign Trade, and Major Kleshchev himself. Hearing that she did not have a map case, he gave her his.[236]

The weather was fine, and every day large formations of German bombers were flying in with fighter escorts to bomb Kotluban Station and the Soviet troops near it. On 16 September the women waited in vain for permission from Kleshchev to fly a mission. Male pilots were flying their aircraft, coming back in the evening after six sorties with strained, bloodshot eyes, and faces "black with fatigue". The regiment's most popular guitar player and songster, Nikolai Parfyonov, a favourite of the women's flight, had not returned from battle.

On their return from the Stalingrad Front in mid-September 1942,

General Zhukov, Deputy Supreme Commander-in-Chief, Georgiy Malenkov, Secretary of the Central Committee of the Communist Party of the Soviet Union, and Alexander Novikov, Commander of the Soviet Air Force, sent Stalin the following outraged memorandum about the conduct of Soviet fighter pilots at the Stalingrad Front.

> Over the last six or seven days we have observed our fighter aircraft in action. On the basis of much evidence we have concluded that our fighter aircraft are performing poorly. Our fighters, even when they outnumber the enemy's fighters several times over, do not engage them in combat. When our fighters are supposedly providing cover for assault aircraft they also fail to engage with enemy fighters and the latter attack the assault aircraft with impunity and shoot them down while our fighters keep their distance or often simply return to their airfields.
>
> What we are reporting are, unfortunately, not isolated incidents. Our troops observe such shameful conduct by fighter aircraft daily. We have personally observed at least ten such incidents and did not observe a single case of good conduct by fighter aircraft.[237]

Even the elite 434 Regiment was no exception. When German planes approached, the pilots would timorously adopt the defensive circle formation. One day in early September, Stepan Mikoyan was on a sortie when he heard a woman's voice from a ground observation post screaming in their headphones, "Messers overhead! Messers!" The pilots had themselves seen German fighters approaching above them and banked into their circle formation. This was a purely defensive grouping and useless for attacking the enemy. The Yaks circled several times, and Mikoyan saw a Soviet aircraft in front. Looking back, he was relieved to see he was being followed by another plane with its nose painted red. Suddenly, a plane with yellow stripes on its wings came at him at an angle of thirty degrees. A Messerschmitt Bf 109! He was under attack.

One Yak flew higher and began vigorously dipping its wings. The regiment's commander was summoning his pilots to stop circling and go into the attack. Stepan recalled how, when they returned to the airfield, they could not look each other in the eye. Passive circling was not the behaviour expected of battle-seasoned pilots.

Seeing even his experienced pilots opting out of engaging Messerschmitts, the commander was in no hurry to let girls loose in the skies. Soon after their arrival, he decided to check their flying skills and conducted a series of practice dogfights. Wing Commander Klava Nechaeva was first up. Initially she almost managed to get on Kleshchev's tail, but he banked steeply and was soon on hers. "After that everything happened at lightning speed," Klava Blinova recalled. "Nechaeva's plane started rolling first one wing then the other, as if trying to make up its mind, but then went into a spin." As a highly experienced pilot herself, Blinova knew it was not too difficult to pull out of such a spin, providing, of course, you had sufficient height. But what if you had not?[238] Stepan Mikoyan recalls all the pilots, terrified because there was already very little height, shouting, "Pull out! Pull out!" as if she could hear them. She did manage to pull out, and the whole airfield, which had been following the duel, heaved a sigh of relief.[239]

The opinion of the male pilots of 434 Regiment was that "the women pilots were quite well trained in the techniques of manoeuvring their fighters, taking off and landing, but there were serious concerns about their readiness for combat." It was clear that "they did not have the understanding of tactics needed to be effective in a dogfight, or use their weapons effectively."[240] They had not received that training in Engels, so would need to be taught it again and again in this front-line regiment. Semyonov could not imagine how they could be sent to fight in the perilous skies around Stalingrad. "It simply did not seem fair to send them into battle." Kleshchev did not rush things. He gave the girls experienced pilots to lead them, but even so did not manage to keep all of them out of harm's way.

*

In 437 Regiment too, despite a shortage of pilots, particularly with extensive experience, Commander Maxim Khvostikov was in no hurry to use the women pilots of Raisa Belyaeva's flight. Belyaeva was furious. There was an element of naive chauvinism in this. Khvostikov explained, "You might get shot down and then the Germans will say we have run out of pilots and are reduced to letting women fly!" Nobody actually said they were not wanted, but every time the assertive Belyaeva went to demand they should be put to use she would be told the commanders did not want to place her at risk because she was such a beautiful woman. When they were allowed to fly, they were most often paired with another female crew. Male pilots were reluctant to lead them, even though they knew of Belyaeva and Budanova from the Tushino Air Shows. Air shows were one thing, aerial combat quite another.

In 434 Regiment, Kleshchev did eventually allow Klava Nechaeva and Klava Blinova to fly, entrusting them to the leadership of Izbinsky and Kotov, who were flight commanders.[241] The group approached the front line, their mission unchanged: to protect the ground troops from enemy bombing. They were to attack fighters escorting the German bombers. Shortly after they took off, the observation centre reported Junkers heading towards Kotluban from the north. As soon as they appeared, Izbinsky led his group into the attack, and immediately he and another pilot, Karnachyonok, each shot down one enemy plane. What followed seemed to Klava Blinova to happen in a dream. From the direction of the sun, they were suddenly set upon by Messerschmitts. "I kept looking round in the cockpit. Crosses, crosses! Which should I get in my sights? Which was my target? Where was my leader?" Remembering that you must not hesitate, that you must strike while the iron is hot, Blinova moved to full throttle and attacked. "Some fascist or other" was already firing at her "with all he'd got" and it might have ended badly had Sasha Kotov not come to the rescue. Klava Nechaeva was less fortunate. Stepan Mikoyan considered Izbinsky a far from ideal leader. "Izbinsky was a great fighter and an excellent pilot, but a bit wild."[242] He had a conviction for fighting and was serving his time at the front. "He was a heavy drinker, of course, but he fought well." The trouble was that in battle Izbinsky "took almost no account when manoeuvring of the pilot he was supposed to be leading, which made it difficult for his wingmate to keep up with him." Baklan recalled that one of the Messerschmitts attacked Klava Nechaeva's plane at close range. The plane caught fire and shortly afterwards crashed to the ground.[243]

When Major Kleshchev's map case was found along with the charred remains of the pilot in the wreckage, a message was sent to battalion head-quarters that "Major Kleshchev has been killed." [244] Kleshchev was there at a meeting and, when this was reported to him, immediately guessed the truth. Eighteen-year-old Vladimir Mikoyan, in love with Klava, outlived her by just one day. Izbinsky had been piloting his lead aircraft too.[245] The whole regiment turned out for Klava Nechaeva's funeral. She was buried in a mass grave that is still preserved in Central Akhtuba. The men had a sombre, guilty look on their faces. "They gave her last military honours with a rifle volley," Klava Blinova remembered. "Now though, years later when I close my eyes and try to imagine Klava Nechaeva dead I cannot. I see a pretty girl striding over the airfield, her blonde hair piled dashingly to one side, and the whole world seems to be reflected in her shining eyes: the Volga with its enchanted meadows above the river; the sky brimming with sunlight; the land wide open in all directions, boundless, infinite; and Klava, so alive."[246] A volley, a closed wooden coffin containing charred remains, a mass grave with a sign written in indelible ink.

Much evidence survives of how concerned Soviet girls in the armed forces were about how they would be buried if fate decreed they were to die. This was true of combatants, nurses, telephone operators, and even the clerks at headquarters. "I know I am dying. In the medical bag you will find a cotton dress with polka dots and short frilly sleeves. Bury me in that," Masha, a nurse severely injured on the Stalingrad Front, told soldiers whose battle wounds she had been bandaging only the day before.[247]

We see from the letter of another girl, written to the mother of a friend who had been killed, that funeral arrangements featured in their conversations. "The area where we were fighting was marshy and muddy. Sometimes I would be sitting talking with the other girls about how we wanted to be buried. Lida and I wanted to be buried with flowers and with our faces washed clean. I carried out her wishes, but who will do the same for me?"

"Of course, it seems odd to be thinking about death, but you cannot ignore reality," was the attitude of these young girls, none of whom believed they would die, but who saw many people around them dying. If their own lives were to end, they wanted to look their best on their final journey.

Girls who were pilots had no such conversations, nor did they prepare dresses for their last public appearance. They were well aware that few pilots would get the chance to be buried in accordance with the rites of the Russian Orthodox Church: mutilated, charred remains could not lie in the open coffin traditional at a Russian funeral. Often enough, there was not even a coffin. "Dead pilots were usually buried in their parachutes, when there was anything to bury." [248]

Klava Blinova, Olga Shakhova, and Tonya Lebedeva were given almost no opportunity to fly before the regiment was disbanded shortly after the deaths of Klava Nechaeva and Vladimir Mikoyan. Its archive contains evidence of only two combat missions flown by the girls. [249] In two weeks of fighting, it lost sixteen aircrew and twenty-five aircraft. Ivan Kleshchev was shot down on 19 September but bailed out of the burning plane with a parachute and survived, only to die a few months later just before the New Year. His plane crashed in obscure circumstances near the village of Rasskazovo. Someone said there had been a mechanical failure, but another view was that the impetuous Kleshchev had been flying in dangerous weather conditions. Behind his bullet-proof seat in the cockpit were two geese he was taking to Zoya Fyodorova in Moscow, with whom he was planning to celebrate the New Year of 1943. [250]

Klava Blinova, Tonya Lebedeva and Olga Shakhova went back to Moscow with 434 Regiment when it was re-formed. They were eager to get into a combat regiment but nobody wanted them. Vasiliy Stalin did his best to help, inviting them to undergo 100 training dogfights, after which they could be enlisted in a front-line fighter regiment. They were delighted and started the training, but Air Marshal Novikov inopportunely arrived at the airfield, noticed them, and ordered them to return to a women's regiment.[251] Only Olga Shakhova did. Tonya and Klava heard from male pilots that 653 Regiment was flying to the Kalinin Front and was short of two pilots. They were later officially accepted, together with their aircraft, to fill these vacancies, but initially they just ran off without any authorisation.

22

"You darling, you've shot down a Heinkel!"

Back in Saratov, their own women's 586 Air Defence Fighter Regiment, from which they were all so eager to escape, suddenly gained nationwide renown. It owed this to Lera Khomyakova, a friend of Belyaeva's since their days in the Central Flying Club, when both of them had for many years participated in the Tushino Air Show. During a night sortie Lera shot down a German bomber that was targeting Saratov.

On 23 September 1942, Khomyakova's mechanic, Katya Polunina, turned twenty-one. Her friends wished her a happy birthday but did not otherwise celebrate because the situation was just too grim. "It is as if I can see the map right now before my eyes. The little red flags marking the front line passed three times through Stalingrad to the Volga," Polunina recalled.[252] They did not know that on 22 September the Germans had broken through to the central crossing, making it virtually impossible to bring in reinforcements and supplies, or that a large part of the city was already in enemy hands. Even so they, like the rest of the country, saw the likelihood that Stalingrad would fall and the war cross the Volga as potentially a disaster. Polunina did nevertheless receive a splendid birthday present from her pilot.

Early on 24 September Zhenya Prokhorova, commander of the Second

Squadron, took off with her wingmate, Lera Khomyakova, on an emergency mission: air observation posts had reported a formation of enemy bombers approaching the Volga crossing. A searchlight picked out a Junkers Ju 88, its gunner began shooting at the Soviet fighters, but it was immediately shot down.[253]

At first it was unclear whether this kill belonged to Zhenya or Lera, but Zhenya landed first, climbed out of the plane in tears, and yelled at her armourer that her weapons had jammed. When Lera Khomyakova landed, she reported she had made two runs at the Junkers and her machine guns and cannon had fired faultlessly.

The Ju 88 she had brought down at night was the first German bomber to be destroyed near Saratov, the first to be shot down by their regiment, and she had become the first woman to shoot down a bomber in a night battle. Only a few of the pilots had received any kind of training in flying night fighters after arriving in Engels.

Lera was told by observers that she must have killed the pilot with her first burst of gunfire. The German plane had gone into a dive, but Lera had continued firing. As the Junkers was on the outward leg of its mission, it was blown up by its own payload of bombs when it crashed into the ground. Lera excitedly described the battle in a detailed letter to her family on 26 September: "He fired at me twice but missed. I was alive and uninjured, but do you know, my dears, I did not at first think I had shot him down. Once I hit him, his plane did not catch fire but banked right and then went into a very steep dive. I fired a few more bursts at him but then it was time to pull out of the dive. 'There,' I thought, 'I shot from too far away and did not see it through. I levelled out too early. He has got away.' Lera's friends in the regiment congratulated her more demonstratively than male pilots probably would. "I landed and my mechanic Polunina ran up and kissed me. She said, 'You darling, you've just shot down a Heinkel!'" Immediately all the others ran up to kiss her.[254]

Lera herself only really believed it when she flew with the regiment's commander to the site where the German bomber had crashed. She could not forget the sight for a long time afterwards. The dead crew members were scattered around in different positions next to their parachutes, which had failed to open. They had bailed out, but not had sufficient height. "The aircraft, such a huge hulk, was scattered in pieces and there were several unexploded bombs." They took the German parachutes, of course, which were highly prized because the silk could be used in different ways.

Lera's superiors were delighted. In the section of the canteen reserved for the upper ranks, tables were laid and glasses filled with vodka.[255] Lera, who often complained about not getting enough to eat, told her family what a great breakfast and watermelon she had. Right there, as she breakfasted, she was handed 2,000 rubles for her kill ("On the orders of Comrade Stalin"). That was a great help for her family. Reporters came flocking, including the poet Yevgeny Dolmatovsky. Institutions in Saratov and Engels sent her congratulatory telegrams and she was promoted. On 5 October she wrote to her family about her trip to Moscow, where she had been awarded the Military Order of the Red Banner by Mikhail Kalinin.

Mechanic Yelena Karakorskaya was also in Moscow on regimental business. She recalls bumping into Lera in the street. Lera "was so happy. She had been presented with her medal by Kalinin." "I've got some great photos," she said. "When we get back to the regiment I'll show you."[256] Karakorskaya returned to the regiment on 5 October and Lera got back the same evening. They did not get a chance to talk because Lera had immediately to stand in on night watch for another pilot who had a headache. Mechanic Klavdia Volkova recalled that, going on duty that evening, Lera complained of being terribly tired and said she really hated having to go out and sit on the alert. She forgot a glove, went back for it, and then went to the plane, started the engine and taxied to the runway.

That night Karakorskaya had a nightmare, which she felt afterwards was an omen. Irrespective of whether or not they were rational members of the Komsomol, all these young women believed in fate's terrible power. "Lera and I were standing on Gorky Street dressed in black opera cloaks trimmed with silver fox fur. The image immediately changed to one of mourning. Lera was dead and I was covering her with a greatcoat." When she woke in the morning, Karakorskaya heard that Lera Khomyakova had not returned from her night mission.

There had been no air raids since 14 September. All was quiet and the crews slept on hay while waiting for an alarm. It was not only to Karakorskaya that Lera failed to talk in detail about her trip to Moscow. She fell asleep in mid-sentence trying to tell her other friends. When the air-raid alert came she took off together with Tamara Pamyatnykh. There was no sign of the enemy in the air and Pamyatnykh soon returned to base. Lera did not. Tamara Pamyatnykh recalled they turned on the searchlights to illuminate the runway and went out looking for her in a car but found nothing.[257] It turned out they needed to look little further than the start. "In the morning a telephonist coiling up wire called out, "Girls, here is your pilot!"[258] They found the wreckage of her plane and Lera Khomyakova nearby, lying dead on the other side of the road among the sunflowers. "I ran there and saw everything," a traumatised Katya Polunina recalled.

According to the official air division account of 9 October 1942, Senior Lieutenant Khomyakova lost her sense of direction at take-off due to a lack of landmarks at night and banked right.[259] Continuing to bank, she veered 270 degrees and lost control of the aircraft, crashing into the ground.

"You don't need to worry about me, Mum," Lera had written home in December 1941. "I fly carefully and the high-speed fighter is a reliable plane." Her mother would often take out and, until the end of her days, re-read this letter, along with forty-nine others Lera had sent her. Lera's friend and commanding officer, Zhenya Prokhorova, who shared a dugout with her, wrote to her family that she was buried at 1600 hours on 7 October with full military honours.

As was usual in the Soviet Union, someone had to be punished for the death of a combatant who had so recently become a celebrity, even if it was not really anybody's fault. The scapegoats in this instance were Kazarinova, who was stripped of her position as commander of the regiment, and the regiment's commissar, Kulikova.

★

Tamara Kazarinova's removal from the post of commander of 586 Regiment ended its time as the only women's fighter regiment in the Soviet Union, and probably in world history. Zhenya Prokhorova's lack of Communist credentials ruled her out and no other suitable female military pilot could be found to replace Kazarinova. Instead the replacement was Major Alexander Gridnev, a good pilot and a good man. When asked how long he would be staying with the regiment, he replied, "For ever." [261] He identified the future of the regiment and its members with his own future, but saw no reason to keep it exclusively female. To Gridnev, what mattered was the combat readiness of the unit entrusted to him.

He set to work, tightening discipline and improving their training. Within a short time he reported that the regiment was ready to undertake duties in the air defence of Voronezh. Vacancies in the regiment were filled by women pilots retrained to fly fighters, but also by men. 586 Fighter Wing became an exemplary combat unit, but 586 Women's Fighter Regiment ceased to exist.

23

"Here goes!"

Lilya Litvyak's first battle in 437 Regiment, on 27 September 1942, went down in the annals of 8 Air Army. She and Belyaeva (in some accounts, Katya Budanova) were included in a mission led by Colonel Danilov, commander of 287 Air Division. According to the official history of 8 Air Army, [262] "The squadron engaged two five-aircraft groups of Junkers Ju 88 bombers" which were on their way to bomb the Stalingrad Tractor Factory. Regimental Commander Khvostikov, paired with Litvyak, attacked the Junkers but was shot down by the gunner of one of the bombers. Litvyak put paid to the bomber, shooting it from a distance of just thirty metres. This technique of firing at close range was one she would come to favour in her future battles. After that, as the authors of *Eighth Air* tell us, Litvyak joined up with Belyaeva and together they engaged enemy fighters approaching to assist the bombers.[263] Working as a team they shot down a Messerschmitt, and credited this as a shared kill. This victory is even mentioned in the memoirs of Andrey Yeryomenko, commander of the entire Stalingrad Front, although he mistakenly names the pilot Nina Belyaeva and omits any mention of Litvyak. Lilya, however, on her third sortie a day or two later, got into another dogfight. It was sensational, had everyone talking about her, and was the beginning of all the myths that were to spring up around her name within less than a year.

Most of the Russian sources state that this dogfight took place earlier, on 13 September. We cannot know for sure because, as the girls were not officially members of 437 Regiment, there is no information about their aerial combat in the regiment's documents. Neither is there anything in the archive of 586 Women's Fighter Regiment because they had been temporarily released. No letters by Lilya have survived describing her triumph, so we can only reconstruct her victory on the basis of the memoirs of mechanics, a couple of lines by a war correspondent, and rumours which circulated in 8 Air Army, of which there were plenty. By word of mouth the legend snowballed, accumulating details.

It was said that Litvyak was being allowed to fly a plane in after repairs and was circling the airfield.[264] German fighters appeared but at first Lilya did not notice them. Khvostikov, the regimental commander, supposedly clutched his head in horror, exclaiming, "They'll eat that girlie for breakfast!" Then, however, Litvyak finally saw the German planes, opened fire, and not only was not shot down herself but brought down a Messerschmitt before landing safely. We can tell this is at least partly fiction, because a plane being flown in after repairs would not be armed. In a short report that appeared six months later, Litvyak informed a reporter that the plane shot down was a bomber, not a fighter. After all this time, there is no telling. Whatever the truth, the regiment's pilots put down the pretty blonde's kill to an improbable stroke of luck. They would soon know better.

The German pilot bailed out and, as the fight had taken place above the airfield or immediately adjacent to it, was taken to the headquarters of the air division. His chest was covered in medals, it was clear he was not just any bomber pilot. At this period Soviet fighters had few victories to boast of, let alone one so spectacular, with a highly decorated German pilot caught alive. The authorities decided to interrogate him and, as they liked to, to introduce him personally to the Soviet pilot who had brought him down. They summoned Anya Skorobogatova, the radio operator who had been in contact with the Soviet pilot, and she confirmed it was Litvyak. When the German pilot was told he had been shot down by a girl of twenty he could not believe it. With great satisfaction they sent for Litvyak. It was the first time Anya had met Lilya face to face. Before she had only heard her voice over the radio.[265]

Her recent redeployment as a radio operator to 8 Air Army had delighted Anya Skorobogatova. Working with ground units near Stalingrad had been very frightening, and she had in any case long wanted to serve with an air unit, even if only as a radio operator. Her task now was to communicate with pilots out on combat missions, at least, with those whose planes were equipped with radio. This included all the foreign aircraft being used by the Soviet Air Force, for example, the Bell P-39 Airacobra, but only half the Soviet-manufactured aircraft. Anya was acutely conscious of the importance of the tenuous human relationship linking her to the boys in the skies of Stalingrad that, in the case of those shot down almost immediately, might last only a day or two. For the young men in these perilous skies, the voice of the girl at the other end of their radio link was all that connected them with the ground and normality. When Anya was instructed to come up with a call-sign to identify herself to the pilots, most of whom never saw her face, she chose "Forget-me-not", the name of a flower as blue as her eyes, cheerful and rooted in the soil, which would remind them, in the hell of Stalingrad and in what might be their last flight, of the ground, girls, and summer meadows.

In recent days, in addition to men's voices she had been hearing those of women on the airwaves. Lilya's voice was high, like Anya's, in contrast to that of Katya Budanova, which was much lower. Anya had no recollection of the voices of Kuznetsova and Belyaeva, possibly because she never

189

heard them while on duty. When flying, Litvyak said very little, probably as a precaution, Anya thought. The Germans were also listening in to Soviet radio communications. Call signs were changed, but Anya remembered Litvyak's was often "Seagull" plus the number of the aircraft she was flying. On the day Lilya shot down the Messerschmitt her call sign was Seagull-15, When they met, Anya discovered that Seagull was a very pretty, short girl with wavy blonde hair, a marvellous figure, and a uniform that fitted her slender waist perfectly. Lilya had evidently tailored it.

Some of the senior officers assembled to interrogate the pilot asked her to describe the dogfight. Soviet "historians" later concocted a story that Lilya described the battle in German, which she supposedly "knew to perfection". In fact she adopted the language of gestures that pilots invariably use when describing such incidents to each other. There is little need for words. Forty, fifty or sixty years later Anya Skorobogatova observed at 8 Air Army reunions that the pilots used gestures far more than words as they recalled past dogfights.[266] Lilya's hands moved, her eyes darted here and there, her face lit up. She described how she had climbed steeply and then attacked from above. This was the moment Anya Skorobogatova heard her say, "Here goes!" An expression she was to hear from Lilya Litvyak several times in the months ahead.

The German pilot was persuaded. Everything had been exactly as this girl described it. As to what happened next, Skorobogatova's memoirs agree with Soviet sources: the German pilot took off his wristwatch and tried to present it to Litvyak but she refused his gift. The Soviet histories also claim he tried to gallantly kiss her hand, but people from her regiment thought this was pure invention.[267]

These first victories inspired the whole flight, but they continued to fly infrequently. "Our planes were taken off us by the men." [268] Four Three Seven Regiment flew Lavochkin La-5 aircraft, which had little in common with the Yak. They did, however, have a number of pilots who could fly a Yak, and it was mainly those who flew the girls' new planes, rarely giving them a chance to take to the sky. They threw the posies of wild flowers she had picked in quiet moments out of the cockpit of Lilya's Yak. She had written to ask her mother to send a postcard with a picture of roses, which she intended to attach to the side of the dashboard.[269]

Faina Pleshivtseva had been intrigued by Lilya Litvyak since the episode with the white fur collar in Engels. Now when they were near Stalingrad she found herself servicing Lilya's Yak, among others. She came to be on closer terms with her, even though their statuses were so different. Pleshivtseva loved flying. She had graduated from a flying club and, although she had few flying hours, had hoped like many others in Raskova's regiments to become a pilot or at least a navigator. Before the beginning of the war, however, she had completed three years at an aviation institute. And since there was a great shortage of mechanics, that was how she found herself employed. Lilya, knowing nothing of the workings of a fighter engine, enjoyed an officer's rations, wore an elegant uniform, and was destined to cover herself in glory. Faina's lot was constantly greasy overalls, hard manual labour which many men could not have coped with, fingers freezing to metal, short naps often snatched at the airfield under an aircraft cover, and no medals. The controversy over rations continued, even in the vicinity of Stalingrad. The pilots remembered almost no shortage of food there. There was butter in their officers' canteens and, as a rule, a piece of cheese to put on their bread. Aircraft mechanics had junior officer status and were considerably less well catered for. More often than not they were served semolina or millet porridge ("blondie") or pearl barley (known as "shrapnel"). In the end they could not bear the sight of porridge. It was barely satisfying, and they used bread to help stave off the pangs of hunger. "You would have a piece of bread and chew it out by the plane while you were working. That stopped you feeling so hungry."[270] Even so, they were much better off than the private soldiers working at the airfields who were alternately served watery soup and porridge, and never as much of either as they wanted.

24

"My sweet, winged Yak is a good machine"

In late September 1942, desperately worried about her mother, Katya Budanova wrote to her favourite younger sister: "If you hear that mother is alive, let me know just as soon as you can, but don't tell me if she is not. Just let me go on thinking it is either or." Then, very laconically, she adds, "Olga, the situation here is extremely tense. If anything should happen, do not tell Valya [her elder sister] immediately. You yourself will be informed at once, as long as you give your permanent address. Love and kisses, my dear, sweet, lovely, unforgettable Olga. Be steadfast and honourable at your post. Do not forget me. Katya."[271] This letter, like Katya's other letters, is faultless, even though she was educated only in a village school. When you read it, you have the feeling it has been written in order to prepare Katya's sisters, who might already have lost their mother, for the fact that they might be about to lose Katya too. Nearly every day her 437 Fighter Regiment was losing pilots and aircraft in relentless fighting. In early October, however, everything changed for them.

Because 437 Regiment was flying the La-5 fighter, they were unable to service Yaks brought by the girls. They did not have the spare parts, and the mechanics had only a hazy understanding of their construction. At the first opportunity the girls were transferred to 9 Guards Regiment, which was being retrained to fly the Yak-1. Why were they not simply returned to the women's regiment? The likelihood is that its commander, Tamara Kazarinova, did not insist on their return, but there was also another consideration. The pilots of 9 Regiment were waiting for new Yaks, and this transfer enabled them to begin training and keeping watch using the planes the girls brought with them. Although the regiment had been relieved of combat duties while it was being retrained, it was nevertheless required to provide cover for Elton railway station, which was a frequent target of German bombers. By now, this branch line was the only rail link with Stalingrad. Four airwomen already fully trained to fly the Yak could

17. Anya Skorobogatova.
"Forget-me-not" radio operator.

18. Pilot Klava Nechaeva.

19. Komsomol organiser Lena Lukina.

20. Zhenya Rudneva.

21. *Above:* Masha Dolina.

22. *Opposite top:* Sergey Yesenin.

23. *Opposite bottom:* Konstantin Simonov.

24. Corporal Alexandra Vinogradova –
I will grow my hair back
after the war.

25. Olga Golubeva.

26. Yevdokia Rachkevich and Yevdokia Bershanskaya.

27. Lilya with mechanic Semyon Nizin, Stalingrad.

28. Mechanics on a Yak, Stalingrad. Nina Shebalina is in the middle.

29. Female anti-aircraft soldiers.

30. Lilya Litvyak, Katya Budanova and Masha Kuznetsova.
Stalingrad, autumn 1942.

31. Mechanic Nina Shebalina.

32. Lilya and mechanics standing beside her Yak, Stalingrad.
Valya Krasnoshchyokova is fourth from the left.

33. *Left:* Stalingrad.

34. *Below:* Vasily Stalin

35. *Opposite:* Galya Dzhunkovskaya
Masha Dolina and Vanya Solyonov
by their Pe-2.

36. Lera Khomyakova with Tamara Kazarinova and a female commissar,
being congratulated on shooting down the German bomber.

be on duty immediately, without the need to wait for the regiment's male pilots to be trained up. It had already been decided to turn 9 Fighter Regiment into an elite unit by allocating it the most talented pilots, so it is not improbable that somebody at headquarters decided it was the obvious home for a flight of the best Soviet female sports pilots. The commander of 9 Regiment demurred. The task his regiment had to undertake was just too dangerous and he did not think it proper to put women at risk. He did, however, agree to take the girls on for a period of training. Although the 27-year-old Major Shestakov had never, unlike Belyaeva and Budanova, taken part in an air show he had become one of the top Soviet fighter aces in aerial combat.

Lev Shestakov, a "stocky commander" with protruding ears and the small features of a typical Slavic face, was "very dynamic" and very young.[272] His colleagues nevertheless respectfully addressed him by his name and patronymic as "Lev Lvovich". Commissar Dmitry Panov, an old acquaintance, was pleased to meet up again with him at the Stalingrad Front. He felt that this "short, grey-eyed, brown-haired strongman" with his authoritative, impulsive personality, was one of the best fighter regiment commanders in the Soviet Air Force and very much needed there.

In action, the young major was intrepid, displaying a combination of initiative and cold calculation. Immediately after interrogating a downed German pilot, he could organise a brilliant raid on a German airfield. Leading a group of fighters, he would seize the initiative in a dogfight, despite flying obsolete aircraft against superior odds. Early in the war Shestakov elaborated his own, innovative principles of aerial combat, and saw to it they were followed in his regiment. It was only when Boris Yeremin was transferred to Shestakov's regiment at Stalingrad that he understood the theory of how best to deploy the pilots in his group during a mission.[273] The first priority was to make sure you were higher than your enemy, because that conferred a speed advantage and made it possible to get into an optimal position. No less important was to range the group at different heights in readiness for battle – this ensured they could react more flexibly in the event of an enemy attack. When attacking, you should ensure the sun was behind you to dazzle the enemy; and so that your own aim was not obscured. Shestakov believed you should open fire at a distance of 100 metres or less, not directly behind the enemy's tail but with a one- or two-quarter profile to give yourself a bigger target. This was not something taught in Soviet flying schools. Yeremin had received prolonged conventional flight training and flown at the front for a long time, but it was only from Shestakov that he heard these and many other "Fighter Pilot's Commandments". These were rules of thumb that Yeremin had largely worked out for himself in months of combat, but it was from Lev Shestakov that he first heard them succinctly articulated.

The high command decided to create another "smashing fist" out of ace fighter pilots and, without more ado, took them away from other regiments. Flight lieutenants and squadron leaders were re-deployed to Shestakov as ordinary pilots and were, for the most part, undismayed by their demotion. The idea of belonging to an elite fighter regiment that was to avenge the Germans' humiliating victories at the beginning of the war appealed to them. Sultan Amet-Khan, famed for his exploits in the Battle of Stalingrad and transferred, together with Vladimir Lavrinenkov, from the terribly depleted ranks of 4 Fighter Regiment, took the view that under Shestakov he would function even more effectively than before.[274]

The four male pilots transferred from 4 Regiment arrived in 9 Regiment at the same time as Belyaeva's flight. Approaching the pilots' quarters, Lavrinenkov was nervously wondering who they were about to meet. He had heard that everybody in 9 Regiment was a Hero of the Soviet Union but, when they entered, the pilots stopped in their tracks, thinking they must have come to the wrong place. The only people inside were two young women in light flying suits. They were sitting on a mattress covered with a blanket and "chatting away".[275] A short, pretty girl with blonde hair noticed them and said, "Come on in! Don't be shy! Have you just arrived?" "Yes," one of the men replied. "So have we. Hello, I'm Lilya Litvyak and this is Katya Budanova."

Before Lavrinenkov and his companions had a chance to talk to the girls, another group of pilots came in. They were the same age as Lavrinenkov, no more than twenty-five, but all had more than one medal on their tunics, and three had the Gold Star. Lavrinenkov's eye was immediately drawn to a fair-haired man of medium height, none other than Mikhail Baranov. Baranov was the best-known fighter pilot on the Stalingrad Front and immediately recognisable from his photographs in the newspapers; he had even had a pamphlet written about him. He was a Hero of the Soviet Union, had shot down twenty-four German planes and, at twenty, was just the same age as Lilya Litvyak. He eyed up the newcomers and asked who had flown in from where. Mikhail Baranov was now 9 Regiment's deputy commander and, introducing the other pilots, he mentioned that both the girls had several kills to their name.

Pointing to a "long row of neatly made-up mattresses", Baranov invited Lavrinenkov and his colleagues to settle wherever they pleased. Amet-Khan, a short Crimean Tatar with a slight stoop, was "stocky, agile, and had curly black hair".[276] He was sociable and witty and could not ignore the presence of the female pilots, immediately throwing his case on the mattress next to where Lilya and Katya were sitting. Lavrinenkov and Borisov reserved places next to him. To their chagrin, however, Baranov invited the girls to his office for a talk and to introduce them to Shestakov.

In terms of popularity in 6 Guards Fighter Air Division, Nikolai Baranov in 296 Fighter Regiment alone could compete with Lev Shestakov. They were the only two men in the entire division to be nicknamed *Batya* (Our Old Man), by the pilots and mechanics. At the front this expressed simultaneously the highest respect, devotion and affection. However, although they had that in common, and were both outstanding pilots, the two commanders were quite different in temperament and the nickname had different overtones for each man. Where Baranov, apart from his weakness for parties and the fairer sex, was an almost ideal commander with a kind and generous nature, Lev Shestakov was hot-blooded, short-tempered, often unreasonably strict and, in the heat of of the moment, could be unfair.[277]

Discipline was fierce in Shestakov's regiment.[278] That first evening, Lavrinenkov and his friends came into the canteen, sat down, and wondered why the waitresses did not come running to serve them. Finally, someone whispered that the pilots never began eating before their commander entered. Shestakov had "only one Hero medal, but even twice-decorated Heroes seated at the table did not start their meal before the regimental commander appeared". When Shestakov came in, all rose. Only after he had greeted them, and the debriefing of the day's flights had concluded, could the meal commence. Proud of their commander, the members of the regiment were also proud of this discipline, which continued even after Shestakov was no longer with them.

The aloof Shestakov was probably the only pilot in the regiment who did not have eyes for Lilya Litvyak. In the three weeks she spent at the steppe settlement Zhitkur, green-eyed Lilya came to embody for them "an ideal of femininity and charm".[279] How many fighter pilots were there in the Soviet Air Force who sported under their greatcoats a "pretty blue or green scarf" fashioned from parachute silk and tinted by their own fair hand with heaven only knows what dye?[280] How many Soviet fighter pilots bleached and curled their hair? Vladimir Lavrinenkov and other young men would sometimes sing her a ditty popular at the time: "She gives me a glance and I feel like she gave me a ruble. She gives me a glance and I feel I've been scorched by her fire." Something else they liked about Lilya was her restraint, and the fact that she gave nobody preference, treating them all alike. She was forward, friendly, and fun. Even the hawk-eyed Belyaeva had no cause to reproach her, while the girl mechanics in their flight, if they dared even to speak to any of the pilots, would find Belyaeva breathing down their necks. Valya Krasnoshchyokova incurred her commander's wrath on account of Vasiliy Serogodsky. "Valya, come and sit on the wing until they send up the flare," he was constantly begging. His plane was one Valya serviced, and she could feel that he did not want her to sit with him just to pass the time while he waited to take off. Vasiliy was a couple of years older than her, already a Hero of the Soviet Union, and "muscular, handsome and slim". He had an expressive face but Valya did not particularly fancy him; he was a simple working-class boy with nothing interesting to say. The mechanics, however, had a special relationship with their pilots that was "part envy, part pity, part tenderness".[281] They were proud of them, and feared for their safety. The mission before which a young man was asking a young woman mechanic to come and sit on the wing of his plane might be his last.

So Valya would sit on the wing while Vasiliy waited for the order to take off, and would chat to him about this and that and answer his questions. Serogodsky was interested in her background, where she came from, and why she was so well read. One fine day, Belyaeva decided it was time to put a stop to this. "If I ever see you with Serogodsky again . . . " As always she was deaf to explanations, like the fact that it was Valya's job to service Vasiliy's plane. She evidently also gave Serogodsky an ear-bashing, because he stopped inviting Valya to sit on the wing. One time, however, as she was walking past, he said, "Valya, I'm about to take off, and I dedicate this mission to you." Valya often remembered that later, because Serogodsky was killed soon afterwards, one of the not infrequent non-combat casualties in the regiment.

Vasiliy died absurdly. Arriving together with Vladimir Lavrinenkov in a U-2 to pick up a repaired Yak from a village in the rear, Serogodsky decided to try it out straightaway. The two of them inspected the plane and tested the engine. Recalling what happened next, Lavrinenkov was baffled that "a front-line pilot who had been through the hell of defending Odessa and Stalingrad could, on an exercise over a quiet village in the rear, lose his sense of height, try to perform a difficult aerobatic manoeuvre at low altitude, and crash into the ground."[282] Vasiliy was, however, only twenty-three, an age when taking risks is addictive. It often happened that a young pilot would emerge unscathed from some desperate situation and lose his sense of danger. It was reported that Serogodsky's low-altitude aerobatics were for the benefit of a local girl who was watching from the ground. It was a ridiculous way to die. Lavrinenkov buried his friend there and gloomily flew back to base in the U-2. The Yak was beyond repair.

"Ladies, smile for the camera!" It was something between an invitation and an order, and all the girls who at that moment happened to be out beside the aircraft would laughingly run to line up.[283] Nine Regiment was still training at Zhitkur, but already reporters were frequent visitors because of the concentration there of Heroes of the Soviet Union. Mechanics, and especially pilots, who were young women were such an unexpected sight that the reporters were eager to photograph them. They were also pleased to find that female pilots, unlike their male counterparts, had no objection to them doing so.

Almost all the male pilots were as superstitious as old women, hardly surprising in a profession where lives were so much in the hands of chance. Each had their own personal quirks, but many superstitions were universal. Pilots would not shave immediately before a flight, preferring to shave the night before. They would fly in old, patched tunics, fearing that a new one would prove unlucky. Many Communists and Komsomol members had a prayer or miniature icon in their pocket, given to them by their mother as they left for the front. Absolutely everybody accepted that under no circumstances should you be photographed immediately before a mission. When reporters came to his regiment, Commissar Dmitry Panov knew in advance the answer he would get if he asked a pilot to be photographed: "You want me in my grave?" As one pilot justified his refusal, "Butov had his photograph taken and now he is dead. Bondar had his photograph taken and he's dead also. Do you really want to photograph me too?" It was Panov who bore the brunt of the reporters' indignation, and he was averse to being photographed himself. He could not help feeling there was some malign force at work. A pilot in his regiment had only to be photographed in flight suit, flying helmet and goggles in front of his plane covered with slogans like, "For the Motherland", "Victory", "For Stalin", and you could be sure he would find himself in the gunsight of a German pilot or a German anti-aircraft gunner and be shot down in flames. Panov had the feeling that fate was "somehow restoring a balance" as it brought its deadly scythe down precisely on those it had just singled out for fame.[284]

The girls, however, Litvyak, Belyaeva, Budanova, and Masha Kuznetsova, readily allowed themselves to be photographed in order to show up the absurdity of the men's superstitions. Lilya was photographed with a neat row of girl mechanics, and also poring over a map with Katya Budanova and Masha Kuznetsova. That photograph was printed in a newspaper, as was a photo of Belyaeva in the front-line paper, along with a note that she had shot down a German plane. They won few victories in 9 Regiment, however. The girls believed this was because they were given little opportunity to fly. The male pilots did not like having one of their girls as their wingman, and Shestakov rarely allowed them into the skies at all, having bluntly made it clear he wanted them out of the regiment, and was reluctant to subject them to risk in the meantime. The only exception while they were at Zhitkur was that, for a few days in early October, their flight was on duty every day because most of the pilots had been sent off to collect the new aircraft.[285]

Faina Pleshivtseva remembered 2 October vividly.[286] The planes had just returned from a mission, the pilots still in the cockpits, but Katya Budanova and Raisa Belyaeva were already at the stands waiting their turn. They themselves hastened to help Faina and another girl mechanic refill the fuel tanks and quickly inspect the aircraft for leaks and damage. The mechanics helped them put on their parachutes, get into the cockpit, and buckle their belts. Belyaeva and her wingman took off to patrol in the direction of the Elton salt lake. As Pleshivtseva was told later, both pilots spotted a group of twelve Ju 88 bombers on the horizon. They attacked, firing first at the lead aircraft then the others until they ran out of ammunition. To their disappointment, they failed to shoot any of them down, but at least the bomber formation was scared off, changed course and, instead of bombing Elton Station, dropped their bombs at random and departed. "They chickened out, the bastards," Katya said later, but was in a bad mood for the rest of the day because she had not notched up a kill. Soon, however she had another opportunity to increase her tally.

On 6 October, Pleshivtseva saw Budanova off on another flight, and this time she returned victorious. It had been a quiet, sunny day, with no sign of Germans, "as if they were hiding".[287] Her spell of duty was nearly over, and she said to her mechanic, "No action today," but just then a flare was fired. Dots on the horizon grew larger and became enemy aircraft.

Budanova started her engine, but the propeller on Belyaeva's plane, with whom she was jointly on duty, would not turn. Katya decided to fly alone, dispersed the formation of unescorted Junkers, and shot one down in a pall of black smoke. A kill! The next day, jointly with Belyaeva, she brought down another.

Her delight at that, however, was as nothing when, the following day, she at last received news of her family. Her mother was alive![288] Up until then Katya had been fighting to avenge her family's deaths, but henceforth she was fighting for them to have a good life. In October 1942, she wrote to her sister, Valya:

> I find myself in the thick of the fighting and am writing from Stalingrad. You know yourself what conditions at the front are like. Now my life belongs to the struggle against the fascist barbarians. I want you to know that I am not afraid of death, but neither do I seek it. If I have to die, I will not sell my life cheaply. My sweet, winged Yak is a splendid machine. My life is inextricably bound up with it, and we will die together only as heroes. Stay well! May your love of our Motherland grow stronger and may you work even better in her cause. Do not forget me.

Katya gave no details of her work as a pilot, and her family learned of her battles only after the war from others in the regiment.

25

Caucasus

In the few free moments the night bomber regiment enjoyed, Anna Yegorova would take out her photographs and wonder how her mother was getting on, little Yury and, most worryingly, Victor. Was he alive?[289] Nobody in their squadron had been receiving letters for a long time. For several months 4 Air Army had been supporting ground troops holding back the German offensive in the Caucasus. In late August, Chairman of the Council of Ministers (equivalent to the Soviet Prime Minister) Lavrenty Beria, flew to Tbilisi and replaced many of the most senior commanders on the Transcaucasian Front, including even the commander of 46 Army. In September the situation on the Soviet side began slowly to improve. German reverses at Stalingrad had an impact: without the expected extra reinforcements they were no longer able to attack simultaneously on all fronts in the Caucasus. The German advance could not, however, be completely halted. By late September the Kuban and a large part of the Crimea were in German hands. Nevertheless, the Germans were unable to advance beyond Nalchik. General Tyulenev, Commander of the Transcaucasian Front, speedily reinforced the area with infantry divisions and armoured brigades and by 5 November the German offensive had been halted. Official sources noted the excellent work of pilots of 4 Air Army.

Despite the difficulty of flying in the mountains, Bershanskaya's 588 Night Bomber Regiment sustained no losses and their bombing was effective. One day, flying with Irina Sebrova over the mountain ridge near Malgobek, Natasha Meklin noticed that most coveted of targets, fuel tanks. They managed to set fire to them on their second run and, as they flew home, Natasha kept looking back. "They're alight!"[290] The success of the Night Witches was noted by Tyulenev, commander of the entire front, who turned up at the regiment's headquarters on 7 November. His unannounced appearance caught Irina Rakobolskaya off guard. Saluting him, she quickly counted the stars on his uniform and addressed him as: "Comrade Colonel General", thereby demoting him. Bershanskaya, summoned by the duty officer, was quickly there but she too addressed him as "Comrade Colonel General". (The same fate was to befall Divisional Commander Popov.) "Why are you all lowering my rank?" Tyulenev asked ruefully.[291]

When the women's regiment was assembled, he told them about the first victories at Stalingrad and that the front was being pushed back westwards. The regiment again infringed regulations by shouting "Hooray!"

and clapping, but that brought no reproach from the commander. The girls' courage was already earning them great respect among the highest circles of the military hierarchy, and many of them were awarded their first medals. Until then they had somehow never thought about awards but, as Natasha Meklin noted, they found that it was in fact "very nice to be given a medal".[292] From then on, the Night Witches received far more attention and medals from the top brass than the other two women's regiments or their fraternal night bomber regiments. There were more Heroes of the Soviet Union in Bershanskaya's regiment than in any other bomber regiment. Only fighter regiments outshone them. These medals were undoubtedly well deserved, and we should probably say not that they were awarded too many but that others were awarded too few.

Shortly after their visit from Tyulenev, Bershanskaya received a letter from Vershinin, commander of 4 Air Army, which began solemnly, "Comrade Bershanskaya and all your fearless eagles, glorious daughters of our Motherland, intrepid pilots, mechanics, armourers and political workers!" Vershinin informed them that the necessary documents had been submitted for them to be awarded the title of Guards Regiment, a matter of immense prestige for any military unit. The same letter went on to mention "the personal concern for all of you of Comrade Tyulenev". It continued, "I am sending certain necessary but non-standard accessories for your personal welfare. Some are ready made while others are material which will require to be made up individually."[293] The commander of the Air Army was personally resolving the problem of underwear for rank-and-file soldiers and junior officers.

The Night Witches were very lucky. Other servicewomen had to wait until 1944 before they were issued underwear adapted to their sex. Previously they'd been supplied with men's vests and underpants and left to get on with it. There was no provision for bras, which you had to sew yourself, if you could find suitable material. In truth, the situation had been little better before the war. In 1929 the Mosbelyo and Lenbelyo enterprise, which had manufactured well-designed underwear, was swallowed by the gargantuan Glavodezhda, which concentrated on producing clothing that might as well have been worn by soldiers, and graceful lingerie became a thing of the past.[294] Glavodezhda produced underwear for everyone: the military, civilians, even for the huge numbers of Soviet prisoners. For all parties the product was much the same, and the range of women's underwear was exceptionally limited. For example, the manual of standards of the People's Commissariat of Light Industry had just one design for a bra, "without darts". Elegant ladies, of course, found a way round this situation, ordering designer lingerie from the Moscow Seamstress experimental atelier, or secretly from private seamstresses who worked from home. Everyone else had to make do with what they could get.

Girls in the forces were dependent on whatever lingerie they had managed to grab at home as they left for the war. Some mothers sent underwear in parcels. Faina Pleshivtseva's mother on one occasion sent a parcel with panties and bras she had run up not only for her daughter but also for her friend, Valya Krashnoshchyokova.[295] That was greatly appreciated. And, of course, during the war girls sewed their own underwear. Parachutes were much sought after because they were made from silk. In the night bomber regiment this practice led to a serious incident, which may have prompted Vershinin to address himself to the matter.

Two girl armourers decided to sew themselves underwear from new parachutes rather than scavenged or captured material. The girls opened an aerial flare bomb (which was normally used to illuminate a target prior to bombing it), removed its parachute, and sewed themselves panties and bras.[296] They were denounced by one of their friends in the regiment. They probably deserved to be found out – it was an act of wanton irresponsibility, particularly in wartime – but, needless to say, the girl who informed on them had no idea of the likely consequences. Pilots would have been reduced to the ranks and left to serve the sentence in their unit, but these girls were only gunners and a military tribunal sentenced them to ten years' imprisonment. Their prospects would have been bleak had not Vershinin, the commander of 4 Air Army, interceded. He referred to it in his letter. "As regards the two girls who were guilty of an error," he wrote, "give them the opportunity to carry on working in peace, and at some later date file an appeal to strike out their criminal record. I am sure that, like all the others, they will ultimately be found deserving of government awards." [297]

This was a far from unique case of an individual with great power intervening in the working of the pitiless and indiscriminate juggernaut of the state. A high-up who came to the rescue of people who were not, in all conscience, guilty of any major crime, came to be seen by his subordinates as almost a magician. Nevertheless, Vershinin's grounds for pardoning them were founded on a shared perception of their feminine weakness, just at a time when Raskova's girls were fighting for the right to be considered the equal of men. As a result of his intercession, the girls had their convictions quashed and both went on to retrain as navigators. One of them, Tamara Frolova, burned to death in her plane during the assault on the Germans' Blue Line.

26

"Are they young women, or scarecrows from the vegetable patch?"

"I'll bake a cake," Nina Shebalina announced, a girl who had her priorities right even at Stalingrad.[298] In their few weeks at the front with 9 Guards Regiment, Valya Krasnoshchyokova had become very close to Nina and felt she could trust her with her life. Nina was fairly hefty, had light brown hair and an agreeable, confident air. She had a great personality, an incisive intellect, a brave heart, and did not say things lightly. But a cake? Where on earth could they find the ingredients? "We'll sort that out," Nina assured Valya. "We absolutely must celebrate the anniversary of the Revolution on 7 November."

The Communists, when they came to power, abolished all "tsarist" holidays except New Year. New, Soviet, holidays soon appeared in their place: International Labour Day, observed on 1 May; Young People's Day; International Women's Day, which was not very international because it was observed only in the U.S.S.R., on 8 March; and, of course, the anniversary of the October Revolution of 25 October 1917. On this day, as on May Day, workers' demonstrations were organised, marching in orderly columns with red flags, portraits of Stalin, and banners with slogans. Bands played, and solemn meetings and rallies were held. In the two decades of Soviet rule people forgot that demonstrations were supposed to be a spontaneous carnival of popular feeling. In the Soviet Union they were planned and attendance was obligatory. The atmosphere was cheerful, and when the official part was over people would go home to celebrate with their families. They would do their best to lay on a festive spread and get hold of vodka. People need holidays, and on 7 November 1942 most Soviet women, just like Nina Shebalina, were determined to bake a cake even if, like her, they lacked the ingredients.

A month previously Stalingrad had been such a hell that it would never have entered the heads of any of Raisa Belyaeva's flight to throw a party but now, in Zhitkur, even though for most people everything was as difficult and chaotic as in any other front-line village, the days were less frenetic for the girls. For the rest of his life, Vladimir Lavrinenkov remembered "its little huts, its watermelons, its camels, and the boundless, open horizon there".[299]

Seeing how hard life was for local civilians, especially evacuees, the girl mechanics did not grumble about their lot, although their work was still just as demanding, their living conditions unsatisfactory, the food bad and, to add insult to injury, there were lice which they just could not get rid of.[300] The pilots were decently fed even here, but the mechanics subsisted on blondie, sometimes with machine oil poured over it. Only on very rare occasions were they given herring. The last time they had seen fresh meat was back in 437 Regiment. On that occasion, when they saw meat and bones on their plates, some guessed they were about to dine on Pashka, their she-camel who had carried water from the Volga. She was wounded during shelling and had to be put down, but provided them with a feast fit for a tsar.[301]

In Shestakov's regiment, pilots they were on good terms with would sometimes slip them something from their own rations. Lilya Litvyak and Katya Budanova, when they were about to go out on a mission, would leave the mechanics bread on a nail in the wall.[302] But nobody ever forgot the cake baked for 7 November 1942, which was the only one they ate in the course of the war. The girls, pilots and mechanics alike, worked together to collect the ingredients. Bread was in short supply locally and rationed, so by hoarding that and other products, the girls had something they could barter for eggs. These were hard to come by and had to be acquired one at a time. In the same way, they got hold of milk and sour cream. In the canteen they drank their tea unsweetened, and asked to be given the sugar separately. The pilots also hoarded the "hundred grams" (of vodka), issued to them daily at the front on the orders of Anastas Mikoyan, People's Commissar of the Food Industry. They swapped the vodka for eggs, milk, and sugar until they had assembled all they needed. It was an all-girl celebration of the revolutionary anniversary: no men were invited. The field post had just delivered a batch of letters and those who had been sent one read it aloud, because those whose home towns and villages were in occupied territory could not receive any. News of their friends' families was almost as important as news of their own. The cake turned out wonderfully and they celebrated the holiday in style.[303] Around them too, the mood was changing. Although nothing had been announced, everyone knew a major Soviet offensive was in the offing. Troops were massing in Zhitkur.

Incredibly, one cold, overcast October day the Soviet St George himself appeared to the girl mechanics. "Girls, on parade!" ordered somebody who ran up to the aircraft very out of breath. With no time to change, they ran straight from the airfield just as they were, "unkempt, in our quilted trousers and mechanics' jackets". They were lined up and "some character in a tall Astrakhan fur hat and with general's epaulettes passed along our ranks, twice". The stranger departed without a word. They learned afterwards that this had been none other than General Georgiy Zhukov, one of the most important figures in the war. As their superiors informed them, this representative of Supreme Command Headquarters had been unimpressed. "Are they young women or scarecrows from the vegetable patch?" he enquired. Their jackets were, as always, covered in grease, and there had been no time to run the several kilometres to their accommodation to freshen up, but evidently no one managed to explain that to him.[304] It was said Zhukov ordered that they should be issued with greatcoats, dresses, and boots the right size, but by the time the requisite items were found, the girls had been transferred to a different regiment.

In peacetime, Zhukov was too dangerous a rival for the U.S.S.R.'s leaders and they kept him well away from power. When, however, the country was teetering on the brink of disaster, they suddenly brought him back, giving him all the powers he needed to save the situation. Something similar occurred after the war. In June 1953 it was Zhukov who was entrusted with arresting Lavrenty Beria, the instigator and executor of Stalin's purges, in the middle of a meeting of the Council of Ministers of the U.S.S.R.[305] Zhukov was warned that Beria was dangerous, might be armed, and was a skilled practitioner of unarmed combat, but Zhukov already knew exactly who he was dealing with. The arrest of Stalin's murderous executioner, who had kept the entire Soviet Union prostrate with terror, was Zhukov's finest hour. A bell was rung, the agreed signal, and Zhukov burst into the meeting with several generals. He pointed his pistol at Beria and ordered him to put his hands up. Beria turned white as a sheet. Looking straight into his enemy's frightened eyes, Zhukov said, with a fine sense of drama, "The game's up, you bastard!"

Drawing on his experiences in the First World War, he spirited Beria out of the Kremlin gagged and lying on the floor of a car. He seated several generals well known to the Kremlin Guard in it to prevent any attempt at rescue by Beria's supporters.[306]

On 11 September 1941, Zhukov was appointed commander of the Leningrad Front, but the situation there was already past saving and he was unable to prevent the Germans besieging the city, although he managed to stabilise the front line and ensure Leningrad held out. Moscow was under threat already, and Zhukov was transferred to the central sector. As commander of the Western Front, he succeeded, together with General

Ivan Konev, in halting the Germans close to the capital itself. Next Zhukov conducted Soviet counter-attacks in the central sector, the Rzhev-Vyazma and Rzhev-Sychyovka offensives. Neither is well known because they failed, but a large proportion of the German forces was diverted from the assault on the capital and the danger to Moscow passed. His next campaign was the Battle of Stalingrad.

In late August 1942, Zhukov was appointed First Deputy People's Commissar of Defence ready for the Soviet counter-offensive. There was good reason for his presence: failure at the Stalingrad Front in November 1942 would have been calamitous.

On one occasion, Dmitry Panov, Commissar of 85 Fighter Regiment, saw to his horror a scowling Georgian soldier outside the Zhitkur barracks, slowly tearing pages out of an already half-depleted copy of the Soviet equivalent of the Bible: *A Short Course on the History of the All-Union Communist Party of Bolsheviks*. He was using them as kindling for a campfire to cook some supplement to his meagre rations. For such sacrilege, you could be shot, but Panov only bawled the soldier out. Completely unfazed, he replied that the Course was "not likely to be needed now, as the cause the Red Army was fighting for was doomed". And indeed, nearly every soldier fated to be sent to Stalingrad really was doomed. Of General Rodimtsev's 10,000-strong division, which played a huge part in the battle, only 320 soldiers survived.[307] The German forces, however, were also melting away. Their divisions, already below strength when they embarked on the battle in the summer, were reduced at a disastrous rate and they had no reinforcements to call on.

Gradually pushing the Russians back to the River Volga, the German troops had at first advanced. In early October, Soviet troops attempted two counter-offensives, both of which failed. By the anniversary of the Revolution on 7 November, only a narrow strip of the Volga's western bank remained in Soviet hands, but a sudden sharp fall in the temperature sapped the morale of the German soldiers, most of whom had no winter clothing. However, the defenders of Stalingrad now faced additional problems as the Volga began to freeze, making it more difficult to deliver ammunition, food and reinforcements to the city. The surviving Soviet troops were split into two narrow encirclements, but resistance continued, mainly in factories in the northern part of the city and on Height 102.0, known to the townspeople as "*Mamaev Kurgan*" (Mamai's Barrow). This was the highest hill in Stalingrad, and commanded a view over the whole city. Boris Yeremin, observing the Stuka bombers pulling so low out of their dives above the barrow he could see the heads of the German pilots, noticed an old woman dragging a goat along on a rope. He spotted she already had some of her belongings in a gap under the railway bridge.

"Where are you taking the goat, Grandma?"

"To that hole under the bridge, to save myself from these villains."

"You should cross to the other side of the Volga," he told her.

"How should I leave my home? I'm old. I'll wait under the bridge for it to be over," the old lady said, and perhaps she was right.[308] What were the chances of her making it safely across the Volga and, if she did, what was there for her on the other side? Nobody had time to look after someone in her situation.

Boris Yeremin returned thirty-three years later to that blood-soaked hill where, it is said, after the fighting 38,000 Soviet soldiers were buried in mass graves.[309] Heaven knows what had happened to the support of the bridge to which the old woman had been dragging her goat. Yeremin did not want to talk to anybody, but stood silently at the sun-drenched monument, remembering those days at the beginning of November 1942.

Recalling that time in his memoirs, Yeremin makes no mention of an article in the newspaper *Stalin's Falcons* that he must have seen, and which must have been of importance to him. "Heroes of Stalingrad" appeared in a special edition marking the twenty-fifth anniversary of the Revolution, and lavished praise on, among other pilots, three of Yeremin's protégés: Alexander Martynov, Ivan Zapryagaev, and Alexey Salomatin.[310] After Stalingrad, all three were made Heroes of the Soviet Union. There were rumours later, when he was himself in command of a regiment, that Yeremin nominated pilots for awards only if he was also being nominated – it was as if he was jealous of other pilots' success.[311] Although Yeremin fought valiantly at Stalingrad, he was not made a Hero.

Stalin's Falcons published a collage of photographs of pilots who had covered themselves in glory at the Battle of Stalingrad: Ivan Kleshchev, Mikhail Baranov, Ivan Izbinsky and ten others, including Zapryagaev and Martynov. There is no photo of Alexey Salomatin, either because of a lack of space, or because, out of superstition, he refused to be photographed. In the article, he has a long paragraph devoted to him. The reporter, S. Nagorny, writes that at Stalingrad Alexey gloriously continued the tradition of Yeremin's renowned group. Salomatin had shot down ten air-craft on his own account and another nineteen jointly. He told the reporter that on one occasion, while pursuing a Messerschmitt, he was attacked from above by another. He went into a dive and pulled out "so close to the ground that the propeller almost sliced the bushes". Wholly engrossed by his pursuit, the German pilot "did not notice he had almost no height left and had no time to level out". He crashed into the ground and his plane exploded. "You see," Salomatin explained with a crafty smile, "My dive was lengthwise along the ravine, while the silly idiot was flying across it. That did for him. Also, I was flying a Yak, which is a lot nippier than a Messer."[312]

Often not even a tenth of what was written in articles about the exploits of Soviet pilots was true. The pilots liked to boast, the reporters to embellish, and editors welcomed that. When you read this paragraph, however, you feel you are hearing Alexey Salomatin's words and that everything written here is true, save for a few forgivable exaggerations by the pilot himself. Nagorny has changed nothing in his not wholly grammatical but graphic description. Salomatin, fearless, a born fighter pilot, was quite capable of bringing his plane out of a dive at the last moment with the propeller "almost slicing the bushes". He loved taking risks, even when there was no need. His death-defying aerobatics were to cost him his life only a few months later.

27

"We did not need to look for the target"

On the night of 18 November 1942, Boris Yeremin was ordered to line up his squadron and read them an address from the Military Council of the Stalingrad Front. People were woken without any explanation, and while they were lining up there was puzzlement. "What's happened?" "Why the parade?" However, when Yeremin started reading, the importance of the moment became clear: the Front had now concentrated all its resources and was preparing to attack. There was a lump in Yeremin's throat as he finished. He had spent four months in this place, living in a constant state of tension. This was a fight to the death in which his friends had been dying one after another. Now, finally, they were going on the offensive! Yeremin well understood why his subordinates, after hearing the order, "exulted and cried and cheered!" He was experiencing the same tumultuous emotions himself, "a mix of pain at our losses, dark memories, and hope of victory".[313]

In the ground forces, sergeants issued their soldiers with clean underclothes. The apathy fell away. "At last we were on the attack! Smoke rose from the kitchens; we were given hot food; we lived again!"[314]

Four days after the start of Operation Uranus, the ring of encirclement closed round the German 6th Army under General Paulus. Soldiers out in the steppes faced a grim ordeal. In the city there were basements where you could shelter, and at least some supplies to be found. The only option for those in the steppes was to dig themselves burrows, primitive dugouts or just holes in the snow if the ground was frozen. They had no heating. It was only in Stalingrad that firewood, in the form of planks from ruined houses, was to be found. There was no way of delivering food to the dying 6th Army other than by air.

A sense of elation spread through the Red Army and the Soviet rear, and people waited eagerly for Soviet troops to get at the Germans in the encircled "Cauldron". Commanders of ground forces set their troops the task of keeping the enemy under deadly pressure. Commanders of the air forces tasked theirs with cutting off airborne supplies to the surrounded German units. Timofey Khryukin, who led 8 Air Army, made it the first priority of the fighter regiments to stop the Germans getting food and ammunition to their besieged army. They were to shoot down all transport aircraft, condemning the 250,000 German soldiers in the Cauldron to death by starvation.

Even without the menace of Soviet fighters, it would have been impossible to fully provision the encircled army by air. That would have required delivery every day of 700 tonnes of freight. Goering knew perfectly well that planning to airlift such quantities was unrealistic, but nevertheless assured Hitler it would be done. The commander of German air transport, who warned that his aircraft could deliver at most 350 tonnes a day, was ignored. On 7 December, the most successful day of the German airlift, 135 aircraft landed in the Cauldron and succeeded in delivering 362 tonnes of supplies. On 9 December, however, of 157 aircraft sent forward not a single one was able to land.[315] The airlift managed to provide the surrounded German units with no more than one-fifth of their minimum requirements. A lack of ammunition meant that tanks and artillery lay idle or could only be used ineffectively, and the soldiers began to starve. In December, the front-line bread ration was reduced to 200 grams a day, and support services in the rear were lucky to receive 100 grams.[316]

The Russian fighter units set about shooting down transport planes without delay, which the pilots of 8 Air Army found "fun". The German aircraft had little or no fighter cover and Soviet pilots were finally able to take revenge. Their fighters and ground attack bombers were soon focusing on Pitomnik, 100 kilometres from Stalingrad, which was the main airfield supplying the Cauldron. To one side of the airfield, a graveyard of shot down or burnt-out German planes began to expand. Emaciated, frostbitten wounded waited to be evacuated. Fighting broke out when the aircraft were being loaded, the walking wounded contriving to sneak onto the planes and throw out the more seriously injured. They had to be forcibly removed. Many of the severely hurt died before it was their turn to be carried to the plane, and their corpses were stacked up near the hospital tents at the edge of the airfield. These sights were so horrific that the transport pilots just wanted to get away as soon as possible from this hopeless situation back to a semblance of normality, even though they knew the Russian anti-aircraft guns and fighter planes were waiting for them.

When flying in groups became too dangerous, the Germans began switching to solo and night flights. A substantial number of their transport planes were lost when the Soviet 24 Tank Corps broke through to their airbase at Tatsynskaya, making the situation of the German units trying to defend themselves in the Cauldron really grim. Attempts were made to drop supplies by parachute, but the huge cardboard cigars as often as not drifted over to the positions held by Soviet troops, who were only too happy to take delivery of such unheard of luxuries as German chocolate, ham and sausage, cigarettes, and French Cognac. Airdrops containing ammunition were met with considerably less enthusiasm.

Dmitry Panov, the commissar of 85 Fighter Regiment, had survived the battles of 1941 and 1942 that he and his comrades had fought with obsolete aircraft. He noted that finally, after so many losses, air superiority was passing to the Soviets, but acknowledged that the German transport pilots he was now fighting were performing "feats of heroism", flying "night and day on suicidal missions across a boundless wasteland of snow".[317]

Pilots from Boris Sidnev's 268 Fighter Aviation Division were continuing to intercept bombers, but were now often also escorting ground attack bombers. These were targeting the troops and ordnance Paulus was assembling for an attempt to break out of the Cauldron and join up with General von Manstein. "We did not need to look for the target," Panov notes. In the freezing weather the German positions were given away by plumes of smoke as they tried desperately to keep warm.[318] It was in any case all but impossible to hide in the barren steppe, where trees and bushes grew only in the ravines. Commanders of the ground attack bombers set goals for their squadrons, assigning each a ravine or concentration of German troops. They now had little difficulty seeing off any Messerschmitts that tried flying to the rescue. For Boris Yeremin and Dmitry Panov, who had been fighting since 1941, this was different. "An enjoyable war," was how Panov described the missions, but that did not salve the pain. "How much we had had to suffer before things became more cheerful!" It was a grim sort of cheer, but the suffering had hardened their hearts. As he flew away after a bombing mission, Panov would look back with satisfaction at the heaps of German corpses strewn over the bottom of the ravines of Stalingrad.

During this period, Raisa Belyaeva wrote to a friend:

> Dear Yevgenia, I am now right on the front line. My wish has been granted. I shot down two enemy fighters, although I got shot down myself once, but managed to parachute out of the burning plane. Yevgenia, all my thoughts are of the one I love. I long for just one thing, to fight for my country and the happiness of many people, and to bring closer the day I see him again when we have driven the last of these vultures from our land.[319]

Years later, Masha Kuznetsova, the only member of Belyaeva's flight to survive the war, expressed her amazement that even in such fraught circumstances, "people were still glad to be alive."[320] They were young! The pilots would gather to sing their favourite songs, wind up the gramophone, "and out over a steppe pitted with craters would ring the strains of foxtrots and tangoes. They would play 'Champagne Bubbles' and 'Rio Rita', then somebody would pick up an accordion and they would dance Tsyganochka, 'The Gypsy Girl'." Katya Budanova danced no less well than her friend Lilya Litvyak, and liked to play the fool if someone invited local girls to a dance. She would ask a girl to dance, introducing herself with the boy's name "Volodya". The girls would immediately fall for this handsome pilot in his well-fitting uniform, with his unruly curls and a broad smile that showed off beautiful teeth. She once laughingly related what her dancing led to. Continuing to play the role of a dashing cavalier, she walked one of the girls home. When they arrived, the girl was in no hurry to say goodbye to "Volodya". Katya's feet were getting cold and she was wondering how to take her farewell when the girl grabbed her and started kissing. Katya fled.[321]

Belyaeva's flight had settled in well with 9 Regiment and they made friends with its pilots, but their future remained unsettled. Shestakov had said long before that they would not be staying in his regiment. One sortie in particular during this period had major consequences for them, but information about it is sparse and contradictory. Belyaeva's whole flight of fighters were airborne at the time, but Masha Kuznetsova left no reminiscences of the episode, and Belyaeva herself, Lilya Litvyak, and Katya Budanova all died within a year. The Germans were mounting one of their regular raids on Elton Station, on this occasion flying Heinkel bombers with a fighter escort. According to Belyaeva, she was hit and bailed out, while Budanova, Litvyak, and Kuznetsova continued to fight. Raisa Belyaeva got back to the regiment only a few days later.[322] Curiously, all the various memoirs give differing accounts of what happened. One writes that Belyaeva was injured during a training flight.[323] Another says her plane was shot down, only she did not bail out but made an emergency landing.[324] Veterans of the women's fighter regiment wrote, based apparently on what Belyaeva told them, that she did bail out.[325] There is no information in the records of 9 Regiment because Belyaeva was not officially part of it. And by the same token, nor is there anything in the records of 586 Regiment, because her flight was considered to have been temporarily assigned to 9 Regiment.

If, before the loss of her aircraft, Belyaeva had probably still been hoping to win the confidence of Shestakov and stay in his regiment, she no longer had any illusions. She was given to understand that there would be no replacement aircraft, and Shestakov did not permit her to fly again, referring to the state of her health. She knew that was not the real reason. In Belyaeva's opinion, there was no point remaining in 9 Regiment. Most likely, with her imperious and ambitious personality, she was simply tired of being treated as second best to the male pilots. It was time for her to take a decision, and she did, resolving to return to the women's regiment and re-form her old squadron from Nechaeva's flight, which had lost its commander, and her own.[326] Alexander Gridnev, the new commander of 586 Regiment, was no less keen to see all his pilots and aircraft returned to where they belonged. After Klava Nechaeva's death, the Belyaeva episode was the last straw and Gridnev swung into action.[327] The top brass of the Air Defence Division duly issued the requisite order but, when they heard about it, Klava Blinova and Tonya Lebedeva informed Olga Shakhova they had no wish to return to 586 Regiment and wanted to stay in the men's regiment. Raisa Belyaeva's own flight had exactly the same reaction: Masha Kuznetsova, Lilya Litvyak, and Katya Budanova were in no hurry to pack their bags.[328]

28

"People are saying Boris Yeremin is scared of us"

In early December, 9 Regiment was informed it would be flying to a new airfield much closer to Stalingrad. The nearest village was Zety, which had just been liberated. Belyaeva's flight was to return a few days later to the women's regiment at Anisovka. Valya Krasnoshchyokova and Nina Shebalina were reluctant to part with the male pilots who seemed somehow to need their support, but they were also looking forward to seeing friends in their old regiment again, and to be with them when the regiment began combat duties, which Belyaeva said was imminent. There were practical considerations too: if they went back to the women's fighter regiment, they would finally get new uniforms. Fate intervened, however, and separated Valya and Nina, who were not to meet again until the war was over.[329]

"Valya, wake up!" Valya opened her eyes to see Faina Pleshivtseva. Why was she being wakened? It was the middle of the night, dark, cold, and completely silent. Everybody else was asleep. Faina explained everything in a whisper, but it was all so strange that Valya, still half asleep, had trouble making head or tail of it.[330] Nine Regiment was flying to its new deployment, and Litvyak and Budanova had decided to flee with it instead of returning to the women's regiment with Belyaeva. They intended to take Pleshivtseva and Valya with them to service their planes and, right now, needed them to come very quietly to the airfield, warm up the aircraft, and keep them ready. As she dressed quickly and quietly, it dawned on Valya just what she was being drawn into. She could not see why Pleshivtseva had asked her rather than anyone else, because they were not on close terms, but Valya was conscientious. It never occurred to her to refuse. Budanova and Litvyak were officers, they commanded their crews, and the responsibility was theirs.

But how had they decided to do something so outrageous? Which of them had taken the initiative in deciding they should run away, and misappropriate combat aircraft into the bargain? In fact, this sort of thing occurred more often than one would imagine, particularly towards the end of the war when young pilots, desperate to see action, would help themselves to a plane and fly to the front. They could be punished, but that was unusual. Such indulgence in the armed forces, where strict discipline was usually enforced, might seem puzzling, but pilots evidently belonged to a caste exempt from the rules that applied to everybody else.

Antifreeze for aircraft engines was not available to Soviet pilots, so Valya and Faina had to sit for a long time in the aircraft heating the engines. Finally Litvyak and Budanova appeared and told them the Lisunov Li-2 transport aircraft (a version of the Douglas DC-3) for the headquarters equipment was about to be loaded. There was a pile of aircraft covers in the tail of this enormous airbus where, they suggested, Valya and Faina could hide. These covers were as warm as quilts, and mechanics and technicians often used them as blankets. Pulling the covers round them, Valya and Faina sat in the tail behind crates of headquarters property, but when the "Douglas" took off and gained height, it became clear they were going to be none too warm. A strong draught was blowing through the tail.[331]

There was, however, no real need for them to hide. Nine Regiment's chief engineer, Spiridonov, had worked out they were there. "Girls, where are you? Come on out!" he yelled. They later heard that his male mechanics had told him they had not readied the planes for Litvyak and Budanova. After a quick consultation, Valya and Faina decided they were unlikely to be thrown out of the hatch and emerged.

It was still dark when they landed at Zety, an almost completely destroyed Kalmyk village. Spiridonov did not tell them off, having many other things on his mind. "Girls, it's up to you to meet the other planes as they arrive!" The transport with the male mechanics had been delayed, so there was no one to service incoming planes. From that early start, Valya and Faina worked straight through the day with nothing to eat. The others had passes for the canteen. Handsome Yevgeny Dranishchev, a hero of the Battle of Stalingrad, gave them a bar of chocolate from his emergency rations. "Let's just eat one square a day, like Raskova did," Valya suggested.

Victor Nikitin, chief of staff of 9 Regiment, called them in that evening after they had done a very full day's work. "You are deserters. You should be court martialled!" he began sternly (having already had the same conversation with Litvyak and Budanova). Valya protested, "We are not deserters! Quite the opposite. We have run to, not from, the front." "Dear me, aren't you the clever one!" Nikitin said sarcastically, but the girls could see he was going to let them stay and that his ire was more for appearance's sake. They were highly trained, hard working, and would be an asset to the regiment. Nikitin put away wrath and replaced it with mercy.

"Have you eaten?"

"Yes."

"What have you eaten?"

"Chocolate, like Raskova."

Without more ado, Nikitin sent them off to the pilots' canteen. There, also for appearance's sake, they were asked where their passes were and Valya said she had no idea. They were fed anyway.

It was late and they were very tired, but the authorities were unprepared when they asked where they should sleep. In the end they said, "Go to the pilots' dugout!" It was large and newly constructed, and the young pilots gave them a friendly if amused reception. They separated off a corner for them with a piece of material and gave them a sleeping bag. Valya and Faina squeezed into it together, were soon warm, and fell asleep.

For the pilots of 9 Regiment, their flight to Zety represented a new experience. They could see this was the beginning of a long advance westwards. Zety was the first airfield they had landed at in an area liberated from the Germans and their regiment was one of the first to return to "land that had suffered much, been traversed by hundreds of tanks, and scorched mercilessly by fire".[332]

All that remained of the village of Zety were three huts in the immensity of the flat landscape. The steppe was white with snow, which made everything around look beautiful and hid from view all the ruins, craters, wrecked tanks and vehicles. The accommodation for aircraft was better than for personnel, in that the Germans had left protective earth-covered shelters at the airfield. One of the three huts was commandeered for the canteen, the headquarters occupied another, and the third was allocated to the pilots and mechanics.[333] Litvyak and Budanova were put up in a small, separate room in the headquarters hut. For the two-thirds of the personnel for whom there was no room in the dormitory hut, dugouts were hastily prepared. Starting in the morning, by evening the men had built a place to live. Each squadron gouged out pits in ground frozen as hard as stone. These were roofed with metal from wrecked planes and vehicles and capped with earth and snow. The sappers installed small iron stoves and their living quarters were complete. There was no wood to be found in the steppe, but the next day the airfield maintenance battalion had "procured hay and heating oil", and it was soon cosy in the dugouts, above which thick black smoke billowed. In the cramped command post the telephone rang incessantly and Chief of Staff Nikitin could be heard talking into it without respite. Maps showing the "operational environment" hung on a boarded wall, stirring as the wind gusted, but demonstrating that the front line had already moved forward almost to Kotelnikovo. Pilots crowded round, awaiting orders. The airfield had been cleared of snow, and it was decided to start flights that same day. It was desperately cold, but Amet-Khan, looking closely at the map, remarked, "If we keep moving at this rate, we should be in Alupka in time for the holiday season." Yevgeny Dranishchev expressed doubt, and Amet-Khan looked closely at him too. The faces of both pilots were grey after a sleepless night and from the cold, and both had their noses hidden in their fur collars. "I fear you are forgetting who rules the skies in this area!" Amet-Khan said in tones of mock menace. "Of that no one is in doubt," Dranishchev retorted. "Nine Guards Regiment, in which there serves that valorous son of Alupka, Sultan Amet-Khan himself." [334]

Those two were the regiment's wits, and all present tuned in to this promising exchange that, however, came to an end almost immediately as Nikitin received details over the phone of their combat mission. They were to attack the airfield at Gumrak.

Vladimir Lavrinenkov waited with bated breath. His plane was ready for take-off and he knew every building and every hard stand at the airfield. Would he be included? Shestakov called out his name, adding, "You will lead a flight of six aircraft." [335]

He went on to warn them that a good half of Paulus's transport aircraft were at Gumrak, and there were plenty of fighters there to protect them. If those were given time to take off, they would have a fight on their hands.

Gumrak was the reserve airfield of the surrounded German troops but, with Russian units already approaching their main airfield at Pitomnik, Gumrak, with its inconvenient short runway, was being used more intensively by the day.

Shestakov ordered his force to approach the airfield from the centre of Stalingrad, the better to take the enemy by surprise. To Lavrinenkov's disappointment, Shestakov, in deploying the group, positioned his flight high above the others so they could act as a screen against any possible German attack. Shestakov himself headed straight for the target with another flight consisting of Amet-Khan, Alelyukhin, Korolyov, Bondarenko, Budanova, and Serogodsky.

The assault on Gumrak was a success. Shestakov set fire to a Junkers Ju 52 transport on the airfield, and five others immediately caught fire. The airfield was covered by a pall of thick smoke, through which flames licked upwards here and there.

For the mechanics, life in Zety went on much as at Zhitkur, with work, work and more work, rest in an overheated dugout, and infrequent trips to the bathhouse. Valya and Faina were no longer servicing the planes of Litvyak and Budanova but working with other crews and meeting other pilots.[336] A plane's crew was a closed community. The mechanic's day was spent working hard and waiting for their pilot to return. If he was in a good mood, he might say what had happened on the mission, but that was by no means certain. How the other pilots were faring was something you might hear from their mechanics, or overhear in a conversation, but Valya generally only got to talk with the other mechanics in the evenings when they came back to the crowded dugout, where they slept side by side, or half asleep in the morning on their way back out to the airfield. Litvyak and Budanova had their work in the sky, while that of Valya and Faina was on the ground, their paths crossing neither in the canteen nor in the dormitory. Valya heard only sporadically about missions flown by the women, or, indeed, by the men.

Shestakov's regiment was sent into battle on 9 December 1942, and already by 11 December a group of pilots, that included Lavrinenkov, Amet-Khan and Dranishchev, together with some from another regiment, had shot down eighteen German transports "which had been proceeding from the direction of Kotelnikovo by way of Zety to the encircled German troops at Nariman". Yeryomenko, commander of the Stalingrad Front, reported this success to Stalin, who expressed gratitude to the pilots concerned.[337]

Not infrequently, the fighters would take off "on sight", when an observer reported the approach of German planes. The regiment's Yaks were well concealed in the shelters the Germans had left them, and German transport pilots, unaware of the airfield's existence, would often fly towards Stalingrad right over their heads. When the enemy was spotted, 9 Regiment's pilots would take off and "attack without even turning to gain height".[338] Days when a Ju 52 laden with food was brought down nearby gladdened the heart of Major Pushkarsky, commander of the airfield maintenance battalion. It made a substantial contribution to the quality of meals.

On one occasion, Lavrinenkov succeeded in shooting down two German transports in succession. One fell near the regimental command post and, when Vladimir landed, he was summoned to meet the German pilot who had parachuted to safety. The tall redheaded officer removed his helmet, goggles, and map case and asked to have his already unloaded pistol returned. He handed them over to Lavrinenkov, as was traditional. Then he started taking out photographs of his wife, children and parents. His eyes and ingratiating smile pleaded for mercy, for his life to be saved for the sake of those in the photos. Vladimir could understand his motivation, but reflected that he himself would never behave like that if captured.[339] He and his comrades felt no personal animosity or hatred towards captured German pilots, and no urge to take the law into their own hands. The only exception was in Commissar Panov's neighbouring 85 Regiment, when a German pilot who had been shot down escaped from captivity and was then shot down for a second time. The pilots conferred briefly before marching him to a nearby ravine and all shooting him simultaneously to make sure he would never fight against them again. The commander and commissar did not intervene, understanding the pilots' logic and judging that, in the context, his blood could simply be written off.[340]

Vladimir's good day with two kills was followed, as was often the case, by a less good one.

That day Lavrinenkov was flying with Katya Budanova as his wingmate.[341] They were advised that a group of Heinkel bombers had been spotted. Most probably, these had been converted into transports and were carrying supplies to the Cauldron. The Heinkels had been camouflaged with white paint and they did not spot them immediately. When they did, Lavrinenkov went into a climb. "Cover me. I'm going in," he radioed Budanova. His burst hit the target, but the German gunner also hit him. He felt his plane suddenly pulling strongly to the left, "as if the left wing had become twice as heavy." Immediately, he heard Katya's voice in the headphones. "Seventeen, you've been hit. I'm covering you!" When Lavrinenkov looked at his right wing, he found it had all but disappeared, only the bare framework remaining. It took immense effort to keep the skewed aircraft on course.

The bomber he had damaged was shot down by another pilot. Budanova could have done the job, but was obliged to remain with her crippled lead aircraft. "Head back to the airfield! I'm covering you," she repeated from time to time to encourage Lavrinenkov, but when he did make it back, he saw it was going to be very difficult to land. On a turn the plane went into a spin. "Jump!" he heard Katya urge, but he had decided to land it.

The landing was "more like falling from a modest height". The first person to come running across the deep snow to him was Budanova. Next the chief of staff drove up. Lavrinenkov had been justified in deciding to try to save his plane. "Roll up your sleeves, Kaparka!" the chief mechanic ordered Vladimir's man. All that was needed for the repair was glue, percale covering material, and a skilled pair of hands.

The regiment was flying sorties ceaselessly. Between 10 and 31 December they flew 349 missions. In other words, every day the pilots took to the air three or four times, and that in December when the days are at their shortest. To be without a plane at just this moment was particularly galling. For the next few days, not knowing what to do with himself, Vladimir mooched about from the hostel to the hard standing where the aircraft were parked, to the headquarters, and back to his plane. He hung around his Yak in the hope of making himself useful to the mechanics repairing it. On one such day, he heard a roar of engines and looked up to see a huge Dornier returning from Stalingrad, but flying very low, its engines labouring, most probably heavily overloaded.[342] After delivering their cargo, these transports would take on board as many sick and wounded as could be crammed in. The field gendarmes charged with organising boarding of the planes had great difficulty maintaining order. They would fire in the air, but still so many people were piled into the aircraft it could barely take off.

Vladimir instinctively ran towards his plane before remembering it was out of commission. Then he ran to phone headquarters, but they had already alerted a group of the regiment's fighters that was approaching Zety. Vladimir and the mechanics observed from the ground as the lead aircraft, piloted by Shestakov, broke away from the group and caught up with the Dornier. He was unable to fire at it because all his ammunition had been used up during the sortie. Another fighter immediately took over the attack and several bursts of machine-gun fire were heard. The giant Dornier went out of control and crashed. Before the fighters had even landed, everyone knew that this formidable aircraft, bristling in every direction with machine guns, had been shot down by Lilya Litvyak.

According to Lavrinenkov's memoirs, Litvyak and Budanova had rapidly gained the affection and respect of his regiment. The men went out of their way to make life easier for them and minimise their risks in combat, but "the reaction on the part of Litvyak and Budanova was completely unexpected: they categorically refused to be fussed over and declined all acts of consideration."[343] Next to broad-shouldered Katya, the diminutive Lilya seemed like a little girl. They were close friends but, Lavrinenkov claims, "Katya was the boss. Lively, direct, and great fun," she soon became the life and soul of the squadron. Nobody was better at organising a dinner or dance than Katya.

Just before the New Year, Faina and Valya went to visit some Kalmyks in their *yurta*, to see what life was like for them. What she saw appalled the intellectual Valya. As soon as they entered, fetid air assailed their nostrils. A Kalmyk woman was sitting, smoking a pipe and rocking a cradle containing a baby covered in urine and faeces. The Kalmyks offered them tea with salt and fat, but they declined.[344]

Valya Krasnoshchyokova remembered their celebration of New Year 1943 for the fact that their food in the canteen was served in a mug and their wine in a bowl. There was a shortage of millet porridge, compensated for by an over-supply of wine. Valya, who had just turned twenty in December, had never drunk wine before, and neither was Faina used to it. Jostling each other with their elbows, they emptied the bowls in one, and on an almost empty stomach the wine acted so effectively that they could not climb the hill on their way back to their digs in the village. The ground was slippery, and whenever they got to the top they promptly slid back down in fits of giggles.

The pilots spent the whole of 31 December in battle and "collapsed into bed" immediately after eating. The cold and their exhaustion left them feeling completely spent. Someone did, however, wake up around midnight, remembered it was nearly the New Year, and woke the others. Amet-Khan suggested greeting the New Year and their successes at the front in his favoured manner, a pistol shot fired into the air. It felt just too cold to go outside, so they pulled the trigger right there in the dugout. Their salute blew out the oil lamp, fashioned out of a shell case, the stove door flew open and embers fell out onto the floor. One of the men dealt with it, and they all immediately went back to sleep.[345]

Did Lilya Litvyak and Katya Budanova celebrate their last New Year, or were they too so tired that they slept through it? What were their emotions and thoughts on New Year's Eve 1943? Perhaps they were worried about the future, because they knew Shestakov was insisting they should be moved from the regiment and there was no certainty they would be accepted by another. Everything was to be decided in the next few days.

According to pilots in the regiment, Shestakov respected and admired the girls as pilots.[346] However, the unit was sustaining incredibly high losses and there was a general feeling that it was too dangerous for them. This tough-minded man with a complex, authoritarian character decided they could no longer fight side by side with the men in his regiment.

Boris Sidnev, commander of 6 Fighter Air Division, personally undertook to find a place for Litvyak and Budanova in a way he would assuredly not have helped ordinary male pilots. He saw the girls as something special. Sidnev followed their successes, considered them good pilots, and was proud to have them in his division. But there was an even more compelling reason behind his support for their refusal to go back to the women's regiment. "Any fool could see he fancied Lilya."[347]

The 34-year-old Major General Boris Sidnev was well educated and handsome. "Quiet-natured and well mannered, an excellent pilot,"[348] but with a pronounced stammer, which was unusual for a soldier of that rank. Sometimes articulating a word would cost him such effort that he was "convulsed, with his jaws chattering". His speech defect did not stop

Sidnev from having a spectacular career. Starting the war as the commander of a fighter regiment with the rank of major, he ended it as the commander of an air corps with the rank of major general. Those who knew him considered him entirely worthy of these exalted positions and ranks. He was a good commander, valued his pilots, and flew in battle himself.

He did, however, have one failing: everybody in 8 Air Army knew Sidnev was a womaniser.[349] It would seem the young general had never been turned down by anyone until he ran into Lilya Litvyak. Young waitresses and telephone operators could not resist his charms. Such romances were nothing out of the ordinary. Khryukin, his superior, also had a "field wife". Many other commanders, high and low, in 8 Air Army had romances. Cohabitation with subordinates was a fact of life in the Red Army.

As a pilot and officer, Lilya Litvyak was in a completely different situation from most girls at the front. Men could ogle her as much as they liked: she was afraid of nothing and no one, and was well able to stand up for herself. She would have been quite prepared to tell a general where to get off, but chose instead to avoid any kind of confrontation with Boris Sidnev. When he summoned her to headquarters, she would often hide, and ask that he should be told she could not be found.[350] When she had no option but to encounter the divisional commander, she was as polite, friendly, and natural as with all the other men in love with her. She could not afford to quarrel with Sidnev, since it was his decision whether she stayed in a combat regiment or was sent back to the women's fighter regiment. Anya Skorobogatova would occasionally see Lilya in there when she came on business to Air Division headquarters. Sitting at a table, Lilya would be chatting to some high-up, often Sidnev himself, and Anya was amazed how relaxed she was, as if it was the most natural thing in the world for a sergeant to be sitting with generals, nibbling chocolate and chatting about Moscow. She responded to their jokes with her unforgettable laugh, and Anya found it wonderfully happy and uninhibited expression: not the "tee-hee-hee" of an affected flirt; or a deliberately sensuous "ho-ho-ho"; but genuine, happy, open laughter – "ha-ha-ha!"[351] Anya took a great liking to Lilya, but there was little probability of their becoming friends. Though both ranked as sergeants, the gulf between them in the unwritten hierarchy of the Air Division was too great.

To be on such friendly terms with senior officers while brushing aside their attempts at sexual harassment was something a girl in Anya's position would never have got away with. She preferred just to keep well out of the way of over-friendly commanders. Once, just once, she and another radio operator were invited to a strange party at divisional headquarters to celebrate a holiday.[352] A well-stocked table had been laid, at which a lot of her superiors were sitting with one or two other girls. Much vodka was drunk and everybody was having a good time until, at a certain moment, Anya suddenly became uneasy. The atmosphere changed. One of the officers started moving closer and closer and Anya decided, despite pressing entreaties, that it was time to leave. Her friend reappeared only the next morning, said nothing about what had happened, and Anya did not ask. She decided that from then on she would accept no invitations to dine with her superiors, whatever the pretext.

By behaving with a certain amount of guile, Lilya secured Sidnev's much-needed support for herself and Katya. While agreeing with Shestakov that the girls should leave his regiment on the grounds that it was too dangerous for them there, Sidnev had no wish to see them leave his fighter division completely. Such were the times: at the request of a girl he was in love with, a divisional commander allowed her to risk her life rather than send her back to the relative safety of an air defence regiment. Besides 9 Fighter Regiment there were three other regiments in 268 Fighter Air Division. These were Nikolai Baranov's 296 Regiment, Boris Yeremin's 31 Regiment, and Ivan Zalessky's 85 Regiment. Sidnev offered Litvyak and Budanova to Yeremin and Baranov.

Boris Yeremin, who knew Shestakov well, had had no doubt a day would come when he would face this choice, and had already decided not to accept them. Yeremin knew how keen Budanova and Litvyak were to stay in a combat regiment and that both were good pilots who only needed to gain more experience in action. His 31 Regiment, however, was a specialised fighter-reconnaissance unit and the pilots sometimes flew missions hundreds of kilometres behind the enemy's front line. When his divisional commander asked him what he thought, he replied diplomatically that he was "not against the idea in principle". In his opinion, both girls had been quite well trained, and "Litvyak was particularly outstanding." Yeremin saw her as a rare example of a born fighter pilot. She "felt the air", she "saw" it, always knowing what was going on around her and reacting to everything in good time, but how could they send any girl deep into enemy-occupied territory? Yeremin reminded Sidnev how difficult it would be for them to get back from there "if anything happened". And if they were caught, they might be raped and tortured. Sidnev agreed. Katya and Lilya heard this news right away, most probably from Sidnev himself. Yeremin recalled Lilya, with her wry sense of humour, administering a pinprick in the canteen: "People are saying Boris Yeremin is scared of us." Yeremin, who was afraid not of them but for them, did not demur.[353]

That left Baranov's 296 Regiment. It had been fighting throughout the war alongside Shestakov's 9 Regiment, whose two female pilots had impressed him. In addition, Lilya had in her favour the story of how she shot down that German ace during the Battle of Stalingrad. It was told half jokingly, half in earnest, some claiming that the German pilot had "flown headlong into her gunfire". Somehow, men could not bring themselves to believe that Lilya had shot down an outstanding German pilot on almost her first sortie. What could be the explanation? Talent? Skill? Or just extraordinary good luck? She had, however, other kills to her name. "I'll take them," Baranov said. He was short of pilots, and short of planes too.[354]

"That's it, girls. Pack your things! We're being kicked out," Katya announced grimly as she came into the dugout where Valya and Faina slept.[355] The mechanics were as sad to part with 9 Regiment as their pilots. Nevertheless, Lilya and Katya's dearest wish had been granted. They would be continuing to serve in a fighter regiment, and a very distinguished one at that. They joined Baranov's 296 Fighter Regiment a couple of days later in Kotelnikovo.

★

The Night Witches of 588 Bomber Regiment tried to tell their fortunes that New Year's Eve, as they had a year earlier in Engels. At midnight they burned a sheet of paper and then looked at the shadow of its charred remains on the wall. Galya Dokutovich joined in, and decided hers looked like a coffin. The other girls all "fell over themselves thinking up all sorts of nonsensical alternative interpretations". Luckily, Galya was not superstitious.[356] She was back with her regiment and felt extremely happy.

Galya had returned one wet, overcast December evening. The crews of 588 Regiment were gathered at the school in the centre of Assinovskaya, ready to go to the airfield. They were standing, looking up at grey sky and the "dark wisps of low cloud". The trees seemed to be waving their bare branches ridiculously, as if slipping in the mud and trying to keep their balance.[357] The girls were waiting for the truck that took them to the airport, but instead round the corner came a mud-spattered car out of which stepped a girl who, at first, no-one recognised. She was wearing a greatcoat that was too small and tight, which someone must have given her, and holding a half-empty rucksack. She got out and stood there, motionless and silent, until suddenly someone said quietly, "It's Galya. Galya Dokutovich!"

Galya rushed headlong towards them, struggling to pull her boots out of the squelching mud. Her friends could hardly believe she had come back from the rear after such a terrible accident. She was hugged and fussed over, she laughed out loud and could not stop talking. Natasha Meklin noticed the tears welling up in Galya's eyes. Then their truck arrived, they all climbed in the back and it moved off, leaving Galya alone on the road, "tall, in her absurdly short coat, looking so lonely, looking after us, waving".

29

"If they get killed, you answer for it to me"

When General Rotmistrov's 7 Armoured Corps broke through into Kotel-nikovo hot on the heels of the enemy, they found fifteen German aircraft at the airfield that had not had time to take off, and a huge number of barrels of aviation fuel. In a dugout were mugs of steaming tea. The Germans had been expecting to greet the New Year here but, caught by surprise, were instead driven out into the icy steppe.

At the station stood trains loaded with tanks, armoured cars, provisions, and German uniforms. The Soviet soldiers were overjoyed. It was their first victory for many long months.

The New Year was celebrated in style by officers and men alike, in marked contrast to the two preceding years. Large quantities of captured delicacies contributed to the jollity. The officers' table was groaning under the weight of food, and there was even champagne which the Germans had readied to celebrate the New Year, as they hoped, in the liberated Cauldron. A captured anti-aircraft gun ceaselessly fired a victory salute, lighting up the sky with the flash of explosions at high altitude. Ordinary soldiers too got German food, and welcomed the chance to celebrate their victory and the New Year with captured schnapps.[358]

Boris Sidnev's entire 268 Guards Fighter Air Division flew into Kotel-nikovo on 3 January, so they were able to make good use of the fuel, the Zwieback dried rusks, and tinned food.[359] Hopefully, Commissar of 85 Air Regiment Dmitry Panov took a good drink of schnapps after what he later referred to as one of the most terrifying experiences in his life.

Commissars having been abolished in October 1941, it was as a humbler "political adviser" that Dmitry Panov, together with technicians from his 85 Air Regiment, was travelling with a spearhead headquarters team in a truck laden with equipment to the new airfield. As they were "racing across the steppe in a fiendish frost on an icy moonlit night", an incident occurred which, to Panov's mind, "showed the terrible wheel of fate coming full circle".[360] "For dozens of kilometres around, the snow glittered in green-tinged moonlight, but suddenly the driver slammed on the brakes, shouting in panic, "Germans!" Panov was struck by a sense of the absurdity of being captured by Germans who were themselves surrounded and doomed to captivity and death. Not far from the road, in a hollow about 100 metres from their truck, stood groups of soldiers in dark uniforms. It was too late to escape. Panov and the technicians snatched up their firearms and loaded them with cartridges. The Germans were standing motionless, as if waiting for something. Five minutes passed. Something strange was going on. No one moved. Finally, one of the technicians decided you only die once and went to investigate. When he came back, he said the Germans were frozen solid. Panov went over and saw that someone had stuck into the snow by their feet the corpses of German infantry who had frozen to death. Such a thing was imaginable "only in some savage theatre of the absurd or a horror movie". Many of the Germans were wearing helmets, some had had rifles stuck in their hands. "The moonlight reflected in their open, frozen eyes. The mouths of some were gaping." Panov was saddened by the thought that what yesterday had been living men were now corpses, frozen "in the name of goals and ideals they had never asked for". His technicians and mechanics were less inclined to philosophise. They "hooted with laughter as they wandered through this macabre forest", knocking the dead men over in the snow.

Flying into Kotelnikovo with 9 Fighter Regiment, Vladimir Lavrinenkov had mixed feelings. It was wonderful to be advancing, freeing his country of its enemies, but painful to see the way the war had changed once familiar places out of all recognition.

He remembered Kotelnikovo as it had been in summer 1942: the white railway station, tall trees along the platform, so many houses around it submerged in orchards. Coming in to land that cold January morning, he saw the station and all the houses were gone. How many charred ruins they had still to see![361]

At the airfield, at least, the Germans had left a welcome legacy. There were bunkers, shelters for the aircraft, workshop and storage facilities. All that was needed was to "clear out the corpses and rubbish".[362] Nine Regiment immediately went to work, flying missions to escort the ground attack bombers. Baranov's 296 Regiment too began operating from the new base.

Lilya Litvyak and Katya Budanova met up with Baranov's 296 Regiment on 4 January, a bright, frosty, sunny day. It was one of those days when, out in the steppe, you do not feel the cold. The air is dry, your face is warmed by bright sunlight, and the snow is blinding. At the airfield they were advised they would have to live in dugouts, but that was nothing new and no one was upset. The men would be accommodated in squadrons, while the women pilots were promised a dugout of their own where they would live with the girl mechanics. Lilya and Katya went off to meet their squadrons.

Lilya Litvyak entered 1 Squadron's dugout together with Faina Pleshiv-tseva and Valya Krasnoshchyokova. Coming from bright sunlight into semi-darkness, they could see nothing at first.[363] Pilots who were not flying that day were lying on their "beds", which were just mounds of earth sculpted when the dugout was built. Aircraft covers were thrown over them, and that was their bedding. Some were playing cards, the inevitable game of Durak ("Fool"). The cards were very well worn and hit the table less with a slap than a tired flop. The young men were startled when girls appeared, but in the darkness Lilya, Faina and Valya could not make out the expression on their faces. "Oh, someone from my home town!" one of the lads exclaimed.

"What makes you think I'm from your town?" Lilya rebuffed him, accustomed to the fact that men always talked to her rather than other girls.

"Not you, her!" the young pilot said, with a nod to Valya who, when she looked more closely, recognised him as Alexey Salomatin from the Kaluga Agricultural College.

There had been more boys at the college than girls, so many local Kaluga girls went to their dances. Valya was taken along to one by a friend, who pointed Alexey out to her. He seemed a rather short, solidly built, blond boy with a curiously prickly look to his eyes, a quality given to them by straight, thick black eyelashes that pointed downwards. Alexey had come to Kaluga from Bunakovo, the village where he had grown up in a peasant family. He was straightforward, sociable and good-hearted but, in Valya's judgement at the time, nothing special. Later, she heard girls from the college say Alexey Salomatin had enrolled at a flying club and was giving himself airs, but then he went off to a flying school and she heard no more of him. Now, only a short time later, here was Alexey Salomatin, a dashing fighter pilot, Hero of the Soviet Union, and squadron leader.

Naturally, they talked about Kaluga, a pleasant merchant town where Valya had been born and grown up, while Alexey spent his teenage years there. It had been liberated already on 30 December 1941, but what had been destroyed in the town, which buildings survived? Which of the people they both knew were fighting in the war, and who had been killed? Most importantly, how were their families? They chatted away, sitting on someone's bed, and Valya was pleased that, even though Alexey was already a captain and a Hero, he talked easily to her as an equal, just as he had in Kaluga. Salomatin and Lilya exchanged a few words, and he told her they would be training together the next day.

The mechanics gossiped that Baranov, having decided to accept the girls in his regiment, had summoned squadron leaders Alexey Salomatin and Alexander Martynov (Martynov was also a Hero of the Soviet Union), and told them, "I'm giving one of the girls to you and the other to you. If they get killed, you answer for it to me."[364]

Later, when Lilya and Alexey were a couple, someone asked Valya if it had been love at first sight. She thought Alexey had immediately found Lilya attractive, as everybody did, but as far as Lilya was concerned, there were other boys more interesting and handsome than Salomatin. Lilya, she felt, had come to love him later, admiring him as an outstanding pilot and a kind, easy-going man. Faina Pleshivtseva disagreed, believing that right there in the dugout "Lilya took a fancy to him."[365] Be that as it may, that meeting in a dugout on a frosty, sunny day is the beginning of their love story.

Galya Dokutovich too was waiting for first love. She had always read a great deal, and confided to her diary that she longed to write if only she had the paper.[366] She was inventing love stories that took place between pilots on the front line. In January 1943, she wrote a story in her diary in which Nikolai, a handsome, dark-eyed pilot, has won a doll in a dancing competition. He gives it to the girl he loves, Olga, who is a pilot flying, needless to say, a U-2. Olga keeps the doll with her on the plane, but before long a girl pilot he does not know brings it to Nikolai. There is a speck of blood on its chin. Olga is no more, and soon Nikolai too is killed.[367]

"Hiya! Are you on the hop again today?" a pilot from a neighbouring regiment asked Galya with a grin. They were going to be flying from a forward airfield again, and those few words and his grin were enough for Galya to want "to burst into song, run headlong down a hill, and jump over a stream!"[368]

30

"Marina Raskova, hero of the Soviet Union, great Russian aviatrix, has concluded her glorious career"

The war correspondent Konstantin Simonov met Marina Raskova in the autumn of 1942 at Kamyshin airfield, halfway between Stalingrad and Saratov.[369] He had never seen her close-up before and had not realised that she was "so young and had such a beautiful face". He was struck by Raskova's "still, gentle Russian beauty". He thought later that the meeting had perhaps been so strongly etched in his memory because she died soon after.

Just before New Year 1943, 587 Heavy Bomber Regiment finally received the long-awaited order to fly at the beginning of January to the Stalingrad Front.[370] Part of the regiment was to fly from the Kalinin Front where they had been active in operations, the rest from Engels. The Second Squadron, led by Klava Fomichyova, suffered an early reverse. They took off and –

what an awful thing to happen – one of Masha Dolina's engines failed.[371] She managed a safe "belly" landing but was terribly upset at being left behind. She was not able to set off in pursuit of her squadron until the morning of 4 January. Raskova and two crews that had been delayed by other difficulties also took off from the other front.

The weather was less than ideal and several times Masha had to put down and wait it out at intermediate airfields. She had no idea where the rest of the regiment's pilots were or which of them had already reached their destination. Landing at one of these airfields to refuel and take a break, she and her crew went to the canteen. Pilots were normally a boisterous, jocular bunch, but today they were subdued and from their sombre expressions it was immediately obvious that something bad had occurred. Masha, her navigator Galya Dzhunkovskaya and gunner Ivan Solyonov looked at them in bewilderment until someone said, "Have you really not heard? Your regimental commander has been killed!"

"What do you mean?" Masha shouted. "That's not something you should joke about!" Even as she was shouting she started to shake. Someone passed her a newspaper that confirmed the terrible news. "On 4 January 1943 while on her way to the Stalingrad Front M. Raskova died in a plane crash."

Raskova had crashed in low cloud while flying from Arzamas to Saratov with the two straggler crews. Before taking off they had received a weather report from the Central Hydrometeorological Centre warning of bad weather along the route.[372] They could fly to Petrovsk, but must land there and wait for the fog to lift. It was dense fog from there on all the way to Razboyshchina Station. The Petlyakov Pe-2 dive-bombers had only basic instruments and in adverse weather conditions were soon helpless. Raskova was well aware that you could not fly them in thick fog, heavy rain or snowfall but decided nevertheless not to wait. She was keen to catch up with the others. As they approached Petrovsk the fog became impenetrable but Raskova decided to fly on. She said it seemed to be clearing. By the time they reached Razboyshchina visibility was zero. It was not the first time the pretty, grey-eyed major had diced with death. She had many times before put her own life, and those of others, at risk. This was to be the last.

Raskova had the regiment's chief navigator, Captain Kirill Khil, flying with her. He was a top-class professional, worshipped in the regiment. Khil could perhaps have saved them but Raskova, also trained as a navi-gator, probably opted to rely on her own judgement. As with many other Russian rivers, the left bank of the Volga slopes gently while the right is steep and high. Raskova sent the aircraft into a dive, intending to break through the fog.[373] Instead they crashed into the right bank of the Volga. The search for them was concentrated far from the scene of the accident, and they were found only after the weather cleared.

The pilot's cockpit took the brunt of the impact and Raskova was killed instantly. A terrible impact with the armour-plated back of the pilot's seat as they hit the bank beheaded Khil. The gunner–radio operator and the chief mechanic of the squadron, who was also travelling with them, would probably have survived if the plane had been found that day. The tail broke off on impact and they were injured. Both men froze to death there beside the aircraft. When they were found, the mechanic was still clutching a bloody towel with which he had been trying to staunch the bleeding from the gunner's injury.

The airwomen Raskova was leading during her last flight were luckier. When the fog began to close in on them they dispersed, since you do not fly in close formation when visibility is low. Both Lyuba Gubina and Galya Lomanova were experienced pilots who before the war had worked as flying club instructors. Lyuba managed to discern the edge of a forest and landed her plane there. Galya Lomanova landed near a railway station. Both were injured and damaged their aircraft, but survived and were able to fly to Moscow to bid farewell to Raskova.

Her body was flown on a U-2 to the Saratov Aviation Plant, which was close to the crash site. The Director, Levin, could not believe this "big-hearted, wonderful, enchanting woman" was dead.[374] Raskova was on friendly terms with his family and, when she came to the plant, would often spend a couple of hours with them, talking, playing the piano, and singing the songs they loved.

Levin reported what had happened to his superiors, and shortly afterwards received instructions to "prepare the body and send it overnight to Moscow". The "preparation" was undertaken by a team led by Sergey Mirotvortsev, a famous academician and surgeon. They did their best to rebuild her face. Raskova's head was intact, but her face was so disfigured it needed more than forty stitches. The initial intention was for Raskova to lie for her final farewell in an open coffin, but this was reconsidered and instead a closed coffin stood in the foyer of the factory's clubhouse. All the workers there and thousands of residents of Saratov and military units went past to pay their last respects to Marina Raskova.

Late that night the body was taken to Moscow in a special carriage attached to an express train. Kirill Khil and the other crew members whose deaths she had caused were buried in a common grave near the scene of the crash.

After hearing the terrible news, Masha Dolina flew on to rejoin her regiment. Everybody there was in mourning.[375] They were all crying, pilots, navigators, gunners and technicians. "There was a painful memorial service at which the entire regiment was in tears," Dolina recalled. The news of Raskova's death was soon passed on to the other two regiments.

Zhenya Rudneva wrote in her diary, "The next day at the squadron's morning inspection we received awful news. Rakobolskaya came in and said, 'Raskova is dead.' There was a gasp. Everybody got to their feet and bared their heads in silence. I was sure there must be a mistake in the newspaper. It could not be true. Our major. Raskova. Thirty-one years old."[376]

Galya Dokutovich wrote in her diary that Raskova was the most remarkable woman she had ever met, her "youthful ideal, organiser and first commander".[377] She was comforted by the thought that, after the other two regiments had ceased to be composed exclusively of women, her own 588 Night Bomber Regiment had become the best embodiment of Raskova's ideal.

The entire country was in mourning. Her death and funeral took up the entire front page of all the national newspapers. *Pravda* wrote in an editorial entitled "Moscow attends Raskova's funeral":

From the high ceilings to the plinth of the funeral urn strips of black crêpe cascade down. In this urn are contained the ashes of one of the most remarkable women of our time, Hero of the Soviet Union Marina Raskova. The Gold Star and two Orders of Lenin glitter on crimson velvet by the plinth.

Members of the Soviet government, People's Commissars, Heroes of Socialist Labour, Heroes of the Soviet Union, the U.S.S.R.'s greatest people stand today beside Raskova's coffin. The hands of the clock approach three. The guard of honour is formed by Moscow Party Secretary A.S. Shcherbakov, Marshal S.M. Budyonny, and V.P. Pronin, Chairman of the Moscow City Council.

It is three o'clock, the time when the funeral urn containing the ashes of Marina Raskova will make its final journey to the Kremlin wall on Red Square.

The urn with the ashes of Raskova moves to the Kremlin wall. A threefold volley and the roar of engines as aircraft fly over Red Square proclaim to Moscow that Marina Raskova, Hero of the Soviet Union, great Russian aviatrix, has concluded her glorious career.

After Raskova's death, as indeed before it, her daughter Tanya was brought up by her grandmother. The command of her orphaned 587 Regiment was entrusted, if only temporarily, to Zhenya Timofeyeva.

Timofeyeva was the most experienced pilot in the Heavy Bomber Regiment. Even before the war she had flown a twin-engined bomber and been a squadron leader, but she had inherited no easy task. After the death of its commander the regiment seemed to lose faith in itself, and others lost faith in it too. At an airfield where 587 Regiment was to land on its way to the Stalingrad Front, on hearing the news that a female bomber regiment was approaching, a mock panic broke out. "Get in the dugouts! Women landing!" the pilots yelled, only half joking.

Zhenya Timofeyeva, like the rest of the unit, was distraught. She kept wondering what future the regiment now had. Would all their hard work in training to fly a complex aircraft have been for nothing? Would they be trusted? They were waiting for the order to move to a front-line airfield on the left bank of the Volga, and in the meantime needed to get on with clearing snow. The snowdrifts were waist high and, leading the women out to the aircraft, Timofeyeva walked backwards because the icy wind bit their faces. When they were hard at work she was summoned to headquarters where she found a representative of 8 Air Army waiting. "Take command of the regiment," she was ordered. Zhenya was shocked. How could she replace Raskova and lead her girls into the first real battle of their lives? She had it on the tip of her tongue to say "No!" but instead heard what sounded like someone else's voice say, "Yes, sir!"

The weather was unchanged over the next few days, with more than forty degrees of frost and a high wind, but they had to get on with their training, flying at high altitude, in formation, and communicating in the air. In the latter half of January she reported that the regiment was ready, and on 28 January they finally set off on their first bombing mission, led by pilots of 10 Bomber Regiment which was stationed at the same airfield. Although her death could not be directly blamed on the Germans, the pilots used a screwdriver to scratch "For Marina Raskova!" on the first 100-kilogram bombs they dropped on their enemy at Stalingrad.

"This will be my last letter for a long time, and perhaps for ever. My friend has to go to the airfield and will take it, because tomorrow the last plane will leave from our kettle of encirclement. The situation is beyond our control. The Russians are three kilometres from our last air base and if we lose that not even a mouse will escape from here, including me. Of course, the same goes for hundreds of thousands of others, but it is small consolation to know that they too are facing death." This letter from an unknown German soldier was airlifted out of the kettle by the last aircraft to land there, but the plane was shot down and the letter never reached its addressee.[378]

Setting out on their first combat mission, 587 Women's Heavy Bomber Regiment was in a state of feverish excitement.[379] Taking to the air at dawn, they peered down at the ground enveloped in freezing mist. They flew over a few villages, saw vehicles driving along roads, and soon had a view of the ruins of Stalingrad, "an endless succession of charred ruins extending along the banks of the Volga". They encountered the first bursts of anti-aircraft fire, small black clouds they had not seen before and which did not, as yet, seem all that frightening. Navigator Valya Kravchenko touched Zhenya's shoulder and pointed towards the ground below. She saw the turn in the road towards the Volga, the skeletons of destroyed buildings, then the Barricades Arms Factory and, finally, their target – the Tractor Factory.

"Keep an eye on the bomb doors of the leading aircraft," Valya said, "and I'll keep an eye on what's happening in the air."[380] At that very moment the hatches of the lead aircraft opened. Zhenya was about to point this out to her navigator when she felt the hatches of her own aircraft open. The leader dived suddenly, straight to where the flak was exploding, and Zhenya followed him. The next explosions were higher and to their right. Bombs rained down from the lead aircraft and Zhenya immediately felt a jolt in her own plane. Their bombs had been dropped. They hit the target.

Masha Dolina's heart too was beating wildly at that moment as she gave herself mental instructions: "Easy, Masha! Maintain height! Bomb hatches opening any minute now." Freed of its deadly cargo her plane bounced upwards. Masha glanced at the navigator, Galya Dzhunkovskaya, the prettiest girl in the regiment who, at that moment, was looking pale. She smiled back and said, "Congratulations on your baptism of fire, Masha!"[381]

On 30 January, when the dark ruins of Stalingrad were shrouded in snow that had fallen overnight, they flew for the first time without lead aircraft, and on 1 February released the last of the 14,980 kilograms of bombs they dropped on Stalingrad.

On 31 January the newly promoted Field Marshal Paulus, who had lost all communication with the outside world, took the decision to surrender. At 0700 hours a German soldier crawled out of the basement of the central department store where Paulus and 6th Army headquarters were holed up, bearing a white flag.

Paulus signed the surrender that same day, but units of his Army, unable to communicate with their headquarters, continued resistance for a further day, so 587 Regiment continued bombing for another twenty-four hours.

Like all who were at Stalingrad in those days, the airwomen were appalled by the sight of a city reduced to rubble. "I suppose my Leningrad looks just the same," Lena Timofeyeva said sadly.[382] Through all the sadness, however, there was joy at the victory, and satisfaction in the sense of having successfully accomplished their mission.

When they had dropped all their bombs, they would often hear the voice of the gunner and radio operator in their headphones: "Ground says thank you for the strike. The tanks are going in."[383] As they left the target area at low level they would see tanks on the move. Behind them Ilyushin ground attack aircraft would flatten the German positions, to be followed by the infantry.

The last German spy plane flew over Stalingrad on 2 February 1943. The pilot reported, "The city is quiet. No signs of continuing hostilities observed." The bomber regiments asked the commander of the Air Army if they could view from the ground the battlefield they had seen only from a height of 2,000–3,000 metres.[384] Permission was granted for all pilots of lead aircraft, and on 4 February they were loaded onto three open trucks (at a temperature of minus twenty-five degrees) and, with stops to let them warm up, travelled to Ilovlya Station, sixty kilometres from Stalingrad. From then on the road was "littered with corpses" of Soviet and German soldiers, interspersed with civilian men, women and children. Before driving into the city they saw armed soldiers and barbed wire entanglements where minefields had yet to be cleared. Beyond was a "battlefield still breathing war. Not all the wounded had yet been gathered up, wrecked aircraft were smoking, tanks burning." Sixty years later, as she dictated her memoirs, Masha Dolina closed her eyes and saw this all again: the dazzlingly white fresh snow, and on it the black hordes of Paulus's encircled army. Looking at the starving, frozen Germans Masha felt only hatred. "Half-dead, frozen Krauts were straggling along and falling. We felt such rage at the sight of these captured fascists, this filth. They were skulking along like a pack of wolves. None of them helped a fallen comrade." She remembered that "monstrous sight" for the rest of her life.

Hatred of the enemy was so overwhelming that Masha's kind heart felt no twinge of pity for these unfortunates. The civilian population too, after all the sufferings and tragedy they had endured, gave vent to their fury.[385] Prisoners tried to march as close to the head of the columns as they could, near the guards. The local women, children and old men would attack them, tearing off their blankets, spitting in their faces, throwing stones at them. Those who were too weak to march any further were vengefully shot by the Russians, just as the Germans had shot Russian prisoners of war. Of almost 100,000 German soldiers taken prisoner only half survived The rest were shot by guards who felt no pity, or died of hunger or sickness on their way to camps, or after they arrived. Some rotted alive in hospitals, where the Russians gave them virtually no medical treatment.

In the ruined city Masha Dolina was treated to a sight of Paulus himself. There were five truckloads of people wanting to see the defeated Field Marshal. When Masha and her comrades arrived, Paulus came out to them pale, haggard, and stony-faced. They wanted to ask questions, but the composed and dignified Paulus refused to talk.

Major Valentin Markov arrived in the women's 587 Heavy Bomber Regiment after Stalingrad. The pilots believed Zhenya Timofeyeva was perfectly capable of leading it, but the senior officers decided a career army commander was needed. As no woman judged capable of leading the regiment was to be found, they sent in the slender, brown-haired, highly-decorated major. Neither he nor the women's regiment was overwhelmed.[386]

Markov was thirty-three and had been commanding a men's dive-bomber regiment. He was shot down and wounded, had a spell in hospital and, emerging to learn what his new appointment was to be, felt as if a bucket of ice-cold water had been poured over his head. He simply could not see himself in command of a women's regiment. These planes were difficult to fly. How could women be expected to cope with them? Markov's first reaction was, "Why me?" When asked whether he would like to command the regiment, he replied that he would not and asked his superiors to find someone else. The question, however, had been purely a matter of form. The order had been signed. He had no choice.

Coming out of the office at headquarters "pale and angry", Markov told his friends waiting outside the door the position he had been given. He recalled, "Their hair stood on end," and they thought trying to command a women's regiment would drive Markov mad.

A thousand questions assailed him. How should he behave towards these women, whom he assumed he would find fickle and over-sensitive? How could he instil the discipline essential on combat missions? And how would they rate him against their beloved Raskova? Markov decided to be "fair, strict and demanding", and hope for the best.[387]

In fact he fitted into his new role admirably, although the girls agreed they could not imagine a greater contrast to Raskova. Their new commander's manner was stern and cold. They saw him as "tall, thin, and gloomy", and immediately nicknamed him "The Dagger". At their first parade his expression conveyed the unambiguous message that he saw his appointment as a humiliation and a cross he would just have to bear.[388]

"Let's start with discipline," Markov said severely, "like a warder talking to convicts", as he surveyed his troops, who had just floundered through three kilometres of deep snow from the village, lined up in the thirty-degree frost. He warned them he would make no allowances for the weaker sex, stuck his finger in a hole in the jacket of a girl mechanic, and caustically pointed out to another girl that her boots were dirty. How they hated him! There began an endless cycle of getting ready for parades, drilling of aircrews, drilling of armourers. Heaven forbid that anyone should fail to march properly on parade; heaven forbid anyone should smear too much grease on their weapon. "Save that for when you are buttering bread at home, young woman," Markov told one with an icy stare.

It was only when they started flying with Markov that they saw he was exactly the kind of commander they needed.

31

"Why would you want to expose yourself to deadly danger?"

At last Anna Yegorova's dream came true: she was going to fly the Ilyushin Il-2, a ground-attack aircraft nicknamed "The Hunchback" by the Russians and "Meat-grinder" by the terrified Germans. She cannot have been the only pilot of the small, defenceless U-2s who fervently hoped one day to fly the death-dealing Il-2. But the losses of Il-2 pilots were even greater than those flying the U-2.

In their new air assault regiment, Anna Yegorova and her friends were called in one by one for an interview by the political adviser.[389] We have no idea what he talked to the men about, but his first question to Anna was, "Why would you want to expose yourself to deadly danger?" "Oh, don't tell me it's deadly!" she threw back at him. The officer told her that their losses were "rather heavy", and added, "I can tell you in confidence that in the recent fighting at Gizel, almost none of our pilots came back."

His fatherly advice to Anna was to be prudent and go back to a training regiment where she would be more useful as an instructor. Flying a ground assault bomber was no work for a woman. He was speaking without hostility or any lack of respect, but lately Anna had been receiving similar advice so regularly that she flew off the handle at the least provocation.

"Well, what is suitable work for women in war, Comrade Commissar?" she demanded. "Nursing? Straining yourself beyond all reason to drag wounded soldiers off the battlefield under fire? Or being a sniper? Spending hours in all weathers stalking enemies, killing them and getting killed yourself?"

The commissar tried to say something, but now there was no stopping Anna.

"Perhaps it would be less dangerous to be airdropped behind enemy lines with a radio? Or maybe it is easier now for women in the rear, smelting metal or growing crops, while trying at the same time to bring up children?"

The commissar did not try to argue, just smiled sadly and told Anna he had an equally crazy daughter. She was a doctor at the front, somewhere near Stalingrad, but he had had no letters from her for a long time.

Soon Anna was travelling by rail with the assault regiment to collect new Il-2 aircraft from the factory. The railway carriage was noisy, the pilots exultant at the Red Army's tremendous success at Stalingrad, only regretting that they would have no chance of fighting there as they trundled slowly on their way to collect their aircraft. On 2 February they heard at one of the stations a loudspeaker announcement from the Soviet Informbyuro news agency that "Hitler's Army Group South, led by Field Marshal Paulus, has surrendered." Soon after that, they reached their destination, expecting to take delivery of the new aircraft that, they were promised, would be ready any day now. This proved to be nonsense. There was also a long queue in the canteen at the factory's airfield. To be issued an aluminium spoon you had first to surrender your fur hat as security because the spoons were constantly being pilfered. The food was unexciting: what they described as "hunter's soup", where you had to pursue isolated pieces of vegetable round the bowl, the inevitable "shrapnel porridge" and, smeared over a large aluminum plate, "dessert à la raspberry". The men joked, "It'll keep you alive, but you won't feel like chasing girls." They were accommodated in a dugout "the size of a tunnel in the Moscow Metro, with two tiers of bunks". It was here that Anna was one day brought a letter from Tanya Fyodorova, a friend from her days building the Metro.

Tanya wrote about new Metro stations, which were still being built in spite of the war – Novokuznetskaya, Paveletskaya, Avtozavodskaya – and about their friends in the flying club, almost all of whom were now at the front. Anna's instructor, Miroyevsky, and Sergey Feoktistov were flying ground attack bombers; Valeriy Vishnikov, Yevgeny Minshutin and Sergey Korolyov were fighter pilots. Many had already been killed: Luka Mirovitsky, Ivan Oparin, Alexander Lobanov, Vasiliy Kochetkov, Victor Kutov . . .

What? Victor? Anna was in shock. Everything faded into darkness, the sun, the people, the war. She was suffocating. Next she saw the kind face of the regimental doctor. He said, "Go ahead, cry, my dear, go ahead. That's going to help . . . " But Anna could not cry. "Something unbearably heavy had fallen on my heart and did not shift for many, many years after that . . . "

Soon, when they were on the Southern Front, she had an unusually vivid, beautiful dream. She had returned that day, tired and very cold, to the little house Dr Kozlovsky had insisted she should be allocated. The stove was warm, the coals had not yet gone out and were glowing prettily with little flickering red, blue and gold flames. Anna warmed herself at it and, without undressing, fell asleep on the bed. She dreamed of Victor, as vividly as if he had been with her. He was wearing a white shirt with a tie and an embroidered Tajik skullcap. Anna was with him, wearing a black velveteen skirt and blue shirt with a white collar and lacing. She had a white beret, white stockings, and white slippers with a blue trim. Her beret, the latest word in chic, was barely managing to cling to the top of her head and her right ear. Anna actually had owned "all this splendour" before the war. She had acquired it in the hard currency Torgsin shop on the strength of an old gold coin her mother gave her. Admittedly, Victor had never been known to wear a tie. Thus attired, they were strolling together over a vast, daisy-covered meadow in Sokolniki Park. How relaxed and happy she felt in this dream! Someone knocked on the door, but she had no wish to wake up. They hammered louder and louder, shouting her name, but her body would not obey her. She got up somehow and began crawling along the wall towards the door but fell before reaching it. She managed to crawl on and, with great difficulty, unlocked it. Some of the pilots had looked in on her quite by chance, and if they had not she would have been dead in the morning, poisoned by fumes from the stove.

They nursed her all night, walking her up and down outside in the fresh air, and in the morning took her to the good doctor in his surgery. She told him about her dream, adding, "It would have been better if I had never woken up."

His kind face became stern and he said, "Death will come to everyone in due course, but not everyone manages to live their life in this world with dignity." The next day, Anna pulled herself together and attended the training session to fly the Il-2 as if nothing had happened. She put powder on her face to hide the scratches from her fall.

On the other flank of the Southern Front, the regiments of Boris Sidnev's Fighter Division took to the sky. January had been a fairly quiet month for them. "Aerial Combat missions – 3," Major Krainov, political adviser of Baranov's 296 Fighter Regiment, noted in his secret report. "During this period, no enemy aircraft were shot down. There were no combat losses in the regiment." Katya Budanova's biographers claim that on 8 January she was paired with Baranov and took part in a dogfight with four Focke-Wulf aircraft, one of which was shot down.[390] There is no mention of this in the regimental records and it is probably another legend. Litvyak and Budanova's successes in 296 Fighter Regiment began only in February 1943, but what victories they were!

The Southern Front was preparing to attack Rostov-on-Don. If the city could be recaptured speedily, the German armies in the Caucasus could be encircled, and in far greater numbers than in the Stalingrad Cauldron. In early January, on the orders of the Military Council of the Stalingrad Front, commanders and political officers "gave talks explaining the heroic exploits of aircrews and the selfless labour of maintenance workers". The advance of Soviet troops was demonstrated on maps, unlike the only too recent retreat. In 296 Fighter Regiment the propaganda campaign involved all Party members, headed by "Batya" Baranov himself who "explained the significance of the attack and of the rout of the German hordes at Stalingrad".

Valya Krasnoshchyokova likened Batya to the Soviet aviation hero, test pilot Valeriy Chkalov: like him, he was an intrepid pilot and a good man. His pupil and friend, Alexey Maresiev who became a great Soviet war hero, felt the same way about him.[391] Shot down over enemy territory and wounded in both legs, Maresiev crawled eighteen kilometres, trying to get back to his unit. Later, after his legs were amputated, he began flying again and returned to his combat unit. "Baranov was my first commander at the front. I can see him as if he was here now: average height, solidly built, with curly, slightly ginger hair. You could see the willpower in his eyes. As a commander he was strict, but liked people and recognised their good qualities. Baranov was the first to teach me what is most important for any pilot, the art of skilfully, resourcefully, and unpredictably conducting a dogfight," Maresiev recalled.

Yevgeny Radchenko of 296 Regiment tells us that Baranov taught the pilots, his subordinates and his students to fight "by personal example. Whenever there was a really difficult mission, he would lead the group himself." [392] Radchenko adds that Baranov was fun-loving, and he really did have a unique personality. From childhood he wanted to ride with the cavalry, but the inexorable march of progress obliged him to adjust his plans and he became a pilot. Nevertheless, there was something of the swashbuckling cavalry officer about him. On one occasion, Timofey Khryukin, commander of 8 Air Army, arrived at the regiment to find Baranov sending his pilots off on their missions in very strange attire. He was barefoot, wearing a peasant shirt instead of a military tunic, and giving them the signal to take off with a sabre. (Heaven only knows how he had come by that.) "Take a look at yourself, Baranov," was all Khryukin said. He was the same age as Baranov and liked and respected him. [393]

In January 1943, Krainov had reported to the head of the political department of 6 Guards Air Division on the propaganda work he had carried out. "The political and moral condition of the regiment's personnel is healthy. All personnel in the regiment and the Party and Komsomol organisation are focused on carrying out the combat orders of the regiment's commanders. The personnel are inspired by the successful advance of our Red Army and are putting all their strength into hastening the rout of the enemy." Suitable topics were selected for talks to be given by the Party members to other members of the regiment, such as: "Revolutionary Vigilance During the Advance of the Red Army". The girl armourers were given a special talk by Major Guskov on the need to "Increase Revolutionary Vigilance!"

The political workers had long been aware of the particular difficulty of indoctrinating women. We do not know what Major Krainov thought about his regiment's female cadres, but Political Adviser Panov in the neighbouring 85 Regiment sometimes lost patience. One evening he was conducting an indoctrination session with the female personnel in which they were being assured that: "America and England will not abandon us in our hour of need, the Japs in the Pacific Ocean are facing total collapse, the Yugoslav partisans have again taught the Germans a lesson they will not forget, and Rommel in Africa is stuck in the sands of the desert. Furthermore, not only does the Red Army now have at its disposal Katyusha rockets and new tanks, but also the heroic traditions of our ancestors, (admittedly counts and princes, but good ones), Suvorov and Kutuzov."[394] The girls, some of whom, after a tiring day and not expecting the political adviser to be dropping in, had already gone to bed, did appear to be listening, but their vacant eyes told him they were thinking about other matters. Suddenly a black-eyed girl called Nadya lifted her blanket and, to the great amusement of her friends, invited him to join her. "Oh, Commissar, Commissar, where do you have to go? Nip in under my blanket!" Panov had no option but to abandon his political indoctrination session and take his leave with some alacrity.

One way a newly demoted commissar could make himself useful was by improving the living conditions of the mechanics and technicians, if he could be bothered. Krainov could be bothered, and often upbraided the commander of the airfield maintenance battalion for various problems and oversights. The victory at Stalingrad brought little improvement in conditions for the technical staff. As one political report noted, while "the regiment's aircrew are always fed well and in a timely and ample manner with hot meals," maintenance staff, often "because of dysfunction in the work of the ASB",* did not have enough to eat. In 1943 and later, especially

---

* The Airfield Support Battalion: functions of the battalion included servicing the pilots and crews as well as organising food, clothing and accommodation.

during the final advance, maintenance staff were often "fed abominably: millet concentrate was boiled which they had to drink without seasoning."[395] All this time, while moving from one airfield to another, they were unable to wash and just could not get rid of their lice. These had appeared at Stalingrad, which was hardly surprising as there was no question there of being able to wash. The regimental engineer remarked one morning to mechanic Kolya Menkov, "Well, Menkov, that's a lot of Messers you've got crawling over you!"[396] But how were they to be dealt with? They used petrol to exterminate the lice on clothing, and picked them off themselves, but within a few days they were back. The command took the matter seriously only after someone caught typhus. At that stage everybody was washed thoroughly and clothing treated, but that was already towards the end of January 1943 when they liberated Zernograd.

32

"Street women and all sorts of madcaps"

"The Germans are in retreat and we are going after them," Zhenya Rudneva of 588 Night Bomber Regiment wrote in her diary. Four Air Army was on the heels of German troops withdrawing from the Caucasus.

She reported to her parents that "because we are constantly on the move the field mail will be even worse than it was. Now it really is our turn to celebrate on our street. We are attacking and will stay here for a day or two before moving on again to a new place, because the Krauts are scrambling to get away at amazing speed."[397] Zhenya wrote in her letters that the girls in her regiment found themselves lodging with the same women as they had last summer. Then, as now, they would only stay in one place for a short while since they were constantly changing airfields as they retreated along with the ground troops. But now they were moving in the opposite direction.[398] Zhenya was sharing with Galya Dokutovich, who felt terribly sorry for the local people and noted in her diary how much the

Germans had destroyed while they were there and how shamelessly they had robbed the inhabitants.

Heaven knows who told them the myth about themselves that was said to be circulating among the Germans. Galya noted, "The Hitlerites have found out about the existence of our regiment" and were supposedly saying that "our regiment recruits street women and all kinds of madcaps, and that we are given special injections which half stop us being women. We are half-women, half-men, sleep during the day and go out bombing at night."[399] There was also a story that when a U-2 from the men's regiment fell into German hands "they all, especially the officers, rushed to the plane to goggle at the woman pilot. The crew were men, but were made to strip naked anyway."

The Night Witches believed this silly story. Even though they had been so many months at the front and seen so many terrible things, they were still very naive and inexperienced. Many had never seen a dead enemy soldier.

Natasha Meklin first saw a German corpse in February 1943 at Rasshevatka Station. The Germans had been driven out just the day before by General Kirichenko's Cavalry Corps. The village was in flames and the bodies of people and horses were everywhere. On the side of the road to the airfield Natasha and her pilot Irina Sebrova came upon a dead German soldier. He was lying behind a mound and Natasha almost fell over him. The girls stopped to look. They were silent. The German was young, without his uniform, in blue underwear. "The body was pale and waxen, the head thrown back and turned to one side. It had straight fair hair frozen to the snow."[400] It looked as if he had just turned round and was staring in horror at the road, expecting something to happen.

Until then the girls had only a vague idea of what the death they sowed every night might look like at close quarters: "Suppress the point of fire," "Bomb the crossing," "Destroy enemy combat resources." It all sounded so abstract and straightforward. They knew that every enemy killed brought the hour of victory closer, and that was why they had gone to war in the first place. Now, however, contemplating the bloodless face of a dead enemy on which the fresh snow was not melting, his arm thrown to one side with its fingers tensed, Natasha experienced mixed emotions: depression, revulsion, but also pity. "Tomorrow I shall be bombing again," she reflected, "and the day after that, and the day after that until the war is over or until I am killed myself."

"We are 150 kilometres from the front line," Galya Dokutovich wrote on 2 February 1943. "Tomorrow we fly on to catch up with it."[401]

They flew again and again in the direction of Krasnodar: 4 Air Army was providing support for the North Caucasus Front, which was advancing rapidly on the capital of the Kuban. "We are flying. I have flown 28 sorties already. At present we are in Dzherelievskaya. We have got used to not sleeping at night, whether we are working or not. It is like being on the front line here. Enemy spies are snooping all the time and they have their aircraft in the sky. The fascists are pulling all their equipment and troops out of the Caucasus to the Kerch Strait. We are pecking at them from the sky. Rostov, Shakhty, Novoshakhtinsk, Konstantinovka have been recaptured, and yesterday we heard the news that Kharkov has been taken," she wrote on 17 February.[402] Events had moved so quickly that the retaking of Krasnodar just five days previously seemed already a thing of the distant past. The newspapers were still writing about it, however, and emphasising the heroic part played by 4 Air Army.

German units withdrew through Rostov, blowing up the bridges behind them. Having begun to retreat on 10 January 1943, within four weeks all formations of the German 17th Army fighting in the Caucasus had descended on the Kuban bridgehead.

At the beginning of the fighting to retake Rostov, Baranov's 296 Regiment had just fifteen serviceable aircraft left, and two that were being repaired in Kotelnikovo.[403] Four planes on the far side of the Volga had to be written off as irreparable. The pilots took turns flying the few aircraft available. Lilya Litvyak now often shared the same plane as Semyon Gorkhiver, an arrangement that suited the mechanics because Gorkhiver was short and only slightly taller than Litvyak, so when one of them flew after the other there was no need to adjust the pedals. Lilya and Semyon enjoyed sharing a joke.[404]

On 10 February, Kutsenko, Salomatin, Budanova and Gorkhiver distinguished themselves by shooting down three German aircraft.[405] Litvyak was not far behind. On 11 February the regiment "flew 20 missions to provide cover for Soviet ground troops". In the course of the day the regiment's commander, Nikolai Baranov, and Lilya Litvyak both shot down a Stuka, and one Messerschmitt was shot down by a group of other pilots. In his secret report, Political Adviser Major Krainov noted the vanguard role of Communists in the operation: "Member of the C.P.S.U.(b) Senior Lieutenant Salomatin and Member of the C.P.S.U.(b) Captain Verblyudov are fearless combatants in the air."[406]

Alexey Salomatin, however, had less and less time to devote to Communist Party activities, because he had fallen in love. You can hide nothing in a regiment, and the relationship blossoming between two pilots in the First Squadron was public knowledge. Salomatin was so popular and admired in the regiment, and Litvyak had performed so well in her first dogfights since joining the unit, that their feelings were treated with great respect even by pilots who loved playing the fool and winding their friend up. Both the pilots and mechanics did their best to "make it possible for them to be alone".[407] At the beginning of March Salomatin and Litvyak applied to Baranov for permission to marry. This was granted, but even then they had little opportunity to be together. The only chance they had to spend time together by themselves was at night. More often than not they would be allocated a small room in a peasant hut, but with the front advancing, their temporary refuges changed frequently.[408] Sometimes though they managed to grab the chance to take a break from the relentless fighting. There is a lovely photograph that must have been taken on one of these precious afternoons. Pilots crowd on all sides round an off-roader – it is strange to see these pilots beside a vehicle other than a plane. Alexander Martynov is to one side, while Alexey Salomatin is closer to Lilya, his elbows on the bonnet, his chin resting on his hands. Batya is sitting on the running board, showing off his new yellow buckskin boots. The pilots had these made from leather stripped off the fuel tanks of downed Junkers. They were purely for show, and hopeless at keeping water out. They look so carefree and happy that it is hard to believe three of them would be dead within months of the picture having been taken.

"This is a time for bombing and bombing," Zhenya Rudneva wrote in her diary.[409] The ground was thawing out and atrocious, impassable mud marked the coming of spring. It caught whole columns of German vehicles retreating on the roads from the Caucasus. The only problem for the Russians was that their planes were also unable to taxi out through the mud for take-off, and there were no fuel deliveries. The airfield maintenance battalion vehicles got stuck in the mud too.

This necessitated some changes to the regiment's routine. They had to go out to the airfield long before it was light in order to drag the aircraft from their stands to the runway. The undercarriages sank deep into the mud, and the mechanics' feet in their canvas boots did the same. "In peacetime," Raisa Aronova reflected, "no one in their right mind would consider flying with this sort of mud." How remote peacetime seemed now. Katya Piskaryova would just stop a local man on the road and say, "Come on, uncle, give us a hand!"

The lack of fuel meant they had to fly less frequently, which created an opportunity for some of the personnel to be sent to a health resort. Yessentuki, the best resort and hospital in the Caucasus, was only 200 kilometres away, and had just been recaptured from the Germans.

"I've been given a pass to the Yessentuki sanatorium," Galya Dokutovich recorded on 24 February.[410] It was unlike her to agree to go to a sanatorium when none of them could wait for the airfield to dry out and the fuel trucks to get back on the roads, but Galya was feeling very ill. "I feel awful. I try not to show it, but I am afraid my endurance may soon fail," she confessed, but only to her diary.[411] She said nothing to her friends, not even Polina. They were not blind, no matter how hard

Galya tried to hide her suffering, but the only time Polina tried to talk to her about it, Galya got very angry and forbade her to mention it again.

After several months of occupation, the sanatorium in the newly liberated town was probably not in a great state to receive visitors, but the soldiers were undemanding. Soon after arriving, Galya wrote in her diary that she was already getting used to conditions there and was not too bored. In addition, she had found someone who was giving a lot of meaning to her stay there.

It is a simple matter to trace her developing relationship with Misha, a blue-eyed pilot, through her diary entries. First there is a note that some officers came into the girls' room, and "behaved too freely", and started saying such things that Galya had to leave. Then she admits to the diary how surprised she is to find that one of them, Misha, is really "a very genuine and profound person". Misha left, and Galya writes that one of the staff told her, "He left his heart with you, Galya." She thought to herself, "He does not know that he also took mine with him!" "Wonderful, blue-eyed Misha with that shock of tousled hair" flew a Boston, an American heavy bomber, in a regiment deployed not too far from where the Night Witches were, so there was a chance they might meet again soon. After Misha's departure, time dragged "unbelievably slowly". She just wanted "to get back to the regiment as soon as possible, back to work". And also, back to where she might "if only in passing" get to see Misha.

The deadly danger she faced every night she was flying seemed to Galya wholly negligible compared to the threat to Misha flying his Boston. Galya was in love.

33

"Despite the pain continued to fight the enemy"

In flying weather the fighter pilots often made several sorties a day and, when they landed, were so exhausted by the stress of combat they did not have the strength to climb out of the plane immediately. Valya Krasno-shchyokova remembered that sometimes, after flying a third or fourth mission, the exhausted pilots would have to be literally pulled out of their aircraft by Pleshivtseva and herself.[412] The Germans were less formidable in the air than a year ago, but still strong.

Baranov's pilots no longer had any misgivings about the girls, especially Litvyak whom most considered an "average to good pilot".[413] In March, her name crops up frequently in the records of the unit, now known as 73 Guards Fighter Regiment after receiving the honorific title of "Guards".

On 7 March 1943, Litvyak "made a forced landing at the Selmash [in fact, Rostselmash] airfield". The cause, as the political adviser reported, was "being investigated".[414] Before it was discovered there had been a mechanical failure, there were many jokes circulating among the men. It was held, and may have been true, that Lilya did not have much of a grasp of technical matters. People recalled the reprimand she received from the regimental engineer when she arrived back at the airfield with only a few drops of petrol left, having failed to take account of the direction and speed of the wind. "Oh, lassie!" he scolded. "As long as the wee stick on the front keeps going round and round you think everything's fine!"[415] Very soon, however, Lilya again proved she was not to be laughed at. "During the period 22, 23 and 24 March the regiment was providing air cover for the city of Rostov," wrote Major Krainov in his routine report to the political department. "At the time of raiding by hostile bombers of the city of Rostov, air battle was conducted, as a result 2 aircraft of the enemy of type Junkers Ju-87 and 1 of type Junkers Ju-88 and 1 Messerschmitt Bf-109 were shot down. In the air battle there distinguished themselves: Member of the Communist Party Lieutenant Kaminsky (shot down 1 Junkers Ju-88, which

37. Vladimir Mikoyan (in the middle) with pilots from his regiment.

38. Klava Blinova with male pilots from her regiment.

39. Pilot Klava Blinova.

40. Galya Dokutovich in Yessentuki.

41. Lilya Litvyak by her plane.

42. Anna Yegorova, Il-2 pilot, summer 1943.

43. Boris Yeremin in his Yak, 1943.

45. *Above:* Pilot Antonina (Tonya)
Lebedeva.

44. *Left:* Pilot Alexey Salomatin.

46. Lilya with pilots of her regiment, Nikolai Baranov (sitting in the car) and Alexey Salomatin (standing behind the car, his chin propped on his hands).

47. Sasha Martynov, Nikolai Baranov, Lilya and Salomatin.
Both this picture and the photograph above were almost certainly taken in early May 1943.

48. Salomatin's funeral.

49. Katya Budanova in military uniform in Moscow, April–June 1943.

50. The photo taken by Yakov Khalip of the refugee family returning to their village, who Simonov encountered in Ponyri.

52. *Above:* Regiment commander Ivan Golyshev.

51. *Left:* Mechanic Nikolai Menkov, 1944.

53. Veterans of the 46 Guards Night Bomber Regiment on Victory Day in front of the Bolshoi Theatre.

54. Valentina Vashchenko with her students, Krasny Luch, Ukraine. For many years, schoolteacher Vashchenko and pupils from her school searched for the remains of Lilya Litvyak and her plane.

fell in the district of Gorodishche), Senior Sergeant Borisenko (shot down 1 Junkers Ju-87 enemy aircraft), Member of the Komsomol Junior Lieutenant Litvyak (shot down 1 Junkers Ju-87), Member of the Communist Party and Hero of the Soviet Union Captain Martynov damaged 1 aircraft of type Messerschmitt Bf-109." Further on, he returns to Litvyak. "Showing courage, Junior Lieutenant Litvyak wounded made a safe landing at her airfield, her plane was hit in the air battle and requires repair." [416]

In his more comprehensive monthly report, Krainov noted that "On 22 March Member of the Komsomol Junior Lieutenant Litvyak courageously engaged in combat a group of enemy Junkers Ju-88 bombers, was wounded in aerial combat, but despite the pain continued to fight the enemy heroically and at close range shot down a Junkers Ju-88, leaving the battle only when her air system was punctured. Of such combat are capable only daughters of the Russian people," Krainov concluded on a note of suitable hyperbole.

Lilya became a celebrity. She was featured in *Komsomolskaya Pravda*. The Tur Brothers, well-known playwrights who went to the front as war correspondents, wrote about her in *Stalin's Falcons*. Needless to say, in an article entitled "The Girl Avenger", they could not omit to describe her appearance. "Lilya Litvyak is 20 years old, a lovely springtime in the life of a maiden! A fragile figure with golden hair as delicate as her very name – Lilya."

The article described how Lilya, on her third sortie at Stalingrad, had shot down a German pilot who had been "awarded three German crosses". It added that she now had a reputation as "one of the Front's outstanding pilots", and related that, after being wounded, she managed to save her stricken plane. Noting that this young woman was quite without affectation, the reporters quoted her as saying, "When I see a plane with those crosses and the swastika on its tail fin, I experience just one feeling – hatred. That emotion seems to make my grip firmer on the firing buttons of my machine guns."

The article was printed immediately, and a day or two after the wounded Lilya was taken to hospital in Rostov, the whole town knew about her and her exploits. Lilya Litvyak did not just have visits from Katya, the girl mechanics and the male pilots in her regiment. There were features about her in the Rostov and regional newspapers, and streams of residents came to see her, bringing gifts and sweets, despite the fact that after the occupation most of them had almost nothing left.[417] Lilya did not stay in the hospital long, however, and within a few days had returned to her regiment with heaps of gifts, happy, proud, and limping heavily. The wound was superficial, to the soft tissue of her thigh, but it hurt.

She really needed a longer stay in hospital but insisted on being discharged. Instead Batya, and possibly Sidnev himself, offered her something she could not refuse: a leave in Moscow, and moreover with Katya Budanova, who was detailed to accompany her friend. They were seen off in style. "They drank, and ate bottled apples Baranov brought," and sang songs.[418]

Lilya's brother Yury was fifteen years old, and remembered the return of his beloved sister from the front very well. The next day, after catching up on all the news with her mother, she ran off and returned with two friends. Katya Budanova joined them after she had spent time with her sister and nieces and given them the food she had brought with her. There was a lot of noise and fun that day in the room where Lilya's family lived. The girls cranked up the gramophone and played "Rio Rita" very loudly. Lilya's mother, Anna Vasilievna, patched her clothes and mended her uniform.[419]

Lilya had returned home in uniform, but Yury recalled she brought in her rucksack "a dress with some green bits". He had no idea what the dress was made of, but we have. "That's right. Our girls were the prettiest in 8 Army," the pilots of 73 Guards Regiment recalled. "Do you remember in Rostov we got them German fishnet stockings? They sewed everything themselves, you understand. They sewed amazingly pretty dresses out of German parachutes. Basket-weave silk! The way they trimmed them was, they took German anti-aircraft shells. The gunpowder in them was in little green bags made of viscose. They chucked the gunpowder out and used the green viscose for trimming their dresses. You couldn't take your eyes off them!" [420] A waitress in the Aerodrome Maintenance Battalion who recalled Lilya very well remembered this dress. In Rostov the Red Army captured such quantities of German air munitions that all the girls in 8 Air Army could have been dressed like that, but Lilya sewed better than any of them.

In the cold Moscow of late March, where it was no warmer in people's apartments than outside in the street, the dress was not very suitable. While her newly laundered uniform was drying, Lilya and her mother together very quickly ran up a suit from an offcut which was either a left-over or which Lilya had brought home with her. Anna Vasilievna kept that suit, and today, faded, it is conserved behind glass in a school museum in Krasny Luch near where Lilya died. [421]

Lilya did not stay home for long, in a hurry to get back to her regiment, her friends, and Alexey. She was too embarrassed to tell her mother anything about her intimate relationship with Salomatin. Even in letters home, she called it a friendship. [422]

Katya Budanova was held up in Moscow, most probably on Komsomol business. "Where is she?" Lilya asked in letters home. [423] She missed her friend, but Katya returned only at the end of June. In Moscow, she met a lot of people, including the poet Samuil Marshak whom she already knew. After Katya's death, Marshak wrote his "Song of Katya Budanova", which was set to music. In June, Katya gave a talk at an aircraft factory where she had once worked. She told her audience, "It is not at all frightening in battle, girls, but afterwards, when you are sitting on the ground and close your eyes and think back through all that happened, that is when you get frightened, and go hot and cold, and shake with fear." [424]

While Litvyak and Budanova were away, Valya and Faina were settling into a community of women, which was something new for them. There were still a few girl armourers in 296 Regiment. One night Batya Baranov descended on the house in Rostov where they were living, drunk and in a sportive mood. He went to every girl's bed, pulled off her blanket, and "watered" her with a kettle. The girls shrieked. Only Faina Pleshivtseva kept her head. She got out of the bed where she slept next to Valya, padded in her bare feet over to the bucket, scooped up a mugful of water and poured it over his head. Batya immediately sobered up and departed. After that he was very wary of Faina and Valya.[425] When drunk he was apt to pinch the bottoms of other girls. Valya, however, had already decided that he was basically a good man and an outstanding pilot, and shrugged it off on the basis that everyone has their weaknesses. Someone living constantly under that level of stress does sometimes just need to get drunk.

Litvyak was back in her regiment within a week. Had she stopped off somewhere on the way back? Gridnev, commander of 586 Fighter Regiment, in memoirs written late in life, claimed that Litvyak had suddenly turned up in the women's regiment. According to Gridnev, she had been seconded back to 586 Regiment and came to demand that he should allow her to return to Baranov's regiment in which her fiancé was a pilot. She was very forward and talked on equal terms with Gridnev, but he understood that he was not dealing with an ordinary pilot: Litvyak was already a celebrity. Gridnev told her he had no authority in the matter, and that the order could only be cancelled by Air Defence Command.[426] No challenge was too great for Litvyak, who promptly went to Moscow to have the order rescinded there. She evidently succeeded, because that was the last the women's regiment saw of her.

The regiment's veterans disagree with Gridnev's account. They did not care at all for his memoirs, and even demanded that the manuscript should be burned.[427] Unfortunately, it seems likely that we will never known for sure how true his often sensational recollections are. Almost no veterans of 586 Regiment are still alive, and those who are decline to talk about this topic, as if they have something to hide. However, bearing in mind how many myths and outright lies proliferated around Lilya's good name, it may be that Gridnev's account is the only true one and that she did not go to Moscow on leave, but to talk to people in positions of power and petition Air Defence Command to let her return to Alexey. Perhaps that is also why Katya Budanova spent so long in Moscow. Was she seeking permission to remain in Baranov's regiment? But why, in that case, did only Litvyak go to speak to Gridnev?

There certainly was an attempt to bring back to Gridnev's 586 Fighter Regiment the other pilots who left it at the time of the Battle of Stalingrad and later refused to go back. These were Klava Blinova and Tonya Lebedeva, and later also Masha Kuznetsova and Anya Demchenko, who joined Kuznetsova heaven knows how. Blinova and Lebedeva had the benefit of knowing Vasiliy Stalin, but Kuznetsova and Demchenko wilfully remained in a male regiment, persuaded by the pilots, who included Masha's future husband, that this insubordination would go unpunished. They were soon summoned to Moscow.[428] Masha and Anya were dripping with sweat in their winter pilots' uniforms, which they had been unable to get changed out of because they were not attached to any regiment. When they reached Air Defence Command headquarters, General Osipenko subjected them to such a barrage of abuse that even Anya Demchenko, not usually noted for her reticence, was abashed. At this point, General Gromadin, commander of Air Defence Forces, himself came to their aid. "Give them aircraft and let them fly," he ordered Osipenko. The girls were given overcoats to change into and sent off to a rest facility in the countryside. Masha managed to get permission to spend a day in Moscow to introduce Anya to her family.

The next day they were summoned and told to be at a reception at the Mongolian Embassy. Mongolian women had raised money for planes, and it had been decided to give these planes to the girls. Only a couple of days before, Osipenko had been giving them a blistering dressing-down and threatened to have them arrested; now they were to be the principal guests at a banquet in the Embassy of Mongolia. There was a meeting in their honour at the airfield where they were to be presented with the new planes, fresh from the factory. These were Yaks, with an inscription along the side reading, "From the women of Mongolia – for the front!" They flew off in the aircraft, albeit reluctantly, back to the women's fighter regiment in Voronezh.

Masha Kuznetsova continued to fly successfully until the end of the war, but had no more victories in the air. The regiment remained on air defence duties in the rear, and it was extremely rare for enemy planes to be shot down.

34

"The worst death"

Lieutenant Colonel Nikolai Baranov was killed on 6 May while escorting Petlyakovs bombing German ground troops. It was a bitter irony that only two days previously he had given a talk to a meeting of Party members on "The State of Discipline in the Unit". According to a report filed by Political Officer Krainov, when Baranov was taking off on his last mission, he was drunk. There were battles on the approaches to Stalino, with German fighters involved. Several other pilots did not return from the mission, which saw intense fighting, so Baranov might have been shot down even if he had been sober. Nevertheless, the commander had broken a golden rule he was always drumming into his pilots: never drink before take-off, wait until you are safely back. According to Krainov, Baranov was leading a group of fighters but, on the way back from their target, lost touch both with the bombers they were escorting and his own fighter group. He engaged enemy fighters solo and was shot down over enemy territory. One of his pilots saw the plane falling, and noted that Baranov did not manage to bail out.

The crash was witnessed by two teenage boys who lived on the western outskirts of Shakhtyorsk, fifty kilometres from Stalino. The description of Baranov's death given by one of them, Vasiliy Ruban, differs marginally from Krainov's account, which was also based on eyewitness testimony.[429] The boys were waiting eagerly for the Red Army to liberate Shakhtyorsk and, early in the morning of 6 May, spotted three Soviet aircraft, a heavy bomber and two fighters, flying at high altitude above them. First one and then a second pair of Messerschmitts intercepted them and a dogfight began. The bomber and one of the fighters made their escape, but the second Yak fought on alone, shooting down one of the German fighters. (There is no confirmation of this in the regimental records.) The Yak was hit by machine-gun fire and caught fire. A speck separated from it. The pilot had bailed out, but his parachute was on fire and he was doomed.

Whether Nikolai Baranov died "the worst death", falling without a parachute, or whether the other pilot was right in saying he never managed to jump, we cannot tell.[430] The boys found the dead pilot next to the wreckage of his plane, took the documents from his shirt pocket, and saw his name was N. I. Baranov. Germans soon drove up, took the documents from the boys, and removed two Orders of the Red Banner from Baranov's tunic. They told the boys to clear off but, as soon as the Germans had gone, Vasiliy and his friend returned, dug a grave, and buried the pilot. They took a propeller blade from the Yak's wreckage and put it on the grave mound in place of a headstone.

Vasiliy Ruban pointed out Baranov's grave twenty years later when he returned to his home village and retold the story. Archival documents were researched and investigators from Shakhtyorsk succeeded in tracking down Baranov's mother, wife and son. In 1963, his remains were reburied.

The regiment waited several days for Batya to return, unable to believe he could have been killed. They felt orphaned, as if they all really had lost their father.[431] Although he had seemed to them an old man, he was only thirty-one. He was mourned by Nina Kamneva, also known as "Tiny Nina", the tall, ample armourer who was his mistress. He was mourned too by everyone else in his unit, which had been fighting under his command since the war began and had become a Guards regiment under his leadership. People said that without Baranov the regiment could never be the same again. "The death of Guards Regiment Commander Lieutenant Colonel Baranov was accompanied by circumstances of personal indiscipline," Major Krainov noted in his report.[432] He must have known that the real cause was the inhuman stress imposed on Batya by the heavy responsibility he carried for the lives of so many people, a strain he had lived with since the outbreak of war. The vodka was a way of coping with that burden.

Batya was succeeded as commander by Ivan Golyshev who, like Baranov, was a fine pilot and good commander, but was otherwise entirely dissimilar. He was well-educated, well-spoken and highly disciplined, but a man of few words.[433] Although many in the regiment were still reluctant to believe Batya was really dead, Golyshev took command on 7 May. That same day Alexey Salomatin and Lilya Litvyak further increased their tally of kills, bringing down one Messerschmitt apiece. The report notes that Salomatin "drove the enemy fighter into the ground". Ivan Soshnikov, a pilot who had only recently joined the regiment but was already on friendly terms with Valya Krasnoshchyokova, also distinguished himself.[434]

Valya's close friend Faina Pleshivtseva was in love and forever disappearing off somewhere, so she was feeling lonely. Fortunately, Valya had already been accepted by the other girls and made friends with some of the pilots, including cheery Ivan Soshnikov and tall, handsome Alexander Yevdokimov who, when they were stuck at an airfield in Chuyevo, gave her his photo.[435] They were friends, but no more. In affairs of the heart, Valya was a complete ingénue. There was plenty of questionable behaviour going on around her, but somehow it all passed Valya by. On one occasion, she and Faina were invited by some of the pilots to join them in wetting their new medals. This was accomplished by dropping the medal in a tumblerful of vodka that had then to be drunk down in one. Valya noticed a small packet on the table and picked it up. "Is this a spare part for the medal?" she asked. There was a roar of laughter and Valya, confused, realised it must be a condom.[436] These were a rarity at the front at that time and had usually been captured from the Germans, who had a more than adequate supply. Needless to say, Soviet condoms bore no comparison in quality with their "fascist" counterparts.

Zhenya Rudneva categorically disagreed with people who took the view that casual wartime romances were perfectly defensible. Her idealism, her childish naivety, and her youthful dogmatism are all reflected in an article "Varya's Error", which she wrote for the in-house literary magazine of the Night Witches regiment.[437]

The Night Witches had wanted to produce a magazine for a long time. Their regiment had its poets, its writers and artists. Polina Gelman even set up a philosophy club, but it did not flourish. It was as if nobody felt they had the time or energy to devote to the kind of intense thought such an endeavour would demand. Publishing a literary journal, however, was self-evidently a good idea. The girls had a backlog of poems, stories, and drawings, and it was time to bring them together in one place.

Galya Dokutovich agreed to be the editor, and the first issue contained two articles by Zhenya. One was about a real or fictional girl called Varya who unwisely put her trust in some gigolo. Varya's error, according to Zhenya, was not that she had forgotten Alexey, the boy she loved, and indulged in a fling, but more seriously that she had not seen fit to renounce all else for the sake of victory. Her error was in failing "to see through him, to know him for what he was, and in failing to see that, even if he had been a really good person, she had given him grounds to hope for something more than just a date. This she should not have done under any circumstances."

Zhenya, who had never been in love before, talks earnestly about a "petty bourgeois understanding of happiness", warning girls against intimacy with their "brothers" in the male regiment that the Air Division constantly placed them next to. "It is no surprise that friendship arises, and sometimes infatuation. That does not make people bad people. It does not mean they lose their dignity and honour. What is far more serious is when we sometimes hear people complaining that their youth is passing and that soon they will be old women. This attitude is a step in the direction of the swamp, and is now one of our greatest enemies." Zhenya rounded off her naive reflections on a rousing note: "Our girls will proudly bear the banner of their regiment, never allowing it to become sullied."

For the present, Zhenya herself was only falling in love with girlfriends. Her romantic heart needed passionate enthusiasms, whether that was for their training exercises, for books or for people. She fell in love first with Galya Dokutovich. Galya found Zhenya's ardent declarations of love an embarrassment. She could do without all that. On 14 April 1943, she noted in her diary:

I am afraid too that I have upset Zhenya. She has given me her photo inscribed, "To my Galya." I did not ask her why she wrote that, but expected she would explain later. But now! She has written a story about two friends who love one another deeply, and cherish that feeling through all the difficulties they face during their entire lives. To one of these friends Zhenya has given the name Galya . . . She has been thinking that perhaps I am the one person she could have that kind of friendship with. It is really like a declaration of love!

Well, what can I say to her proposal to be her friend? If I said, "Fine," that would be a lie. We are just very different. Zhenya is a splendid, intelligent, affectionate, sincere girl, and a much better person than I am, although I think I am stronger than her. We simply won't be able to be lifelong friends. I can see that clearly, but why can't Zhenya?

Anyway, if you respect someone and love them and want to be their friend, why would you talk about it? Polina and I have never said a word about our being friends. We have taken no oaths and promised each other nothing.

In fact, Galya was inseparable from Polina, whom she also considered weaker than herself, often criticised, and had done so for the past ten years. Now, however, even Polina no longer had pride of place in her heart. That she had given to blue-eyed Misha, to whom she wrote often in letters, and in her diary which was for nobody's eyes but her own. When Misha was ill and unable to fly, she wrote an unsent message to him in her diary: "How is life treating you there? Are you better yet? Oh, Mishka, my sweet imp, stay well! When you are ill I feel sorry for you, and I don't like it myself when people are sorry for me. Right now, though, I am not worrying. I know you are alive and not in danger and no enemy bullet can hurt you. Perhaps I would think about you less, and I would definitely worry about you less, but I would also be less proud of you if you were never facing danger." That same day, she continued, "Oh, Misha, do you love flowers? There are so many roses around now, red, and white."

One time, just as she was about to take off on a sortie, she was brought a letter from Misha. She had no time to read it and, during the mission, when the German anti-aircraft guns started up, her heart suddenly sank at the thought that, if she died, she would never get to know what he had written.

<h1 style="text-align:center">35</h1>

"Undue self-confidence, self-regard and lack of discipline"

Alexey Salomatin outlived his friend and teacher, Regimental Commander Nikolai Baranov, by just two weeks. Those who were with him on that warm, cloudy day in May grieved for the rest of their lives that this young, brave, kind boy who was in love should have died in such a useless, dreadfully absurd manner.

In later years a succession of people writing sketches and stories about Lilya Litvyak described the touching scene of the death of Salomatin. Shot in battle by the fascist invaders, he limps back in his stricken plane to the airfield where Lilya is waiting, and then expires. The less mendacious wrote that Salomatin was killed during a training dogfight because of a serious technical fault in his plane. Not one of the authors of the dozens of articles written about this couple has told the truth. His disorderly conduct in the air did not fit the propaganda image of a Communist and Hero of the Soviet Union, even if he was still just a boy of twenty-two. Here the story is told for the first time without invention, on the basis of evidence documented by the regiment and of eyewitness memoirs. That day Lilya was on duty, sitting in her cockpit and waiting for the signal to take off. It was warm on the ground and she was over-dressed, uncomfortable, bored and generally fed up. Valya and Faina, who were servicing her plane, sat on the wings at Lilya's invitation.[438] Alexey, they knew, was currently somewhere in the clouds engaged in a training dogfight with a new pilot. The girls were already familiar with Lilya's peculiarities. When she had nothing to do, which was usually only when she was on duty in readiness to take off, she liked to moan. Nothing was right. It was boring, and probably in any case there would be no signal to take off today, and she had not had any letters from home for ages. They got depressed themselves just listening to her.

Suddenly they heard the sound of an engine, barely audible at first but quickly rising to a deafening roar. The mechanics jumped down from the wings. It was not the kind of sound a plane made unless something was wrong. The growl of the engine suddenly ceased and the ground trembled under a terrible impact. Valya and Faina rushed towards the far end of the airfield where the crash had occurred. "Find out who!" Lilya shouted after them. She needed to unstrap herself from the cockpit before she could follow.

It never occurred to the people running from all directions that the victim in the wreckage could be Alexey Salomatin, Hero of the Soviet Union, squadron leader and flying ace. Obviously it must be somebody from the new reinforcements, somebody inexperienced who had lost control in the course of the aerobatics.

That, at least, was what Kolya Menkov thought as he ran towards the wreckage.[439] He had seen someone flying a Yak come out of the clouds and start doing rolls: a first, a second, then a third when he was already near the ground. "He isn't going to make it!" flashed through Kolya's mind in the split seconds that sealed the pilot's fate. He did not make it. The plane smashed into the ground. When they reached the crash Valya and Faina saw to their horror that the dead pilot was Alexey. Lilya arrived just after them.[440] People who witness a catastrophe often have a detail etched in their memory for the rest of their lives. Kolya Menkov remembered the light brown hair on Alexey's shattered skull was very short. He had probably just had a haircut.[441]

Major Krainov wrote, "Undue self-confidence, self-regard and lack of discipline on the part of Hero of the Soviet Union Guards Captain Salomatin was the cause of his death."[442] Probably everybody serving in the regiment, deeply saddened as they were by the death of Salomatin, would have had to agree with that harsh verdict. Alexey liked to fool around, to try to pull off outrageous tricks in his plane, but that kind of aerobatic hooliganism was reckless and irresponsible.

Members of the regiment later recalled Alexey's funeral in detail. They were rarely able to be present at the funerals of comrades, who usually died far from where the regiment was deployed and were buried by local people. Often they simply disappeared without trace, so that not only was there no grave, but it was not even known whether the pilot was dead or living in captivity.[443] The entire regiment turned out for Alexey's funeral as well as other soldiers who were in Pavlovka, and all the residents of the village. His family would have been proud to see how well it was organised. Wailing mourners even came from the settlement to accompany Alexey to his final resting place with traditional Russian peasant lamentation, as they did also in his home village.

The photograph of the funeral is blurred, but we can recognise the stern, grim faces of the regimental commander Golyshev, Alexey's friend Sasha Martynov, and next to them, in profile, much shorter than the others, Lilya Litvyak. Her numerous biographers later made groundless claims that she wailed and flung herself on the coffin. The less dramatic truth is that she just cried quietly, standing in the line-up of soldiers according Alexey his final honours.

She cried a lot after the funeral too.[444] Alexey was buried in the central square of the village and the path to the airfield passed his grave. Faina and Valya tried to be there for her and were very worried: Lilya would often "hide away from everybody and cry".

After Alexey's death, Lilya asked the regimental commander to transfer her to the Third Squadron under Captain Grigorovich. After that, Valya Krasnoshchyokova saw little of her and knew almost nothing about the work she was doing. There was not much coming and going between the squadrons. Faina Pleshivtseva liked to claim she had been Lilya's mechanic right up until her death, and that it was she who saw her off on her last flight. These tales, which have misled biographers, are pure fiction that Faina, after she had repeated it often enough, probably came to believe herself. She did have a great fondness for Lilya, and after the war was involved for many years in searching for the wreckage of her aircraft and her remains. The reality, however, is that from late May Lilya was in the other squadron, her plane serviced by a different mechanic. By June Pleshivtseva was no longer in the regiment at all but in hospital after an illegal abortion went wrong.[445] She never returned to the regiment and went instead to study at the Air Force Academy. Some thirty years after the end of the war, at a reunion of the veterans of Baranov's 296 Regiment, someone ridiculed her storytelling. Somebody else took pity on her, but still chided her gently, "Really, my dear, how can you say these things when you know they are untrue!" She never attended the reunions again.[446]

In the Third Squadron Litvyak flew almost invariably on a plane serviced by Kolya Menkov. This young man, almost the same age as her, got to know a little better the "small, blonde girl with wavy hair" he had previously seen occasionally at the airfield. Lilya was amiable enough, although naturally, as a decorated pilot and officer, she talked down to him rather.[447]

At Stalingrad, and indeed after it, the mechanics worked long and hard in freezing cold, in wind and rain, and in blazing heat. Nikolai Menkov had no fear of hard work or bad weather. Tall and slender, this raven-haired, brown-eyed boy had been well used to both since childhood. In 1943, Nikolai was just twenty-one, but was already familiar with all the things urban lads had to learn in the war: to work tirelessly, never to complain, often to go hungry, to mend your own clothes, and always to look out for your mates. He was born near Belozersk in northern Russia, a region of mossy pine forests, lakes, and long, light summer nights. His parents were simple people who had to feed a large family by the sweat of their brow. The northern summers are short, the land infertile, and all they could store up for the winter was mushrooms and berries gleaned from the forest. Summer and winter, the people who lived in Nikolai's village went out to the lake to catch fish. It was backbreaking work that could only be done if everybody worked together. If anybody slacked, they would not be included in the group next time.

Kolya was initially a bit sceptical about Litvyak, a petite blonde who took so much trouble over her appearance and who trailed in her wake the myth of having accidentally shot down a German ace. However, she immediately demonstrated the kind of pilot she really was.

In early June, still operating from Biryukovo airfield close to Pavlovka where Alexey was buried, Lilya, with Sasha Yevdokimov as her wingmate, brilliantly executed a tricky mission to set fire to two enemy artillery observation balloons.[448] The balloons were tethered behind the front line and observers on them were very effectively helping the German artillery with its range-finding. German anti-aircraft guns made sure Soviet aircraft were unable to approach them. Litvyak asked her regimental commander, Ivan Golyshev, for permission to try to bring them down by flying along and then over the front line, approaching the balloons from behind and taking the Germans by surprise. Golyshev and her squadron leader agreed. Lilya's manoeuvre was successful, and she and Yevdokimov each set fire to a balloon.

When she returned, Litvyak excitedly described seeing the observer fall to the ground. Senior Sergeant Borisenko used the same manoeuvre later that day to set a third balloon on fire. The operation was the talk of the whole battalion.

There was constant heavy fighting. Lilya was flying a great deal, most often as lead pilot with Sergeant Yevdokimov as her wingmate. She instructed the young pilots reinforcing the squadron, and continued to notch up kills. Anya Skorobogatova's heart stood still when she heard over the radio the familiar voice of Seagull say, "Here goes!" as Lilya attacked.[449] Anya was desperate for this girl pilot to survive. She was the radio contact for several flying units and boys she heard in the ether were dying almost every day. She would see the young pilots in the canteen where, after a sortie, they would ask the waitresses to bring them borshch that was "really hot and so thick the spoon stands up in it!" She sensed that for them the soup was a symbol that they had lived to fight another day.

In mid-June Litvyak was already commanding a flight, having earned the confidence of Golyshev and her squadron leader. They praised her highly for her attack on 16 June, again paired with Sasha Yevdokimov, when they flew out to intercept a Frame range-finding aircraft. Even though the engagement proved fruitless, it was regarded as a win. The pair was met by four Messerschmitts, the Frame flew off, and Litvyak and Yevdokimov attacked the fighters. Sasha's plane was hit and he was lightly wounded, but managed to land safely.[450] Litvyak got back to base with ten bullet holes in her plane, which Menkov and another technician patched up overnight.

If Lilya had not died in the summer of 1943, she would certainly have been put forward for the title of Hero of the Soviet Union. She was hugely popular throughout 8 Air Army: loved, respected and admired not only by her fellow pilots and the technical staff, but also by her superiors. So much so that she even got away with a very serious incident for which another pilot would have been severely punished, perhaps even sent to a penal battalion.

On the morning of 16 June, before she flew out to intercept the Frame, Litvyak, taking off in response to a call from the airspace monitoring service was, by all accounts, responsible for the death of Sergeant Zotkin, her young wingman.[451] The airfield at which they were stationed, near the village of Vesyoly Khutor, was so small that both taking off and landing were hazardous. As she became airborne, Litvyak veered off the approved course to the left and so, behind her, did Zotkin who had only recently arrived in the regiment. He apparently deviated just slightly from the in-correct path set by Litvyak, snagged one aircraft hangar with his wing, lost control and crashed into another. "The plane caught fire. The pilot was killed and is buried in the centre of the park in Vesyoly Khutor," Major Krainov reported, but even he kept quiet about the real cause of the trag-edy, covering up for Litvyak. "The cause of Sergeant Zotkin's death was a lack of personal discipline in ignoring the foresight and instructions of the regimental commander to take off singly, and of Flight Commander Guards Junior Lieutenant Litvyak who did not demand that her wingman repeat the instructions for taking off."[452] He mentioned that a penalty was imposed on Litvyak, but that was a pure formality. The other pilots and technical staff in the squadron tacitly held her responsible for what had happened. They had no need to say anything. Lilya herself was deeply upset. Her comrades saw how she cried over Zotkin's death, how despondent she became, and tormented by guilt at the senseless death of a wingman entrusted to her care. It was also a gratuitous accidental loss of an aircraft at a time when the regiment was losing so many in combat on the obstinately unyielding Mius Front.[453]

36

"Move it will you? She's going to blow up"

The sector next to the Mius Front was called "The Blue Line" by the Russians and "*Gottenkopf*" ("Godhead") by the Germans. It was vital for the Germans to retain the Taman peninsula as a starting position for any future offensive so, using the locals as slaves, they built a series of extremely strong fortifications. There were two defence lines 20–25 km apart, saturated with pillboxes, machine-gun posts and artillery trenches, all connected by communication trenches. The main line of defence was covered in minefields and several lines of razor wire. The German positions were bolstered by a number of almost impenetrable natural fortifications: bogs, coastal lakes and flooded lands on the northern sector, and forested mountains on the southern sector. As a result of their swift retreat in the spring of 1943, the Germans had avoided significant losses and were gathered in strength. After some desultory skirmishing, the fighting started in earnest once the Soviet troops decided to make a determined effort to break through the Blue Line. However the Soviets did not commit soldiers in sufficient force, and the assault soon degenerated into a bloody stalemate.

For eighteen-year-old novice navigator Olga Golubeva this was her tenth sortie over the "Blue Line".[454] Her U-2's little 100-horsepower engine was clattering away with the strain. Under the wings and belly of the aircraft bombs hung from simple hooks, Olga's ordnance. She leaned over the side, peering down at the woodland, the fields, the roads, looking for places where they might be able to make an emergency landing if they had to. She was not thinking about anti-aircraft guns or fighters, and had no idea what they would be flying into in a few minutes. She had never been under fire.

The western outskirts of the Novorossiysk were where they saw most of the flashes coming from and heard the incessant roar of gunfire, and that was where they were to drop their bombs. Olga pulled the knobs to release them and the plane jolted. Moments later they saw bright flashes below as the incendiary bombs burst at an altitude of 100–300 metres, setting fire to large areas. Nina Altsybeeva turned the plane to fly home, but Olga could not stop looking back to where their fire was blazing. What a sight!

By ill luck they faced a strong headwind on their return journey. Their little aircraft was almost stationary and simply could not escape from a sudden barrage of anti-aircraft fire. Huge spheres hurtled towards them, "exploded, and turned into sinister clouds". One of the shells burst very nearby, and it felt as if the plane had been hit by a battering ram. "They are aiming too high," Olga reflected, but immediately realised that against the moonlit clouds their plane was highly visible and the German gunners were just finding their range. Nina was weaving the plane about so they presented a more elusive target. "We need to hold out another five minutes," Olga said, hoping that by then they would be out of the firing zone. They had no time to be scared. After a second's respite, there was another exploding shell, and then another, this time right next to them. The plane was hit and fell in a spin. Nina pulled them out of it, but evasive action was no longer an option; the stricken plane could barely fly in a straight line. A new squall of fire flung the plane to one side and Olga realised that their only choice was to fly with the wind. "Nina, head for the fire. We'll piggy-back on the wind!" she said, and Nina circled back and flew towards the German rear, soon leaving the anti-aircraft fire behind. They needed to change direction, but the plane would not obey until Nina contrived a flat turn with no banking. They adapted to what their wounded plane could still manage and flew back, Nina never taking her eyes off the instruments, and Olga keeping hers on the ground below, checking it against the map.

The work was too demanding to give them time to think about anything else. People probably never do think so clearly as when they are in mortal danger. At last, they saw their airfield, with a signal lamp shining to them from the perimeter.

The girl mechanics examining the plane gasped periodically. "Half the surface skin is gone," "And look at the holes in the spar bridge." "The cockpits! The cockpits are riddled!"

Nina told Olga to report to the commander, and she went cheerfully to the take-off point, where she found another person with Bershanskaya. This man, when Olga showed on the map where the flak had been coming from, asked what armaments were being used. Olga only shrugged in response, whilst snarling silently to herself: "Not a catapult!" The stranger repeated his question: "So what was it coming from?" "It went b-boom and then there was a grey cloud," Olga said, prompting a guffaw from what turned out to be the chief navigator of the entire Air Division. "Why don't you try it yourself!" Olga thought darkly. She had just undergone her baptism of fire.

On 2 June 1943, the weather over the Blue Line was bad, worse than the Pe-2 dive-bombers could cope with.[455] It was not a plane you could fly blind, as they were well aware at headquarters, but that day caution had evidently been thrown to the winds because the ground troops were taking a beating. Unexpectedly, Masha Dolina's 587 Heavy Bomber Regiment, recently renamed 125 Guards Regiment, was ordered to bomb Height 101 in the village of Krymsk on the Taman peninsula. "The damnable height had already twice changed hands" that day and failure to hold it was preventing the infantry from going on the offensive. A group of nine aircraft was led that day by Yevgenia Timofeyeva, and Senior Lieutenant Masha Dolina led the left flight.

They flew at an altitude of 1,000 metres instead of the usual 2,000, under the lower edge of the cloud cover. Height 101 greeted the squadron with "a solid wall of flak". All around them there opened up "the white and black flowerheads of exploding shells, like a forest of giant dandelions".

Piloting heavy bombers called for strong nerves. In close formation it was almost impossible to take evasive action, and you could not turn back until you had completed your mission. Such a large machine was an inviting target for enemy gunfire and the pilot had to put her trust in luck and the aircraft's armour. Masha's plane was playing up. One of the engines started cutting out just as they reached the target. The bomber had a bias to one side and began falling behind. Masha's wingman did not abandon her, but also reduced speed and stayed on her tail. She had taken a hit from an anti-aircraft shell. The crew felt only a slight bump at the time, and realised what had happened only when the left engine began to smoke. They were minutes away from the target, but every second seemed like an eternity. "The sound of my heart beating filled the cockpit, blocking all the sounds of war from outside." Summoning all her willpower, Masha waited for the navigator's command. Finally it came: "Dive!" The bombs were released and the Pe-2 jerked upwards. Masha clearly saw columns of smoke and fire down below where their bombs had fallen on the German troop formations.

Heading for home, she realised they would not make it back to the air-field. With only one engine the aircraft was losing height. "Commander, I see Messers," she heard her gunner, Ivan Solyonov, warn. There was no sign of their fighter escort: somewhere in the clouds above, abandoning the crippled Pe-2, they had a battle of their own to fight. Vanya and Galya Dzhunkovskaya were firing at the fighters, but were no match for them. The other two aircraft of her flight, providing cover to the rear, had also been damaged. Masha Kirillova had flown on to catch up with the main group, but the second slave, Tonya Skoblikova, stayed with Masha, trying to provide cover even though her own fuel tank had been punctured and petrol was streaming from it. The left wing of Masha's bomber was on fire now, but she hoped somehow to make it back over the front line.

They were out of ammunition, and a German fighter flew right up alongside, so that Masha could see the pilot's face. Laughing, he showed her first one finger, then two. Later, in the hospital, Soviet fighter pilots told her he was asking whether she would prefer to be shot down with one approach or two. Masha's second engine caught fire and, hoping to blow out the flames, she went into a dive. They were nearing Russian anti-aircraft guns and the German fell back.

Miraculously, their burning plane managed to limp over the front line of the River Kuban and land. The plane was on fire but the escape hatch had jammed. Smoke was clouding their eyes and choking them, and the inferno was coming closer. They were frantic, beating their heads against the immovable hatch. With hundreds of litres of fuel on board, the plane was likely to explode at any moment. They were saved by the wounded Ivan, who forced the hatch open with a screwdriver. He dragged Masha out, then Galya, whose flying suit was already on fire. She fell to the ground and began rolling to put it out, but Ivan shouted, "Galya! Masha! For fuck's sake, move it, will you? She's going to blow up!" Ivan, "Solyonchik" as Masha called him affectionately, a simple, very young boy, counted fifty-one steps as he ran before the plane blew up behind them and chunks of aircraft flew through the air. The men from the anti-aircraft battery ran to help and drove them to the field hospital, wounded, burnt, but alive. Although Masha Dolina was born in December, after this escape she made sure she celebrated a second birthday every year in early summer on the day she scored a victory over death.

In 1941, Nikolai Baranov had given Masha leave to visit her family just before their village was occupied by the Germans. In 1943, as Soviet troops were advancing, driving the Germans out of the Ukraine, his successor, Commander Markov, already known as "Batya" himself, promised Masha leave again when Mikhailovka was liberated.[456] The news came while she was still in hospital. She knew nothing of the fate of her family, whom she had been completely unable to support during those two years of occupation.

Over that period, prevented from sending them money, she had saved up 19,000 rubles, a bigger sum than she had ever seen before in her life. (The pilots were financially rewarded both for successful combat missions, and for bringing back their planes in one piece.) After receiving the cash, a pile of 190 hundred-ruble banknotes, Masha was perplexed as to how to transport it. First she stuffed as many as she could into her map case and pockets, and wrapped some in paper and shoved them inside her tunic. These preparations were watched by the regimental doctor and Yevgenia Timofeyeva, who said nothing at first, but then asked, "Are you crazy? The first train you board you'll get your bags stolen and your pockets picked!"

The doctor, Maria Ivanovna, brought some wide bandages and a needle and thread. "Okay, spin round, beautiful!" They sewed banknotes into the bandages and wrapped them round Masha. She soon had reason to be grateful to them, because her map case with 4,000 rubles was stolen from her in the crush at the platform.

At one of the stations, she bought gifts. "A headscarf for my mum, a hat for Vera, scarves and tunics for the boys." She finally reached home, but the dugout was empty. Inside "everything had been turned upside down and there was not a soul to be seen." Her heart sank. The neighbours said her family were in a nearby village, and there Masha found them, desperately thin, pale, and exhausted. Her parents had aged as if an eternity had passed. Her mother wailed and rushed to embrace Masha, as her father chided, "She's alive, for heaven's sake. Why are you wailing as if she was dead?" His hair had gone completely grey and tears coursed down the deep wrinkles on his cheeks.

37

Katya's return

"Dear Mother," Katya Budanova wrote on 25 June 1943, "I am back at the front. I flew back safely. I am well. I am returning to combat duty. Mum, four of my comrades have been killed. I am readying myself to avenge them mercilessly. Please do not worry about me. I will write to you often, and you write to me." [457]

Katya, who learned of the deaths of Commander Baranov, Alexey and Grigory Burenko only after returning to the regiment, wrote in more detail to her sister.

My dear, sweet sister Valya! I have flown back safely but you cannot imagine how sad I am. Besides the Old Man, our commander, and his deputy, two others have been killed, Squadron Leader Alexey Salomatin, a Hero of the Soviet Union, and Grigory Burenko. You can imagine how I feel, how it hurts to lose the people you most love in the regiment, your own family. It has all happened in a single month, while I was away. I could feel it in my heart. That must have been why I was so desperate to get back to the front.[458]

When Katya returned, her regiment was stationed at a different airfield not at all far from the one she had left, though the front line had been static for many months. The village of Matveyev Kurgan had changed hands a number of times in the course of the war and now, for several months in 1943, was once more on the front line, constantly shelled and bombed. In March, people who had remained because they had nowhere else to go witnessed, when darkness fell, trucks covered with tarpaulins arriving with the bodies of Soviet soldiers. "All night the headquarters staff were at work, writing reports, and in the early morning the bodies were buried." The village women also had husbands and sons away in the war, and came to look at the dead in search of family members, but the numbers were enormous. Great pits, like those used for silage, were dug by excavator, and in each a thousand bodies were stacked, one row on top of another.

Ivan Domnin, the commander of a flight in Second Squadron, in his brief memoir about Katya Budanova wonders why she was not awarded the title of Hero of the Soviet Union. In his own recollection and that of others in her regiment she was a real hero. Domnin often took Katya as his wing-mate, and considered that she saved his life on at least two occasions. One time as he was landing at the airfield at Mius, Domnin had "a lapse of air awareness" and very nearly suffered the fate that befell his friend, Grigory Burenko, who had been shot down by an enemy he had failed to spot. As he later realised, four German fighters had been following him and Katya ("like thieves", Domnin said, although trying to catch out enemy aircraft during take-off or landing was entirely standard practice). Domnin was already on approach to land when shells began exploding around him and he thought their own anti-aircraft gunners were mistakenly targeting them. Katya quickly understood what was happening and saved the day by remaining airborne and fighting off the attack. When she landed, she reported to her chastened commander, "You know, Comrade Commander, those Germans were really after me. It was a big sweat getting rid of them." Domnin appreciated her sense of humour, but admitted he had not noticed them. "Thank you very much for not letting them shoot me down."[459]

The second time Domnin considered that Katya saved his life was shortly before her death. The two of them were escorting attack bombers flying to a target near the River Mius. Some Messerschmitts attacked and, in the heat of fighting them off, Domnin failed to notice he was in the firing line of another pair of German fighters. Again, in his own words, he had let his "air awareness" slip. Katya managed to fight them off and, like Domnin that day, also took down a German fighter.

It was a blazing hot summer in the steppe and the airmen and air-women of 296 Regiment, just like the previous year, were flagging. The Germans, because of the reduced number of aircraft at their disposal, began to move their air groups from one front to another. In mid-July, taking advantage of bad weather over Kursk, they redeployed part of the Udet air fleet from that front. The pilots of 296 Regiment sometimes made five sorties a day. They had difficulty sleeping at night, had no opportunity of eating between flights, and when meals were brought to the airfield they were inedible because of "meadow fleas" which constantly swooped down in swarms and fell into the borshch. Her fellow squadron members were impressed that Katya never complained.[460]

Perhaps surprisingly, despite the terrible stress to which they were subjected during the day, after their meal in the evenings, whenever they could find any other enthusiasts, Lilya Litvyak and Katya Budanova were still only too happy to dance. They managed to arrange two or three such parties and, as in the past, Katya often danced the man's part.[461] Lilya's biographers omit any mention of them. If the writers are to be believed, after the death of Alexey Salomatin, Lilya wanted only to "fight and be avenged". But if Lilya went to dances, it does not necessarily follow that she was not still mourning the death of Alexey. Valya Krasnoshchyokova felt these entertainments were just a way of letting off steam after the terrible tensions of the day, as well as giving support to her colleagues in the regiment.[462] The return of the courageous, indomitable Katya Budanova, who Lilya had missed greatly, changed everything. Alas, they were not to have long together.

38

"I cried like I had never cried before"

By the summer of 1943, pilots who had been at the front for a few months were considered battle-hardened, and only a few of those who had been fighting since the outbreak of war survived. When the fighting at Kursk began on 12 July, Political Adviser Major Georgiy Prokofiev of 65 Guards Fighter Regiment was reporting casualties on a daily basis: two pilots had not returned, one had been lost, four . . .[463] On 17 July seven out of the nine pilots who had taken to the air to provide cover for ground troops failed to return. The report was signed by a different officer. Prokofiev was among the seven missing, as was Tonya Lebedeva.[464]

Tonya Lebedeva and Klava Blinova had always been kept back, in conformity with an unwritten order from the divisional commander that they were to be protected. They found this upsetting, considering themselves experienced pilots, which they undoubtedly were in comparison with the new recruits arriving in the regiment. Both were fearless. "Yes, both of us were daring and reckless and did not want to lag behind the men," recalls Klava.[465] Tonya, a fanatical Communist, was particularly anxious to give nobody any grounds for accusing her of exploiting her Party position to stay safely on the ground. In July 1943, however, it was no longer possible to shield them; the losses were simply too heavy. Even the newcomers with only minimal training were sent out more than once every day. On both sides there was the greatest concentration of aircraft at any time during the war, and with the highest rate of attrition.

Tonya Lebedeva was remembered by others in her regiment as a small girl, as thin and angular as a teenager, and far from pretty. Her hair, which she had again grown to shoulder length after Raskova's depredations, was noticeably going grey. They recalled her clever, observant eyes, and a wonderful, disarming smile that lit up her face. She was a good pilot too, more skilful, they thought, than Klava Blinova. All in all, she was a well-educated, dedicated Communist, and a good and reliable comrade.[466]

Having been with 65 Guards (formerly 653) Fighter Regiment for over six months, Tonya Lebedeva and Klava Blinova were fully accepted. They were readily taken on missions as wingmates, trailing and supporting a lead plane, and on occasion themselves flew the lead aircraft. If they did not fly as many missions as they would have liked to, it was because their commander wanted to spare them. The girls were close friends and shared all their joys and sorrows, but were temperamentally very different. Klava was lively, gregarious, and loved dancing, while Tonya was serious-minded and treated the young pilots as younger brothers whom it was her job to instruct and educate. She was almost the oldest in the squadron and was its Party administrator. In the summer of 1943 Tonya often organised meetings, with the pilots and mechanics sitting round her on the dry, dusty grass or, when it rained, on the bunks in a cramped dugout. It was not up to her to choose what to talk about: she was given the topics by the political adviser.

Unlike most political advisers in air regiments, Georgiy Prokofiev did actually fly on missions and had shot down enemy aircraft himself. On the Kalinin Front he even made a present of one he had winged to Tonya. She was flying in support and he let her finish the German plane off, crediting her with the success in his report. There were not many other political advisers who died in battle, rather than at their desk: his plane was hit by anti-aircraft fire and crashed as he attempted to land it. In spite of this, most of 65 Fighter Regiment's pilots considered him a waste of space. He gave lectures about the situation at the front and internationally, gave instructions to the Komsomol and Party administrators regarding their work with pilots and the technical staff, and wrote reports to his superiors. Needless to say his job included "keeping tabs on everybody".[467] Happily, Prokofiev did not detect any treachery in the squadron and ruined no lives.

In July 1943 Party Administrator Tonya Lebedeva gave the pilots and mechanics of Third Squadron talks related to a new order from Stalin that differed markedly in tone from Order No. 227 published the year previously.[468] Now the emphasis was on the need for maximum support and wholehearted devotion from the population to the Red Army as it drove the Germans back westward, not forgetting the Soviet state, which was credited with turning the war around. In the light of Stalin's order, Tonya paid particular attention to collecting for the Red Army Fund,* but also dealt with more abstract topics. Among the topics recommended by the Main Political Directorate of the Workers' and Peasants' Red Army (GlavP.U.R.K.K.A.) were discussions and lectures on the patriotism of the great Russian writers Pushkin, Gogol, Tolstoy and Chekhov, and also tales about great Russian generals like Kutuzov, whose name was primarily identified with the victory over Napoleon in 1812.[469] It mattered little that Leo Tolstoy had been a count, or that for Kutuzov his country was inseparable from the tsar and the Russian Orthodox faith. What mattered now, with the war at its height, was to raise the patriotic spirit of the Soviet people by reminding them of heroic figures of the Russian past. Tonya Lebedeva, the former Moscow University student from a family of intellectuals, was in her element speaking about Russia's history and literature. By the end of June, however, she no longer had time for morale-raising talks.

---

* The Red Army Fund, or Defence Fund, consisted of money or valuables contributed by Soviet citizens to the state to help support the war effort. They were said by the authorities to be strictly voluntary, but we now know that often people were given no choice.

The air became tense in July. There was cloudless, hot flying weather almost every day and the skies were full of planes. Both sides were preparing for one of the biggest engagements of the Second World War, the Battle of Kursk. The spring thaw, when melting snow made most roads impassable, had given both sides a chance to reinforce their troops and receive materiel. Now the Germans, looking to recover the territory they had lost since Stalingrad, aimed to launch a crushing new offensive.

At that moment, the front line ran from the Barents Sea to Lake Ladoga, then along the River Svir to Leningrad and on towards the south. It turned south-east by Velikie Luki and made a huge bulge in the area of Kursk that intruded deep into the German-occupied area. From Belgorod the front line went east of Kharkov, along the rivers Seversky Donets and Mius and to the east coast of the Sea of Azov; then east of Temryuik and Novorossiysk on the Taman peninsula. The German leadership concluded that the bulge in the Kursk area – the "Kursk Salient" – was the best spot for the crucial blow. They planned to cut the bulge off and encircle the armies of the Central and Voronezh Fronts that were operating there.

The German command codenamed this operation "Citadel". They allocated almost a million men, three thousand tanks and two thousand aircraft for the assault. According to the memoirs of Anastas Mikoyan, Stalin was aware of the enemy's plans as early as late March, and used the intervening months to devise a defensive strategy of attrition.

The Soviets replied to the beginning of the German offensive on 4 July with a murderous artillery barrage and an air raid conducted by over 400 assault aircraft and fighters. This brutal show of concussive mechanical force set the tone for what would follow. Battles went on non-stop with both sides suffering huge losses. The Germans advanced only a few kilometres in the next days. They had planned to take Kursk in under forty-eight hours, but a week later were still far from their goal, having advanced just thirty kilometres. More and more men were thrown into the battles. The front-line writer Bykov wrote: "The reinforcements were moving towards the front in a never-ending flow from numerous training locations in the rear; masses of people, starved and exhausted by drills, who could barely handle a rifle and often hardly spoke any Russian." Within a few days, a bloodbath at Prokhorovka, site of one of the largest tank battles in history, had turned the weapons and ammunition unloaded at Skuratovo and Vypolzovo stations under the protection of planes from Tonya and Klava's regiment into heaps of burnt and twisted metal. The losses of men and women were equally devastating.

After a week of fighting, 65 Air Assault Regiment had just eighteen pilots and seven operational aircraft left. Starting combat missions on 12 July, the regiment flew 175 sorties in a week. They carried out every con-ceivable mission, protecting the river crossings from German bombers, undertaking reconnaissance flights, and providing cover for ground troop operations, but mostly escorting Il-2 bombers flying to attack enemy troops.

Junior Lieutenant Tonya Lebedeva flew her last combat mission on the afternoon of 17 July 1943 as a member of a group of nine aircraft.[470] In order to muster such a large force, which would improve their chances of fending off attacks by Messerschmitts and Focke-Wulfs, even Major Prokofiev and the regiment's chief navigator Major Plyonkin were pressed into service. Their task was to provide air cover for ground troops in the area of Prosetovo, Gnezdilovo and Znamenskoye to the southwest of Bolkhov.

Soviet troops were slowly moving forward, trying to encircle several groups of German troops and break through to the railway. The Germans were sending such reinforcements as they could. Luftwaffe bombers were flying in from the direction of Oryol to bomb the advancing Soviet troops. For several days now the Russian pilots had noticed that their appearance was always heralded by large groups of Focke-Wulf fighters.

Of the nine pilots who set off, only two returned to base. No one in Tonya's flight returned. She and Gavriil Guskov, a Hero of the Soviet Union, were the lead pilots, with newcomers Ponomaryov and Albinovich as wingmen. As they were approaching Oryol, near the village of Betovo, they were attacked by a group of Focke-Wulf fighters. What happened after that, nobody knows for sure, but all four pilots were killed. Pilot Adil Kuliyev, in another flight, later reported seeing Lebedeva parachute from her plane. He claimed a German pilot had begun shooting at her as she descended, but was evidently mistaken. Tonya died in her aircraft. Majors Prokofiev and Plyonkin were among those missing, believed shot down over enemy-occupied territory. In fact three airmen who made a crash landing, including Prokofiev, returned to the regiment the following day.

There is no telling how the rumour that Tonya had been captured arose. After the retaking of Oryol it was claimed someone had seen her injured in the hospital there. She had already been reported missing to her family, but the regimental adjutant evidently decided it was better to give the family unverified information than to leave them in uncertainty. He wrote to Tonya's father in Moscow:

Dear Vasiliy Pavlovich, I have received your letter asking me to tell you what happened to Tonya. I cannot at present give you a precise answer, but will pass on what we know so far. After the liberation of Oryol, I learned that Tonya had been in the hospital and had been taken away with them by the Germans when they evacuated the city. The hospital staff told me that when interrogated by German officers she conducted herself like a Bolshevik and a patriot. When they said, "We shall win anyway," she spat at them. We know nothing more after that. All our fighting comrades remember Tonya and will never forget her. She was exceptionally courageous and an inventive pilot in combat who shot down three enemy aircraft. We honour the memory of Tonya in our hearts.

Yevgeny Pestryakov, No. 35428

Her father, mother and sisters hoped for many years that Tonya would return and searched tirelessly for her. Her bed in their Moscow apartment was kept made. Her father, Vasiliy Lebedev, died shortly before Tonya's body was finally found.

*

Boys play at war even when there is a real conflict going on all around them. Although Mtsensk District was occupied by the Germans, who were present in almost every large village, the boys in Razinkino loved collecting spent cartridge cases and pretending to shoot. They competed to see who could find most. Whenever there was a dogfight in the sky above, they would run out to be first to find the spent cartridges, with little thought of the fate of the pilots fighting it out overhead. There was plenty of fighting: every evening German heavy bombers escorted by fighters flew from the direction of Oryol towards Bolkhov. They flew at low altitude, the German crosses clearly visible on their wings, and were often confronted by Soviet fighters.

On 16–17 July three pilots of the Normandy French volunteer regiment were shot down in that area.[471] After it was retaken, local residents pointed out roughly where the two aircraft had come down, but a thorough search was carried out only thirty years later. This was looking for one of the pilots near Betovo, when it found instead where Tonya Lebedeva had crashed.

Schoolchildren excavating the site found among the wreckage the remains of the pilot, a parachute, pistol, knife, and documents that included the pilot's logbook and medical card. In both it was still possible to read the name Antonina Lebedeva. They also found a notebook with preliminary notes for a Party meeting and a well-preserved machine gun whose serial number confirmed that this was indeed Tonya's plane. Among the debris they found a headset with skull fragments and two short braids of greying hair.

They buried the remains nearby and erected a small obelisk on the grave fashioned from the pilot's armoured seat back.[472]

As the Germans were being driven westward, people were returning to their destroyed settlements and burnt villages in the Kursk area. Konstantin Simonov, who in 1941 and 1942 had witnessed armies retreating in disarray and bewildered old men and women wandering the roads with children, wrote lines filled with pain:

No help to weep. The summer heat
Bakes yellow steppes and trampled tracks.
As then, the crowds of refugees,
As then, the children on their backs.[473]

The heart of Simonov, a soldier and a poet, was filled with the same terrible pity, the same sense of guilt of a man powerless to bring aid and comfort to defenceless women and children.

On his way back to Moscow, where as a reporter he had to write up all his observations, Simonov and photographer Yakov Khalip returned again to Ponyri in Kursk province where they saw "the sad fields unharvested", "German artillery with mangled barrels, mountains of empty artillery ammunition baskets", bodies of the fallen, "unnoticeable at first in the thick rye".[474] Local people were trudging home along dusty tracks, or "against peasant custom", taking shortcuts straight through fields. The journalists stopped their vehicle beside a woman walking with her children along a path trampled through a field of rye. Simonov counted five children, and then noticed a sixth, a baby, in its mother's arms. The woman and all her children were carrying immensely heavy loads, barely able to walk under the weight of their bundles. She stopped and set down two sacks tied together, or rather, they were so big that she "climbed out from underneath them". "Wearily wiping her brow", she sat down on one, and the children too put down their burdens and sat beside her. "Have you come far?" Simonov asked. The woman replied that they had travelled thirty kilometres and had no strength left. "But I can't leave our belongings," she said, pointing to the sacks and much patched bundles. "I expect the Germans will have burned everything where we are going. There will be nothing in the village. We can't leave anything, and we still have forty versts to walk."

She began to cry, her face that of an old woman. Simonov asked if all the children were hers and she said they were, telling him their names in turn. The oldest was ten and the youngest eight months. Her husband was missing in the war.

Simonov was silent. There were four of them in the jeep and they were going in the opposite direction. Even if they went out of their way, they still could not squeeze the whole family and their belongings into the vehicle.

"We'd better be off," the woman said, and again slipped her shoulder under the sacks which, when she stood up, were "almost the same size as she was herself".

Simonov watched the children, "also silent and serious, take up their sacks and small bundles like porters or loaders. Even the second littlest, who was three, like a big boy slung his bundle over his shoulder." They went off along the path, and Simonov "stared vacantly and helplessly" after them. He had thought he "already hated the fascists as much as it was possible to hate", but suddenly another iota was added to all that hatred.

Soviet troops were advancing on Oryol. Only eighteen pilots in 65 Fighter Regiment had survived the fighting in July and they took it in turns to fly the seven remaining aircraft.[475] After Tonya's disappearance the authorities were reluctant to allow Klava Blinova to fly, but she was determined to avenge her dearest friend. Desperately lonely, she was chilled when she thought of the fate that might have befallen Tonya. To be taken prisoner was considered a terrible disgrace for a Soviet citizen. A soldier was expected to fight to the death or be counted a traitor, and everybody was familiar with tales of the terrible things that were done to prisoners by the Germans. Soviet newspapers were full of reports, lavishly illustrated with appalling photographs of the degradation meted out to those in captivity. And Tonya was a woman. It was, however, Klava who was about to experience the fate she considered worse than death.

"Losses on our side: aircraft – 6; Airmen – 5 failed to return from their mission," Major Prokofiev, now back at his desk, wrote in his latest report. He went on to mention briefly that lead pilot, Communist Party Member and Guards Senior Lieutenant N.I. Koventsov and his wingmate Guards Junior Lieutenant and Komsomol Member K.M. Blinova had not returned to base from a mission to escort attack bombers. "According to a statement by

Guards Lieutenant Sychev", he noted, "two Yak aircraft were shot down in aerial engagement FW-190. The pilot (believed to be Blinova) bailed out of one of our stricken aircraft. The other pilot, flying at low altitude, banked, the wing of the aircraft made contact with the ground, the plane crashed and the pilot (believed to be Koventsov) was burned to death."[476] The pilot who bailed out was indeed Klava Blinova.

Klava had no idea when her attention flagged or how she managed to get herself shot down. She remembered only a dry crack and the grinding of metal. Klava was thrown hard against one side of the plane and it began to disintegrate. For a time she was falling together with the cockpit, clutching a now useless joystick. She felt no fear, only a clear-headed determination to live. She undid the cord of her headset and seat straps and the next moment an invisible hand seemed to pluck her violently out of the wreckage of the plane. Her parachute opened and she suddenly saw a Luftwaffe fighter firing tracer bullets rapidly increasing in size and apparently hurtling straight at her. The German almost snagged the canopy of her parachute and Klava was thrown to one side. She heard someone shriek, realised it was herself, quickly wound the parachute cords round her fist to hasten her descent, and plummeted towards the ground as the plane with its white crosses disappeared from view.[477]

The next moment the alarming thought occurred to her that, as the dogfight had been taking place behind enemy lines, she was parachuting into enemy-held territory. Just before hitting the ground she noticed woodland nearby and decided to run there to hide. She freed herself from the parachute in a matter of seconds but, as she ran, Klava heard something "snapping and churning up the ground with a strange, predatory whistling sound". Klava had been at the front for almost a year but this was the first time she had been under fire on the ground, and it was only when she felt a sharp pain in her leg she realised she was being shot at. Though she had been hit in the foot, she ran on a little, crouching down, but then could no longer put any weight on it and had to crawl. A German soldier suddenly appeared standing directly above her.

When she stood up, covered in dust and soil, and pulled off her flying helmet, the German soldiers who ran up exclaimed in surprise and sympathy to find the pilot was a very young woman. The sympathy was not sufficient to stop them claiming their trophies. They soon stripped Klava of her watch, her epaulettes, and ripped from her tunic her Guards insignia and medal "For Valour" together with some of the material. They then sent her off in a passing car to the military police and from there, after interrogation, she was packed off with other pilots to a prisoner-of-war camp in Karachev. This was already close to the advancing Soviet front line. In Karachev everything was on fire, shells were exploding, "motorcyclists were dashing everywhere in a panic", and at crossroads, traffic regulators were yelling furiously. By the time they left Karachev, Klava knew their group was being sent to Bryansk.

Only a small minority of the 80,000 prisoners at Bryansk were accommodated in the former repair workshops that formed the centre of the camp; the majority were out in the open air. Incredibly, someone in this great mass of humanity recognised Klava and called to her. Like everyone else there, the tag hanging round the prisoner's neck gave only a number and it was impossible to tell who the burnt, disfigured face belonged to.

"It's me, Anatoly Golovin, your commander," the stranger muttered barely audibly. It was only then that Klava broke down. "I cried like I had never cried before."[478]

Twenty-four-year-old First Squadron Leader Anatoly Golovin had shown himself a highly capable pilot in the battle of Kursk. Reports confirm that he shot down eight German planes, but was himself shot down by a Focke-Wulf on his last sortie, providing cover for ground troops in the same region near Znamenskoye.[479] In the two weeks since the death of Tonya and her colleagues, Soviet troops had made almost no progress. Reporting that Golovin had bailed out of his burning aircraft over enemy territory, Major Prokofiev added that the attack bombers had passed on their official thanks to Golovin, who had saved their skins a few days previously. Golovin's group had been due to provide them with cover but his wingman's plane got stuck in mud before take-off and the entire group was ordered to turn back. Golovin was already in the air and had to provide cover on his own for the duration of the bombers' mission. He shot down two Focke-Wulfs and also received a commendation from the command of his fighter battalion. He was in line for a major military award, but fate decreed instead that he should find himself wounded and with terrible burns sitting in the dust along with thousands of other Soviet prisoners of war.

Soon Klava and her fellow pilots were dispatched to the railway station. They heard they were to be sent westwards and, aided at great personal risk by local women, decided to try to escape on route. The women had made their way close to the platform and threw the prisoners bread and potatoes. In a paper bag containing tobacco and a saucepan of boiled potatoes Klava and her fellows in misfortune also found two knives. They decided to cut a hole in the side of the wagon to enable them to flip open the latch on the door.

It took them three days to achieve this, and they then jumped one after the other from the speeding train into the dark. Klava hesitated for a moment, trying to work out how not to land on her wounded foot. She landed safely, stood up, and walked back along the track until she met the others. The five of them headed east through a field of summer wheat.

Klava had three brothers. The eldest was Sergey, then Stepan and Pavel. All three of them went voluntarily to the front the day after the outbreak of war. Stepan had been killed near Smolensk, Sergey at Stalingrad. She knew that Pavel, the youngest, was still alive and fighting recently, but who could tell? What if he too was dead? Klava just had to make it back.

They walked for eleven days, picking berries and gathering mushrooms and roots, avoiding villages and roads. Only after ten days did they venture for the first time into a village where they were given potatoes, tobacco, and a little bread. Here they discovered the front line was now only twenty kilometres ahead.

They crossed a river, whose name they did not know, on planks of wood from a wrecked bridge and, on the bank on the Soviet side, were at last able to stand up straight.

Klava had never been happier than when she heard a sentry's challenge,

"Halt! Who goes there?" She thought all her trials were behind her, but she was in for a surprise.

They were taken to the headquarters of one of the regiments of 21st Army by two soldiers with submachine guns, where they were interviewed by an officer from S.M.E.R.S.h. He responded suspiciously to every answer they gave. They were each given a sheet of paper to write an explanation of where they had been, and were fed only after they finished writing. Their "special assessment" took two weeks, after which they were sent to a filtration camp. Conditions there were little better than those in the Germans' prisoner-of-war camp. The bunks were the same, the food almost as meagre. The only real difference was that, if before they could hate their jailers, here they were baffled. The jailers were Soviet citizens just as they were themselves.

Air gunner Nikolai Rybalko, who had escaped from the Germans together with Klava and who also found himself in a Soviet prison camp, recalled how many people passed through the camps "which imprisoned a huge military force capable of taking any obstacle the enemy might present". They all adapted to living and working in the camp. Many had been there for a year already.

Klava was rescued from Soviet imprisonment by someone she knew from the past, Vasiliy Stalin, who did his best to shield pilots from the consequences of his father's policies. Shortly after she had miraculously managed to get a letter back to her own regiment, her good friend, Squadron Leader Vasiliy Kubarev, came to take her away from the camp. When the regiment had received her letter, they had contacted Vasily Stalin, who used his influence to secure her release. Very soon, with tears in her eyes, she was again sitting in the cockpit of a fighter aircraft.

Almost none of the new friends Klava Blinova left behind in that camp managed to return to fly and carry on fighting for their country. The lives of most were wrecked for good. Many languished for years in Stalin's prison camps.

39

"I want to fly a mission. This is no time to rest"

On the evening of 16 July 1943, taking to the sky to patrol the area around the village of Kuibyshevo, Lilya Litvyak and seven Yaks from other units engaged some thirty German bombers which, the Soviet pilots reckoned, were escorted by eight Messerschmitt fighters. It was an evening sortie, the last of the day. Litvyak shot up a Ju 88 bomber which "after the attack banked steeply and at low altitude and with flames appearing from its surfaces flew off in a westward direction". The pilot, the report mentions, "did not see the plane crash as she was attacked by Messerschmitts". Litvyak was lucky. She managed to land her plane safely in rough country near the village of Darievka, not at all far from her airfield. Lilya's plane had taken punishment. Another document details that, "The plane has perforation of the fuselage, the left fuel tank, the water and air systems." Because of this major damage it was sent off for a factory repair. It was not the plane Lilya usually flew. The following day she climbed into the cockpit of her own Yak, No. 16131 that Kolya Menkov serviced and in the cockpit of which, while on standby, she had scratched "Mum" and her initials, "LL". Despite an injury she refused to take a day's rest, saying, "I want to fly a mission. This is no time to rest."[480]

Eight Air Army continued to support the armies of the Southern Front, who were regrouping for a counter-offensive against the Germans on the Mius. At first the forces – tens of thousands of soldiers, thousands of guns and hundreds of tanks – were moved up only under cover of darkness, but the nights are short in July, and from 14 July the commander allowed the troops to march during the day.[481] Twenty-four hours a day huge columns of vehicles were moving along the roads at the front, and they needed protection from the air. They were being attacked by major groups of bombers redeployed by the Germans from many areas, including Kursk. The troops were required to be fully ready by 17 July to strike at a thirty-kilometre-long section of the front extending through Dmitrievka, Kuibyshevo and Yasi-novsky and to break through the enemy's defences.

On the afternoon of 18 July there remained only a small Soviet bridge-head of about ten-square kilometres on the right bank of the Mius. In support of 5 Assault Army, 2 Guards Army was brought into action. This was to attempt to extend the attack and reach the line of the River Krynka. It was there, while providing cover to the ground attack bombers, that Katya Budanova was killed.

Lieutenant Katya Budanova and Junior Lieutenant Alyokhin provided an escort of just two fighters for eight attack aircraft flying to the area of Pokrovskoye, not far from Artyomovsk, where they were engaged by six Messerschmitts. The fate of Budanova and Alyokhin was described by pilots of the attack aircraft, which the two Yaks successfully defended, seeing off all the enemy planes. Alyokhin's damaged Yak headed "home", accompanying a stricken Ilyushin, but did not make it back to the air-field. The second Yak, according to the report, "after the Messerschmitts had left, at an altitude of approximately 2,000 metres, nosedived, hit the ground and burst into flames".

A secretary from the field hospital of the Second Assault Army, Ye. Shvyrova, was the first to reach the crash site. She described what she found in a letter to No. 63 School, Moscow which set up a Katya Budanova museum. She wrote, "In July–August 1943 there was an assault on the Mius River when we were stationed in the village of Novokrasnovka."[482] Shvyrova recalled that the fighting was so intense that the shell explosions and roar of aircraft meant that in the headquarters they could make them-selves heard only by shouting into each other's ears.

"I happened to be outside," she continued, "and saw an aircraft coming down fast. I realised the pilot was wounded or already dead. It crashed and instantly burst into flames. The village is situated in a hollow and the plane crashed on a hill. When I reached the top the plane was already almost burnt out and the pilot (it was Katya Budanova) was lying next to it covered in blood, as was her parachute."

It was not until they discovered her documents that the people who found Katya learned the charred corpse was that of a woman. The village women buried her, and Shvyrova and her colleagues read and reread the letters they found with Katya, and looked again and again at the photos, only some time later sending them on to her sister, Valya, in Moscow. Among the letters, they found one from Mikhail Baranov and an unfinished letter from Katya to her mother. There were several pictures of Katya herself, in uniform beside the plane, in civilian clothes, and one when she was very young wearing a pretty hat. Shvyrova remembered these photographs well. It was hard to believe the girl in them was the broken and bloodied body she had found by the wreckage of the plane.

The girls at army headquarters had seen many terrible sights, but were deeply affected by the death of this young woman pilot. Just one day later a German plane came down on the same hill and burst into flames. "As one, we all muttered, 'That's for Katya!'"

Katya's obituary in the newspaper *Stalin's Warriors* was signed by the senior officers, the pilots, her comrades in the regiment including Lilya Litvyak, and others who had known her at the front.[483]

The biographers of Litvyak and Budanova have written, supposedly citing others in her regiment, that a few days after Katya's death a short, blonde girl flew to Novokrasnovka, asked where she was buried and went to the grave.

Alas, there is no truth in this. Novokrasnovka had no airfield, and a Yak did not have the same capability as the U-2 for putting down on rough terrain; there was nowhere it could have landed there. A woman drove a truck with several people from the regiment, pilots and mechanics, everybody who was able to go at this moment of intense fighting, to Katya's funeral.[484] Lilya was not among them. She was flying constantly. On 19 July, the day of the funeral, she shot down another German aircraft.[485]

After Katya's death Valya Krasnoshhyokova saw almost nothing of Lilya Litvyak. She was in a different squadron and the fighting was so ceaseless there was no time to breathe.[486] Valya often thought about her, and felt deeply sorry for her. She was now completely alone. Valya decided that when there was a free moment she would ask the commander of their regiment to transfer her to the same squadron. Two days after Katya Budanova, however, Golyshev was himself killed.

The 21st of July 1943 was a bad day. Commander Ivan Golyshev, Lilya Litvyak, and her wingman Dimitry Svistunenko did not return from their mission of escorting Ilyushin Il-2 attack aircraft. Major Krainov wrote in his report that the commander had been drunk as he took off. Attempts to stop him were made by Chief of Staff Smirnov and the regiment's N.K.V.D. officer, Lieutenant Perushev, but Golyshev "told Perushev to stuff himself". This was highly unusual behaviour for the educated and disciplined Golyshev, but evidently the intolerable stress of recent weeks, the dangers of escorting the attack aircraft, and the endless losses in the regiment had taken their toll.[487] Golyshev, no doubt because he was drunk, considered himself in great shape to fly and brushed aside the N.K.V.D. official whom, like most other members of the regiment, he strongly disliked.

They escorted six Il-2s to the vicinity of Krinichka, a village near the River Krynka. The aircraft came under attack from a large group of Messerschmitts.

When the mechanics back at base calculated that the plane they looked after would be running low on fuel, they would start looking out for its return. They were somehow able to recognise them while still far away. "Here comes mine," someone would say. Those whose aircraft had not returned would wait for some time more, even after the point when they knew that their plane must already have run out of fuel. Eventually they would walk back from the stand despondently, clinging to the hope their plane had crash-landed somewhere and that the pilot would return. That day it was the turn of Nikolai Menkov. His plane did not come back, and he could only wait and hope for the best.

Litvyak, with her face scratched but otherwise unharmed, appeared back in the regiment the following day.[488] She related that they had encountered a large group of Messerschmitts and taken them on, but could give no specific information about the fate of Golyshev and Svistunenko. Chief of Staff Smirnov duly reported, "Litvyak returned to the unit on 22/07/43 and stated she had been winged in combat and pursued by a

Messerschmitt Bf 109 to ground level. She crash-landed on the fuselage near Novikovka."[489]

Nikolai Menkov went with a woman truck driver to recover the plane. There was no one to ask for information because they were very close to the front line and all the local people had been evacuated, so they drove cluelessly around until Menkov stumbled by chance on the right village. Nearby, lying in tall grass, was Yak 16131, which he knew like the back of his hand.[490]

It was obvious that the plane had been in combat. The radiator was punctured, the engine damaged, and the propeller had been bent when it landed on its belly. Some signallers appeared who had witnessed the crash landing. One of them from Central Asia told Nikolai, "The plane come down. Like it just fall down in the weeds." They ran to help and called out, hoping to find the pilot. Then, as they laughingly told him, they heard a piping voice say: "I am the pilot." They could not see anyone because the grass was much taller than Lilya. It was probably also the grass that had saved her life by concealing the aircraft from German ground troops. Her face had been smeared with blood and engine oil because in the bumpy landing her nose hit the gunsight. She had a meal with the signallers, spent the night with their unit, and in the morning got a lift on a passing vehicle.

"The plane's right assembly and crankcase were broken," Nikolai recalled. The signallers told him Litvyak had barely made it back over the front line, landing just 700–900 metres on the Soviet side. Nikolai and another mechanic brought the plane back, lifting it with air bags and attaching its tail to the truck. "No. 16131 is being repaired within the unit," Smirnov reported. They replaced the plane's engine and airframe belt, and five days later it was again ready for service. Nikolai Menkov remembered very exactly that Litvyak flew seven more sorties on his plane before her disappearance.

The fate of Dmitry Svistunenko, who came to the regiment after fighting at Stalingrad on a U-2 night bomber and was remembered as a very nice lad, only became known in September. Following the breakthrough at the Mius Front, the regiment's representative of S.M.E.R.S.h., Guards Senior Lieutenant Perushev, was able to visit the approximate area of his crash that Lilya Litvyak had indicated. The local people to whom he turned for help showed him Svistunenko's plane by Mikhailovsky hamlet: the Yak-I, with a "28" painted on the tail. There was a "decomposed corpse next to it" which had not been buried because that same night the local people were evacuated to the rear.

According to the villagers, Svistunenko's plane was apparently hit, by a machine-gun burst from a German tank. He turned back to the east but the engine started to misfire so he crashed the plane on a slope. Two German motorcyclists approached him and he raised his hands as if to surrender. As the Germans started getting off their motorcycles, he took his pistol and shot both of them. German submachine gunners were already running towards him. Svistunenko bade farewell to his aircraft before shooting himself: "The pilot turned round, took off his cap, waved towards the plane, then shot himself." Perushev buried Svistunenko, who would have turned twenty-two in November, at the village cemetery, and fired a salute over the grave. As for Regimental Commander Golyshev, nothing was known about him until thirty years after the war. He was found by a school expedition that was looking for the remains of Lilya Litvyak and her plane.

Anna Zakutnyaya from the village of Artyomovka told the expedition she had seen a plane catch fire in the area of Krasnaya Gora after it was hit by a German anti-aircraft battery. It fell straight on top of the battery. The pilot did not bail out. The explosion threw him out of the cockpit and he was still alive when the Germans came running. They immediately shot him. Once they had gone, the local women buried the body next to his crashed plane, which became, as was often the case, a memorial to its dead pilot. His face remained in Anna's memory, and she recognised it at once when, many years later, she saw him in a group photo of pilots: "Oh, look, children, that's him!" The chairman of the village soviet gave them a horse and cart and the old woman took the schoolchildren and their teacher, Valentina Vashchenko, to a high cliff. At the bottom of it and scattered around were fragments of an aircraft. There they later found the remains of Ivan Golyshev, commander of 73 Guards Fighter Regiment.

40

"Every word brings back again and again the grief and pain"

The night of 31 July 1943 was the most terrible of all those in which the 588 Night Bomber Regiment served.[491] The following morning's situation report stated, "In the combat area the crews met active countermeasures from the enemy's air defences, and in particular from its fighter aircraft and searchlights. Four crews did not return from the mission: Pilot Vysotskaya, Navigator Dokutovich; Pilot Krutova, Navigator Salikova; Pilot Polunina, Navigator Kashirina; Pilot Rogova, Navigator Sukhorukova. Three crews were shot down by fighter aircraft and one apparently by anti-aircraft fire. The mission was not fully accomplished and was terminated on orders from divisional headquarters."[492]

After the German counter-offensive on the Taman peninsula, a number of villages passed into enemy hands. For a time the front did not move. The women pilots bombed German defences, while Soviets troops massed in anticipation of a major attack on the right flank of the German in the region of Novorossiysk.

On the night Galya Dokutovich died, Chief of Staff Irina Rakobolskaya and Yevdokia Bershanskaya saw off fifteen aircraft in succession on their first sortie of the night. Their target was not far away, and the beams of searchlights trying to fasten on them were clearly visible from the airfield. Suddenly, Rakobolskaya saw one of her planes burst into flames and begin to fall "slowly, like a fireball". She rushed to the logbook to see "who that was in flames". Then the first aircraft to have left returned, the crew reporting they had seen a plane burning at 2218 hours. Another crew that managed to return safely reported seeing another plane on fire at 2300 hours. Two similar reports followed. All the returning crews confirmed that the German anti-aircraft guns had been silent.[493] Bershanskaya was baffled, but quickly realised that, for the first time, the Germans had used a night-fighter to attack her regiment. The anti-aircraft guns had not been firing because their compatriots were overhead. In the beam of a searchlight, Bershanskaya's slow-flying planes were a perfect target.

Natasha Meklin, who had been a navigator before she was retrained, was flying one of her first combat missions as a pilot that night. When they were about seven minutes away from the target she and her navigator, Lida Loshmanova, saw the plane ahead of them caught by a searchlight beam. Natasha thought how closely the U-2 in the intersecting beams resembled "a silvery moth caught in a spider's web".[494] She too was puzzled by the anti-aircraft guns' silence, but soon everything became clear. A yellow flare lit up the sky as a German night-fighter signalled to those on the ground that it was one of theirs. Immediately "a bluish trail of lights" flew towards the aircraft caught in the spotlight as the fighter fired tracer bullets. Missing the first time, it corrected its aim. The second burst hit the plane.

The U-2 began to fall towards the ground in flames, "leaving behind a winding trail of smoke". A burning wing broke off, it crashed to the ground and exploded.

Though not yet an experienced pilot, Natasha instinctively veered away and began to climb, gliding back down to the target with her engine turned off. She began her return from the target at low altitude, eluding the searchlight. The other crews that did not fall prey to the fighter had adopted a similar tactic.

The thought of friends burned alive, a fate that could so easily be your own, was very painful. Zhenya Rudneva, who had agreed to provide Anya Vysotskaya, an inexperienced pilot, with "a more experienced navigator", felt partly to blame for Galya Dokutovich's death.[495] She did not see Anya and Galya shot down in flames, but "they burned Zhenya Krutova and Lena Salikova" in front of her eyes. At that moment Zhenya had been over the target and saw the U-2 of Krutova and Salikova with its canvas burning, not plummeting but gliding downwards. When it blew up near Kievskaya in enemy territory it had already landed. Rudneva received a report that another plane had been shot down in flames at 2300 hours, but it was unclear whether it was piloted by Vysotskaya or Rogova. In the event both their planes were destroyed.

Zhenya ran to each plane as it landed, but Galya was not in any of them. "There is only emptiness in my heart. Everything is over!" she wrote. The last entry in Galya Dokutovich's diary dates from 6 July 1943. She was twenty-three years old.

Rakobolskaya wrote to the families of the ten girls – eight died that night, and two had been killed a day or two previously – who had been shot down in flames to inform them that their daughters were missing. Even without any evidence to hand it was clear that they could not have survived. Yevdokia Rachkevich only managed to find their graves after the war.

In 2003, Irina Rakobolskaya learnt the name of the German fighter pilot who, on the night of 31 July, shot down no fewer than three "sewing machines", as the Germans called the U-2 planes. He was Oberfeldwebel Josef Kociok, and he in turn was killed some six weeks after his successful night's hunting.[496]

When the Germans' Blue Line was finally broken and a vain search for Galya's body was undertaken in the area where her plane had crashed, Polina Gelman wrote a letter to her friend's family, full of love and sorrow but with a remarkable restraint in its expression of grief which testifies to her own strength of personality:

It is hard for me to write to you about the irreparable loss of the person nearest and dearest to me. Every word brings back again and again the grief and pain. I know that you more than anyone else will understand me. It is so very hard. Our Galya did not return from her mission on 31 July. Everybody is now reconciled to the view that this girl who was everybody's favourite is no longer among the living, because it is undeniable. I stubbornly waited and waited for news of her and even wrote letters to send her the instant there was any. Alas, when our troops recently liberated the area where she was shot down our fears were confirmed. I could write you words of comfort but they would be as useless as the words people offered to me and I know how pointless it would be to write them or try to comfort you.

That is all I can say. Galya probably wrote to tell you she had been awarded the Order of the Red Star. She has also posthumously been awarded the Order of the Patriotic War, Second Class. That award will be made to you. In a day or two I will send you her possessions and photographs, and will also transfer her money through the accounts department.

Write to me. I will always be glad to hear everything about the family of my dear, unforgettable friend. The shining memory of her will never fade in my mind. If no enemy bullet kills me and some day I have a daughter, I shall call her Galya and bring her up to be noble and wonderful like our Galya.[497]

Polina Gelman died in 2005, having outlived her dearest friend by sixty-two years. She graduated from the Institute of Military Translation, specialising in Spanish. Polina did have a daughter and, as she had promised, called her Galya. She worked in the Central Komsomol School, took a doctorate in economics, and worked for two years in Cuba. Until she was very old she gave lectures in Spanish. She was an active member of the Jewish Anti-Fascist Committee, the only Jewish woman to be awarded the title of Hero of the Soviet Union, and an active member of the Veterans Committee. Throughout her long, busy, inspiring life the thought never left her that she was living simultaneously for herself and for her Galya.

Zhenya wrote her last entry about Galya on 15 August. "Now that Galya is no more and will never come back . . . Oh, how dreadful that sounds, my own dear Galya who was so full of life!"[498] She still could not bring herself to move Galya's photograph to the small white envelope in which she kept the photos of other friends who had died. "Everything points to the fact that she is dead . . . " Zhenya continues, and yet again analyses their relationship, which now is no more than a memory. "Oh, how I would like now to really know what she thought about me. I know she sometimes found me tiresome. I know that, and that because of the goodness of her heart she was too forgiving towards me, more than I was of her stubbornness. She never showed petty jealousy, perhaps because she never loved me. For all that, she did genuinely feel warmly towards me and, strangely enough, like an older friend might feel for someone younger, although there were no grounds for that."

Life went on. Very soon Zhenya fell in love with a pilot, Dina Nikulina, just as she had with Galya. She fell head over heels in love, and was jealous and wept when another navigator claimed Dina. It was only in Polina's heart that nobody could replace Galya.

41

"Wh-what kind of men are you not to be able to keep one g-girl safe?"

Anya Skorobogatova had been on duty on the evening of 1 August. It was the last time she heard Lilya Litvyak's voice over the radio. Lilya said, "Here goes!" and fell silent.[499] Anya was not particularly surprised, because that was a common occurrence. The radio signal was unreliable and Litvyak tended to be taciturn while she was flying. It was only when Anya finished her tour of duty that she learned Lilya had not returned.

Nikolai Menkov, who had seen Lilya off on her last flight, was there to meet the other pilots of her group and carried on waiting for the return of his plane, although he knew it would have run out of fuel long ago. Eventually, crushed, he had walked away from the airfield.

When in 1979 a Moscow publishing house brought out Valeriy Agranovsky's semi-documentary, semi-fictional novella about Lilya Litvyak, her disappearance, and the search for her remains and aircraft, Lieutenant Colonel (Retired) Nikolai Menkov wrote the author a long letter which began, "I have been very moved to read *The White Lily*, because for two months in June and July 1943 I worked in the same Third Squadron of 73 Wing as fighter pilot Lilya Litvyak." Menkov decided to contact Agranovsky in the hope that his information would assist in the search. Menkov, the father of two children, a former army engineer and now a schoolteacher, after all these years still remembered the minutest details of the missing plane in which he had invested so much effort, and of the pilot who had vanished along with the aircraft.

The top of the joystick had the letters "LL" scratched on it (for "Lilya Litvyak". She scratched them on with a knife while on call one time). On the top of the instrument panel she had scratched "Mum". In the cockpit the foot controls were set as far back as possible because Litvyak was quite small. The skin of the aircraft was grey. The tail wheel guards had plates with hidden rivetting. The tank had been repaired and must have had welded seams on it. The number on the tail of the aircraft was "18".

On the middle finger of her left hand Lilya Litvyak had a gold-plated signet ring. She had two gold crowns (visible when she smiled) on the teeth on the left side of her upper jaw. Lilya's clothing at the time of the flight was: chrome leather boots with short tops, dark-blue flying breeches, a khaki tunic, and she always tucked her dark-blue beret away in her map case.

On the day she disappeared Lilya made four sorties, mostly in support of Ilyushins attacking German ground troops. The Germans threw all their operational reserves at the area of the Soviet breakthrough. They redeployed substantial numbers of aircraft from the Belgorod-Kharkov sector to the Donetsk coal-basin.[500] The Southern Front regrouped urgently in order to counter-attack on 31 July, but this plan was foiled by the transfer of three German armoured divisions from Kharkov. On 30 July the Germans succeeded in inflicting major damage with a large number of tanks, repeating the manoeuvre the following day. According to Soviet reports the Germans had 400–500 tanks. These were given effective air support. The troops of the Southern Front were ordered to retreat to the left bank of the River Mius.

Attack aircraft continued their missions with fighter escorts. On her third sortie Lilya shot down a Messerschmitt.[501] When she came out to her aircraft to fly a fourth sortie, Menkov felt obliged to try to talk her out of it, even though as a mechanic he had no right to question the judgement of a senior officer. He commented that it was "very punishing for one person to fly so many missions in this heat", and added, "Do you really need to do so much flying? There are other pilots!" Litvyak told him, "The Germans have started using weaklings. They are wet behind the ears and I feel like blasting one more of them!"[502] Before taking off, Lilya as always said goodbye to her mechanic, "smiled and nodded her head". Then she raised her left hand to close the canopy and moved to take off.

Six Yaks had been allocated to escort a group of eight Ilyushins. Lilya, as she often did, was leading Alexander Yevdokimov. Without waiting for them, the Ilyushins took off for the front line and, as they approached, the fighter pilots could see they were already engaged in combat near the River Mius. The fighters managed to take out two Messerschmitts and keep all the Ilyushins safe. Their only loss was Litvyak, who was shot down as they were leaving the battle zone. The crash was witnessed by Sasha Yevdokimov and Borisenko, who saw her plane falling out of control but not on fire. Its pilot did not bail out, manifestly having been killed or seriously injured in the air. On returning from the mission, Yevdokimov reported to their commander that Litvyak had come down behind enemy lines in the vicinity of Dmitrievka. Borisenko reported that he saw a Messerschmitt suddenly emerge from the clouds, fire off a round at the tail of the nearest Yak, which was unprotected, and promptly vanish. He believed the plane fired on was that of Litvyak.

A regimental document entitled "Information on Aviation Incidents, Combat and Non-Combat Losses of 73 Guards Stalingrad Fighter Regiment. 1–9 August 1943" contains an entry reporting that Guards Flight Commander Junior Lieutenant Litvyak, Lidia Vladimirovna "did not return to base after accomplishing a combat mission at 1040–1150 hrs providing cover for Soviet troops". There are already two mistakes evident here: the sortie took place in the evening, and the flight was not to cover troops but to escort attack aircraft. The document goes on to assert, "In the vicinity of Marinovka they engaged in combat several groups of Me-109s totalling up to 12 attack aircraft and up to 30 Junkers Ju 87s." The likelihood is that the author has confused this sortie with a mission flown on 16 July, when Lilya really did engage with a group of thirty bombers.[503] The information about the location of her crash does, however, agree with the observations of Yevdokimov and Borisenko. "Crews engaged in the battle saw one Yak-1 fall 4–5 km northeast of Marinovka." The author of this document concludes that the aircraft was "evidently shot down and the pilot is presumed to have perished".

Veterans' memoirs tell us that the whole regiment was in mourning. Almost no one had the stomach for dinner.[504] In spite of all the evidence, people waited and hoped, but Lilya did not return. The next day Boris Sidnev, commander of 6 Guards Air Division (formerly 268 Fighter Aviation Division), appeared in the regiment and stutteringly reproached one of the flight commanders, "Wh-what kind of men are you not to be able to keep one g-girl safe?"[505] The whole of 8 Air Army grieved for her.

A day later, when Soviet troops had been able to advance a little, Alexander Yevdokimov and Nikolai Menkov went in search of the crashed aircraft.[506] They scoured the area where the fighting had occurred, from Dmitrievka to Kuibyshevo. They went round all the villages and gullies, but found nothing. There were almost no civilians remaining in the frontline villages, and soldiers "offered contradictory explanations". They were, after all, engaged in fierce fighting right on the front line and had no great interest in a missing plane. Many aircraft had crashed there in those days.

Lilya's last letter to her mother, which she dictated to the squadron's adjutant while sitting on call in the cockpit of her fighter, contains no suggestion of weariness or anxiety. Just that she was greatly missing her mother and home. She wrote:

Everything here, the meadows and the sparse woodland, remind me now of our own dear countryside around Moscow where I grew up and spent so many happy days. It has been a long time since I heard the bustle of the streets of Moscow, the clattering of the trams, and the cars hurrying everywhere. Life in the army has completely swallowed all that. It is even difficult for me to snatch a moment to write a letter to tell you I am alive and well, and that what I love most in all the world is my Motherland and you, my dear mother.

I have a burning desire to drive those German reptiles out of our land just as soon as may be, so that once again we can live a happy, peaceful life, so I can come home to you and tell you all the things I have been through in the days since we parted. Dear Mum, this letter has been written by our adjutant while I was on call. So long. I love and kiss you. 28.7.43[507]

Lilya's mother, Anna, was forever asking Valya Krasnoshchyokova when she came to visit after the war, "Valya, was Lilya ill? How did she look? Was she terribly tired?"[508] There was nothing Valya could tell her. People who wrote about Litvyak claimed that in the last weeks before she died she was exhausted and depressed, the death of Katya having affected her so much that she was acting out of character. Their source is a tale told by Faina Pleshivtseva, but as we have seen, Pleshivtseva left the regiment in late May or early June, and did not return. None of the mechanics or pilots who were working with Lilya in those last days said anything about her being tired or depressed. She was fighting with the same determination as ever. Menkov tells us that her mood as she took off on her last flight was "bright and cheerful".[509]

In August 1943 Kharkov was retaken and the Soviet Army moved deeper into the territory of the Ukraine. Aircraft with red stars on their wings now invariably outnumbered those with German crosses. The fighter regiment flew to the airfield at Makeyevka and Menkov and Yevdokimov again went out looking for any sign of Lilya, but again found nothing.[510] On 25 August Alexander Yevdokimov was killed as they were moving to another new airport, his "air awareness" having lapsed. He and Pilot Byvshev were shot down over Soviet territory by a pair of Messerschmitts. When the regiment learned that he jumped with a parachute that failed to open everyone was terribly saddened. He was such a young, handsome and likeable man and this was "the most terrifying death, hurtling earthwards, fully aware of your situation".[511] After Alexander died they undertook no further searches, and registered Lilya's name in perpetuity in the list of 73 Guards Fighter Regiment. *Komsomolskaya Pravda*, where she had been so warmly received just four months before, wrote about her death. Everyone was expecting that she would be posthumously awarded the title of Hero of the Soviet Union, but things took a different turn.

It all changed about a month and a half later, when a pilot from a neighbouring fighter regiment who had been taken prisoner returned and unexpectedly claimed he had seen Litvyak in captivity.

Valya Krasnoshchyokova now faced an ordeal. After the death of Lilya and Katya, she was very lonely, and then in September she found herself being called in for questioning by the Special Department who, for some reason, were suddenly taking an interest in Lilya.[512] What kind of Komsomol member had she been? What did she talk about? Could she have gone over to the side of the Germans? Valya indignantly told them exactly what she thought. Lilya had been a devoted Komsomol member. She could only have been captured if she had been seriously wounded. There was no way she would have gone over to the Germans; it was ridiculous even to suggest it. Nikolai Menkov also found himself summoned, but only once. The other mechanics and pilots were called in too, one by one. At first no one could understand what was going on.

The rumours spread and multiplied. The ground was only too fertile: a beautiful girl fighter pilot had vanished without trace. There had been no shortage of gossip about Lilya while she was alive, and even now someone could not leave her in peace. It was asserted that local people had said a plane landed behind the front line right on the road. The village was even named. A diminutive girl pilot with a straight nose and blonde hair had climbed out and been driven off in a car with Germans.

Others swore they had heard someone say the Germans buried Lilya in Kramatorsk with full military honours. There had supposedly been a parade through the town with a band because "the fascists wanted to keep up their own troops' failing morale" and decided to show them the example of a "Russ heroine".

There was even a rumour that someone had seen a German leaflet with her photograph that said the aviatrix Lilya Litvyak was well and happy with the Germans.

Gradually, however, it became known that all this bizarre nonsense was based solely on the testimony of a pilot who had escaped from captivity. Officially, of course, nobody could say anything out loud, but they whispered his name: Vladimir Lavrinenkov.[513] That was difficult to believe. Anyone else, but surely not brave, honest Lavrinenkov. He just did not look like a man capable of slandering a fellow soldier.

Lavrinenkov was a famous fighter pilot who had shot down twenty-six German planes. He was a Hero of the Soviet Union and was a favourite of Timofey Khryukin, commander of 8 Air Army. Khryukin personally had ordered him at the end of August to shoot down a Frame spy plane that was conducting reconnaissance overhead.[514] Proud and excited, Lavrinenkov took off to perform the task, watched from the ground by the high command. It manoeuvred so adroitly that he was finding it difficult to make the kill. Remembering his lessons, he pursued the Frame, guns blazing. He was not entirely sure what happened next. Whether he hit the plane and it went out of control, or whether he underestimated his own speed, at all events Lavrinenkov collided with it, damaging the Frame and also his own Airacobra. The Frame fell earthwards, but one wing came off his own plane. His biographers later claimed he had deliberately rammed the German plane, but in his memoirs the pilot describes the incident more honestly. Bailing out, he found himself drifting helplessly behind enemy lines.[515]

He did not conceal his identity in captivity and was well treated, not beaten or starved like others. After the initial interrogations it was decided to send him to Germany; he was evidently considered an important potential source of information. On the way there, he and other fellows in misfortune escaped from the train and walked for many days back towards the front.

They did not make it to the front line, instead coming upon a partisan guerrilla unit that, after they had been questioned, they were invited to join. Soon their detachment joined up with the advancing Red Army and Lavrinenkov, wearing a greatcoat taken from a dead German, returned to 8 Air Army. Seeing Khryukin's joy at his return, Lavrinenkov was met with open arms as a hero by the others. His awards were returned to him without further ado and he was promoted. Soon he was back in his own regiment.

Lavrinenkov says in his memoirs that he was very lucky; even after his heroic participation in guerrilla operations he might not have been believed, sent to a Soviet prison camp for interrogation, or been "exposed" as a spy. Another famous Soviet fighter pilot, Mikhail Devyataev, was less fortunate. For his feat of escaping from captivity in a German plane and bringing a number of other Soviet prisoners back with him he was rewarded by his homeland with ten years in a prison camp, his interrogators having decided that a fighter pilot could not possibly know how to fly a bomber and must, therefore, have been sent back as a spy by the Germans.

In his memoirs Lavrinenkov mentions that for a month and a half after his return to the regiment he was not allowed to fly while he was investigated by the Special Department. They contacted the partisan detachment he had fought with and Lavrinenkov had to write many pages of detailed testimony explaining where he had been and what he had done. Is this evidence still extant? Will it ever be made public? What did the Special Department ask Lavrinenkov and what did he volunteer on his own initiative? In his own memoirs and in memoirs about him there is not a single word about any incrimination of Lilya Litvyak.

Could Lavrinenkov, unquestionably a fearless soldier, have slandered his dead comrade-in-arms, a girl he greatly admired? Would he have done what was demanded of him, perhaps under duress? It is difficult to believe, but for Vladimir Lavrinenkov flying was his life. He knew that pilots who returned from captivity were not allowed to continue to fly. As for Litvyak, she was dead and he might have reasoned that he could not hurt her personally, only her reputation. "There is something fishy about the whole business," Boris Yeremin, commander of 31 Fighter Wing, was to remark many years later, but without saying he believed the story told by a pilot in jeopardy after returning from captivity was a lie.[516] In his last days Lavrinenkov himself repudiated what he had said.[517]

Many years have passed and none of those involved in this story are any longer alive, but we know that almost certainly Lavrinenkov lied, smearing the reputation of a deceased pilot. If Litvyak had agreed to cooperate with the Germans, or had even still been alive and their captive, their propaganda would assuredly have trumpeted the fact to the world. However, there was no mention of her, no photograph of her on a German leaflet, not a word from any of the radio transmitters which broadcast in Russian to Russian soldiers, not a single remark by prisoners returning from prisoner-of-war camps about a girl the like of whom they would assuredly have remembered. Lilya, almost certainly, died and, like 800,000 other Soviet soldiers, lies unburied in the earth of the Mius Front.

The myth of the captive Lilya was confirmed, as was later discovered, also under duress, by Andrey Golyuk, an 85 Regiment pilot who was returned from German captivity after the war.[518] He too claimed to have seen Litvyak as a prisoner, which appeared to discredit her conclusively. He subsequently made no secret of the fact that he had been compelled to make this false assertion. At a veterans' reunion Valya Krasnoshchyokova found an opportunity to talk to him in private and ask why he had done so. Golyuk made no attempt to justify himself and replied that he had been forced to defame Lilya. He had been warned that failure to do so would entail major unpleasantness for him, as his own conduct in captivity could be called into question. Valya was incensed. As she walked away from him, she contemptuously amended his surname: "*Govnyuk!*" she hissed. "Shithead!"

So Golyuk was forced to defame Lilya Litvyak, confirming false testimony which somebody, most probably Lavrinenkov, had given earlier. But if he too had been coerced, what was going on? Was there a leaflet? Had some informer claimed Lilya was planning to defect? Did the Special Department know her father had been purged? Why did Sidnev not stamp on this campaign of defamation against her? Or Khryukin, who also followed her fighting career with admiration? If they decided to take no action, was it because they were uncertain Lilya had died?

When these rumours reached Lilya's own women's 586 Fighter Regiment, many were only too ready to believe them. Valya Krasnoshchyokova found that unsurprising. Other girls envied Lilya her looks, her popularity, her skill as a pilot and, after summer 1943, her national celebrity.[519] They whispered that her victories had been ascribed to her only because she had pretty eyes, and even many years after the war were still writing and talking in this vein, unashamedly vilifying her memory. When one of the pilots of the women's Fighter Regiment many decades after the war thought she had recognised Lilya in a Swiss or Swedish TV programme about a Soviet aviatrix who had been captured and gone on to live a prosperous life in Sweden or Switzerland, many agreed that of course it must have been Lilya.[520]

Faina Pleshivtseva, or Inna Pasportnikova as she became known after her marriage (Inna was a more fashionable variant of Faina), revered the memory of Lilya Litvyak and for many years joined schoolchildren from the town of Krasny Luch in the Ukraine and their teacher Valentina Vashchenko in organising expeditions to find the remains of Lilya and her plane. They discovered many other pilots, including Commander Golyshev, but were unable to locate Lilya. They did learn that in the 1970s the remains of an unknown woman pilot had been found by village boys when they were trying to pull a grass snake out of its hole. This was near the village of Marinovka, but what was left of the plane had long been sent to the scrapyard. The school expedition discovered that the find had been registered and the remains then buried in a mass grave. According to Valentina Vashchenko, the list of items included fragments of underwear – namely a brassiere made from parachute silk – and, in addition, fragments

313

of a flying helmet and bleached hair.[521] Alas, today a copy of that list is nowhere to be found and nobody has any suggestions as to where to begin looking for it.*

Poetry, particularly lyric poetry, was something the girls in Marina Raskova's regiments needed desperately. They dreamed of love, their hearts longed for tenderness, and their feelings were the more acute because they were risking their lives. Men fighting in the war had the same experiences, but for girls the longing was even stronger. Konstantin Simonov's poem "Wait for Me", published in *Pravda* on 14 January 1942 and copied out in notebooks hundreds of thousands, and probably even millions, of times, was the voice of their generation, the song of those at war who longed for home, and of those who were waiting for them at home. It was the prayer of those who might be killed, and of those who waited.

The poem was written in the early months of the war when Simonov, as the reporter of a front-line newspaper, saw the horror and chaos of the retreat, bade a last farewell to friends he had only just met, and narrowly escaped death himself. "If I had not written it, somebody else would have," he once said of this front-line anthem. He added, "There is no great backstory to 'Wait for Me'. I went away to war, leaving behind the woman I loved, so I wrote her a letter in verse." Writer Lev Kassil, at whose dacha he was staying at the time, told Simonov that it was a good poem but that this was not the time to publish it. The editor of the Army's *Red Star* newspaper, for which he was working, had a similar reaction. "This poem has no place in an Army newspaper," he said. "There is no point

* We cannot just take the word of "Pasportnikova". If we were to believe everything she said, she not only saw Litvyak off on her last flight but even sewed that bra for her. It was supposedly Pleshivtseva Lilya sent to get the peroxide bleach. She claimed Litvyak also told her shortly before her death that she could not afford to go missing because then the purging of her father would resurface. In fact, Faina Pleshivtseva was not there shortly before Lilya died, and in any case in those years nobody would have discussed such things with anyone, no matter how close to them. As so often happens, Faina Pleshivtseva played an ambiguous role in the posthumous reputation of Lilya Litvyak. By devoting herself to perpetuating her memory, she did much that was positive; but in the process she surrounded Lilya's reputation with so many fictions that caused no small amount of damage herself.

in unsettling our soldiers." [522]

The poem, however, made its own way. Wherever Simonov went, the soldiers at the end of a stressful day would ask him to read them poetry. After once reading "Wait for Me" on the Northern Front, he went on to read it many times more. In December 1941 he read it on the radio and on 14 January it was published in *Pravda*. The poem moved an entire nation, and after it was published Simonov was a celebrity, known even to those with little interest in literature. People came to believe that, if they just waited faithfully enough, no harm would come to those they loved.

From then until the end of the war on trips to the front to gather material for his reports, Simonov, thawing out after the cold and the dangers with a front-line vodka ration or some diluted spirit in the company of officers at the front, was happy to read them his poetry invariably including, of course, "Wait for Me".

> Wait for me, and I'll return,
> Only really wait.
> Wait for me when autumn rains
> Make you sad.
> Wait when snows sweep over the land,
> And in the summer's heat.
> Wait when others are not waited for,
> Just yesterday betrayed.[523]

It was rumoured that the actress Valentina Serova, for whom the poem was written, did not wait too long for Simonov, embarking on a romance with the dazzling young Marshal Rokossovsky, but how much does that really matter? She was still the muse of a poet who wrote the most important Russian poem of the Second World War.

Many years after the war Simonov would receive letters from those whose wait had been rewarded, and from others who had waited in vain. Some women whose husbands or sons did not return wrote that his poem had left them feeling guilty all their lives that they must not have waited hard enough.

Lilya Litvyak's mother, left without a death certificate and thus without the pension automatically paid to anyone whose breadwinner had died at the front, lived in penury after the war. For her, however, the words "lost without trace" in the official letter she received from 73 Guards Fighter Regiment were infinitely preferable to "died a hero's death", because it left room for hope. Around her, if only very rarely, miracles did happen. Some people whose families had been sent notification of their death in action came home safe and sound. Every time she saw Valya and Faina she would ask the same unanswerable question: "If she's alive, why has she not let us have some news at least about herself?" Then she would shake her head and say, no, Lilya could not still be among the living. And yet, right to the end of her life she lived in hope. Others around her were waiting too for their loved ones to come back from the war, thousands, hundreds of thousands, millions of people.

Konstantin Simonov went on to read "Wait for Me" at literary evenings for twenty years after the war, but then decided it was time to stop. "Everybody who was going to come back had come back. There was no longer anyone to wait for." [524]

Dramatis Personae

Sultan Amet-Khan, pilot in 9 Guards Fighter Regiment

Nikolai "Batya" Baranov, commander of 296 (73 Guards) Fighter Regiment

Raisa Belyaeva, pilot in 586, 437, 9 Guards, 296 (73 Guards) Fighter Regiments

Yevdokia Bershanskaya, commander of 588 (46 Guards) Night Bomber Regiment

Klavdia (Klava) Blinova, pilot in 586, 434, 65 Guards Fighter Regiments

Senior Sergeant Borisenko, senior sergeant in 296 (73 Guards) Fighter Regiment

Katya Budanova, pilot in 586, 437, 9 Guards, 296 (73 Guards) Fighter Regiments

Anya Demchenko, pilot in 586 Fighter Regiment

Galya Dokutovich, navigator in 588 (46 Guards) Night Bomber Regiment

Masha Dolina, pilot in 587 (125 Guards) Heavy Bomber Regiment

Yevgeny Dranishchev, pilot in 437, 9 Guards Fighter Regiments

Irina Dryagina, pilot in 588 (46 Guards) Night Bomber Regiment

Galya Dzhunkovskaya, navigator in 587 (125 Guards) Heavy Bomber Regiment

Polina Gelman, pilot in 588 (46 Guards) Night Bomber Regiment

Olga Golubeva, navigator in 588 (46 Guards) Night Bomber Regiment

Ivan Golyshev, commander of 296 (73 Guards) Fighter Regiment after the death of Baranov

Alexander Gridnev, commander of 586 Fighter Regiment, replaced Kazarinova

Lyuba Gubina, pilot in 587 (125 Guards) Heavy Bomber Regiment

Nina Ivakina, Komsomol administrator for Air Group 122

Militsa Kazarinova, chief of staff in 587 (125 Guards) Heavy Bomber Regiment

Tamara Kazarinova, first commander of 586 Fighter Regiment

Lera Khomyakova, pilot in 586 Fighter Regiment

Timofey Khryukin, commander of 8 Air Army

Maksim Khvostikov, commander of 437 Fighter Regiment

Ivan Kleshchev, commander of 434 Fighter Regiment

Major Krainov, political adviser in 296 (73 Guards) Fighter Regiment

Valya Krasnoshchyokova, armourer in 586, 296 (73 Guards) Fighter Regiments

Masha Kuznetsova, pilot in 586 Fighter Regiment

Vladimir Lavrinenkov, pilot in 4, 9 Guards Fighter Regiments

Tonya Lebedeva, pilot in 65 Guards Fighter Regiment

Lilya Litvyak, pilot in 586, 437, 296 (73 Guards) Fighter Regiments

Natasha Meklin, navigator, subsequently pilot, in 588 (46 Guards) Night Bomber Regiment

Kolya Menkov, mechanic in 296 (73 Guards) Fighter Regiment

Klavdia (Klava) Nechaeva, pilot in 586, 434 Fighter Regiments

Sonya Ozerkova, chief mechanic in 588 (46 Guards) Night Bomber Regiment

Dmitry Panov, commissar of 85 Fighter Regiment

Faina Pleshivtseva, mechanic in 296 (73 Guards) Fighter Regiment

Yevgenia (Zhenya) Prokhorova, pilot in 586 Fighter Regiment

Georgiy Prokofiev, political adviser in 65 Guards Fighter Regiment

Yevdokia Rachkevich, senior commissar in 122 Air Group

Irina Rakobolskaya, chief of staff in 588 (46 Guards) Night Bomber Regiment

Zhenya Rudneva, navigator in 588 (46 Guards) Night Bomber Regiment

Alexey Salomatin, pilot in 296 (73 Guards) Fighter Regiment

Nina Shebalina, mechanic in 586 Fighter Regiment

Lev Shestakov, commander of 9 Guards Fighter Regiment

Boris Sidnev, commander of 268 Fighter Aviation Division (6 Guards Air Division)

Anya Skorobogatova, radio operator in 8 Air Army

Vasiliy Stalin, Head of the Inspection of the Soviet Air Force

Dmitry Svistunenko, pilot in 296 (73 Guards) Fighter Regiment

Yevgenia (Zhenya) Timofeyeva, pilot in 587 (125 Guards) Heavy Bomber Regiment

Anna Yegorova, pilot in 805 Assault Aviation Regiment

Boris Yeremin, pilot in 296 (73 Guards) Fighter Regiment

Alexander Yevdokimov, pilot in 296 (73 Guards) Fighter Regiment

Notes

1. "Girls – pilot a plane!"

1 Lubianka v dni bitvy za Moskvu. Po rassekrechennym dokumentam FSB RF (Moscow, 2002), p. 10.
2 Marina Raskova, Zapiski shturmana (Moscow-Leningrad, 1941), pp. 145–63.
3 Raskova, pp. 161–2.
4 Ibid., pp. 168–9.
5 Oleg A. Shushakov, I na vrazh'ei zemle (Moscow: Veche, 2012) p. 2.
6 Gennadii Tokarev, Vesti dnevnik na fronte zapreshchalos (Diaries Were Banned at the Front) (Novosibirsk, 2005)
7 Raskova, pp. 70–71.
8 V. Kar'kov, "Oborvannyi polet", Serovskii rabochii, 14 May 2004, p. 2.
9 Kar'kov, p. 2.

2. "How can you photograph such misery?"

10 Mariia Dolina, Docheri neba. Dnevnye ved'my na pikirovshchikakh (Kiev, 2010), p. 32.
11 Konstantin Simonov, Raznye dni voiny. 1942–1945 (Moscow, 2005), pp. 225–6.
12 Dolina, p. 19.
13 Ibid., p. 41.

3. "When you get to the front you can wrap your feet in newspaper"

14 Valentina Nikolaevna Krasnoshchekova, author's interviews, Kaluga, 2009–12.
15 Rumours circulated among people sheltering in the stations that there were secret branches of the Metro which led to special, luxuriously appointed bomb shelters with lavish supplies of food for members of the Government. These improbable rumours later proved to be true.

Leonid Repin, "Molchalivaia drama v zloveshchei tishine Moskvy v 1942 godu", Komsomol'skaia Pravda, 15 October 2011, www.mosmetro.ru
16 I. Rakobol'skaia and N. Kravtsova, Nas nazyvali nochnymi ved'mami (Moscow, 2005), p. 12.
17 Krasnoshchekova interviews.
18 Rakobol'skaia and Kravtsova, p. 159.
19 Irina Krauze, "Dnevnik Iriny Krauze iz arkhiva obshchestva Memorial", Izvestiia, 16 October 2009.
20 Ibid.
21 L. K. Brontman, Voennyi dnevnik korrespondenta "Pravdy" (Moscow, 2007), p. 140.
22 Repin, "Molchalivaia drama". In October 1941, Muscovites were hurriedly burning their Party membership cards. Leonid Repin, "Kak chut'ne sdali Moskvu". Komsomol'skaia Pravda, 13 October 2011
23 Lubianka v dni bitvy za Moskvu, pp. 31–2.
24 Ibid., pp. 42–4.
25 Ibid.

4. "So, they are taking even young girls?"

26 Krasnoshchekova interviews.
27 Evgeniia M. Rudneva, Poka stuchit serdtse. Dnevniki i pis'ma Geroia Sovetskogo Soiuza Evgenii Rudnevoi (Moscow, 1995), pp. 157, 11.
28 Valentina Petrochenkova-Neminushchaia, author's interview, Chkalovskaia, September 2009.
29 V nebe frontovom (Sbornik vospominanii sovetskikh letchits – uchastnits Velikoi Otechestvennoi voiny) (Moscow, 2008), p. 18.

30 Valya Aban'kina, in E.K. Polunina, comp., *Devchonki, podruzhki, letchitsy* (Moscow, 2004), p. 93.
31 Sasha Makunina, in ibid., p. 93.
32 Newsreel footage of the Tushino Air Show, YouTube, no longer accessible.
33 *V nebe frontovom*, p. 15.
34 ibid.
35 Anna Timofeeva-Egorova, *Nebo. Shturmovik. Devushka* (Moscow: Yauza, Eksmo, 2007), p. 99.

5. "Why are you leaving us, children?"
36 Order No. 813 of the State Defence Committee, on a state of siege. Rossiiskii Tsentr khraneniia i izucheniia dokumentov noveishei istorii (RTsKhIDNI), fond 644, op. 1, d. 12, ll. 167–8.
37 Fedor von Bock, *Ia stoial u vorot Moskvy* (Moscow, 2009), p. 204.
38 Konstantin Bykov, *Kievskii kotel*, (Moscow: Yauza, Eksmo, 2008), p. 457.
39 Field Marshal Erich von Manstein, *Uteriannye pobedy* (Lost Victories) (Moscow: Astrel, 2012), p. 187.
40 Timofeeva-Egorova, *Nebo. Shturmovik. Devushka*, p. 31.
41 Vladimir Grigorian, "'Dva neba konstruktora Polikarpova', 'Ia s gordost'iu nesu po zhizni svoi krest', Beseda s issledovatelem zhizni i tvorchestva N.N. Polikarpova V.P. Ivanovym", *Vera. Khristianskaia gazeta Severa Rossii*, http://www.rusvera.mrezha.ru/645/5.htm
42 Vladimir Beshanov, *Letaiushchie groby Stalina* (Moscow, 2011), p. 32.
43 Valerii Tsagaraev, "Odin vek Andreia Tsagaraeva", http://www.anaharsis.ru/kultur/tsagar/tsag_5.htm Accessed 19 February 2014. "Cola" chocolate was issued to U-2 pilots, particularly if they were flying night missions, to keep them alert.
44 Anna Makarovna Skorobogatova, author's interview, St Petersburg, June 2011.
45 Dmitrii Shevarov, "O Vladimire Pivovarove", *Druzhba narodov*, No. 5, 2010, Internet version.
46 Anya Makarovna Skorobogatova, interviewed by Oleg Korytov, www.iremember.ru

6. "She's just a young girl, hasn't seen people die"
47 *V nebe frontovom*, p. 18.
48 Krasnoshchekova, author's interview, September 2011.
49 Krasnoshchekova interviews.
50 Mariia Koz'mina, "Stanovilos' golodno", author's interview, Krasnyi Luch, January 2011.
51 Nina Ivakina, "Dnevnik komsorga", *Devchonki, podruzhki, letchitsy*, supplement, p. 4.
52 Aleksandra Arkhipovna Vinogradova, author's interview, Yaroslavl, June 2011.
53 Rakobol'skaia and Kravtsova, *Nas nazyvali nochnymi ved'mami*, pp. 160–1.
54 Vinogradova interview.
55 Krasnoshchekova interview, September 2011.
56 Ivakina, "Dnevnik", p. 4.
57 Ibid., p. 2.
58 Letters of Lera Khomiakova, in *Devchonki, podruzhki, letchitsy*, pp. 24–33.
59 Elena Ivanovna Lukina, author's interview, Saratov, September 2009.
60 Ol'ga Timofeevna Golubeva-Teres, author's interview, Saratov, 2010.
61 Ol'ga Golubeva-Teres, *Nochnye reidy sovetskikh letchits. Iz letnoi knizhki shturmana U-2. 1941–1945*, Internet version.

62 E. S. Seniavskaia, *Psikhologiia voiny v XX veke: istoricheskii opyt Rossii* (Moscow: RossPEN, 1999), Internet version.

7. "No talking in the ranks!"
63 Ol'ga T. Golubeva-Teres, *Bogini frontovogo neba* (Saratov, 2008), p. 46.
64 Ibid., p. 73.
65 Nina Ivakina, "Dnevnik".
66 Golubeva-Teres, *Bogini frontovogo neba*, p. 77.
67 Irina Viacheslavovna Rakobol'skaia, author's interview, Moscow, 2011.

8. "Stop flirting, there's a war on!"
68 *Devchonki, podruzhki, letchitsy*, p. 11.
69 Ibid.
70 Stepan Anastasovich Mikoyan, author's interview, 14 July 2009.
71 Aleksandr Iakovlev, *Tsel' zhizni* (Moscow: Respublika, 2000).
72 Dolina, *Docheri neba*, p. 51.
73 Nina Ivakina, "Dnevnik", p. 7.
74 Krasnoshchekova interviews.
75 Nina Ivakina, "Dnevnik", p. 2.
76 Ibid., p. 7.
77 Golubeva-Teres, author's interview, p. 46.
78 Ibid.
79 Ivakina, "Dnevnik", p. 8.
80 Iosif Vissarionovich Stalin, *O Velikoi otechestvennoi voine Sovetskogo Soiuza (1941–1945)* (Moscow, 1947), Internet version.
81 *V nebe frontovom*, p. 333.
82 Inna Kalacheva, ex-servicewoman of 586 Fighter Regiment, author's interview, Moscow, 2010.
83 "The evacuation of Kerch by Soviet soldiers has been undertaken on orders from Central Command on strategic grounds, to enable our troops to consolidate their positions on territory better suited to

defence." Informbiubro communiqué quoted from www.great-victory.ru
84 Skorobogatova, author's interview.
85 Skorobogatova, author's interview.
86 A. V. Isaev, *Kotly 41-go. Istoriia VOV, kotoruiu my ne znali* (Moscow: Yauza, Eksmo, 2005), Internet version.
87 Skorobogatova, author's interview.
88 Rudneva, *Poka stuchit serdtse*, p. 94.
89 Dakutovich, Galina, *Sertsa i kryly. Dzennik shturmana zhanochaya aviyatsyinaga palka* (The Heart and the Wings: Diary of a Navigator of a Women's Aviation Regiment) (Minsk, 1957) [Fragments used in this book are translated from the Belorussian by Veronika Gorbyleva and Olga Vashkova].
90 Evdokiia Borisovna Pas'ko, author's interview, Moscow, winter 2010.
91 Ivakina, "Dnevnik", p. 8.
92 Ibid., p. 5.
93 Ibid., p. 21.
94 Valentina Krasnoshchekova learned of this only when she read Nina Ivakina's diary in 2011.
95 Ivakina, "Dnevnik", p. 8.
96 Liudmila Ovchinnikova, "Stalingrad, devushki, samolety", in *Stoletie. Informatsionno-analiticheskoe izdanie Fonda istoricheskoi perspektivy*, 16 October 2012.
97 Ivakina, "Dnevnik", p. 9.
98 Golubeva-Teres, interview.

9. "An aircraft you could use to fight"
99 Ivakina, "Dnevnik", p. 10.
100 Boris Nikolaevich Eremin, interview with Artem Drabkin, www.Iremember.ru
101 Eremin, interview with Drabkin.
102 *V nebe frontovom*, p. 333.
103 *Devchonki, podruzhki, letchitsy*, p. 24.
104 Raisa Aronova, *Nochnye ved'my*

(Moscow: Sovetskaia Rossiia, 1980), Internet version.

105 Dakutovich, *Sertsa i kryly*, p. 14.
106 Dolina, *Docheri neba*, p. 50.
107 Galina Markova, *Vzlet. (O Geroe Sovetskogo Soiuza M.M. Raskovoi)* (Moscow, 1986), Internet version.
108 Dolina, *Docheri neba*, p. 53.

10. "You ask how we drop bombs?"

109 Ivakina, "Dnevnik", p. 12.
110 Daniil Fibikh (Luchaninov), *Dvuzhil'naia Rossiia. Dnevniki i vospominaniia* (Moscow, 2010).
111 Ol'ga Golubeva-Teres, *Ptitsy v sinei vyshine* (Saratov, 2000), Internet version.
112 Golubeva-Teres, *Bogini frontovogo neba*, p. 29.
113 Ibid., p. 42.
114 Ivakina, "Dnevnik", p. 16.
115 Ibid., p. 17.
116 Aronova, *Nochnye ved'my*, p. 42.
117 "Tekhnicheskoe opisanie samoleta Po-2VS", www.airwar.ru
118 Rudneva, *Poka stuchit serdtse*, p. 236.
119 Rakobol'skaia, author's interview.
120 Rudneva, *Poka stuchit serdtse*, p. 98.
121 Ibid., p. 92.
122 Ibid., p. 157.

11. "It's simply wonderful! Imagine the speed!"

123 Ivakina, "Dnevnik", p. 14.
124 A. Gridnev, Unpublished memoirs, furnished by Reina Pennington.
125 Letters in the collection of Muzei Voennoi Slavy pri Gimnazii No. 1, Krasnyi Luch.
126 Litvyak, Letters.
127 Ekaterina Fedorovna Terekhova, author's interview, Krasnodar, September 2010.
128 Comment by Lilya's brother, Yury, author's interview with Valentina Ivanovna Vashchenko, director of Muzei voennoi slavy pri Gimnazii

No. 1, Krasnyi Luch, 8–9 January 2012.

129 Rakobol'skaia, author's interview.
130 Galya Dakutovich, *Sertsa i kryly*, p. 20.
131 *V nebe frontovom*, p. 334.
132 Liudmila Agafeeva, author's interview, Moscow, July 2012.

12. "A whole lifetime older"

133 Litvyak, Letters.
134 Rakobol'skaia and Kravtsova, *Nas nazyvali nochnymi ved'mami*, p. 24.
135 Aronova, *Nochnye ved'my*, p. 43.
136 Ivakina, "Dnevnik", p. 16.
137 Ibid., p. 16.
138 Pas'ko, author's interview. Moscow, winter 2010.
139 Ivakina, "Dnevnik", p. 13.

13. "See that? Your planes have proved themselves"

140 Ivakina, "Dnevnik", p. 21.
141 Ibid., p. 20.
142 Ibid., p. 21.
143 A. S. Abramov, *Muzhestvo v nasledstvo*, Sverdlovsk, 1988, p. 24.
144 Andrei Smirnov, *Boevaia rabota sovetskoi i nemetskoi aviatsii v Velikoi Otechestvennoi voine*, Moscow, 2006, p. 83.
145 Simonov, *Raznye dni voiny*, pp. 56–60.
146 Iakovlev, *Tsel' zhizni*, p. 260.
147 *Pravda*, 7 November 1942.
148 Eremin, interview with Drabkin.
149 Iakovlev, *Tsel' zhizni*, Internet version, p. 260.
150 Vasilii Semenovich Grossman, *Gody voiny* (Moscow: Pravda, 1989), Internet version.

14. "Nails should be made out of people like these"

151 Ivakina, "Dnevnik", p. 21.
152 Ibid., p. 23.
153 *Devchonki, podruzhki, letchitsy*, p. 26.

154 Ivakina, "Dnevnik".

155 Dolina, *Docheri neba*, p. 72.

156 Rakobol'skaia and Kravtsova, *Nas nazyvali nochnymi ved'mami*, Internet version.

157 The honorific "guards" title was awarded to military units who had displayed mass heroism, courage or outstanding military skills. Guards regiments had special banners and soldiers and officers wore a distinctive badge. Soldiers were paid double, and officers too were given a salary one and a half times above the standard rate.

158 Rakobol'skaia and Kravtsova, *Nas nazyvali nochnymi ved'mami*, Internet version.

159 Ibid., p. 26.

160 Galya Dakutovich, *Sertsa i kryly. Dzennik shturmana zhanochago aviiatsyinaga palka* (Minsk, 1957), p. 24.

15. Poetry and prose

161 Nikolai I. Bukharin, "Zlye zametki", *Pravda*, 12 January 1927.

162 Golubeva-Teres, author's interview.

16. "But we'll beat them, we just have to not go soft"

163 Dakutovich, *Sertsa i kryly*, p. 32.

164 *Rostov ofitsial'nyi*, No. 17 (908), 25 April 2012.

165 Rudneva, *Poka stuchit serdtse*, p. 105.

166 Dakutovich, *Sertsa i kryly*, p. 31.

167 Rakobol'skaia and Kravtsova, *Nas nazyvali nochnymi ved'mami*, p. 172.

168 Golubeva-Teres, *Bogini frontovogo neba*, p. 109.

169 Ibid., p. 117.

170 Rakobol'skaia and Kravtsova, *Nas nazyvali nochnymi ved'mami*, p. 179.

171 Ibid., 181.

17. "What a misfortune, what a useless death"

172 When she completed a highly successful transfer flight to Syzran and Seidmamedova, the regimental navigator, congratulated her, Smirnova burst out, "You mean you really do trust me?" and kissed her. *Devchonki, podruzhki, letchitsy*, p. 150.

173 Ibid.

174 Ibid.

175 Seniavskaia, *Psikhologiia voiny v XX veke*, p. 131.

176 *Devchonki, podruzhki, letchitsy*, p. 150.

177 Ibid.

178 Ibid.

179 Sergo L. Beriia, *Moi otets – Lavrentii Beriia*, (Sovremennik, 1994), pp. 195, 225.

180 Ibid., pp. 195, 225.

18. "Not one step back"

181 K.A. Vershinin, *Chetvertaia vozdushnaia*, (Moscow, 1975), Internet version.

182 Informbiuro, Communiqué, www.great-victory.ru

183 ru.wikipedia.org

184 Rakobol'skaia and Kravtsova, *Nas nazyvali nochnymi ved'mami*, pp. 172–3.

185 Ibid., p. 174.

186 Dakutovich, *Sertsa i kryly*, p. 33.

187 Timofeeva-Egorova, *Nebo. Shturmovik. Devushka*, p. 99.

188 Skorobogatova, author interview.

189 Smirnov, *Boevaia rabota sovetskoi i nemetskoi aviatsii v Velikoi Otchestvennoi voine*, p. 83.

190 Timofeeva-Egorova, *Nebo. Shturmovik. Devushka*, p. 138.

191 Ibid. pp. 139–40.

192 Ibid.

193 "Zashchitnitsam neba", website "Pamiatniki Dona", 4 October 2010, http://www.voopiik-don.ru/

19. "We can do anything, we never surrender"

194 Dakutovich, *Sertsa i kryly*.
195 Rakobol'skaia and Kravtsova, *Nas nazyvali nochnymi ved'mami*, p. 53.
196 Dakutovich, *Sertsa i kryly*, p. 34.
197 Ibid.

20. "Falling like vultures"

198 Leonid Fialkovskii, *Stalingradskii apokalipsis. Tankovaia brigada v adu* (Moscow: Yauza, Eksmo, 2011), p. 26.
199 Boris Eremin, *Vozdushnye boitsy* (Moscow: Voenizdat, 1987), p. 109.
200 Ibid., p. 110.
201 Ibid., p. 111.
202 Ibid., p. 113.
203 Iurii Panchenko, *163 dnia na ulitsakh Stalingrada* (Volgograd, 2006), p. 24.
204 Natal'ia Sholokh, Interview, www.pomnivoinu.ru, 13 March 2012.
205 Natal'ia Yur'ina, "Stalingrad, letom i osen'iu 1942-go", *Pomni voiny: vospominaniia frontovikov Zaural'ia* (Kurgan Parus-M., 2011), Internet version.
206 Eremin, *Vozdushnye boitsy*, p. 113.
207 Ibid., p. 114.
208 Ibid., pp. 120–21.
209 Ibid.

21. "Blazing away in all directions"

210 B. Gubin and V. Kiselev, *Vos'maia vozdushnaia. Voenno-istoricheskii ocherk boevogo puti 8–i vozdushnoi armii v gody Velikoi Otechestvennoi voiny* (Moscow, 1980), pp. 59–60.
211 *V nebe frontovom*, p. 333.
212 Ibid.
213 Ibid.
214 Krasnoshchekova interview, September 2011; V.A. Agranovskii, *Belaia liliia* (Moscow: Sovetskaia Rossiia, 1979).
215 Gubin and Kiselev, *Vos'maia vozdushnaia*, p. 60.
216 Reina Pennington, *Wings, Women and War* (University Press of Kansas, 2001), p. 109.
217 A. Gridnev, Unpublished memoirs.
218 *Asy protiv asov* (Moscow: Veche, 2007), pp. 263–4.
219 Krasnoshchekova, author's interview, September 2011; author's telephone interview with Nina Nikolaevna Shebalina, February 2009.
220 Shebalina, author's interview.
221 *Devchonki, podruzhki, letchitsy*, p. 105.
222 Ibid., p. 104.
223 Krasnoshchekova interview; Shebalina interview.
224 *Devchonki, podruzhki, letchitsy*, p. 103.
225 Vasilii Grossman, *Za pravoe delo*.
226 Shebalina interview.
227 Tsentral'nyi Arkhiv Ministerstva oborony Rossiiskoi Federatsii (TsAMO), fond 113IAP, op. 383416, d. 1, ll. 48 ob–53.
228 Irina Viktorovna Khvostikova, "Maksim Khvostikov", www.allaces.ru
229 *Devchonki, podruzhki, letchitsy*, p. 105.
230 Stepan Anastasovich Mikoian, *My – deti voiny* (Moscow, 2006), p. 101.
231 Ibid., p. 102.
232 M. Aleksashin, *Poslednii boi Vasiliia Stalina* (Moscow, 2007), Internet version.
233 *Devchonki, podruzhki, letchitsy*, pp. 104–11.
234 Stepan Mikoian, author's interview.
235 A. F. Semenov, *Na vzlete* (Moscow: Voenizdat, 1969), Internet version.
236 Stepan Mikoian, author's interview.
237 Smirnov, *Boevaia rabota sovetskoi i nemetskoi aviatsii*.
238 *Devchonki, podruzhki, letchitsy*, pp. 104–11.

239 Mikoian, My – deti voiny, p. 103.
240 Semenov, Na vzlete, Internet version.
241 Klava Blinova, in Devchonki, podruzhki, letchitsy. pp. 204–11.
242 Stepan Mikoyan interview, 14 July 2009.
243 A.Ia. Baklan, Nebo, proshitoe trassami (Leningrad, 1987), p. 72.
244 S. A. Mikoian, My – deti voiny, p. 103.
245 Ibid., p. 106.
246 Klava Blinova, in Devchonki, podruzhki, letchitsy, pp. 104–11.
247 A. V. Glichev, Korotkie rasskazy o voine (Moscow: OOO "Premium Engineering", 2009).
248 Valerii Petrovich Ponomarev, Iz vospominanii aviatekhnika 451–go shturmovogo aviapolka, www. airforce.ru (Not on open access.)
249 TsAMO, fond 32GvIAP, op. 213332, d. 1, ll. 5–7.
250 Mikoian, My - deti voiny, p. 109.
251 Klava Blinova, in Devchonki, podruzhki, letchitsy, pp. 104–11.

22. "You darling, you've shot down a Heinkel!"

252 Katya Polunina in Devchonki, podruzhki, letchitsy, pp. 26–7.
253 Devchonki, podruzhki, letchitsy, p. 28.
254 Ibid., p. 29.
255 Ibid., p. 30.
256 Ibid., p. 31.
257 Ibid.
258 Ibid., p. 32.
259 Document No. 085, 144 Air Defence Fighter Division, 9 October 1942. Quoted in Devchonki, podruzhki, letchitsy, p. 31.
260 Devchonki, podruzhki, letchitsy, p. 22.
261 Gridnev, Unpublished memoirs.

23. "Here goes!"

262 Gubin and Kiselev, Vos'maia vozdushnaia, Internet version.

263 Ibid.
264 Nikolai Men'kov, author's interview, Cherepovets, September 2009.
265 Skorobogatova, author's interview.
266 Skorobogatova, author's interview.
267 Men'kov, author's interview.
268 Shebalina, author's interview.
269 Pennington, Wings, Women and War, p. 136; Vashchenko, author's interview.
270 Shebalina, author's interview.

24. "My sweet, winged Yak is a good machine"

271 Katiusha. K 90-letiiu so dnia rozhdeniia Ekateriny Budanovoi (Viaz'ma: Tsentr razvitiia obrazovaniia, (no date)), p. 7.
272 D. P. Panov, Russkie na snegu. Sud'ba cheloveka na fone istoricheskoi meteli (L'vov: Spolom, 2003), Internet version.
273 Eremin, Vozdushnye boitsy, pp. 139–40.
274 Vladimir Lavrinenkov, Vozvrashchenie v nebo (Moscow: Voenizdat, 1983), p. 41.
275 Ibid., pp. 42–3.
276 (Sultan Amet-Khan) Profile, in www.airaces.narod.ru
277 Eremin, interview with Drabkin.
278 Lavrinenkov, Vozvrashchenie v nebo, p. 45; Men'kov, author's interview.
279 Ibid., pp. 57–8.
280 Krasnoshchekova, author's interview.
281 Krasnoshchekova, author's interview.
282 Lavrinenkov, Vozvrashchenie v nebo, p. 61.
283 Krasnoshchekova, author's interview.
284 Panov, Russkie na snegu, Internet version.
285 I. Driagina, Zapiski letchitsy U-2 (Moscow, 2007), p. 44.

286 Unfortunately, Faina Pleshivtseva's memoirs are often inaccurate. Caution needs to be exercised in respect of dates and even facts.

287 Ovchinnikova, "Stalingrad, devushki, samolety".

288 *Katiusha*, p. 47.

25. Caucasus

289 Timofeeva-Egorova, *Nebo. Shturmovik. Devushka*, p. 145.

290 Rakobol'skaia and Kravtsova, *Nas nazyvali nochnymi ved'mami*, pp. 185–6.

291 Ibid., p. 46.

292 Ibid., p. 196.

293 Ibid., p. 46.

294 Vita Sevriukova, "Pro ispodnee: sovetskii uniseks", *Nezavisimaia gazeta*, 1 March 2008.

295 Krasnoshchekova, author's interview.

296 Rakobol'skaia and Kravtsova, *Nas nazyvali nochnymi ved'mami*, p. 41.

297 Ibid., p. 48.

26. "Are they young women, or scarecrows from the vegetable patch?"

298 Krasnoshchekova, author's interview.

299 Lavrinenkov, *Vozvrashchenie v nebo*, p. 42.

300 Shebalina, author's interview.

301 Krasnoshchekova, author's interview.

302 Krasnoshchekova, author's interview.

303 Krasnoshchekova, author's interview; Shebalina, author's interview.

304 Krasnoshchekova, author's interview.

305 Aleksandr Kochukov, "Beriia, vstat'! Vy arestovany!", *Krasnaia zvezda*, 28 June 2003.

306 Nikolai Iakovlev, *Marshal Zhukov (stranitsy zhizni)* (Moscow, 1988), Internet version.

307 Antony Beevor, *Stalingrad* (London: Penguin, 1999), p. 135.

308 Eremin, *Vozdushnye boitsy*, pp. 123–4.

309 www.pomnivoinu.ru

310 "Geroi Stalingrada", *Stalinskii sokol*, 7 November 1942.

311 Panov, *Russkie na snegu*, Internet version.

312 "Geroi Stalingrada".

27. "We did not need to look for the target"

313 Eremin, *Vozdushnye boitsy*, pp. 141–2.

314 Fialkovskii, *Stalingradskii apokalipsis*, p. 260.

315 G. F. Korniukhin, *Sovetskie istrebiteli v Velikoi Otechestvennoi voine*, Internet version.

316 Joachim Wieder, *Katastrofa na Volge. Vospominaniia ofitsera-razvedchika 6–i armii Pauliusa*, Internet version.

317 Panov, *Russkie na snegu*, Internet version.

318 Ibid.

319 *Devchonki, podruzhki, letchitsy*, pp. 116–17.

320 Ovchinnikova, "Stalingrad, devushki, samolety".

321 Krasnoshchekova, author's interview, January 2011.

322 Driagina, *Zapiski letchitsy U-2*, p. 44.

323 S. V. Ivanov, comp., *Razvitie istrebitelei Iakovleva* (Moscow, 1999), Internet version.

324 Lavrinenkov, *Vozvrashchenie v nebo*, Internet version.

325 *Devchonki, podruzhki, letchitsy*, p. 116–17.

326 Shebalina, author's interview; Krasnoshchekova, author's interview.

327 Gridnev, Unpublished memoirs.
328 *Devchonki, podruzhki, letchitsy*,
     p. 107.

28. "People are saying Boris Yeremin is scared of us"

329 Krasnoshchekova, author's
     interview; Shebalina, author's
     interview.
330 Krasnoshchekova, author's
     interview. February 2011.
331 Krasnoshchekova, author's
     interview, February 2011.
332 Lavrinenkov, *Vozvrashchenie v nebo*,
     p. 52.
333 Ibid.
334 Ibid., p. 54.
335 Ibid.
336 Krasnoshchekova interview,
     February 2011.
337 Krasnoshchekova, author's
     interview.
338 Lavrinenkov, *Vozvrashchenie v nebo*,
     p. 61.
339 Ibid., p. 62.
340 Panov, *Russkie na snegu*, Internet
     version.
341 Lavrinenkov, *Vozvrashchenie v nebo*,
     pp. 58–9.
342 Ibid., pp. 59–60.
343 Ibid., p. 57.
344 Krasnoshchekova, author's
     interview, 2012.
345 Lavrinenkov, *Vozvrashchenie v nebo*,
     p. 63.
346 Eremin, interview with Drabkin.
347 Krasnoshchekova, author's
     interview, 2012.
348 Panov, *Russkie na snegu*, Internet
     version.
349 Men'kov and Krasnoshchekova,
     author's interviews.
350 Krasnoshchekova, author's
     interview, 2011
351 Skorobogatova, author's interview.
352 Skorobogatova, author's interview.
353 Eremin, interview with Drabkin.
354 Eremin, interview with Drabkin.
355 Krasnoshchekova, author's
     interview, 2011.
356 Rakobol'skaia and Kravtsova, *Nas
     nazyvali nochnymi ved'mami*, p. 200.
357 Rakobol'skaia and Kravtsova, *Nas
     nazyvali nochnymi ved'mami*,
     Internet version.

29. "If they get killed, you answer for it to me"

358 A. V. Kozlov, "1943 – samyi
     schastlivyi Novyi god", *Materialy
     konferentsii "Marshal Vasilevskii i ego
     vklad v pobedu"* (no date or place).
359 Lavrinenkov, *Vozvrashchenie v nebo*,
     p. 64.
360 Panov, *Russkie na snegu*, Internet
     version.
361 Lavrinenkov, *Vozvrashchenie v nebo*,
     p. 64.
362 Ibid.
363 Krasnoshchekova, author's
     interview.
364 Men'kov, author's interview, April
     2010.
365 Ol'ga Vladimirovna Pasportnikova,
     author's interview, Zhukovskii,
     winter 2009.
366 Dakutovich, *Sertsa i kryly*, p. 52.
367 Ibid., pp. 53–4.
368 Ibid., p. 62.

30. "Marina Raskova, Hero of the Soviet Union, great Russian aviatrix, has concluded her glorious career"

369 Simonov, *Raznye dni voiny*,
     pp. 156–7.
370 Dolina, *Docheri neba*, p. 75.
371 Ibid., p. 76.
372 Ibid.
373 The version of events according to
     Maria Dolina – Ibid. p. 77.
374 I.S. Levin, *Groznye gody* (Saratov,
     1984), pp. 110–11.
375 Dolina, *Docheri neba*, p. 78.

376 Rudneva, *Poka stuchit serdtse*, p. 145.
377 Dakutovich, *Sertsa i kryly*, p. 51.
378 Collection of the Diorama Museum of the Battle of Kursk, Belgorod Direction.
379 *V nebe frontovom*, p. 26.
380 Ibid.
381 Dolina, *Docheri neba*, p. 90.
382 *V nebe frontovom*, p. 27. The commander of a flight of 587 Heavy Bomber Regiment, Lena Timofeeva was killed in action at Smolensk in summer 1943.
383 Dolina, *Docheri neba*, p. 91.
384 Ibid.
385 Ibid., p. 93.
386 Ibid., p. 109.
387 *V nebe frontovom*, Internet version.
388 Dolina, *Docheri neba*, p. 110.

31. "Why would you want to expose yourself to deadly danger?"

389 Timofeeva-Egorova, *Nebo. Shturmovik. Devushka*, p. 152.
390 *Katiusha*.
391 *Vospominaniia o Nikolae Baranove, Shakhterskii gorodskoi internet-portal. Shahtersk.com*
392 Ibid.
393 Men'kov, author's interview.
394 Panov, *Russkie na snegu*, Internet version.
395 Ibid.
396 Men'kov, author's interview, April 2010.

32. "Street women and all kinds of madcaps"

397 Rudneva, *Poka stuchit serdtse*, p. 144.
398 Ibid.
399 Dakutovich, *Sertsa i kryly*, p. 63.
400 Rakobol'skaia and Kravtsova, *Nas nazyvali nochnymi ved'mami*, pp. 204–5.
401 Dakutovich, *Sertsa i kryly*, p. 65.
402 Ibid., p. 68.

403 TsAMO, fond 73GvIAP, op. 273351, d. 2, l. 31.
404 Krasnoshchekova and Men'kov, author's interviews.
405 TsAMO, fond 73GvIAP, op. 273351, d. 2,
406 TsAMO, fond 73GvIAP, op. 273351, d. 2, l. 32.
407 Krasnoshchekova, author's interview, March 2011.
408 Krasnoshchekova, author's interview.
409 Rudneva, *Poka stuchit serdtse*, p. 144.
410 Dakutovich, *Sertsa i kryly*, p. 73.
411 Ibid., pp. 48–9.

33. "Despite the pain continued to fight the enemy"

412 Krasnoshchekova, author's interview, winter 2009.
413 Men'kov, author's interview, September 2009.
414 TsAMO, fond 73GvIAP, op. 273351, d. 2, l. 34.
415 Men'kov, author's interview, August 2011.
416 TsAMO, fond 73GvIAP, op. 273351, d. 2, l. 67 ob.
417 Men'kov, author's interview, August 2011.
418 V. Agranovskii, *Belaia liliia* (Moscow, 1979), p. 40.
419 Ibid., p. 41.
420 Ibid.
421 Vashchenko, author's interview.
422 Litvyak, Letters.
423 Litvyak, Letters.
424 *Katiusha*, p. 23.
425 Krasnoshchekova, author's interview, 2011.
426 Gridnev, Unpublished memoirs.
427 Kalacheva, author's interview.
428 *Devchonki, podruzhki, letchitsy*, p. 65.

34. "The worst death"

429 *Vospominaniia o Nikolae Baranove*.

430 Men'kov, author's interview, August 2011.

431 Men'kov and Krasnoshchekova, author's interviews.

432 TsAMO, fond 73GvIAP, op. 273351, d. 2, l. 93, 93 ob.

433 Men'kov, author's interview.

434 TsAMO, fond 73GvIAP, op. 273351, d. 2, l. 88.

435 Krasnoshchekova, author's interview, March 2011.

436 Krasnoshchekova, author's interview, March 2011.

437 Driagina, Zapiski letchitsy U-2, pp. 92–5.

35. "Undue confidence, self-regard and lack of discipline"

438 Krasnoshchekova, author's interview.

439 Men'kov, author's interview.

440 Krasnoshchekova, author's interview.

441 Men'kov, author's interview.

442 TsAMO, fond 73GvIAP, op. 273351, d. 2, l. 93, 93 ob.

443 Men'kov and Krasnoshchekova, author's interviews.

444 Krasnoshchekova, author's interview.

445 Krasnoshchekova, author's interview, March 2011.

446 Men'kov and Krasnoshchekova, author's interviews.

447 Men'kov, author's interview.

448 Men'kov, author's interview, September 2009, etc. TsAMO, fond 73GvIAP, op. 273351, d. 2, l. 95.

449 Skorobogatova, author's interview.

450 TsAMO, fond 73GvIAP, op. 273351, d. 2, l. 109.

451 Men'kov, author's interview, April 2010.

452 TsAMO, fond 73GvIAP, op. 273351, d. 2, l. 109, 109 ob.

453 Men'kov, author's interview, April 2010.

36. "Move it, will you? She's going to blow up!"

454 Golubeva-Teres, Bogini frontovogo neba, pp. 119–25.

455 Dolina, Docheri neba, p. 98.

456 Ibid., p. 103.

37. "Katya's return"

457 Katiusha, p. 15.

458 Ibid, p. 9.

459 Ibid, pp. 29–32.

460 Ibid.

461 Ibid, p. 32.

462 Krasnoshchekova, author's interview, January 2012.

38. "I cried like I had never cried before"

463 TsAMO, fond 65GvIAP, op. 168041, d. 1.

464 TsAMO, fond 65GvIAP, op. 168041, d. 1, ll. 19, 19 ob.

465 Ovchinnikova, "Stalingrad, devushki, samolety".

466 V. N. Kubarev, Atakuiut gvardeitsy (Tallin, 1975).

467 V. N. Kubarev interview, www.iremember.ru

468 TsAMO, fond 65GvIAP, op. 168041, d. 1, l. 13.

469 TsAMO, fond 65GvIAP, op. 168041, d. 1, l. 13.

470 TsAMO, fond 65GvIAP, op. 168041, d. 1, l. 19 ob.

471 Devchonki, podruzhki, letchitsy, p. 133.

472 Ibid, p. 134.

473 Simonov, Raznye dni voiny, p. 137.

474 Ibid., pp. 256–7.

475 TsAMO, fond 65VvIAP, op. 168041, d. 1, l. 19 ob.

476 TsAMO, fond 65VvIAP, op. 168041, d. 1, l. 24.

477 Devchonki, podruzhki, letchitsy, pp. 104–11.

478 Klavdiia Blinova, in *Devchonki, podruzhki, letchitsy*, pp. 104–11.
479 TsAMO, fond 65GvIAP, op. 168041, d. 1, l. 24.

39. "I want to fly a mission. This is no time to rest"

480 Men'kov, author's interview, September 2011.
481 M. Zhirokhov, *Srazhenie za Donbass* (Moscow: Tsentrpoligraf, 2011), p. 161.
482 *Katiusha*, p. 28.
483 Ibid., p. 27.
484 Men'kov, author's interview, September 2011.
485 TsAMO, fond 73GvIAP, op. 273351, d. 2, l. 108, 108 ob.
486 Krasnoshchekova, author's interview, winter 2010.
487 TsAMO, fond 73GvIAP, op. 273351, d. 2, l. 109.
488 Men'kov, author's interview, September 2009.
489 TsAMO, fond 73GvIAP, op. 273351, d. 2, l. 109.
490 Men'kov, author's interview, September 2011.

40. "Every word brings back again and again the grief and pain"

491 Rakobol'skaia and Kravtsova, *Nas nazyvali nochnymi ved'mami*, p. 78.
492 Ibid., p. 79.
493 Ibid., p. 78.
494 Ibid., pp. 244–5.
495 Rudneva, *Poka stuchit serdtse*, pp. 179–80.
496 Rakobol'skaia and Kravtsova, *Nas nazyvali nochnymi ved'mami*, p. 81.
497 Dakutovich, *Sertsa i kryly*, p. 102.
498 Rudneva, *Poka stuchit serdtse*, p. 189.

41. "Wh-what kind of men are you not to be able to keep one g-girl safe?"

499 Skorobogatova, author's interview.

500 Zhirokhov, *Srazhenie za Donbass*, p. 167.
501 TsAMO, fond 73GvIAP, op. 273351, d.2, l. 114, 114 ob.
502 Men'kov, author's interview, April 2010.
503 TsAMO, fond 73GvIAP, op. 273351, d. 2, l. 110.
504 Agranovskii, *Belaia liliia*, p. 39; Skorobogatova, author's interview.
505 Agranovskii, *Belaia liliia*.
506 Men'kov, author's interview, 2009.
507 Litvyak, Letters.
508 Krasnoshchekova, author's interview.
509 Men'kov, quoted in Agranovskii, *Belaia liliia*.
510 Men'kov, author's interview, 2009.
511 Men'kov, author's interview.
512 Krasnoshchekova, author's interview.
513 Krasnoshchekova, author's interview.
514 Lavrinenkov, *Vozvrashchenie v nebo*, p. 102.
515 Ibid., pp. 103–58.
516 Eremin, interview with Drabkin.
517 Krasnoshchekova, author's interviews, including September 2012.
518 Krasnoshchekova, author's interviews, including September 2012.
519 Krasnoshchekova. author's interviews.
520 *Devchonki, podruzhki, letchitsy*, p. 146.
521 Vashchenko, author's interview.
522 Simonov, *Raznye dni voiny*, p. 36.
523 Later, at the request of editors, Simonov changed this to "Just yesterday forgotten . . ."
524 Simonov, *Raznye dni voiny*, Internet version.

Bibliography

Books

Abramov, A.S., *Muzhestvo v nasledstvo* (The Heritage of Courage) (Sverdlovsk, 1988)

Adam, Wilhelm, *Trudnoe reshenie* (Hard Decision) (Moscow, 1967)

Agranovsky, V.A., *Belaya Liliya* (The White Lily) (Moscow, 1979)

Aleksashin, M., *Poslednii boi Vasiliya Stalina* (The Last Battle of Vasily Stalin) (Moscow, 2007)

Aronova, Raisa, *Nochnye vedmy* (Night Witches) (Moscow, 1980)

Baklan, A.Ya., *Nebo, proshitoe trassami* (The Sky Pierced with Tracer) (Leningrad, 1987)

Beevor, Antony, *Stalingrad* (London, 1999)

Beria, Sergo, *Moi Otets Lavrenty Beria* (My Father Lavrenty Beria) (Moscow, 1994)

Beshanov, Vladimir, *Letayushchie groby Stalina* (Stalin's Flying Coffins) (Moscow, 2011)

Von Bock, Feder, *Ya stoyal u vorot Moskvy* (I Reached the Gates of Moscow) (Moscow, 2009)

Brontman, Lazar, *Voenny dnevnik korrespondenta "Pravdy"* (The War Diary of a Pravda Correspondent) (Moscow, 2007)

Bykov, Konstantin, *Kievsky kotel* (The Kiev Cauldron) (Moscow, 2008)

——, *Posledny triumf Vermakhta. Kharkovsky kotel* (The Last Triumph of the Wehrmacht: Kharkov Cauldron) (Moscow, 2009)

Chechneva, Marina, *Lastochki nad frontom* (Swallows Over the Frontline) (Moscow, 1984)

Dakutovich, Galina, *Sertsa i kryly. Dzennik shturmana zhanochaga aviyatsyinaga palka* (The Heart and the Wings: Diary of a Navigator of a Women's Aviation Regiment) (Minsk, 1957) [Fragments used in this book are translated from the Belorussian by Veronika Gorbyleva and Olga Vashkova]

Dolina, Mariya, *Docheri neba. Dnevnye vedmy na pikirovshchikakh* (Heaven's Daughters: The Day Witches on Dive Bombers) (Kiev, 2010)

Dryagina, Irina, *Zapiski letchitsy U-2* (Notes of a U-2 Pilot) (Moscow, 2007)

Egorov, Georgii, *Rasskazy o razvedchikakh* (Stories about Reconnaissance Men) (Barnaul, 2007)

Eremenko, A., *Stalingrad: Zapiski komanduyushchego frontom* (Stalingrad: Notes of a Front Commander) (Moscow, 1961)

Eremin, Boris, *Vozdushnye boitsy* (Air Soldiers) (Moscow, 1987)

Fialkovskii, Leonid, *Stalingradskii apokalipsis. Tankovaya brigada v adu* (The Stalingrad Apocalypse: Tank Brigade in Hell) (Moscow, 2011)

Fibikh, Daniil, *Dvuzhilnaya Rossiya. Dnevniki i vospominaniya* (The Sturdy Russia: Diaries and Memoirs) (Moscow, 2010)

Glichev, Aleksandr, *Korotkie rasskazy o voine* (Short Stories About War) (Moscow, 2009)

Golubeva-Teres, Olga, *Bogini frontovogo neba* (Goddesses of the Frontline Sky) (Saratov, 2008)

——, *Nochnye reidy sovetskikh letchits. Iz letnoi knizhki shturmana U-2. 1941–1945* (The Night Raids by Soviet Female Pilots: From a U-2 Pilot's Logbook, 1941–1945) (Moscow, 2009)

——, *Ptitsy v sinei vyshine* (Birds in the Blue Sky) (Saratov, 2000)

Granin, Daniil, *Leningradskii katalog* (Leningrad Catalogue) (Leningrad, 1986)

Grossman, Vasily, *Za pravoe delo* (For the Just Cause) (Moscow, 1954)

——————, *Gody voiny* (The Years of War) (Moscow, 1989)

Gubin, B., and Kiselev V., *Vosmaya Vozdushnaya* (The Eighth Air Army) (Moscow, 1980)

Isaev, A.V., *Kotly 41-go. Istoriya VOV, kotoruyu my ne znali* (Cauldrons of 1941: The Unknown History of the Great Patriotic War) (Moscow, 2005)

——————, *Kogda vnezapnosti uzhe ne bylo* (When the Enemy Was No Longer Taken By Surprise) (Moscow, 2007)

Ivanov, S.V. (ed.), *Razvitie istrebitelei Yakovleva* (The Development of Yakovlev's Fighter Aircraft) (Moscow, 1999)

Katyusha. K 90-letiyu so dnya rozhdeniya Ekateriny Budanovoi (Katyusha. On the 90th Anniversary of the Birth of Ekaterina Budanova) (Viazma: Tsentr razvitiia obrazovaniia)

Kornyukhin, G., *Sovetskie istrebiteli v Velikoi Otechestvennoi voine* (Soviet Fighters in the Great Patriotic War) (Smolensk, 2000)

Kubarev, Vasily, *Atakuyut gvardeitsy* (Guards Troops Attacking) (Tallinn, 1975)

Lavrinenkov, Vladimir, *Vozvrashchenie v nebo* (Back in the Sky) (Moscow, 1983)

Lebina, N., *Povsednevnaya zhizn sovetskogo goroda* (Daily Life in a Soviet City) (Moscow, 1999)

Levin, I. *Groznye gody* (Stormy Years) (Saratov, 1984)

Von Manstein, Erich, *Uteryannye pobedy* (Lost Victories) (Moscow, 2002)

Markova, Galina, *Vzlet* (Take-off) (Moscow, 1986)

Mikoyan, Stepan, *My – deti voiny* (We Are the War's Children) (Moscow, 2006)

Nekrasov, Viktor, *V Okopakh Stalingrada* (In Stalingrad's Trenches) (Moscow, 1995)

Ortenberg, David, *God 1942* (The Year 1942) (Moscow, 1988)

Panchenko, Yurii, *163 Dnya na ulitsakh Stalingrada* (163 Days in the Streets of Stalingrad) (Volgograd, 2006)

Panov, Dmitry, *Russkie na snegu. Sudba cheloveka na fone istoricheskoy meteli* (Russians In the Snow. A Person's Fate Against the Background of a Historical Storm) (Lviv, 2003)

Polunina, Ekaterina (ed.), *Devchonki, podruzhki, letchitsy* (Girls, Friends, Pilots) (Moscow, 1999)

Rakobolskaya, Irina, and Kravtsova, Natalya, *Nas nazyvali nochnymi vedmami* (They Called Us Night Witches) (Moscow, 2005)

Raskova, Marina, *Zapiski Shturmana* (Notes of a Navigator) (Moscow–Leningrad, 1941)

Rudneva, Evgeniya, *Poka stuchit serdtse. Dnevniki i pisma Geroya Sovetskogo Soyuza Evgenii Rudnevoi* (For As Long As My Heart Is Beating. Diaries and Letters of Hero of the Soviet Union Evgeniya Rudneva) (Moscow, 1995)

Semenov, A., *Na vzlete* (On the Take-off) (Moscow, 1969)

Senyavskaya, Elena, *Psikhologiya voiny v XX veke* (Psychology of War in the 20th Century) (Moscow, 1999)

Shushakov, Oleg, *I na vrazh'ei zemle my vraga rasgromim* (We Will Smash the Enemy Even on Enemy Soil) (Moscow, 2010)

——————, *I na vrazhei zemle* (On the Enemy Land) Moscow 2010

Simonov, Konstantin, *Raznye dni voiny: 1942–1945* (Different Days of War: 1942–1945) (Moscow, 2005)

Smirnov, Andrei, *Boevaya rabota sovetskoi i nemetskoi aviatsii v Velikoi Otechestvennoi voine* (Combat Performance of Soviet and German Aviation During the Great Patriotic War) (Moscow, 2006)

Smyslov, Oleg, *Asy protiv asov* (Aces Against Aces) (Moscow, 2007)

Stalin, Joseph, *O Velikoi Otechestvennoi voine Sovetskogo Soyuza (1941–1945)* (On the Great Patriotic War of the Soviet Union (1941–1945)) (Moscow, 1947)

Timofeeva-Egorova, Anna, *Nebo. Shturmovik. Devushka* (Sky. Attack Aircraft. A Girl) (Moscow, 2007)

Tokarev, Gennadii, *Vesti dnevnik na fronte zapreshchalos* (Diaries Were Banned at the Front) (Novosibirsk, 2005)

V nebe frontovom (Sbornik vospominanii sovetskikh letchits – uchastnits Velikoi Otechestvennoi voiny) (In the Skies of War. Collected Memoirs by Soviet Female Pilots Who Participated in the Great Patriotic War) (Moscow, 2008)

Vasilevsky, A.M., *Delo vsei zhizni* (My Cause) (Moscow, 2002)

Vasiliev, N.I., *Tatsinskii reid* (The Raid at Tatsinskaya) (Moscow, 1969)

Vershinin, Konstantin, *Chetvertaya vozdushnaya* (The Fourth Air Army) (Moscow, 1975)

Vinogradov, V.K., Zhadobin, V.I., Markovich, V.V., Peremyshlennikova, N.M., and Sigachev, Yu.V., *Lubyanka v dni bitvy za Moskvu* (Lubyanka During the Battle For Moscow) (Moscow, 2002)

Weltz, Helmut, *Soldaty, kotorykh predali* (The Betrayed Soldiers) (Moscow, 2011)

Wieder, Joachim, *Disaster on the Volga* (Moscow, 1965)

Yakovlev, Aleksandr, *Tsel zhizni* (The Mission in Life) (Moscow 2000)

Yakovlev, Nikolai, *Marshall Zhukov (stranitsy zhizni)* (Marshal Zhukov (Pages of Life)) (Moscow 1988)

Zamulin, Valerii, *Zasekrechennaya Kurskaya bitva* (The Classified Battle for Kursk) (Moscow, 2008)

Zhirokhov, M., *Srazhenie za Donbass* (Battle for Donbass) (Moscow, 2011)

Zhukova, Lidiya, *Vybirayu taran* (I Choose Ramming) (Moscow, 2006)

Newspaper articles and academic papers

Altukhov, P.V., "Interview" *Rossiiskaya Gazeta*, 9 May 2012

Bukharin, Nikolay, "Zlye Zametki" (Angry Notes) *Pravda*, 12 January 1927

Ehrenburg, Ilya, "We Understood That the Germans Are Not Humans" *Pravda*, 24 July 1942

Gorinov, M.M., "Zoya Kosmodemyanskaya (1922 –1941)" *Otechestvennaya Istoriya*, 2003 No. 1

Grigoryan, Vladimir, "Dva neba konstruktora Polikarpova" ("Two Heavens of Designer Polikarpov") *Vera, the Christian Newspaper*, 19 February 2014

"Heroes of Stalingrad" *Stalinsky sokol*, 7 November 1942

Karkov, V., "Oborvannyi polet" ("The Interrupted Flight") *Serovskii rabochii*, 14 May 2004

Khlystalov, Eduard, "Death in the Vagankovskoe Cemetery" *Literaturnaya Rossiya* No. 50, 14 December 2001

Kochukov, Aleksandr, "Beria, Stand Up!" *Krasnaya zvezda*, 28 June 2003

Kozlov, A.V., "1943 – samyi schastlivyi Novyi god", *Materialy konferentsii "Marshal Vasilevskii i ego vklad v pobedu"* (1943 Was the Happiest New Year. Materials from the conference "Marshal Vasilevskii and His Contribution to the Victory")

Krauze, Irina, "Diary" *Izvestiya*, 16 October 2009

Monetchikov, Sergey, "Attack at the Blue Line" *Voennoe obozrenie*, 7 December 2013

Ovchinnikova, Lyudmila, "Stalingrad, Girls, and Aircraft" *Stoletiye. Iformatsionno-analiticheskoe izdanie fonda istoricheskoi perspektivy*, 16 October 2012

Pravda, 25 January 1939

Pravda, 7 November 1942

Prokushev, Yu., "Poslednii adresat Esenina" ("Esenin's Last Correspondent") *Moskva* No. 10

Repin, Leonid, "The Silent Drama", *Komsomolskaya Pravda*, 15 October 2001

Rostov ofitsialnyi No. 17, 25 April 2012

Sevryukova, Vita, "About Underwear: Soviet Unisex", *Nezavisimaya gazeta*, 1 March 2008

Shevarov, Dmitrii, "About Vladimir Pivovarov", *Druzhba narodov* No. 5, 2010

Tsena pobedy. Rossiiskie shkolniki o voine. Sbornik rabot pobeditelei V i VI vserossiiskikh konkursov istoricheskikh issledovatelskikh rabot starsheklassnikov "Chelovek v istorii. Rossiya – XX vek" (The Price of Victory. Collection of Works by Laureates of 5th and 6th All-Russia Competitions of History Research Papers for Upper-Form Students "A Person in History. Russia, 20th Century") Moscow

Yurina, Natalya, "Stalingrad in the Summer and Autumn of 1942" *Pomni voinu: vospominaniya frontovikov Zauralya Kurgan*, 2001

Websites

www.airaces.narod.ru Profile of Sultan Amet-Khan

www.airwar.ru *Tekhnicheskoe opisanie samoleta Po2VS* (Technical Description of Po-2VS Aircraft)

www.allaces.ru Maksim Khvostikov by Irina Khvostikova

http://www.anaharsis.ru/kultur/tsagar/tsag_5.htm ValeriiTsagaraev, *Odin vek Andreya Tsagaraeva* (One Lifetime of Andrei Tsagaraev)

www.great-victory.ru Informburo Bulletins

www.iremember.ru Interviews with Boris Eremin, Artem Drabkin, Anna Makarovna Skorobogatova (Oleg Korytov), Nikolai Tsibikov,

klee-klaus.business.t-online.de/vermisst.htm Klaus Klee, "*Vermisst! Das kurze Leben des Soldaten Walter Michel*"

http://www.peoples.ru/military/colonel/ilchenko/ Interview, Fedor Ilchenko

www.pomnivoinu.ru Interview, Natalya Sholokh, 13 March 2012

www.shahtersk.com *Vospominaniia o Nikolae Baranove, Shakhterskii gorodskoi internet-portal*. (Memoirs About Nikolai Baranov on Shakhtersk Town Internet Portal)

www.voopiik-don.ru *Zashchitnitsam neba* (To the Defenders of the Sky), The Don Memorials website, 4 October 2010

Archive and Unpublished Material

Order No. 813 of the State Defence Committee, on a state of siege. Rossiiskii Tsentr khraneniia i izucheniia dokumentov noveishei istorii (RTsKhIDNI), fond 644, opis' 1, delo 12, ll. 167–8

A. Gridnev, Unpublished memoirs, kindly sent to me by Reina Pennington

Letters of L. Litvyak from the collection of Muzei Voennoi Slavi pri Gimnazii No. 1, Krasnyi Luch.

Letters from the Collection of the Diorama Museum of the Battle of Kursk, Belgorod Direction

Tsentral'nyi Arkhiv Ministerstva oborony Rossiiskoi Federatsii (TsAMO), fond 113IAP, opis' 383416, delo 1

TsAMO, fond 32GvIAP, op. 213332, d. 1

TsAMO, fond 73GvIAP, op. 273351, d. 2

TsAMO, fond 65GvIAP, op. 168041, d. 1

Author's Interviews

Agafeeva, Lyudmila, Interview July 2012, Moscow

Golubeva-Teres, Olga, Interview September 2011, Saratov

Kalacheva, Inna, Interview by telephone, winter 2009

Kozmina, Mariya, Interview January 2011, Krasny Luch

Krasnoshchekova, Valentina, Interviews 2010–2012, Kaluga

Lukina, Elena, Interview September 2011, Saratov

Menkov, Nikolai, Interviews 2009–2011, Cherepovets

Mikoyan, Stepan, Interviews 2009 and 2011, Moscow

Pasko, Evdokiya, Interview 2010, Moscow

Pasportnikova, Olga, Interview 2009, Zhukovskii

Petrochenkova (Neminushchaya) Valentina, Interview 2009, Chkalovskaya

Rakobolskaya, Irina, Interview 2011, Moscow

Shebalina, Nina, Interview by telephone 2009

Skorobogatova, Anna, Interview June 2011, St Petersburg

Terekhova, Ekaterina, Interview September 2011, Krasnodar

Vashchenko, Valentina, Interview January 2012, Krasny Luch

Picture credits

akg-images / RIA Nowosti: p1 *bottom*; p11 *top, bottom*

akg-images / ullstein bild: p16 *top left, top right*

akg-images / Universal Images Group / Sovfoto: p6 *top, bottom*

From the private archive of Artem Drabkin: p5 *bottom*; p8 *top*; p19 *bottom left*; p20 *top*

From the private archive of Olga Golubeva-Teres: p12 *top right*

From the private archive of Elena Lukina: p9 *bottom left*

From the private archive of Nikolay Khalip: p23 *top*

From the private archive of Nikolai Menkov: p23 *bottom left*

From the private archive of Stepan Mikoyan: p18 *top*

From the private archive of Evdokiya Pasko: p9 *bottom right*; p12 *bottom*

From the private archive of Anna Skorobogatova: p9 *top left*

From the private archive of Alexandra Vinogradova: p12 *top left*

From the collection of the Gomel Museum of Military Glory, Belarus: p3, *top right*; p19 *top*

From the collection of the Museum of War Glory of No. 1 Secondary School, Krasny Luch, the Ukraine: p2; p3 *top left, bottom*; p4 *top, bottom*; p5 *top*; p7 *top, bottom*; p8 *bottom*; p9 *top right*; p13 *top, bottom*; p15 *bottom*; p18 *bottom right*; p20 *bottom left, bottom right*; p21 *top, bottom*; p22 *top*; p23 *bottom right*; p24 *bottom*

From the collection of the Russian State Archive of Film and Photo Documents: p1 *top*; p10; p14 *top, bottom*; p15 *top*; p16 *bottom*; p17; p18 *bottom left*; p19 *bottom right*; p24 *top*

From the collection of the museum of the Tumanovo Secondary School, Smolensk province, Russia: p22 *bottom*

Acknowledgments

As is probably the case with any new project, I had no idea where to start with my research. Of course I did have some idea of what might interest the readers – thanks to my work as a researcher with Western historians, in the first place Antony Beevor and Max Hastings, the two people that showed me how interesting history can be, for which I am immensely grateful. Now, however, I was on my own. After discovering that most of the women pilots were already dead I felt somewhat disheartened. But, as a Russian saying goes, "The world is not without kind people". My Moscow friend, the great historian Anatoly Chernobaev, editor of the journal Istoricheskii Arkhiv, encouraged me to look for materials at the Central Archive of the Ministry of Defence of the Russian Federation (TsAMO) and assured me that whatever happened with the book project, he would publish my article about these girl pilots in his journal.

The Russian "Aviatrissa" club that brings together female pilots did all they could to help me, with both contacts and informative literature. I deeply admire these women for the care and attention they pay to those of their fellows who are elderly and in poor health. A member of "Aviatrissa", Lidiya Zaitseva, famous Soviet pilot and holder of many records, set to help me from the minute we met. She shared contacts, recommended literature and even personally took me to Kaluga to meet armourer Valentina Krasnoshchyokova. I cannot thank her enough.

It was also the "Aviatrissa" club that put me in touch with Anatoly Kanevsky, pilot and journalist, great enthusiast of aviation. Anatoly was extremely supportive and helped with advice, contacts and information.

I do not know how I will ever repay the kindness of several historians who helped me. After reading the book Wings, Women and War by American scholar Reina Pennington, I wrote to her. Reina was kind to me and generously shared whatever materials and information she could provide. For example, she shared an absolutely unique document, the unpublished memoir of Major Alexander Gridnev, who commanded the female fighter regiment from 1942.

Academic Mikhail Rudenko pointed me to the diary of Communist youth administrator Nina Ivakina, which was published as an appendix to another book and therefore was not listed in any catalogues.

I wrote to Artyom Drabkin who compiled the best-ever Russian collections of interviews of war veterans and, in spite of being a very busy man and the author of bestsellers, Artyom immediately replied and has been most generous and helpful.

Two school teachers, amazing enthusiasts of their work, were of enormous help to me and made a very strong impression – Emiliya Gaidukova and Valentina Vashchenko. Both of them were in charge of school museums and dedicated spare time to organising their students and conducting research in order to commemorate the soldiers who died while fighting for their area of the U.S.S.R. – Vyazma oblast for Emiliya and Donbass for Valentina. Each had one particular person who was the main focus of their work: for Emiliya Gaidukova it was Katya Budanova and for Valentina Vashchenko it was Lilya Litvyak. After meeting these women I knew so much more about my heroines.

My heart is filled with gratitude to all those I have mentioned above. Another person to thank is my agent Andrew Nurnberg. He received the idea of such a book with great enthusiasm and encouraged me whenever I needed encouragement.

The person who I would like to thank most of all though, is my husband Martin. He is a pilot with a lot of experience and great enthusiasm, and it was he who explained the technical details, corrected what I wrote and even sent me flying a Yak. Not only that. Martin encouraged me to research and to write this story when both the timing and our location seemed absolutely unsuitable for both.

Index

Donetsk coal-basin 54–5, 131
Dranischev, Yevgeny 218, 219–20, 221
drill practice/ marching 75
Dryagina, Irina 69–71, 157–8, 159
Dzhugashvili, Yakov 175
Dzhunkovskaya, Galya 240, 276, 277

E
8 Air Army 167, 169–70, 176, 187–8, 189,
  212, 226, 239, 272, 307
  see also 434 Air Regiment; 437 Air
  Regiment
85 Regiment 208, 222, 227, 230–1, 312
Engels airbase 17, 20, 39, 62–71, 73–7,
  78–121
Engels town 63
engine technicians see mechanics
escapees from occupied territory 144–5,
  292–3, 311
evacuation of Moscow 40–1

F
Fedutenko, Nadezhda 74
Fedyayev, Alexander 139
female air force
  586 Fighter Regiment at Anisovka
    airbase 127–8, 129, 146–8, 168–9,
    183
  586 Fighter Regiment at Engels
    airbase 32, 65, 66–9, 79–80, 110–12,
    116, 121–2
  586 Fighter Regiment at
    Razboyshchina airfield 121–2
  586 Fighter Regiment join 8 Air Army
    (see Fighter Regiment, female; 434
    Air Regiment; 437 Air Regiment;
    9 Guards Regiment; 73 Guards
    Fighter Regiment; 296 Fighter
    Regiment)
  587 Heavy Bomber Regiment at Engels
    airbase 32, 65, 66, 67–8, 70, 74, 81,
    101, 128
  587 Heavy Bomber Regiment at the

Front 234–5, 238–9, 240, 242–4,
  254, 275–7 (see also 125 Guards
  Regiment)
588 Night Bomber Regiment at Engels
  airbase 18, 32, 65, 66, 68, 75–6, 90,
  97–9, 105–9, 116–20, 128
588 Night Bomber Regiment join 4 Air
  Army (see Night Bomber Regiment,
  female)
aeroplanes 80, 81, 95–7, 98–101, 105–6
armourers 66, 91, 169, 203–4, 249
bad behaviour and discipline 83, 84,
  94, 104–5
disputes and disagreements 90–2
drill practice/marching 75
Engels airbase 62, 63–71, 73–7, 78–121
entertainment and socialising at
  Engels airbase 77, 82–3, 85
fatalities 118–20, 146–8, 181, 186,
  286–7, 295–6, 301–3, 304–9
first orders for deployment to the
  Front 115–16
food/ rations 47–8, 91, 121, 191, 205–6,
  250
formation of 17–18, 24–5, 31–2, 36,
  37–40
haircuts and personal appearance 52,
  64–5, 112, 113–14
inequality amongst the ranks 91, 121,
  169, 191
interrogations by SMERSh 144–5
journey to Engels airbase 45–50, 52–3
mechanics and technicians 66, 75–6,
  90–1, 96, 97, 121, 169, 172, 191, 205–
  6 (see also Krasnoshchykova, Valya;
  Pleshivtseva, Faina)
military oaths 76–7
Muscovite new recruits 37–40, 43–5
navigators 66, 89, 90, 99, 109–10, 140
New Year celebrations 85–6, 224–5,
  229, 230
prisoners of war 290–1
Razboyshchina airfield 121–2

LYUBA VINOGRADOVA was born in Moscow in 1973. After graduating from the Moscow Agricultural Academy with a PhD in microbiology, she took a second degree in foreign languages. In 1995 she was introduced to Antony Beevor and helped him research *Stalingrad*. Since then she has worked on many other research projects, and is the co-author (together with Beevor) of *A Writer at War: Vasily Grossman with the Red Army*.

ARCH TAIT has translated many leading Russian writers of today. For his translation of Anna Politkovskaya's *Putin's Russia* he was the winner of the inaugural P.E.N. Literature in Translation Prize 2011.